BRUCE SPRINGSTEEN
Blinded By The Light

Patrick Humphries and Chris Hunt

Plexus, London

All rights reserved including the right
of reproduction in whole or in part in any form
This edition copyright © 1985 by Plexus Publishing Limited
Text copyright © 1985 by Patrick Humphries and Chris Hunt
Published by Plexus Publishing Limited
30 Craven Street
London WC2N 5NT
First Printing 1985

Humphries, Patrick
Blinded by the light.
1. Springsteen, Bruce   2. Rock musicians—
United States—Biography
I. Title   II. Hunt, Christopher
784.5′0092′4   ML420.S77

ISBN 0-85965-086-3

Lyrics by Bruce Springsteen
printed by kind permission of
Zomba Music Publishers Limited

Cover and book design by Ken Kitchen

Manufactured in Great Britain by Hollen Street Press

PART 1

NO SURRENDER

by Patrick Humphries

PART 2

THE BRUCE FILES

by Chris Hunt

Introduction

'We're gonna take a short break, then come back and do another whole set for you' must be the most encouraging words you can ever hear from a rock stage. But only one man can say it, mean it and really do it. His name is Bruce Springsteen. He is 36 years old, and the only ceiling to his ambitions is his own exacting standards. For those who believe that rock'n'roll can be a route to salvation, Bruce Springsteen has become its prime exponent. To the fans, he has come to be the music of the present, the inheritor of the past, and the symbol of hope for the future. But to understand that, to understand him, you really ought to have been there . . .

In my case 'there' was Madison Square Garden, New York City, Thanksgiving Night 1980. November 27, Gate 3, Section J, Row 21, Seat 3. It's a long walk from the entrance, but after coming 3,000 miles and waiting five years, it doesn't seem that far. Thanksgiving is a time to be spent with the family, not to be alone, particularly in New York. The wind whips off the East River, and everyone I know in this strange town is gathered around the ceremonial turkey. Home is five hours and an ocean away. All I am is a figure filling a seat 360,000 others wanted. But it's okay. I may be a stranger in a strange land, away from the things and people I know and love, but tonight this is definitely the Promised Land!

My mind goes back to how it all began, when a neighbour the other side of the ocean pressed a copy of *Born To Run* into my arms. But then, I am wrenched back into the present. A tape of the Crystals' 'Then He Kissed Me' blares from the PA, and sets the seal on the atmosphere of eager excitement. The capacity crowd is restless in the vast auditorium, geeing itself up on the waiting. Madison Square Garden takes on the appearance of a rock venue as might have been staged by Cecil B. de Mille: frisbees cascade around the auditorium and the fans are divided into tribes, each

bearing banners, like medieval Crusaders. Each wears its own colours, each pledging its devotion to 'The Boss'. Much as my own reserve mistrusts the ceremony, it's hard to remain uninvolved. Then the lights dim, and there's a roar that rattles your fillings. Seven figures race onstage and take their places – the roar gets even louder, welcoming. Your eyes seek out the little guy, the figure who shuffles around stage centre, who carries himself like a bantam-weight, who's scuffing his feet, who skips on tiptoe, who's hungry to start. He's ready. And, after everything you've read, heard and experienced, so are you. It could be anywhere in the world; fortunately for me, it happens to be on his home turf, only a bus ride from Asbury Park.

Bruce Springsteen and the E Street Band *start* on an ovation most bands would kill to finish with! The little guy grins delightedly as the lights burst on, pinpointing the band. He turns to them, stomps his foot with an exultant 'Ah-one-two-three-four . . .' and they crash, as one, into 'Born To Run'. They're off and running before the flag's even dropped. And, within seconds, we're into passion and intensity. Nothing has prepared you for the blitzkrieg that is to follow. *Opening* with 'Born To Run'! It's like Sam Goldwyn's advice: 'Start off with an earthquake, and build up to a climax!' Then out come the songs, dozens of them, each played with an energy and commitment which propels them off the albums you've lived with for years. They span Springsteen's career, pouring out, cataclysmic; they barely pause for breath – 'Growin' Up', 'Fire', 'Rosalita', 'Promised Land', 'Because The Night', 'Hungry Heart', 'Sherry Darling'. All the dreams you've hoarded are suddenly made vivid and real. Everything you've heard about those legendary shows is true: the crowd really does cry out 'Brooooose' after each number (and the first time it *does* sound like booing, then you know better); they *do* play for four hours; they *do* play everything you want to hear, and then some. They (we) chant along with every song, and remain silent at his bidding. It's like there's 22,000 people trying to reach him, focusing everything on that scrawny little figure. It's frightening. It's also unique and elating.

So totally involving is the music that every mention of 'New Jersey' and 'Asbury Park', I, a stranger from another continent, belonged there, an honorary citizen. During 'I Hear A Train', I diligently trilled 'Whoo whoo', much to my later embarrassment. In 'Independence Day' tears fell like rain. By the end of the show, the audience was as drained as the band. Four hours of high energy, high intensity rock'n'roll, which took you to the heights of elation.

In concert, Bruce Springsteen and the E Street Band are simply the best there is. That show piloted you through a vast range of emotions. It gave you the possibility to forget your fears, to revel in the camaraderie, to realise your dreams, to be transported away from reality. But it also took you back to reality, clarifying your aspirations, charting your losses, celebrating your victories. By the end of the show, it was the audience's music. We chanted along to the throaty rockers, and remained pensive during the ballads. What made it more than just a great rock'n'roll spectacular was that you could learn something about yourself; the music reflects back on you, stopping the experience being mere worship.

Springsteen knows he is the best, and his conviction convinces you too. So much has been written about his power in concert that

the hysteria has to be placed in some sort of context. Even his harshest critics admit that he does put on one hell of a show. At Madison Square Garden, I felt a revitalisation, a sense of regaining everything I'd ever wanted from rock'n'roll. For four glorious hours, I experienced its restorative power. In the calm afterwards, the only question was, just who *was* that man up there?

Bruce Springsteen is the single most important rock star to have emerged during the 1970s, but his reputation is built on an astonishingly small recorded output, although fuelled by numerous bootlegs. Unlike most other rock stars, it is his live shows that have made his name. And it is in these that he comes over as rock's great unifier, a performer who remembers the power and passion of early rock'n'roll, and who is burning with the desire to preserve and pass on that excitement in his own music. He zealously revels in rock's rich past, and stands as one of the few artists who can positively affect its future.

This excitement and commitment only fully come across in live performance. Despite the meticulous care he attaches to recording, such is the intensity of a Springsteen performance that afterwards the albums simply become pale souvenirs.

It can be said that rock'n'roll is one of America's greatest contributions to the twentieth century. Ally that to Hollywood's domination of the cinema, the sharpness and vitality of its literature and the country's dominance in the Free World, and you have a powerful culture, unparalleled in its modernity. Through his commitment to the roots and traditional qualities of rock'n'roll Springsteen is linked to the full vitality of that culture, and in his music we can hear the authentic voice of modern America. If the term has any meaning, Springsteen is a particularly American artist. In music his best work can be said to have the same qualities as Thomas Wolfe in writing, of John Ford and Martin Scorsese in the cinema, of Edward Hopper in painting and of Woody Guthrie and Robert Johnson in folk music. His America is twofold – the America of urban New Jersey, and the vastness of the frontier country, the America (particularly on *The River* and *Nebraska*) familiar from the images of Hollywood and popular songs. He conjures up the American Dream, where every man can be a king, and the only ceiling to ambition is the extent of your dreams. The realisation runs through his songs, but the songs also dwell on the underside of the Dream, of the losers that never made it to the mansion on the hill or the house up in Fairview. Springsteen's characters are descendants of those who populate the songs of Guthrie and Hank Williams, and, before them, the figures of the country and blues worlds. His songs evoke the America described in the conclusion of Scott Fitzgerald's *The Great Gatsby*: '(It) had once pandered in whispers to the last and greatest of all human dreams; for a transitory enchanted moment, man must have held his breath in the presence of this continent, compelled into an aesthetic contemplation he neither understood nor desired, face to face for the last time in history with something commensurate to his capacity for wonder ... his dream must have seemed so close that he could hardly fail to grasp it. He did not know that it was already behind him, somewhere back in that vast obscurity beyond the city, where the dark fields of the republic rolled on under the night.'

This 1981 performance portrait perfectly captures the dynamism that Springsteen fans have come to expect in live performance.

Born In The U.S.A.

Bruce Frederick Joseph Springsteen, the only son of Douglas and Adele, was born in Freehold, New Jersey, on 23 September 1949. He was their first child, and was later to acquire two sisters – Virginia, born the next year, and Pamela, who did not appear until 1962. Bruce's father was mainly of Irish extraction and his mother of Italian – a volatile combination – although the family name is Dutch.

Freehold is a small town in mid-New Jersey. It is about fifteen miles from the coast. For Freehold's young it was overshadowed for both vitality and opportunity by the nearest town, Asbury Park. Freehold itself offered little to anyone with aspirations, or even a keen desire to enjoy himself. By Bruce's birth it was already in decline, the filling station next to the Springsteen home offering the main social centre for the local kids during Bruce's youth.

Bruce's father worked at various jobs, including as a factory hand, a gardener, and a prison guard, although he was to settle primarily for driving coaches. Money was usually scarce – eating out, for example, was out of the question, and Bruce was 22 years old before he went into a restaurant. •

Douglas and Adele were both Catholics, so Bruce was sent to local Catholic schools. He hated them and antagonised the nuns with his strong streak of individuality (so much so that on one occasion, in an often-repeated story, one of them made the young Springsteen sit in a rubbish bin under her desk).

Springsteen's upbringing was pretty normal for someone from that background – unadventurous, unscholastic, his only escape being via the radio or TV. There was little intellectual stimulus in his home life, and he once claimed only ever to have read three books for pleasure.

In remembering those early years, there is only really one potent, deeply etched memory. He told *Crawdaddy*: 'Rock'n'roll, man, it changed my life. It was ... the Voice of America, the real America coming to your home. It was the liberating thing, the way out of the pits. Once I found the guitar, I had the key to the highway!'

The Castiles, featuring the 17 year-old Bruce Springsteen, shown second from the right in this picture.

This discovery came with seeing Elvis Presley on the *Ed Sullivan Show* when he was nine years old. He was so excited afterwards that he persuaded his mother to buy him a guitar. But he could not get his fingers round it, so it was put aside. Nevertheless, the experience lay dormant, resting under the surface ready to reassert itself when the time was right.

From then ('Man when I was nine, I couldn't imagine anyone *not* wanting to be Elvis Presley!') Bruce was a fan, and he decided that for him it was rock'n'roll glory, or nothing. That single-minded intensity, which, at times, has proved infuriating, has been a dominant force in his adult life. The urge that won him to rock'n'roll in the first place is now reflected in his attitude to recording and performing, of offering nothing but the best.

School was not the only source of trouble for the young Bruce. His father was as strong-willed as the son would be, and they often clashed, particularly when Bruce was in his teens. These early experiences at home and school were to appear later in the words of some of his songs – the loathing of Catholic values, his edgy relationship with his father, rock'n'roll as the way out of the drudgery.

The tensions in the Springsteen household echoed those across the country during the turbulent sixties. Bruce resented his father's championing of the work ethic, never able to understand his adherence to what he regarded as a corrupt and valueless system. It was the time of Vietnam, student riots, drugs and hippies, and parental values were widely flouted. Although Bruce himself has always been vehemently anti-drug, hasn't smoked, and has only ever drunk in moderation, and has never been overtly political, he shared in the rejection of parental authority. In later years, his attitude towards his father was to mellow, and his adolescent arrogance was to be remembered with guilt on certain crucial songs like 'Factory', 'Independence Day', and 'My Father's House'. Nevertheless, his interests and ambitions encountered encouragement from his mother, who acted as a buffer, while his father offered scorn and derision. In those early years in Freehold, Bruce and Douglas Springsteen were typical examples of the 'generation gap'.

The feeling of guilt evident in the songs shows just how bitterly Bruce and his father must have argued, and also how Bruce still feels attached to his roots. But as he grew up, Springsteen could realise just what made his father the way he was, but as an angry, dissatisfied adolescent, like all such youths, he did not have that perspective.

Bruce's acrimonious relationship with Douglas was, in fact, little different from that of other teenagers, but rebellion has always been at the roots of rock'n'roll, and without it Bruce would perhaps never have become the musician he is. That tension was to be the specific force behind a series of fine songs. On 'Factory' he understood the bitterness and resentment which shaped his father, watching him leave work 'with death in his eyes', half-deafened, simmering, resentful, and all for 'the working life'. At times on record, almost embarrassingly, Springsteen atones for the sins committed against his father. On the Gothic 'My Father's House' he dreamed of those distant days, then: 'I awoke and I imagined the hard things that pulled us apart/Will never again, sir, tear us from each others' hearts.' On 'Independence Day' it all came together: 'There was just no way this house could hold the two of us/ I guess we were just too much of the same kind'. Here he made the realisation, confirmed on 'Highway Patrolman': 'Man who turns his back on his family, well he just ain't no good.' And on the unreleased 'Song Of The Orphans', Springsteen sang poignantly of 'The sons return for fathers/But the fathers are all gone/The lost souls search for saviours/But saviours don't last long.'

In concert Springsteen has offered long, ruminative raps about his father. When in Britain on the 1981 tour, he told an audience in Newcastle about how his perception of his father's way of life came to influence his whole outlook. 'I grew up in this little town, and we lived on this main street next door to this gas station . . . and at 6am every morning I used to watch my old man, I'd hear him out back, fiddling with the hood of the car so he could get it started . . . And as I grew older, I watched around, and I didn't see how my life was going to be much different than his, because it seemed that if you were born in a certain place that things didn't change much for you . . . When I got older I never had a picture of him laughing – all I could remember him doing was sitting at the kitchen table at night with the lights out, smoking a cigarette, waiting . . . for it all to go away, or something. And I tried to think what was the thing that we all had in common, why did it – time after time – end up that way? And that we didn't have enough knowledge about the forces that were controlling our lives. I started reading this book, *The History Of The United States*, and it seemed how the way that things were, weren't the way they were meant to be; like the way my old man was living, and his old man, and the life that was waiting for me – that wasn't the original idea. But even if you find those things out, it's so hard to change those things. And it wasn't until I started listening to the radio, and I heard something in those singers' voices that said there was more to life than what my old man was doing, and the life that I was living; and they held out a promise – and it was a promise that every man has a right to live his life with some decency and dignity. And it's a promise that gets broken every day, in the most violent way. But it's a promise that never, ever fuckin' dies, and it's always inside of you. But I watched my old man forget that, and don't let it happen to you.'

Springsteen, perhaps, talks so much about his father because he was the dominant influence on his adolescence. The image of the American Dream was becoming apparent to him there in the example of his father – not the Dream realised, but instead the Dream frustrated and forgotten. Bruce watched his father, like many of his generation, and has never let himself forget what he saw. The themes of many of his later songs were already forming in his youthful mind.

Douglas offered another instance of the Dream, that of free-wheeling mobility, though again, to Bruce, it seemed that the ideal was soured. He told Marc Didden in 1981 of a typical Sunday of his youth, which obviously was the basis for 'Used Cars' on

CLEARWATER SWIM CLUB
ROUTE 36
ATLANTIC HIGHLANDS

SUNDAY, JUNE 21
8:00 PM – OUTDOORS
ADMISSION: 2.50
INSIGHT LIGHTS
GLORY ROAD

rock concert rain date june 28

the first annual
Nothing's
Festival

steel mill mercy flight
jeannie clark
and many others!

AUG. 8, BEACHCOMBER
LONG BRANCH, 50¢ 700 PM

STEEL MILL
FORMERLY CHILD OF N.J.

THURSDAY   NOV. 20
the center 313 N. LAUREL
TICKETS 2.00 IN ADVANCE
MORNING DISASTER & LIGHTS by AIRE FLOW
STARTS 9 PM   FREE V.

PLEASE DONT BE A PIG. Leave it up until after the show.—THEN rip it off!

Nebraska: 'I used to dislike cars. That was because of my father, he was obsessed by cars. When I would be listening to records in my room on Sunday, he would come and bang on the door: "Come on Bruce, let's go for a ride." And then, no matter how much we disliked it, my mother, sister and I had to tear across the highways because my father thought it was the most beautiful entertainment. I think he liked to show off his car because he had worked so hard to buy it. The bad thing was that he liked to drive so much, we never stopped anywhere! We would drive around the whole damned Sunday and come home in the evening all exhausted. And he would just beam. Perhaps that kind of action was the only thing he needed after working the whole week at his machine in the plastics plant ...' That parental dissension was not unusual, but Springsteen's single-mindedness about his music was.

A scrawny youth, non-academic, an unenthusiastic sportsman, and dissatisfied with his parents' lives, Springsteen turned to the radio and the record deck for sanctuary. Like so many of his generation, he found that rock'n'roll offered some sort of escape from the ordinariness of his existence. However, few bands ventured down to Freehold, so listening to music was essentially a solitary experience for him. To this day, Springsteen is still basically a loner; while he thrives on audience contact in his concerts, he is prone to long, solitary drives in his car, and many of the characters in his songs are individuals, refusing to be ground down by a system which had all but destroyed his father.

When Bruce was 13 years old the most exciting music coming out of the record player and radio was British. American pop in the early sixties was emasculated, until it was rescued by the British Invasion. Like so many young Americans, Springsteen was mesmerised by the style and musical ebullience of the Beatles (the first song he ever learned was 'Twist And Shout') and remained captivated by the Animals, the Rolling Stones, Manfred Mann, the Searchers, Them and the Who. Then the music of Tamla Motown blasted across the airwaves, the compelling rhythms of Martha and The Vandellas, the Supremes, Stevie Wonder, Marvin Gaye. To these the avid listener added the soul music of Sam and Dave, Otis Redding, Aretha Franklin and the gritty R&B of Gary 'US' Bonds and Mitch Ryder. Anything good was gratefully received by the young Springsteen, who not only listened but absorbed and remembered. The effect of these groups can be heard still – Bruce Springsteen in concert is a one man history of rock'n'roll, a human jukebox, lovingly replaying the old rock classics.

The power of rock reasserted itself on the 13-year-old and the desire to play re-emerged. Springsteen went out and bought himself another guitar, this time spending all of $18 on a secondhand one from a pawnshop. For two years he listened and he learned, teaching himself to play. Then in 1965 he heard that a local teenage group, the Castiles, needed a new guitarist. He offered his services to Tex Vinyard, whom the group somewhat grandly had appointed manager. Tex was initially impressed by the stringy kid, and asked him to come back when he had learned five songs. He was even more impressed the next evening when Springsteen not only came back with five songs, but played them fantasically – and then offered a couple more. He was in.

The Castiles, named after the soap, were modelled on the fashions of the time (there's a photograph of a 17-year-old Springsteen, with a haircut that looks as if it was grown for an audi-

A rare glimpse of Bruce, circa *1970, mischievously exuding all the attributes of the hippy lifestyle.*

tion for George Harrison's role in *A Hard Day's Night*). For a high school band the Castiles were quite successful. They gave Springsteen his first professional gig, at the Woodhaven Swim Club, when the five of them shared a princely $35 with Tex Vinyard. Springsteen had quickly made his mark as a composer as well as a player, for the closing number was his arrangement of Glen Miller's 'In The Mood'. They went on to play the normal round for local groups of teen clubs, high schools, supermarket openings and drive-ins, generally finding the New Jersey shore more fruitful territory than their native Freehold. During 1966 the

THE BRUCE SPRINGSTEEN BAND

IN CONCERT WITH SOUTHERN CONSPIRACY AND POWER HOUSE

DECEMBER 17, 1971 AT 7.30 AT THE LEDGE ON RUTGERS CAMPUS GEORGE ST. NEW BRUNSWICK

group's playing had improved sufficiently to win various local competitions, and Tex bought stage uniforms for them. Then in May 1966 they hired time in a local studio to cut a demo disc, 'That's What You Get' and 'Baby I', written by Springsteen and lead singer George Theiss.

A series of gigs in New York's Greenwich Village followed in December 1966 and January 1967, but then, like so many hundreds of bands formed in the wake of the Beatles, when the members left high school in 1967 they drifted apart. No one really noticed and few people really cared. The group's drummer was to enlist and go to Vietnam. He never came back.

Springsteen's next move was a group called Earth, formed while he was at Ocean County College where he went when he left school. It was a combo heavily influenced by the extended blues riffing of Cream and the dominant psychedelia of the period. Earth didn't last long, but while with them Bruce came more and more to regard Asbury Park as his musical home, and after they broke up he played with several scratch Asbury bands. At this time he met 'Miami' Steve Van Zandt, who was to become one of his closest friends and musical associates.

Springsteen formed his next band, Steel Mill, in 1969. They were to prove more durable, as their name suggested. According to Springsteen, they were 'a Humble Pie type band', and it was there that the nucleus of the E Street Band was formed, with Springsteen joined by drummer Vini 'Mad Dog' Lopez and organist Danny Federici. Fashionably hippy in appearance – Bruce sporting hair below his shoulders – though not in attitude, Steel Mill played a tough, driving blues-based music. The group gained a new level of popularity for Springsteen, playing in clubs and colleges, and has become something of a New Jersey legend.

Steel Mill marked Springsteen's first serious efforts at songwriting – 'Goin' Back to Georgia' was reminiscent of Them *circa* 1965, 'Resurrection' was bitterly anti-Catholic, and 'American Song' was a lengthy indictment of militarism.

In early 1969, Springsteen's parents and sisters had moved to California, but the 20-year-old Bruce defiantly stayed put on the Jersey shore, squatting in the family home. That streak of self-determination was already apparent. It was a determination that helped him to avoid the draft in 1969 by the crude, but obviously effective, method of faking madness. He capitalised on the concussion he had suffered in a motor bike accident two years before, and filled in the forms deliberately irrationally.

Another New Jersey musician and friend, Southside Johnny, recalled the crisis points his group, the Jukes, went through at the same time about whether to stick with a day job, or go all out for the music: 'Everyone went through it, except Bruce. Bruce always knew. There was never any question about it as far as he was concerned.' So little question, in fact, that Bruce readily left college, where he did not feel particularly at home, without a degree in order to concentrate on his music. Miami Steve remembered that intensity that Bruce and all the other Asbury musicians felt: 'Rock'n'Roll is not entertainment; it is motivation. No drugs, no alcohol, no lasting diversion!'

Steel Mill were not satisfied with having only local fame, and in winter 1969 Bruce and his band followed his parents west to California. In the first three months of 1970 they got several bookings supporting big name groups in San Francisco. They even cut a demo tape at Bill Graham's Fillmore Recording Studio and were offered a recording contract, but by now the group was sufficiently confident and mature not to be tempted by the poor sum offered. They returned to Asbury Park in spring 1970 with some good notices but little money to show for their trip.

By now, Asbury Park is as potent a piece of rock mythology as Penny Lane – for which the residents are permanently grateful to Bruce Springsteen. Although compared with Freehold it was a Mecca, Asbury had, in fact, always been a joke, a crumbling beach stop, which – out of season – was pretty desperate. Asbury is 53 miles from New York City, a derisory sort of resort of which the locals said: 'If you never had enough gas to get to Atlantic City, you'd stop at Asbury!' From New York, you get to it via the Lincoln Tunnel and the New Jersey Turnpike. That gave the place its first taste of rock fame: 'Counting the cars on the New Jersey Turnpike' was the memorable image of departure on Simon and Garfunkel's 'America'. The Turnpike was also the place – as legend has it – from where Jack Kerouac set out 'on the road'. Atlantic City is further on down the road, supposedly the last resort (as evinced by Louis Malle's film and Bruce's song of the same name) but Asbury Park was even lower down the scale. The boardwalk (of 'Sandy' fame) runs from Ocean Avenue straight down to the cold, grey Atlantic. As an urban centre, it distinctly lacked charisma, but for a musician it had one great asset. The clubs were hot – like Southside Johnny the nascent E Street Band eked out a living and built up a reputation at the Upstage and the Student Prince.

Inspired by Springsteen's later success, there have been attempts to promote 'The Sounds Of Asbury Park' (there was even a compilation album of that name), but, in truth, that sound lies on 'Sandy (Asbury Park, 4th of July)' and Southside Johnny's first album (complete with suitably effusive sleeve notes from Springsteen). What inspired the musicians from Asbury Park was desperation. Its seediness brought that glittering American dream into even sharper focus.

The mythology of Asbury Park as evoked by Springsteen on songs like 'The E Street Shuffle' and '10th Avenue Freeze Out', was rooted in reality. Clarence Clemons, the E Street Band's saxophonist, literally bumped into Bruce at the Student Prince one night: 'A cold, rainy night on the boardwalk in Asbury, windy, raining like crazy,' recalled Clemons, 'and I opened the door, the wind just blew the door right off the hinges and down the street, and it was like "Here I am! I came to play!" and he couldn't say no. When we jammed, it was like we'd been together forever, like a team.' As Miami Steve told me: 'There ain't nothing magic about Asbury. You could do the same with . . . Brighton! All it takes is a band.' But you do need a rather special band.

In the summer of 1970 Asbury Park gained unaccustomed and unwelcome national publicity and scrutiny when the town exploded in race riots. In the desolation that followed Steel Mill was allowed to fall apart. It was a situation that called for either depression or humour and Springsteen responded by forming the cumbersome Dr Zoom and the Sonic Boom, which only managed two gigs before folding. Everyone in the band acquired nicknames, some of them, like 'Mad Dog' Lopez and 'Miami' Steve Van Zandt (who became members of the E Street Band) sticking. The Bruce Springsteen Band that followed only lasted 12 months, but it was all experience, and the rigorous playing and gigging helped forge a commitment which then bound together several of those who were later to form the E Street Band. The friendships made in Asbury play an important role in Spingsteen's music, and it was then that an affinity was established with Van Zandt, Danny Federici, Garry Tallent, David Sancious and Clarence Clemons.

It was in the Upstage club in Asbury that Springsteen cut his musical teeth, from the hard days grinding on the Jersey shore, playing rock'n'roll when he could, and almost with whom he could, often with no money and with necessity promoting his passion for junk food. In those clubs he met the people who were to play with him around the country, and it was in their joint experiences that a sense of community was forged – a community evidenced in his contract where it says that his name and the band's are to appear in equal type on hoardings. And whatever city they now play in, there's a slice of Asbury Park up on stage.

New Jersey's most famous son. Asbury Park has become Springsteen's spiritual home and source of inspiration. Here our hero is photographed on home ground.

The New Dylan

Springsteen's professional career can be said to have begun in earnest when Mike Appel appeared on the scene in early 1972 and signed him to a management contract. Springsteen would later bitterly regret it, but at the time it represented the turning-point he needed. Appel and his partner Jim Cretecos were strictly small time (their chief moment of glory prior to meeting Springsteen had been a Top 10 hit for the Partridge Family), but they *were* in the record business. Springsteen's audition was a decisive moment for the three men. Having seen his band dwindle away the previous winter, Bruce had decided to go it alone. 'He sang as if his life

When John Hammond first heard Springsteen he envisaged some kind of new Dylan, but Bruce refused to put on that mantle.

depended on it,' Appel told Dave Marsh of the audition. In many ways it did, for here was the opportunity to make it. If Springsteen blew this one, he might have no alternative but 'the working life' which had gutted his father.

Mike Appel has since been castigated for his heavy-handed approach in nurturing Springsteen, but when Springsteen was a struggling 23-year-old, scraping a living in the bars of Asbury Park, it was Appel who saw his raw talent. However brash and tactless his method, he went on to achieve the vital breakthrough by impressing that raw talent on John Hammond at CBS. This was a crucial development for it landed Springsteen a record deal – in fact with the company he has stayed with. Appel went on to act as overseer on Springsteen's first three crucial albums, and *Born To Run* itself was a co-production between Appel and Springsteen.

When Springsteen was taken to the audition the significance of John Hammond was not lost on him. One of the three books he claimed to have read for pleasure was Anthony Scaduto's biography of Bob Dylan, so he recognised Hammond's name, and recalled that in the film of *The Benny Goodman Story* Hammond had been played by the actor who played Dennis the Menace's father on TV! John Hammond stands as one of the most venerated figures in the history of American popular music. His track record speaks for itself – he recorded Benny Goodman, Bessie Smith and Billie Holiday. He had gone out in search of the legendary Robert Johnson. He had signed the young Aretha Franklin and Bob Dylan to CBS. He had also numbered Charles Laughton and Sergei Eisenstein among his friends.

When they met on 2 May 1972, Hammond immediately saw that Springsteen had talent, and was keen to have him on CBS, even though he found Appel overbearing, and had to shut him up in order to listen to his protégé. When Bruce started with 'It's Hard To Be A Saint In The City' Hammond sat up, and in no time had booked him into the Gaslight Club that evening so he could hear him perform before an audience. The next day Bruce was at the CBS Studios recording 14 tracks.

Hammond was keen to cast Springsteen in the role of an acoustic poet, much as he envisaged the young Bob Dylan over ten years before. Although Bruce's experience was mainly playing with bands, there was logic in this as he auditioned solo, accompanying himself on piano or acoustic guitar. Of the two, Springsteen struck Hammond as being more mature than the unknown Dylan. He told *Crawdaddy's* Peter Knobler: 'When Bobby came to see me he was Bobby Zimmerman. He said he was Bob Dylan, he had created all this mystique. Bruce is Bruce Springsteen. And he's much further along, much more developed than Bobby was when he came to me.'

It is to Hammond's credit that he recognised Springsteen's potential at that early stage (Springsteen remembered Hammond's faith in him, and dedicated 'Growin' Up' to him during his 1980 Thanksgiving Show.) If one examines the evidence contained on the bootleg of *The Hammond Demos*, the songs are clumsy and cluttered, wordy and unwieldy, with Springsteen nervously accompanying himself on guitar and piano. That wordiness was a trait that Springsteen was to carry on well into his recording career, as if syllables and images piled on top of each other could enhance the intensity of his performance. But the song, 'If I Was The Priest', held Hammond spellbound, loaded with its virulent anti-Catholic imagery, and steeped in the myths of the Wild West: 'And Jesus, he's standing in the doorway/With his six guns drawn, and ready to fan/He says "We need you, son, up in Dodge City"/ But I'm already overdue in Cheyenne.'

Inevitably, comparisons with Dylan spread as soon as it was heard that John Hammond had signed another young singer/songwriter. In terms of impact and influence, Dylan is, indeed, the obvious comparison to make with Springsteen (Springsteen acknowledged that Dylan 'was the guy who made it possible to do the things I wanted'), but the differences are immense. Two years into his recording career Dylan was already addressing himself to 'every hung-up person in the whole wide universe'. In contrast, Springsteen hadn't even cast his net beyond New York City by that time! The comparisons are, in fact, tenuous, for the only Dylan 'period' which had any real effect on Springsteen was the immaculate quick burn 'folk rock' years of 1965–6, and Springsteen's most Dylan-like album, *Nebraska*, was not released until 1982, 20 years after Dylan's debut and ten years after his own. The comparisons are further stretched when you compare the two: Dylan has gone out of his way to be anyone *but* Bob Dylan, presenting a chorus line of characters – the concerned social poet of 1963, the 'spokesman of a generation' in 1964, the iconoclastic folk-rocker of 1965, the contented married man of 1970, the aggressive evangelist of 1979 and the born-again Jew of 1983. Springsteen has never attracted any of Dylan's sort of mystique, seeing his job as being

USA, the E Street Band supported the then fashionable Chicago, working at establishing a reputation. They were an odd bunch; drummer 'Mad Dog' Lopez lives up to his nickname, and seems determined to be remembered as America's answer to Keith Moon. Clarence Clemons, 'Big Man', is a 6ft 4ins ex-college football player who amply justifies his nickname. Danny Federici, once dubbed the 'mystery man' by Bruce, is a careful and warm keyboard and accordion player. And holding them all together was the mercurial and indefatigable 5ft 10ins, 155lb frame of Bruce Springsteen.

The tour was not a success for the Springsteen outfit. Their rough tough style did not go well with the smooth jazz-rock sound of Chicago and audiences did not warm to them. The nadir came in June 1973 when they gave a wretched performance at New York's Madison Square Garden, watched by several CBS executives. It was particularly bad timing as they needed to improve their stock with the company because CBS's president Clive Davis, who had personally backed the promotion of Springsteen, had left the company the previous month. One highlight, however, was three nights at Max's Kansas City where they headed the bill with Bob Marley and the Wailers.

Nevertheless, before the end of 1973, the motley E Street Band was back in the studio. Springsteen had a clutch of songs ready for recording, many of which even at that early stage would never see the light of day, officially (bootlegging is another matter, of which more later). Eventually, the selection was narrowed down to seven songs, which constituted *The Wild, The Innocent And The E Street Shuffle*, which was released in February 1974.

Springsteen's second album marked a musical maturity, although the breezy 'E Street Shuffle' sounded like a hangover from the first album; despite being enlivened by a snappy brass arrangement, it didn't offer anything new. But 'Sandy (4th of July, Asbury Park)' emphatically did. While the song was, and remains, Springsteen's finest love song, it also helped establish Asbury Park as a myth. 'Sandy' pinpoints a time, a place, a girl in an idealised youth. The places mentioned in Asbury are real (you can still see Madame Marie's fortune-telling booth on the boardwalk), but Springsteen portrays it as a 'Little Eden', a place of lost innocence. The song describes the passing of not only a relationship but of that whole time for which everybody has nostalgic memories which is always associated with a particular place, but is different from person to person – in this case, the New Jersey shore. Springsteen's evoca-

tion is conveyed without sounding precious or twee; it sounds like a drunken message left on the girl's answering machine. Unable to face her, the song's narrator pours out fragments of memory and bitter resignation, recalling the wizards and fortune-tellers, and realising that for him 'this boardwalk scene's through'. Asbury Park, that Independence Day, is a special place. Evelyn Waugh wrote of another place in *Brideshead Revisited*: 'I should like to bury something precious in every place where I've been happy and then, when I was old and ugly and miserable, I could come back and dig it up, and remember.' That feeling is what Asbury Park meant to Springsteen, that Fourth of July, when he was young and uncluttered; it is a touching farewell to youth.

'Wild Billy's Circus Story' is one of Springsteen's most uncharacteristic songs, which offers an all-too-rare outing for Danny Federici's accordion. The circus has always exercised a fascination for rock writers: the Everly Brothers, the Beatles, Bob Dylan and Richard Thompson have all tried their hand at a circus song. Springsteen's is a curious exercise, a sort of veiled homosexual paean – or not so veiled when you consider lines like: 'The hired hand tightens his legs on the sword swallower's blade. . . . And the strong man Samson lifts the midget . . . way up, and carries him on down the midway . . . past the sailors, to his dimly lit trailer!' More realistically, it's an impressionistic fairground fable, which significantly ends with: 'All aboard, Nebraska's our next stop!'

The most mature song on the album is the sweeping 'Incident On 57th Street'. While Springsteen still romanticises the street gangs ('little heroes', 'romantic young boys') the song has a genuine narrative thread, with fully realised characters, soaked in atmosphere. It stands as archetypal Springsteen, conveying a drowsy big city day, with plenty of astute vignettes: 'Upstairs the band was playing, the singer was singin' something about going home. . . . And the sister prays for lost souls, then breaks down in the chapel after everyone's gone.'

'Rosalita' is the album's outstanding rocker, and became Springsteen's show-stopper for years. It was, perhaps, the song most associated with him in Britain, as for six long years it was the only film clip available of him there. Filmed in Phoenix Arizona in July 1978 by Malcolm Leo, 'Rosalita' is a full-throated celebration, with Springsteen exulting that 'the record company, Rosie, just gave me a big advance'. The mythologising continued, with his car stuck out 'somewhere in the swamps of Jersey'. However, the song has the verbosity of 'Blinded By The Light', with a whole new cast of characters – 'Weak Knee Willie . . . Sloppy Sue and Big Bone Billy'. The lengthy 'New York City Serenade' was a jazzy excursion, influenced by pianist David Sancious, and based on an earlier Springsteen song 'Vibes Man'.

The Wild, The Innocent And The E Street Shuffle was vinyl proof of Springsteen's development, and his concerts to promote the album laid the foundations for his epic gigs of later years, dipping into the musical reservoir that made up rock history, and performing a number of his own new songs, like 'The Fever', 'Born To Run' and 'Jungleland'. After the release of the album there was a change in personnel. In February 1974 Bruce sacked Vini Lopez, replacing him with Ernest 'Boom' Carter, a friend of David

'Springsteen . . . a rock'n'roll punk, a Latin street poet, a ballet dancer, a joker, a bar band leader. . . .'

Sancious . He had agonised for a long time over dismissing Lopez, who was an old friend from Asbury Park, but the move strengthened the group. Carter stayed with the band until only August 1974 when Sancious himself left in order to follow a solo career.

They took to touring again, building up their numbers so that by the end of 1974 they were playing 90-minute sets. During a break between shows on this tour, in Massachusetts in April 1974, Springsteen met Jon Landau for the first time. Landau was to play a crucial role in the development of Springsteen's career, and when they met he already had a reputation as one of America's finest rock writers. At *Rolling Stone*, along with Greil Marcus and Dave Marsh, Landau's exhaustive interviews and thoughtful features had helped elevate rock writing to a respected critical level. Landau had already dabbled in record production, with the MC5 and Livingstone Taylor, but was – by the time he met Springsteen – reconciling himself to growing old gracefully in a young man's business. He was 27 when he saw Springsteen perform for the first time, and was blown away by his energy and enthusiasm. The two men continued to see each other over the next few months. In Jon Landau Springsteen intuitively recognised someone whose academic (albeit heartfelt) approach to rock'n'roll mirrored his own fervent enthusiasm.

Even with two albums to his name, and a decade of performing under his belt, Springsteen was still a virtual novice when it came to the intricacies of the music business. Mike Appel oversaw Springsteen's management as well as his record production. The two had developed a mutual trust, and despite the hostility Appel and his sometimes heavy-handed methods attracted, Springsteen had faith in him. He adhered to the Western code that if you gave a man your trust, it was a stronger bond than any written contract.

CBS were plainly unhappy with Springsteen's sales. While he garnered all sorts of critical eulogies, good notices didn't shift albums in the quantity a major record company required, and Springsteen's first two albums had all but stiffed. Then Landau ran a piece on Springsteen in Boston's *Real Paper* in May 1974. It was, at times, hyperbolic: 'Springsteen . . . is a rock'n'roll punk, a Latin street poet, a ballet dancer, a joker, a bar band leader . . .' but more often thoughtful: 'I saw my rock'n'roll past flash before my eyes. . . . On a night when I needed to feel young, he made me feel like I was hearing music for the first time.' CBS executives gleefully rubbed their hands, and singled out the one line, 'I saw rock'n'roll future and its name is Bruce Springsteen!', and used it as the cornerstone of a massive marketing campaign, designed to bring Springsteen to the nation's attention. The campaign worked better than anyone had dared hope. Landau's quote echoed round the world. Sensing a story, other publications also ran features. This blitz was an indication of just how desperate the media were during the early seventies, lavishing such attention onto a relatively unknown quantity, but it had an enormous effect on Springsteen's status. Suddenly, from being a struggling musician up against massive indifference, he was becoming known. Springsteen himself was understandably upset on account of the accusations of hype: 'I was always the kind of guy who liked to walk around and slip back into the shadows. What you dig is the respect of doing what you do, not the attention. Attention, without respect, is jive.'

Within months Springsteen was being hailed as America's rocking salvationist. While the fame was most welcome, to an

THUNDER ROAD

Bruce Springsteen: guitar, vocals, harmonica
Garry Tallent: bass guitar
Max M. Weinberg: drums
Roy Bittan: Fender Rhodes, glockenspiel
Clarence Clemons: saxophones
Background vocals: Roy Bittan,
Mike Appel, Steve Van Zandt

TENTH AVENUE FREEZE-OUT

Bruce Springsteen: guitar, vocals
Garry Tallent: bass guitar
Max M. Weinberg: drums
Roy Bittan: piano
Clarence Clemons: tenor saxophone
†Randy Brecker: trumpet, flugel horn
†Michael Brecker: tenor saxophone
**Dave Sanborn: baritone saxophone
Wayne Andre: trombone

NIGHT

Bruce Springsteen: guitar, vocals
Garry Tallent: bass guitar
Max M. Weinberg: drums

Stereo
Can also be
played on mono
equipment

CBS

69170

SPRINGSTEEN
THE BOTTOM LINE—AUG. 13-17

Wild and Innocent

extent the massive media coverage rebounded on him. Many people felt it was simply an opportunistic method of inflating a minor talent into a major one, with little real proof of talent or durability. While it undoubtedly helped bring him to the attention of a vast new audience, and was essential in ensuring his position at CBS, the whole exercise smacked of 'hype', particularly in Britain, where such excessive zeal in marketing a new talent was regarded with cynical caution. The coverage also exerted other less salutory pressures on Springsteen himself. He had begun recording his third album, which, conventional wisdom has it, is the crucial one in an artist's career. If he makes it with that, then he's there to stay. If he fouls up, then the first two can be seen as flukes. Springsteen was as aware of that as anyone, and was experiencing problems himself with the album. Now there was all this extraneous pressure bearing down on his work. On the other hand, it did now mean that people were paying attention.

Springsteen ushered Landau into his inner circle, feeling he could supply the objectivity crucial in finishing the album. It had been taking months, and progress was excruciatingly slow. But Appel also had his own forceful ideas on how the record should sound, and Springsteen was caught between the two of them. Further delays were inevitable. The months threatened to drag on into years, and all concerned were growing tired with the delays, which they saw as the product of Springsteen's unrealistically painstaking approach to recording. Everybody urged him to get

the record out. But Springsteen would not be moved. 'Listen,' he said, 'the release date is one day. The album is forever.' When it was finally released in August 1975, a year had passed since he had employed Ron Bittan (piano) and Max Winberg (drums) to replace Sancious and Carter to work on the album. But the finished record proved Bruce right. The surging, urgent power chords which usher in *Born To Run* are classic rock'n'roll. Its thrashing, restless energy takes the listener back to America of innocence and drive, of Phil Spector and the lost highway, of Buicks and Thunderbirds, of a time before Watergate and Reaganomics. Perhaps that time of innocence never really existed, except in our imagination, but the sheer joy of *Born To Run* is enough to convince one that it should have done.

Despite numerous attempts at emulating it (Bob Seger, Meat Loaf, John Cougar) and subsequent efforts at deriding it, *Born To Run* stands as a classic rock album. Like *Sergeant Pepper* it had become synonymous with its time, and like *Pepper*, it has worn less well than the maker's later works. At its worst, it sounds like bargain-bin Spector, with songs populated by clichéd characters, and Springsteen already sounding like a parody of himself. At its best, it is exultant, full-throated rock'n'roll, with lyrics that ably display Springsteen's ability as a narrator and storyteller.

It found its audience in those who were looking for a reassertion of rock values, for whom rock had lost its way, and for whom the current rock heroes were deficient: Bowie was too aloof and mercurial, Dylan was all wrapped up with nowhere to go, and Elton John was gutless.

The reputation of Springsteen's concerts was spreading. After Madison Square Garden in 1973 Springsteen stuck to smaller venues, seating about 3,000, where he could feel in touch with the audience, resounding with genuine commitment and concern for them. His gigs came across as accessible and desirable. Springsteen found himself swiftly propelled right onto the front grid. The tour which accompanied *Born To Run* saw Springsteen established as a virtuoso performer; his sets began to expand, frequently running to over 20 songs, and attracted celebrities like Jack Nicholson, Carole King, Robert de Niro, and Warren Beatty. After *Born To Run*, there was no looking back. In the audience rush to share that experience, to celebrate the new contender, the weak spots of the album were overlooked.

All over the world, the effect was shattering. Here was an album which evoked that genuine feel of authentic rock'n'roll, which many had feared was lost forever. *Born To Run* reasserted all rock's promises. It spoke the traditional language of rock'n'roll, of highways and cars, of love and redemption in burned-out Chevrolets, sunshine and salvation over the Jersey state line. From the opening punch of 'Thunder Road', invoking the spirit of Roy Orbison's 'Only The Lonely', through to the song's exultant, defiant 'It's a town full of losers, and I'm pulling out of here to *win*!' the album sounds a triumph of ideals over circumstance. A line like 'Your graduation gown lies in rags at your feet' speaks of the lost ideals and tarnished hopes of a generation. *Born To Run* was a shining clarion call at a time of grey mediocrity.

'Jungleland' can be seen as a climactic expansion of 'Incident On 57th Street'. Springsteen casts an eye over a vivid city, sprawling beneath that giant Exxon sign. He over-reaches himself with the appalling line 'There's a ballet being fought out in the alley.' But the stark conclusion about the poets reaching for their moment, and winding up 'wounded, not even dead' echoes the conclusion to T. S. Eliot's 'The Hollow Men': 'This is the way the world ends, not with a bang but a whimper.' Springsteen sees something glorious in the achievement of death in the pursuit of something *worth* dying for, but the street poets aren't even allowed the dignity of death. For them it remains the ignominy of a life compromised by lost ideals and a weary acceptance of the routine.

On the bootlegged 'Contessa' (properly known as 'Hey, Santa Ana') from 1973, Springsteen sang of: 'Some punk's idea of a teenage nation'; in 'Jungleland' lies the realisation of that bitter ideal. Appositely, Charles Shaar Murray quoted extensively from 'Jungleland' in his excellent *New Musical Express* piece on the punk phenomenon two years later, singling out urgent lines like 'Kids *flash* guitars like switchblades ... *hustle* for the record machine ... *explode* into rock'n'roll bands'. But above that street level sincerity, Springsteen's writing isolates character and incident in rock'n'roll *film noir*, the song's focus shifting like a camera – a tracking shot down Flamingo Road, parallel with the Magic Rat burning over the state line. A crane shot over the Exxon sign, swift cutting to the streets, throbbing with action, with lovers crying and gangs slicing into each other, and all the while the soundtrack is rock'n'roll radio. Then the final, slow pull away from the ambulance, and the 'girl shuts out the bedroom light'. A dark screen, the credits roll.

The 'theme' of the album is one of escape. On 'Backstreets' the forlorn love is lived out in movie houses, the streets, the beach. On 'Night' it is the union between a man and his motor 'with all the wonder it brings', and an escape into the velvet darkness. On 'Born To Run' it is escape with the dream heroine, and even though 'broken heroes' clog the highways, salvation lies 'out on the streets tonight in an everlasting kiss'. Even on the uncharacteristic 'Meeting Across The River' there is some sort of hope offered, even though it is salvation through a sordid drug deal, a last desperate chance.

According to Springsteen himself, though, escape is only one aspect of the album; it was also about searching. He told *Musician* magazine in 1984 of the feelings that motivated *Born To Run*: 'I think that what happened during the seventies was that, first of all, the hustle became legitimised. First through Watergate. That was a real hurting thing, in that the hustler, the dope pusher on the street – that was legitimisation for him. It was: you can do it, just don't get caught. Someone will ask, what did you do wrong? And you'll say, I got caught. In a funny kind of way, *Born To Run* was a spiritual record in dealing with values.' In answer to the corruption endemic to the Watergate era it praised the values of hope, faith, friendship and optimism. Those very qualities also gave Springsteen's critics plenty of ammunition. They singled out his efforts at mythologizing his characters, his 'everything but the kitchen sink' style of production. At a time when America was dead from the feet up musically, Springsteen's album revelled in Americana. Springsteen glamorized the common-place, relied on Chuck Berry imagery, and celebrated a past most were happy to forget, or have moved on from.

Immediately following the album's release at the end of August 1975, Bruce Springsteen had made it. The album hit *Record World's* Top 10 in its first week and went gold (500,000 copies sold) a few weeks later. Following the media build-up that had started with Landau's piece 18 months previously, Springsteen achieved the unique scoop of simultaneous covers on *Time* and *Newsweek* on 27 October. The accusations of hype upset *Newsweek* and were to colour its coverage of rock for years after, but at the time the accolade meant that Springsteen had definitely arrived.

Springsteen's 1975 dates carried him around the States and into Europe. The critical and commercial success of the album inspired him, and spurred by that enthusiasm, Springsteen poured everything into his live shows. In Britain, the hype had preceeded him and posters blossomed around the capital proclaiming 'Finally, London is ready for Bruce Springsteen'. Springsteen was incensed by this heavy-handed campaign and personally tore down as many offending posters as he could lay his hands on. The publicity affected his performances and he later recalled that his first show at London's Hammersmith Odeon was one of the worst he had ever given.

With the E Street Band honed as a performing unit, Springsteen kept on running. Fans accustomed to distant and clinical 'concerts' by groups could not believe their energy and strength. By the end of 1975 Springsteen could well look back, and smile that familiar broad grin of his. It was apparent that his real energies were devoted to performance or studio work. After a rigorous tour, he took a well-earned rest, then slowly set about work on the follow up to *Born To Run*. It proved to be a long and frustrating wait for all concerned.

Streets Of Fire

Springsteen has always been a notoriously methodical person when it comes to recording. He first went into the 914 Studios in New York to start recording *Born To Run* in May 1974 but the album was not ready for release until August 1975. It is not that he is unaware or does not care about his fans' desire to have the fire and energy they enjoy in his concerts repeated in albums for home consumption, but his drive for perfection has always made himself his own harshest critic when it comes to fixing the music on vinyl. He told *International Musician and Recording World* in October 1984 of how he does not understand himself why it takes so long to produce his records: 'Well it's a bizarre thing. If I knew that, I'd probably put 'em out faster. I just kinda wait till I feel there's something going on there. The only bad thing about it is that I feel kinda like a friend that goes away and doesn't write. But it's

unbelievable how great the kids are. I'd see a kid like a year afterwards, and he'll say, "How ya doin'?" "Still working on it." "Aw, take your time. We want it to be right." It's amazing. The funny thing about the record is that we don't do any more than five or six takes on a song.'

However, after *Born To Run* a far more serious problem than his own working methods was to prevent Springsteen recording.

A growing estrangement between Mike Appel and Springsteen (with Landau's increased involvement, much to Appel's dissatisfaction) came to a head in July 1976, when Springsteen sued Appel for mismanagement. On 2 July, when Springsteen was thinking seriously about recording a fourth album, he received a letter from Mike Appel which said that under the terms of his contract he could not use Jon Landau as producer. This brought home to

Bruce just how circumscribed he was, and on 27 July he filed his mismanagement suit. In his enthusiasm to get into the music business, Springsteen had only read his original contract with Appel cursorily, and had signed it on a car bonnet in the parking lot of a club.

But for a very long time Bruce Springsteen's faith in Mike Appel – his mentor, the only man to place any faith in his nascent talent – was such that he would not have it redrawn. However, this trust was not to persist indefinitely; by 1976 Springsteen was reckoned to have earned around two million dollars, but had actually only received $100,000. Moreover, the contracts gave Appel control over most of Springsteen's creative work, so that when he countersued on 29 July he was able to gain an injunction preventing Springsteen from entering a recording studio without him.

Springsteen's original naivety was to cause a protracted and rancorous dispute. He told journalist Peter Knobler in 1978: 'What did I know? I didn't know what publishing *was*! What's publishing? Ask the guy down the street, he isn't gonna know. You're gonna think it's what happens in books. It's one of those words. I knew no one who had ever made a record before. I knew no one who had ever had any contact whatsoever with the music business.' The essence of his charge was that this innocence had been exploited, and he sued for 'fraud … undue influence and breach of trust'.

Springsteen felt that he had been betrayed, and – worst of all – betrayed by a friend. That undermined one of the basic features of Springsteen's way of working – the camaraderie on which the E Street Band had been founded and run. What particularly incensed him was the discovery that he did not even control his songs, and that the material he had written himself could only be used with Appel's permission. For all his faults, there was, however, no denying Mike Appel's devotion to Springsteen, and his guidance of his career. But Springsteen was aware that he had outgrown him creatively, and was torn between the man who had got him his start in the business, and the man he felt could help him develop as a musician. The battles were fought out in court, and, as is inevitable in such cases, were bitter. They kept Springsteen out of a recording studio for almost exactly twelve months. The ban hurt him considerably and he fought against it throughout the proceedings, appealing in both September and December 1976 against it, but without success. In the December appeal he even asked to be allowed to record with Landau as his producer on the condition that the tapes were deposited with the court until such time as the case was settled.

In the first hearings Appel had the upper hand. He could afford for the case to be long and drawn-out, but Springsteen was both eager as a committed musician to get back into the studio and needed the money. Then in October Springsteen changed his lawyer and took on Michael Tanner, who specialised in rock musicians, numbering Paul Simon, the Rolling Stones and John Lennon among his clients. It was a turning-point, and on 28 May 1977 both parties agreed to settle their differences out of court. The terms were never officially made public, but it was a compromise that satisfied both men. Springsteen was free of his management contract and was able to record with whatever producer he wanted; Appel received a flat payment and kept a share in the profits of the records Springsteen had already made. Four days later Springsteen and Landau were in New York's Atlantic Studios to start work on *Darkness On The Edge Of Town*.

During the layoff from the studio Springsteen poured all his energies into touring and performing. They started him on an energetic programme that was to keep going through 1976, 1977 and 1978, when he covered the USA as comprehensively as a mapmaker: Los Angeles, Philadelphia, Ohio, Tennessee, Cleveland, Poughkeepsie. … These gigs saw the establishment of his marathon set, and by the end of 1978 a typical performance would be pushing four hours, including something like 26 songs. He also came to be lionised, joined onstage by such luminaries as Gary Bonds, Patti Smith, Eddie Floyd, Ronnie Spector, Southside Johnny and Gary Busey.

The 1976 tour saw Springsteen and the E Street Band become the first rock'n'roll band to play the legendary home of Country and Western music – Nashville's Grand Ole Opry on 28 April. The following night found Springsteen trying to bluff his way into Elvis' home, Graceland, in Memphis. From that first glimpse of Elvis on the *Ed Sullivan Show* in 1958 he had been Springsteen's idol. 'Fire' had been written specifically for him, and the 1981 song 'Johnny Bye Bye' was written about Presley's death. In it Springsteen spoke movingly of his hero's death, prefacing the song in concert with: 'It's hard to understand that somebody who had so much and seemed to loom so large, could in the end lose so bad!' In addition as a tribute to the King, Springsteen regularly included two Presley ballads – 'Follow That Dream' and 'Can't Help Falling In Love' – in his shows, and recorded 'Johnny Bye Bye' as a B-side of his 1985 single 'I'm On Fire'.

Those lengthy and flexible shows and the dearth of official albums were a Godsend to bootleggers. There had been bootlegs of him before, but the legal battles and the tour of 1978 opened the floodgates. Fans of any star (real fans) will go to incredible lengths to obtain rare material; whether studio recordings, or, more usually, live tapes of gigs, primarily as souvenirs. And Springsteen was exactly the performer to fuel this demand. In his live shows from the 1975 to 1978 period he performed countless new or rarely heard songs, many of which he was never to record.

Bootlegging is, of course, criminal. It denies an artist his royalties, and offers the fans sub-standard recordings of songs which were never intended for official release. It gives a wholly distorted idea of how a song develops. Jon Landau has called it 'out and out theft', stating: 'These people come along and confiscate material that was never intended for release on an album, sell it, and make a profit.' He and Springsteen were obviously concerned that songs which were intended to be heard professionally recorded and produced, in sequence, on an official album, were being stolen, duplicated and sold on inferior quality vinyl.

In addition, Dave Marsh has contended: 'It is no more fair or just to release the scraps and fragments of a performer's work without his consent than it would be to publish the crumpled first draft of a book, or the cutting room out-takes of a movie.' However, there is another case. Legally, Marsh is right but artistically he is wrong. Who would deny that Ezra Pound's annotated

A 1975 portrait of a rock'n'roll giant in the making.

version of T. S. Eliot's *The Waste Land* has given an audience a greater understanding and insight into the writer's craft, or that Rembrandt's sketches are great works of art in themselves? Of course, the fans resent having to fork out extortionate prices for inferior recordings. But as a loyal fan, who has dutifully played (and paid) along with CBS, is it theft to want a souvenir of the best live rock show you have ever seen – or are likely to see – when there is a marked reluctance to release any official souvenir?

With the growth of home videos, the threat of bootleg videos has also presented itself to the Springsteen organisation. In these times when a promo video for a record has become recognised as an art form in itself, fans now have the opportunity to hear and *see* their heroes in action. The package is usually either a wildly over-inflated collection of promos, or a straightforward film of an artist in concert. Typically, neither had surfaced from Springsteen, until 'Dancin' In The Dark' in late 1984, when he belatedly realised the impact of video and authorised a number of TV specials. The promo video for 'Atlantic City' in 1982 was an atmospheric black and white effort in which Springsteen did not appear. However, low-quality bootleg videos are available in the same way as bootleg records and it is now possible to see *rehearsals* for 'The River' tour (real fly on the wall stuff!) and badly shot hand-held films of concerts.

Only Bob Dylan has been more bootlegged than Springsteen, and like Dylan, Springsteen has some infuriating characteristics. Much of his finest material has never been (quite possibly, never will be) released. Dylan's attitude to bootlegging was ambiguous; he shrugged off the eight-year delay accompanying the legendary *Basement Tapes* with 'I thought everyone had 'em anyway!' Springsteen's attitude, too, has been ambiguous. Initially, he wryly acknowledged the industry he had spawned, but latterly he has been clamping down with a vengeance. At the height of his exhaustive gigging, at San Francisco's Winterland in 1978, he can be heard exultantly crying 'Bootleggers . . . roll your tapes!', and later in that same show, as he introduced 'Racing In The Street': 'This is for all the guys in Asbury Park, who I am sure will hear this one day through the magic of bootlegging.' In Europe, fans were particularly attracted to bootlegs, because prior to 1981 not many people had seen him live.

Springsteen's perfectionism feeds the bootleggers. He applies massive dedication to everything he does, aiming for both the highest quality recordings, and the best live shows. But to achieve that is a lengthy and frustrating process. Even after the Appel lawsuit had been resolved, and with a stockpile of songs, enough for a double album, there was still a year's delay before his fourth album was released. And there has never been a live album by the man that many consider to be the finest living exponent of rock'n'roll. There has never been an official opportunity to hear records of the composer's own versions of Southside Johnny's 'The Fever', the Pointer Sisters 'Fire', Patti Smith's 'Because The Night' (which he co-wrote with her), Dave Edmunds' 'From Small Things . . .', Gary Bonds' 'Rendezvous'. We have yet to hear Springsteen's interpretations of John Fogerty's 'Who'll Stop The Rain', Woody Guthrie's 'This Land Is Your Land', Jimmy Cliff's 'Trapped', Jackie de Shannon's 'When You Walk In The Room'

Left: *Bruce and his girlfriend, Karen, hit the limelight.*

BRUCE SPRINGSTEEN
AND THE E STREET BAND

Sunday
March 20, 1977
8 p.m.

Providence
College
Alumni
Hall

All Seats Reserved
$7.00 & $7.50
Available at:
Ladd's
Roth's
Beacon Shop
Midland Records (Midland Mall)
Brown, R.I.C., P.C.

Presented By
the BANZINI BROS
and the P.C. B.O.G

Photo: David Stahl
Graphics: Uneeda Design

and hundreds more. Springsteen seemed to be waiting for the ideal live show for release, when everything coagulates. Such is his frustrating search for perfection that we may never get to hear such an album. Hundreds of shows have been legitimately recorded, but, even with judicious editing, such an album has never even come close to official release.

By 1984 Springsteen was to cool entirely on the idea. He told BBC television's 'Whistle Test' that he was unlikely to make a live album because the essence of his performances was being present at them and because a live album would create a distance between the audience and the band: 'Our band is about breaking down distance.' He also felt it would be boring to record his old songs.

Springsteen himself is aware of the criticisms of his slowness, telling Dave Marsh : 'In the studio, I'm slow, I take a long time . . . I'm lucky because I'm in there, I'm seeing it every step of the way. I would assume that if you didn't know what was going on, and you cared about it, it would be frustrating . . . I got into a situation

where I just said "Hey, this is what I do, and these are my assets, and these are my burdens." I got comfortable with myself being that kind of person. . . . So at this point, I just settled into accepting certain things that I've always been uncomfortable with. I stopped setting limits and definitions – which I always threw out anyway, but which I'd always felt guilty about. Spending a long time in the studio, I stopped feeling bad about that. I said: "That's me, that's what I do. I work slow, and I work slow for a reason. To get the results that I want."'

And again, to *Point Blank*, in discussing his responsibility as an artist: 'Of course I could have done an album a year, but would they have been good? I have a responsibility to myself and the fans. I won't release anything I'm not satisfied with, that I don't have my heart and soul in. . . . If people aren't ready to wait, then they weren't interested in the first place.' Perhaps these are admirable sentiments, evincing a genuine sense of responsibility and concern, but they are frustrating too, as anyone will testify who has heard

Bruce
Springsteen
Darkness
on the Edge
of Town

any of Springsteen's studio out-takes, or seen him in concert. It is the quantity, as well as the quality, of material which seems to be lost forever.

Even by the time of *The Wild, The Innocent And The E Street Shuffle* in 1974, Springsteen had already accrued a backlog of material which would never find its way officially on to record. He has always been a prolific writer, but he grew increasingly selective as the pressures on him mounted. Memorable songs from that 1973/74 period include the chilling 'Ballad Of A Self-Loading Pistol' ('Papa, you showed me the beauty of buckshot/The love song a bullet sings as she whistles ...') 'Hey, Santa Ana' (bootlegged as either 'Contessa' or 'Guns of Kid Cole'), 'Thundercrack' (a.k.a. 'Angel From the Inner Lake'/'Heart Of A Ballerina') with its marvellous vocal harmonies from the E Street Band. The same period saw 'Zero And Blind Terry', a tale of renegade children pursued by an avenging father, which recalls Terence Malick's film *Badlands* (which in turn was the inspiration for the title track of *Nebraska*). 'Jeannie Needs A Shooter' (which was covered by Warren Zevon on his *Bad Luck Streak In Dancing School* album) is in a similar vein, about the love for a lawman's daughter, which finds the hero in the final verse in the best outlaw tradition, shot down by the border, and lying in the darkness 'with a pistol by my side'. And there is the beautiful 'Southern Son': 'And though the Western plains are still stained/with the blood of great cowboys/It's a Southern sun that shines down on this Yankee boy.'

Between 1975 and 1978, Springsteen was writing furiously, and the songs which appeared on *Born To Run* and *Darkness On The Edge Of Town* were only the tip of the iceberg. Even the officially released versions have fascinating antecedents, like a version of 'Thunder Road' which only features a piano accompaniment, enforcing the quality of the lyrics, or the plethora of renderings of 'Born To Run'. 'Streets Of Fire' and 'Racing In The Street' can be seen to have undergone massive lyrical alterations.

'The Promise' is a moody ballad, which comes dangerously close to self parody ('Johnny works in a factory and Billy works downtown') and was held from *Darkness* because a number of people interpreted it as Springsteen's comment on his acrimonious court battle with Appel, although Springsteen snapped: 'I don't write songs about lawsuits!' During these three years Springsteen's concerts became practically potted histories of rock'n'roll itself. Those four-hour shows encompassed his own three albums, as well as generous slices of the Bobby Fuller Four, Sam and Dave, Creedence Clearwater Revival, Buddy Holly, Eddie Cochran, the Ronettes, Dylan, Chuck Berry, Mitch Ryder, Jerry Lee Lewis, the Beatles and others. Even familiar songs from his own albums took on a life of their own. 'Thunder Road', 'Growin' Up', 'Badlands' and 'The Promised Land' sounded even better in concert than on vinyl.

After the long delays since *Born To Run* it would have made perfect sense for a live double album to be issued next, or after the album that was eventually to be issued, or, failing that, in the wake of the dynamic 1981 shows. But Springsteen refrained, so much of the fine work of those years, such as an official version of his own composition 'Because The Night', or his dramatic reworking of Jimmy Cliff's 'Trapped', did not appear. Small wonder then that

Above and below: *Springsteen, the private and public figure.*

the Springsteen bootleg industry is such a thriving concern, particularly when you consider such a lavish package as the triple *Teardrops On The City* set. Having tolerated them for a long time Landau and Springsteen eventually moved into action in August 1979, when they took five bootleggers to court, which served as a warning and stemmed the flood momentarily.

However frustrating the layoff of 1976–77 proved, it gave Springsteen an opportunity to assess himself and the position he found himself in. Catapulted to the top after *Born To Run*, the year gave him time to gain a perspective on himself and his career. As an artist, it gave him the opportunity to chart the changes his country was undergoing – how the characters in his songs were coping with maturity and a recession; how dreams were stifled, but never died. The result of those deliberations was *Darkness On The Edge Of Town*, which finally appeared on 2 June 1978, a year and a day after recording work had started. There had been innumerable problems sifting through the songs which were to constitute the final album and, in the meantime, Springsteen had changed studios, from Atlantic to the Record Plant. He had caused a further delay just before the scheduled release, because he was unhappy with the proofing of the sleeve. Even after all the time spent in the studio Springsteen remained dissatisfied with the recording quality and later said he would like to re-record it, especially as the album contained some of his best stuff.

   In the album a sense of resignation was apparent in Springsteen's writing. Up until then he had eulogised the punks who kicked against the system, but his belief in 'the pursuit of happiness' remained intact. But from this album on, he was to look at the underside of the Dream. The Promised Land was still there, alluring at the end of the highway, but to obtain entry, an arduous journey had to be undertaken, through suffering to salvation. Springsteen's new songs were manifestly aware of the rigours facing man in society. He now knew the characters he wrote about, and there was no need to turn them into Magic Rats or Spanish Johnnys.

   Of that change in his writing, and how his perspective had altered, Springsteen told Dave Marsh in 1981: 'I guess it just started after *Born To Run* somehow. I had all that time off, and I spent a lotta time home. We were off for three years, and home for a long time. It came out of a local kind of thing – what my old friends were doing, what my relatives were doing. How things were affecting them, and what their lives were like. And what my life was like.'

   This emphasis on apprehending ordinary life was important to him. He later told *Musician* magazine: 'I wanted the record to feel like what life felt like. You know, not romantic and not some sort of big heroic thing. I just wanted it to feel like an everyday, Darlington County kind of thing.'

   The album was originally to have been called 'American Madness', after Frank Capra's 1932 film about the effects of the Great Depression on small town America. But Springsteen eventually settled for the sombre *Darkness On The Edge Of Town*. By the time of its release, in June 1978, he was edging 30, a tricky age for anyone, but for a rocker, a boundary. It was to that darkness that

Above and below: *two sides of the Springsteen character.*

Springsteen found himself drawn. The face that stared bleakly out from the album cover was one that had endured three years of bitter wrangles, self-doubt, gruelling touring and soul-searching. The mistrust and self-doubt were, inevitably, reflected on the finished album. *Darkness* stands as one of rock's bleakest testimonies, not wallowing in self-pity, but permeated by a sense of realisation, tinged with bitter experience.

Of the ten new songs, seven dwell on darkness. They speak of trust, betrayal, faith and belief. The cars are still there, but only as a means of escape. All of the songs are intensely autobiographical, but in the cases where Springsteen casts himself as observer ('Factory', 'Candy's Room') the results are moving, following the narrative exposition of 'Incident on 57th Street' and 'Meeting Across The River'. The heroine of 'Candy's Room' is no idealised Wendy, to die with on the streets in an everlasting kiss. She's an embittered hooker, dealing in dreams, provided the dollars are upfront in subsidising those dreams. The litany on 'Factory' comes from the poignant observation by an only son of the indignity of his father's life seen slipping away in front of his eyes. It is on 'Factory' that Springsteen sings with unashamed sympathy, for the first time, of his father, undergoing the numbing repetition of a factory job for a living wage, making sacrifices which remain unrecognised by his family. The implicit message was that there *must* be more to life – any life – than this. By the time of *Nebraska* in 1982, and the economic depression it reflected, the dignity of work was to take second place to the job itself.

The key lines from the album are to be found on 'Racing In The Street': 'Some guys just give up living/And start dying, little by little, piece by piece/Some guys come home from work and wash up/And go racing in the street.' It's where the world is split in two: on one side of the line slump those who have been crushed by the system, on the other side stand those who can still see the dream, and are willing to pursue it. The street is still sacred, but not because it's populated by gangs – that's adolescent time. This time it's the road that stretches to the Interstate, which propels them towards a destiny which is a blessed relief from the stifling conformity of their lives. Where a Spanish Johnny, four years on, can express his individuality, or cling to the camaraderie of his youth. Where, in a closed shop of car parts, he can escape the monotony of TV dinners, his hollow marriage and the scream of the factory whistle. Where he can prove himself, if only *to* himself. The song's chorus acts as a gloomy counterpoint to Martha and the Vandellas' 'Dancing In The Street'.

The song from *Darkness* that most typifies the whole album is 'The Promised Land' (again, surely no coincidence that Springsteen filched the title from Chuck Berry?). It is here that the evidence of Springsteen's maturing as a writer is apparent – driving all night, but only chasing a mirage, and knowing it's a mirage. It describes a smouldering resentment of time, place and circumstances, to 'take a knife and cut this pain from my heart/Find somebody itching for something to start'. Searching, again, even if only for a mirage, someone, something, that offers salvation. 'The Promised Land' is where you escape to – it may be a girl, a jukebox, a stretch of road – but it's where you have what is your own, and to enter it you have to have a faith in yourself and your own abilities. When Springsteen sings 'I *believe* in a Promised Land', he can persuade his audience to sing along with him and seize his belief as their own, because if you haven't got that belief, there isn't anywhere else to go.

Of the characters on the album, Springsteen told *Crawdaddy*: 'They're 28 to 30 years old, like my age, they're not kids anymore. . . . On *Born To Run* there was the hope of a free ride. On *Darkness* there ain't no free ride – You wanna ride, you gotta pay! And maybe you'll make it through, but you ain't gonna make it through till you been beat, you've been hurt, until you been messed up. There's hope, but it's just the hope of, like, survival.' *Darkness* shows Springsteen struggling to come to terms with life, and with the lives of his contemporaries, and charting those changes in his songs. He is learning to see the world in shades of grey, instead of starkly divided black and white. It marks his maturing.

The album's title track describes the line that has to be walked. Pleasures and salvation which can only be found on the edge, in the darkness, away from the bright lights of suburbia and conformity. The singer drives to his ex-lover's home where she lives in middle-class respectability, with 'that blood that never burned in her veins' – blood should *burn* not just flow. Springsteen calls her to the place where their dreams are buried, ''neath Abram's Bridge'. To regain those precious dreams, you have to leave the light, and scrabble around in the darkness. It may not work, maybe they're buried too deep. They may not be able to rekindle that old flame, but they've got to *try*. For the old times, they've got to try for what they had, for what they've lost. To try for what they are still searching for.

On 'Prove It All Night', he scornfully asks 'If dreams came true, oh *wouldn't* that be nice?' He's enough of a realist to know now that dreams are dreams and have to be kept like that. But all those sacrifices are worth it, if 'you want it, you take it, you pay the price'. There is redemption, but it's redemption which is won through bitter experience, not a prize on a TV game show. (An early version of 'Something In The Night' finds Springsteen still 'riding down Kingsley', but on the recorded version, he picks up a hitch-hiker who's looking 'to die or be redeemed'.)

'Badlands' was an apocalyptic vision (with which Springsteen appropriately opened his set the night Reagan was elected). 'I don't give a damn/For the same old played out scenes/I don't give a damn/For just the in-betweens/Honey I want the heart, I want the soul/I want control right now', stands as a statement of intent on the album's opening track. Ultimately, though, there is that residual strand of hope which Springsteen offers: 'I believe in the love that you gave me! I believe in the hope that can save me! I believe in the faith! And I pray that someday it may raise me above these Badlands!'

The production of the album reflected its stark lyrical feel. There were no strings, no embellishments, just hard, thunderous rock'n'roll. Springsteen's singing, too, had changed. It was more assertive, more prominent. The aching howl on 'Streets Of Fire', which lapses almost into incoherence, sounds like some wounded animal sloping through the city streets, injured, but defiant.

In the turbulent America of the times, *Darkness On The Edge Of Town* reflected that changing society, and firmly established Bruce Springsteen as *the* American rock star of the seventies.

Bruce asked his ex-girlfriend, photographer Lynn Goldsmith not to photograph him at this particular concert.

The Price You Pay

The impending release of *Darkness On The Edge Of Town* prompted a new surge of touring, starting on 23 May in Buffalo, his first live performance for five months. While mega-bands like Aerosmith, Kiss, Rush and Kansas plugged round the large venues, and stuck pretty close to the same line, Springsteen's itinerary encompassed the whole country, playing in 37 states and Canada. From East Coast to West, and back via the neglected heartland of the Mid-West, the tour careered across the States for six solid months, with the band playing shows usually in excess of three hours *every* night, then on the bus, and further on down the road. It was a gruelling slog which exacted a high physical price – Springsteen would lose between three and five pounds a show – and it says much about his dedication that he both undertook it so comprehensively, and did not skimp on any show. He told *Sounds* in 1978 why he never let up: 'You may be playing 80 shows in eight months, but this kid out there, it's his money, and it's his one night. He may not see you again for a year. So you mustn't let him down. ... You've got a lot to live up to when you walk out on that stage – a certain tradition from the early rockers up to now that I believe in a lot. It's like, you've got to be your own hero, find it out

for yourself – I'm just sort of like the catalyst.'

Springsteen still shunned large auditoriums, preferring the clubs, where the audience could fully appreciate the excitement and intensity of an E Street Band show. It was as if he was repaying a debt, for it had been clubs like Asbury Park's Upstage, New York's Bottom Line and the LA Roxy which had helped establish his live reputation. He felt he could communicate better with a small audience than a large one. This community of response was what the shows were about, with Bruce interspersing the numbers with long monologues about his past. An E Street Band concert wasn't a matter of the group just playing and the audience receiving the sounds; it was meant to be a shared experience. Once when a French journalist went backstage to ask him for an interview after a concert, Springsteen replied: 'But haven't I just been talking to you for the last four hours?'

The only exception to the small venues was three nights in August at New York's Madison Square Garden, the scene of the disastrous set five years previously when he had opened for Chicago. History did not repeat itself. The three nights were a triumph, culminating on the last night in Bruce's mother herself

appearing on stage to drag him back in mock reluctance for an encore.

Springsteen was taking his music to the people it was meant for, the people who were the characters in his songs. He was singled out at this time as the prime exponent of a new musical development, 'Blue Collar rock'. Cynthia Rose wrote a telling essay on the phenomenon for the *History Of Rock* magazine: '[It] is a critical term, disseminated by various rock critics who possess "white collar" credentials. It was coined to deal with a number of American artists who were selling solidly (in the case of Bruce Springsteen, spectacularly) and had achieved somewhat heroic stature; all with "traditional" rock songs, whose lyrics featured girls, cars, rebellion and the radio. . . . Several supposed similarities linked those artists (Springsteen, Tom Petty and Bob Seger). The great unspoken, unwritten one was that they lacked "proper" (i.e. white collar) educations: that their smarts were street smarts, their language limited to that of the truck stop, shopping mall or suburban housing tract. That they were tough and randy rockers in the guise of people's heroes – spokesmen and role models for the little guy and his girl.'

In Springsteen's case, that is certainly applicable. He was almost cocky about his lack of real education, revelled in his role of rock's noble savage (expressing direct emotion without the hindrance of proper education) and phrasing his message and narratives in 'traditional' rock terms. It was a point which David Hepworth amplified in a 1982 essay: 'Springsteen has been called a reactionary . . . he has shamelessly poured every last iota of his craft, enthusiasm, humour and passion into giving back to the people what he himself got from the likes of the Drifters, Smokey Robinson and the Who . . .'

Indeed, in America in the late seventies, people were looking for someone who offered hope, a figure of integrity following the chicanery of Watergate. In politics they got Jimmy Carter, who at least got off on the right foot by quoting Bob Dylan in his inaugural address. In rock'n'roll, they got Bruce Springsteen. His concerts offered more than just good value for money; they became group expressions of solidarity and hope, with Springsteen placing trust in his audience, making spontaneous leaps into the heart of the crowd.

In Britain on the other hand, by the time of the release there of *Darkness On The Edge Of Town* the majority of people had all but written Springsteen off. They remembered the hype of 1975, and there had been nothing since then on record to substantiate the pretender. Certainly, there were stories of the marathon gigs in the States, and a steady trickle of bootlegs. Certainly, there were pieces, too, like Tony Parsons' heartfelt *New Musical Express* interview of October 1978: 'Kid, I've seen 'em all. . . . But this ain't just the best gig I've ever seen in my life, it's much more than that. It's like watching your entire life flashing by, and instead of dying, you're dancing!' But at the end of 1978 UK fans had other things on their mind. The punk revolution of 1976 had entirely altered the face of the British music scene. By 1978 the economic sky had become darker and gloomier than that which had seen the Technicolor panache of *Born To Run* three years before. The New Wave

By 1978, despite radical changes in the nature of rock's musical direction, Springsteen was considered a new wave spokesman.

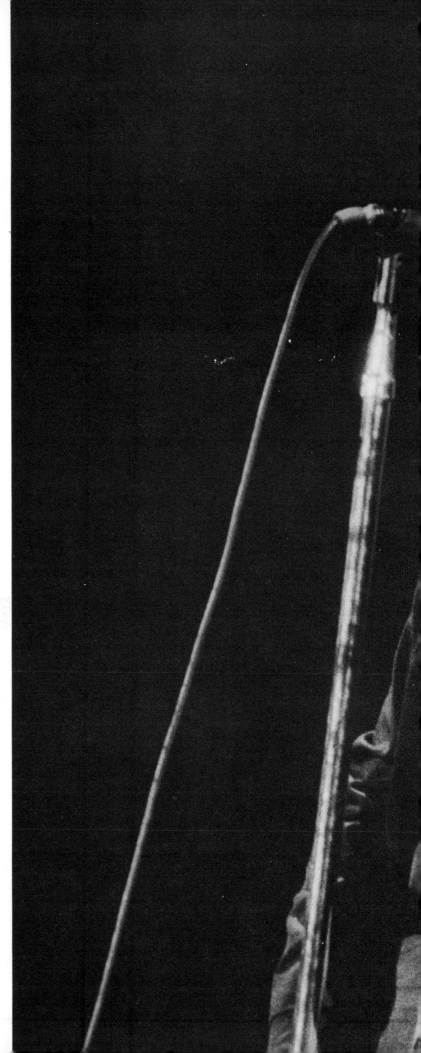

had throbbed on its own manic energy, and had produced its own spokesmen. There was the feeling that the hero worship of remote American superstars – particularly those that sang about cars and cruisin', and called every woman 'baby' – was over. There were instead, *real* issues and dangers, which the young punks confronted. A political swing to the Right, overt racism in British society, the intolerable level of growing unemployment, all had to be confronted and indeed were confronted by the new generation of musicians: Tom Robinson's scathing 'Winter of '79', Elvis Costello's biting indictments of fascism on 'Less Than Zero' and 'Night Rally', the Clash's accusatory 'I'm So Bored With The USA', the Jam's attack on the odious National Front on 'Down In The Tube Station At Midnight' and the Sex Pistols' howl for 'Anarchy In The UK'.

By now many British bands were no older than their audiences. Heavily political, eagerly embracing reggae, spurning orthodox rock venues, scornful of fashion, lambasting the established old guard of rock notables (Rod Stewart, Mick Jagger, Elton John, Genesis), the New Wave had no need for museum pieces like Bob Dylan or the Pink Floyd. After the initial Luddite assault, which recalled the heady days of Merseybeat, with every week throwing up dozens of new bands, the New Wave established its own hierarchy, populated by concerned and articulate writers like Elvis Costello, Paul Weller, Joe Strummer, Ian Dury and Difford and Tilbrook. Punk had given rock'n'roll a necessary kick in the right direction, and the last thing anyone needed then was *Born To Run II*. But that is not what was delivered, and the new sounds were dark and unlike the previous Springsteen. Rather than writing him off, *Darkness* gave Springsteen a lot of new UK fans. It mirrored the turmoil at the end of the seventies, and confronted contemporary issues head on. At a time when many rock idols were dismantled and rendered obsolete, Springsteen proved in the tough British musical climate that he had weathered the storm, and emerged with his principles and credibility intact.

This son of a New Jersey coach driver showed that he could convey sentiments and emotions which would reverberate around the world. It was, in fact, his origins which enabled him to do this. Tired of pretentious concept and flimsy philosophical albums, the fans found a gritty honesty and straightforwardness in Springsteen. Tired of arrogant and aloof stars, they found a singer who was affable and courteous offstage. Tired of rock music hung around with 'art' labels, they found a non-intellectual who once said, 'I was brought up on TV. . . . I didn't hang round with no crowd that was talking about William Burroughs!' This was a man who shared their disillusionment, who also said, 'When the guitar solos went on too long at the end of the sixties, I lost interest!'

Although political in its broader sense, Springsteen had never allied himself directly with any political cause. His songs revealed a humanitarian, an artist with a concern for the issues of his time, but never along orthodox party lines. So it was with some surprise that it was learned that Bruce Springsteen and the E Street Band had agreed to play two charity shows on behalf of MUSE (Musicians United for Safe Energy) in September 1979. The concerts were a response to the near-disaster at Three Mile Island in Pennsylvania earlier in the year, when the nuclear process plant leaked and threatened to explode, causing a hasty evacuation from the area. Springsteen had been friendly with Jackson Browne, one of the organizers, for a number of years, and it was at his suggestion that he agreed to appear on a platform campaigning against nuclear energy.

Springsteen's immediate reaction on hearing of the incident had been to write a song called 'Roulette'. It speculated on how Three Mile Island would have affected a man and his family if they had lived in the area. However, it is not a good song. While managing to evoke a feeling of eeriness and threat, it is far too paranoid, and subsequently suffers by concentrating on such a specific incident. The broader aspects of the song, and the possibility of nuclear holocaust, are clumsily tacked on at the end. Wisely, Springsteen never officially recorded the song, and did not even perform it at the MUSE concerts at Madison Square Garden.

The MUSE shows of September 1979 were a watershed for the music of the seventies. There were five concerts. Springsteen closed each of the last two, and on both occasions stole the show. He played a particularly energetic hour-and-a-half set in the second one, giving everything he had as if to challenge time itself in defiance of the fact that the next day was his thirtieth birthday. But perhaps the event was looming over him, because in an uncharacteristic burst of temper he swooped on his photographer ex-girlfriend, Lynn Goldsmith, in the front of the crowd, and had her ejected for taking photographs of him in spite of an agreement that she wouldn't.

A selection from the concerts appeared as a film, *No Nukes*, featuring three of Springsteen's songs, accompanied by a *No Nukes* triple album, which featured two of the other songs he performed – 'Stay' and 'The Devil With The Blue Dress Medley'.

Lined up were the rock establishment of James Taylor and Carly Simon, Crosby, Stills and Nash, Jackson Browne and the Doobie Brothers, with Springsteen there to provide the shock of the new. Even for the unconverted, it's no contest, with Springsteen winning hands down. From the moment he makes his first appearance in the *No Nukes* film, primed backstage, he is the undoubted star of the event. The resultant film and triple album amply demonstrate just how entrenched and out-of-touch the old guard had become. Graham Nash, who performed an embarrassing version of 'Our House', unwittingly offered an epitaph for the occasion when he was asked what it was like playing before Springsteen: 'Never open for Bruce Springsteen!' Only Gil Scott-Heron's passionate 'We Almost Lost Detroit' and Jackson Browne's haunting 'Before The Deluge' come anywhere near matching Springsteen's intensity.

He shook the concert to life with an energetic 'Thunder Road'. But it was the newly written ballad 'The River' which was the real revelation. Couched in sombre blue light, and singing with an intensity that surpassed even *Darkness*, Springsteen performed 'The River' at his most sensitive and charismatic.

The album package was released in December 1979, and the film followed in August of the next year. The LP was the sole live recording of Bruce Springsteen and the E Street Band at the time.

With the now customary two-year lapse between albums the

usual rumours circulated: Springsteen was to play the Marlon Brando role in a re-make of *The Wild One*; he was paralysed in hospital; he was making albums with Rickie Lee Jones and Stevie Nicks; he was to be chosen as New Jersey's 'Youth Ambassador' (he wasn't, but 'Born To Run' was chosen as the state's 'unofficial Youth Rock Anthem'). In fact, there was a whisper of truth in the hospital rumour as he had hurt his leg in a minor motor cycle

Bruce and singing star Rachel Sweet. She and Bruce share a deep love for the great history of rock'n'roll, and both constantly dip into the rich repertoire of the past in their music.

accident, but this did not stop him getting back into the studio to record his fifth album.

It was another long job. Work on *The River* started in April 1979, but the record did not see the light of day until October 1980. As a reward for the time since *Darkness On The Edge Of Town* it was a two-record set. In fact, it is one of the few double albums in rock to fully merit four sides, and still stands as the best available insight into the Springsteen phenomenon. This was recognised by its selling 2 million copies. Its strength lies in its diversity, with twenty songs covering the spectrum of his writing, from the pensive 'Independence Day' and 'Wreck On The

Highway' to the exuberant 'Sherry Darling' and 'You Can Look (But You Better Not Touch)'. Its span ranges from a chilling 'Point Blank' to a throw-away 'Cadillac Ranch'. It was a return to the intensity of his first album seven years before, as if this was the one that Springsteen had to prove himself with, and as a result poured everything into it. As Paolo Hewitt wrote in his *Melody Maker* review: 'Listening to it is like taking a trip through the rock'n'roll heartland as you've never experienced it. It is a walk down all the streets, all the places, all the people and all the souls that rock has ever visited, excited, cried for and loved.'

Springsteen had never sounded cockier or brasher on the

rockers, or more reflective on the ballads. As if marking his turning thirty during recording, *The River* offers a reconciliation between the glorious optimism of *Born To Run* and the sombre introspection of *Darkness On The Edge Of Town*. It marks a bridge between innocence and experience. The songs find Springsteen viewing the lives and circumstances of his contemporaries with compassion, but with an objectivity which makes them universally applicable. It acknowledges that the stark issues which were so clearly defined in youth, grow blurred and confused with age.

Springsteen saw the album as an austere reflection of the times, but characterised by occasional delights. The characters here are in danger of being crushed, of standing, drained of motivation and ambition, but sustained by the possibility of dreams. He told Robert Hilburn of the *Los Angeles Times* soon after the album was released: 'Rock'n'roll has always been this joy, this certain happiness that is, in its way, the most beautiful thing in life. But rock is also about hardness and closeness and being alone. With *Darkness* it was hard for me to make those things coexist ... I wasn't ready, for some reason within myself, to feel those things. It was too confusing, too paradoxical. But I finally got to the place where I realized I had paradoxes, a lot of them, and you've got to live with them. ... What happens to most people is when their first dream gets killed off, nothing ever takes its place. The important thing is to keep holding out for possibilities. ... There's an article by Norman Mailer that says, "The one freedom people want most is the one they can't have: The freedom from dread." That idea is somewhere at the heart of the new album, I know it is.'

Springsteen recognised that as people grow older – or, indeed, grow up – they have to make compromises, and learn to live with them. It's inevitable, whether in relationships, jobs, aspirations, dreams. But there was still a vestige of the romantic clinging to him, saying that you must have dreams, something to aim for, otherwise life itself loses all meaning, and becomes an empty charade. He said to the *New York Sunday News*: 'You can't just be a dreamer. That can become an illusion, which turns into a *delusion*, you know? Having dreams is probably the most important thing in your life. But letting them mutate into delusions, wow, that's poison.'

Dreams are there to be attained, not sustained, plateaux on the way up our individual Everests. Yet, ironically, the essence of dreams is their ability to remain untouched or unattainable. The lines from the album's title song are especially significant: 'Is a dream a lie if it don't come true/Or is it something worse?'

However, the lighter side of Springsteen was amply represented in *The River*, from the glorious Searchers-influenced opening chords of 'The Ties That Bind', through an exultant 'Sherry Darling', a defiant 'Out On The Street' and a gleeful 'Crush On You' and 'I'm A Rocker'. Songs like 'Hungry Heart', 'Ramrod' and 'Cadillac Ranch' are supremely crafted examples of high energy rock'n'roll. But Springsteen's strength has always been his variety, the ability to alter moods simply on the strength of his songs. The contrast imbues the darker side of the album with a greater power and durability.

The characters on the album are people who have been ground down, but are still kicking. They recognise the bitterness of the system which produced them, and how they have virtually outlived their usefulness, so they escape, or try to escape, whether to the

Bruce gets a helping hand as he headlines the Musicians United for Safe Energy concerts in September 1979.

river, the highway or the edge of town. What Springsteen so admires is their *trying*. If any one line from the album epitomises Springsteen's realisation of those changes, it is 'Point Blank's' valedictory: 'I was gonna be your Romeo, you were gonna be my Juliet/These days you don't wait on Romeos, you wait on that welfare check.' In those two bitterly resigned lines, Springsteen bids a sad farewell to that era of lost innocence, goodbye to Spanish Johnny ('Like a cool Romeo, he made his moves') and the Romeo of 'Fire'. A goodbye, too, to his youth. It was now time to face the harsh realities of adult life.

membered the letters I wrote/When our love was young and bold/ She said last night she read those letters/And they made her feel one hundred years old.' And 'Out In The Street' finds Springsteen at his most brash and feeble: 'When I'm out in the street, I walk the way I wanna walk . . . I talk the way I wanna talk.'

It is on a song like 'Wreck On The Highway' that Springsteen displays his strengths. It is stripped down to the bone lyrically and musically, and acts as an iconoclastic coda to the album. The scope and implication of the song are far broader than the story of a man witnessing somebody dying in the aftermath of a car crash. By implication, Springsteen raises questions about our ideas of mortality, of 'the ultimate question' of life and death, of the haphazard snuffing out of an individual candle. But so restrained is his performance, and so deft his writing, that the song never becomes pretentious.

'The Price You Pay' is an epic song, in both ambition and achievement, from the crashing drums which introduced it, to Springsteen's triumphant vocal finish. It touches on the Western myth so beloved by John Ford, and sounds as if it was intended to be set in Monument Valley: 'Do you remember the story of the promised land/How he crossed the desert sands/And could not enter the chosen land/On the banks of the river he stayed/To face the price you pay?' The song touches on the compromises we must make, and the dreams which sustain their purity. A man stands alone, defiant, determined to fight for what he believes in, aware that sacrifices have to be made, and willing to undergo purgatory for the glory and the dream.

The title track sprang from Springsteen's conversations with his brother-in-law, and shows a complete understanding of the realities of the new recession. His sister had married before she was 20, and started a family soon afterwards. Her husband, a construction worker, lost his job and the family went through a terrible time. 'The River' is about their experiences, and the fortitude that enabled them to pull through and later to thrive. To Springsteen such people are the real heroes of today. The song is full of bitter intensity, and is very much of its time, but one which accommodates the past, recalling carefree younger days in the final verse, without glamorising them. It is an acute piece of narrative, conclusive proof that Springsteen had overcome the sentimentality which had threatened to choke his development.

It was one from the heart, as was 'Independence Day' – a white flag flying over the no man's land which exists between parents and their errant children, which lasts through the years, as successive generations try to come to terms and cope with that distance. The very understatement of the song exonerates Springsteen from many of his previous excesses. He carefully, touchingly, delineates that feeling, that time, when all men must make their way, come Independence Day.

As ever, with any Springsteen album, there was a lengthy, agonising search to decide the final running order, made doubly difficult because of the 20 songs intended for it. Finally, Springsteen himself, Jon Landau and Miami Steve managed to agree on the sequencing. So the Drifterish resignation of 'I Wanna Marry You' slots neatly between the exuberance of 'You Can Look . . .' and the melancholy 'The River', just as 'Fade Away' fits perfectly between 'I'm A Rocker' and 'Stolen Car'.

The River gave Springsteen his first real hit single – 'Hungry

Even the rockers are peppered with marvellous throwaway lines: 'So you fell for some jerk who was tall, dark and handsome/Then he kidnapped your heart, and now he's holdin' it for ransom' ('I'm A Rocker'), 'She makes the Venus de Milo look like she's got no style/She makes Sheena of the Jungle look meek and mild' ('Crush On You') and the ironic last verse of 'You Can Look (But You Better Not Touch)'. But although *The River* contains the best of Springsteen's recorded work, it also has some low points. It is difficult to take 'Drive All Night' seriously – driving all night for a pair of *shoes*? The song's length, and Springsteen's hammy delivery, pall beside earlier versions of a similar theme, like 'Streets Of Fire' or 'Something In The Night'. 'Stolen Car' descends quickly into predictability, with the unconvincing lines: 'She asked if I re-

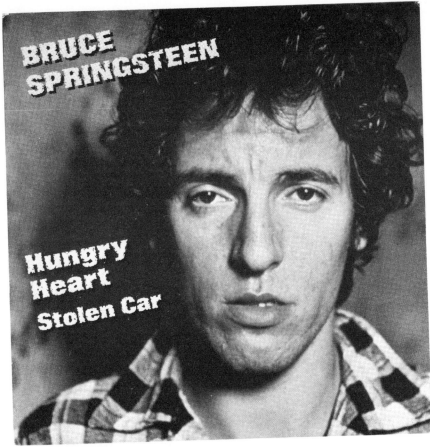

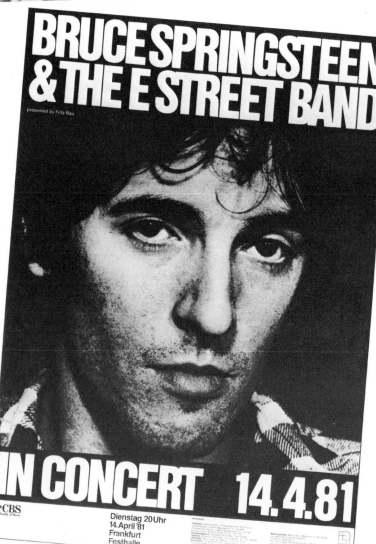

Heart' reached number 5 in the US charts in November 1980; 'Born To Run' had, incredibly, only got to 23. It also brought him a whole vast new audience. The album was awarded a Platinum disc (for selling over one million copies) and entered the *Record World* Top Ten at number 2, and *Billboard's* at number 4. Such was his success that only five albums into his career the press gave him one of their greatest accolades, and started looking out for 'New Springsteens'!

Not everyone was convinced, though. *New Musical Express's* Julie Burchill remarked that 'There's no bore worse than a Bruce bore!' and several other critics had a go at him: they thought he was sentimental and juvenile. He was accused of male chauvinism, constantly referring to women with the demeaning 'baby'. These critics viewed his coy attitude to fame as a sham, and remembered the 'future of rock'n'roll' quote with bitterness. They also found him tiresomely evangelical about rock'n'roll itself in interviews, Frances Lass wryly asking in London's *Time Out*: 'What *would* he have done if he'd failed his driving test?' Some of those who had previously liked his work carped about the constant overpowering use of car imagery and symbols in the new album.

The criticism of him for excessive use of car imagery has been made against other albums. The justification is that the car is a prime American symbol, and Springsteen has countered: 'I don't write songs about cars. My songs are about people *in* those cars.' Certainly, he uses the car and the highway as recurrent symbols, but this springs from his background and environment. It is unfair to criticise a writer for his stock of imagery if he expresses deeper emotions through it. Springsteen simply takes a recognisable icon of America – the car – and utilises it to his own imaginative ends. It can work to dazzling effect ('Racing In The Street', 'Wreck On The Highway') or be numbingly amateurish ('Drive All Night').

The hostile critics were, however, in a minority, and the album was well received by the public. With *The River* in the shops and on the charts, Springsteen hit the road for his most gruelling tour to date. It was to last twelve months, cover thirteen countries, and include 132 gigs. Two months into it, in Philadelphia, he took the stage on the day after one of the most fateful dates in rock history – 8 December 1980. That night, John Lennon had been murdered in New York. Clearly shaken, Springsteen addressed the crowd: 'It's a hard night to come out and play when so much has been lost … if it wasn't for John Lennon, we'd all be in a different place tonight. It's a hard world that makes you live a lot of things that are unlivable. And it's hard to come out here and play, but there's nothing else to do!' Springsteen was visibly shocked by the death of a man he had never met, but whose music had started him on his own career – 'I got the same musical background as most 31-year-olds: Stones, Beatles, Kinks.' He finished that night with 'Twist and Shout'.

Appropriately, when *The River* tour coiled into Europe in April 1981, the first date was in Hamburg, the city where the Beatles had paid their dues in cellars along the Reeperbahn two decades before. Promoter Fritz Rau called Springsteen's visit 'the most successful in German rock history'. It was a promising beginning, and the promise was not to be confounded.

1980 saw 'Hungry Heart' reach number 5 in the U.S. charts, and the tour which continued well into 1981.

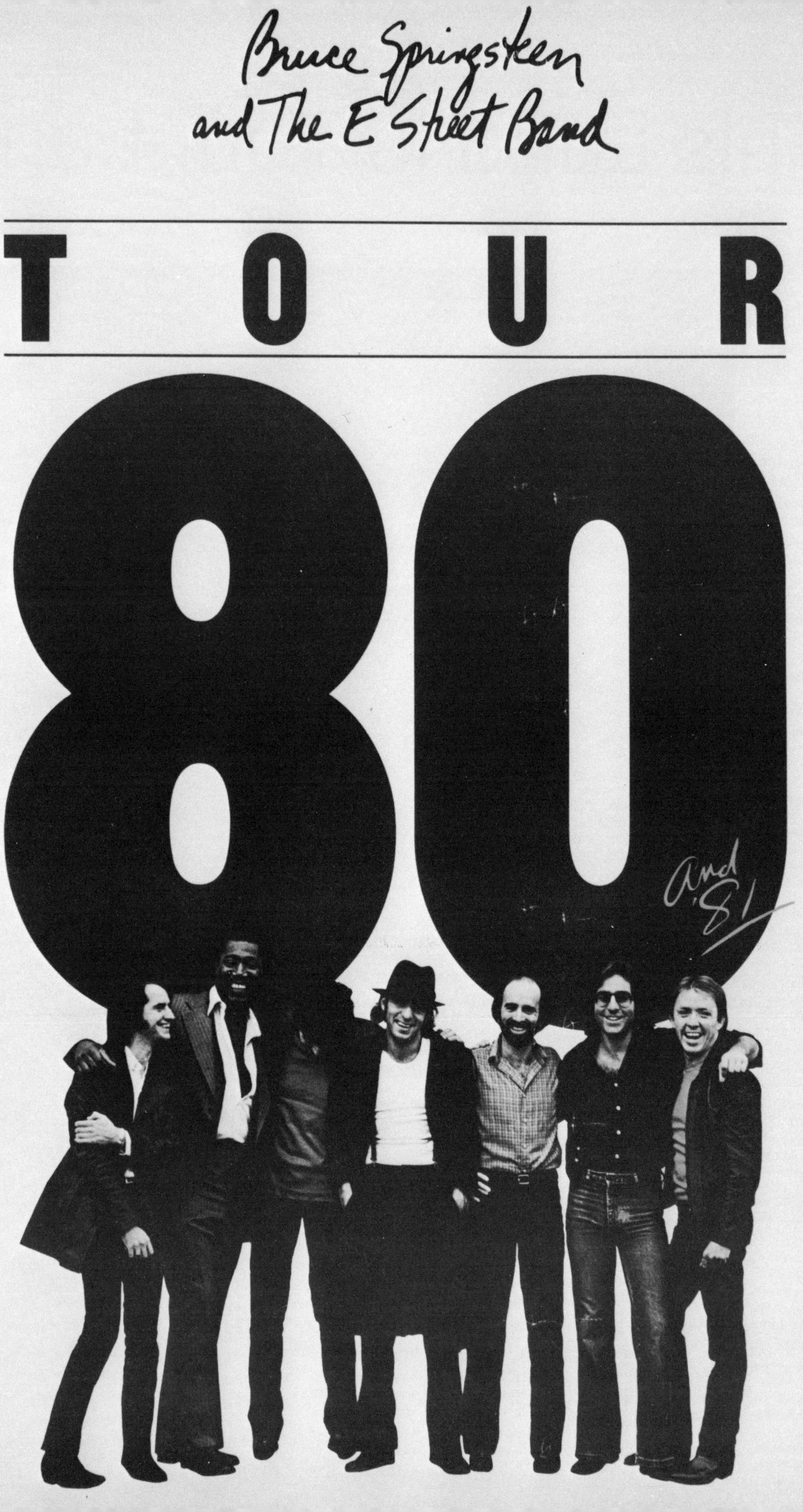
Bruce Springsteen
and The E Street Band
TOUR
80
and '81

This Land Is Your Land

The tour was gathering momentum. From Germany it went to Switzerland, France, Spain, Belgium, Holland, Denmark, Norway, Sweden, and finally to Britain.

Any doubts as to whether Springsteen was right for the current climate were soon confounded. In Britain alone over 600,000 applications were received for the total of 100,000 seats available at his UK shows. Although the deliberate ugliness of the punks was being replaced in a process of reaction by the narcissism of the New Romantics, Springsteen survived the backlash that had had those who sympathised with old-style rock'n'roll branded as 'rockist'. Everyone involved was determined that there would be no repetition of the 1975 debacle. Jon Landau told *Billboard*: 'There was a great deal of promotion around then. The situation wasn't properly controlled. This time we wanted people to know we were here, to see the records, but beyond that we didn't want to

do anything especially elaborate.' Where earlier he had met coolness and scepticism, he was now greeted with enthusiasm. Promoter Harvey Goldsmith, who handled the 1975, 1981 and 1985 shows, remembered how sobering that first visit had been: 'We went out to dinner afterwards, and he just couldn't understand it all. He was used to playing clubs in the US where audiences knew his songs, and went up the walls for him, but here was an audience just sitting there, saying, "Okay Brucie baby, show me".' But this time it was different.

In the midst of a depression British audiences found a song like 'The River' just as applicable to their own experiences as it was in the USA. During the European leg of his tour Springsteen added Woody Guthrie's 'This Land Is Your Land' to his set; it seemed entirely appropriate at the start of a summer that had already seen riots in one black ghetto and was to see a lot more. On the night of

Bob Marley's death, he altered a line to run 'From California to the streets of Brixton'.

The songs Springsteen performed in these concerts were an especially eclectic example of the range he now presented regularly. As well as his own songs, he gave a liberal selection of rock classics: the Elvis ballads 'Follow That Dream' and 'Can't Help Falling In Love', John Fogerty's 'Who'll Stop The Rain' and 'Rockin' All Over The World', Bobby Fuller's 'I Fought The Law', Arthur Conley's 'Sweet Soul Music', the Beatles' 'Twist And Shout', and Jerry Lee Lewis' 'High School Confidential', as well as Guthrie's democratic anthem. However, unaccountably, he only performed one song from his first two albums, 'Rosalita'.

Springsteen's reason for including the classics in his shows was not to preserve them in some sort of rock'n'roll museum, or to show off his knowledge of music. It is because rock'n'roll is his life, and they are included as a homage, to pay tribute to the great liberating influence the music had on him. He told *Crawdaddy*: 'Sometimes people ask me who are your favourites. My favourites change. . . . For me the *idea* of rock'n'roll is sort of my favourite. . . . We don't play oldies. They may be older songs, but they're not nostalgic. . . . It's great right now, it's great today, and if somebody plays it and people hear it, they'll love it tomorrow.' Once again, Springsteen showed that in rock you have to move on, but in doing so you also have to be aware of what has been before.

Springsteen's fascination with rock history is not just a matter of memories from his own past. The past is there for constant exploration. He told Dave Marsh: 'I go back, further all the time, back into Hank Williams, back into Jimmie Rodgers. . . . What mysterious people they were. There's this song, "Jungle Rock", by Hank Mizell. Where is Hank Mizell? What happened to him? What a mysterious person. What a ghost. And you can put that thing on and see him. You can see him standing in some little studio, way back when, and just singing that song. No reason. Nothing gonna come of it. Didn't sell. That wasn't no Number One record, and he wasn't playing no big arenas after it either. . . . But what a mythic moment, what a mystery. Those records are filled with mystery; they're shrouded with mystery. Like these wild men come out of somewhere, and man they were so *alive*. The joy and abandon, inspiration. Inspirational records.'

The European and Scandinavian concerts impressed even his critics with their commitment and their length. It was a refreshing change after years of American stars going there with no apparent desire other than to make money, and after several tours by inferior musicians with less integrity. Springsteen's performance style, his long monologues, and his affability particulary captivated European audiences, who had never experienced anything like it before. After the European concerts Springsteen and the E Street Band returned to the States for an anti-nuclear benefit at the Hollywood Bowl, followed by another three months of touring, once again crossing the country from New Jersey to California. He added several new interpretations to the set – Woody Guthrie's 'Deportees', the Byrds' 'Ballad Of Easy Rider', Creedence Clearwater Revival's 'Proud Mary', Frankie Ford's 'Sea Cruise' and Tommy

The sense of community which the E Street Band have brought to Springsteen's life is an integral part of his success, security and appeal. They are a major part of the Springsteen phenomenon.

James' 'Mony Mony'. By the time they had finished they had been seen by more than a million people, performing to capacity crowds. But Springsteen tours are not just planned as financial ventures. Touring for a large group like the E Street Band was an expensive business, and when Jon Landau was asked about this, he replied: 'Bruce Springsteen doesn't usually make decisions on a profit and loss basis.'

In the lull after the tour, Clarence and Miami Steve worked on solo albums, and Max Weinberg was hard at work on a book about rock drummers. Of all the E Street Band, Miami Steve was closest to Springsteen in his devotion to rock'n'roll, and missed being on the road. He created an alter-ego, Little Steven and the Disciples of Soul, which produced one fine album *Men Without Women* (and a great single, 'Solidarity'). But Springsteen himself kept a low profile for most of 1982, emerging for occasional jam sessions with musicians passing through New Jersey – The Stray Cats, Mitch Ryder, Dave Edmunds, Nils Lofgren – and for a duet with Jackson Browne at a Rally For Disarmament concert in New York's Central Park in June. Otherwise he was involved in lengthy stints in the studio with the E Street Band, where they stockpiled numerous songs for the follow-up to The River. He was also spending time in a recording studio in a different role. The week after finishing *The River* he had set about producing Gary US Bonds' album *Dedication*, which was released in 1981. In early 1982 he was working on the next one, *On The Line*, which was released in June of that year. This desire to help an old friend shows that Springsteen's dedication to rock heritage wasn't simply limited to including 'oldies' in his stage set. This was all part of that Asbury camaraderie: if someone influenced you, or inspired your music, you owed that person a debt – which saw Miami Steve, literally, pulling Lee Dorsey out from under a car in the garage where he worked; and which also saw Springsteen rescuing Bonds from McDonalds' openings, and including Ben E. King of the Drifters on the finished *Dedication* album. Of the two albums, *Dedication* was the one that garnered the critical plaudits, with soulful renderings of songs by Dylan, the Beatles and Jackson Browne. It also had three new songs by Springsteen himself. There were also two cracking rockers, 'Dedication' and 'This Little Girl', and a Bonds/Springsteen duet on 'Jole Blon', a song which Buddy Holly had produced for Waylon Jennings in 1959. But by the time of *On The Line* the formula was wearing thin, and Springsteen's songs were distinctly sub-standard. Only the exuberant 'Angelyne' sounded genuine, while 'Club Soul City' was a clumsy attempt at a big soul ballad, and 'Out Of Work' was almost offensive in its flippancy. The album prompted accusations that Springsteen was simply using Bonds albums as a dumper for his own below-par material, and Springsteen did not do any more work with him.

Much more successful was 'From Small Things, Big Things Come', which Springsteen gave to Dave Edmunds backstage after one of the concerts at the Wembley Arena during the British Tour. It can be found on Edmunds' *DE7th* album. In Edmunds' capable hands, the song is a classic, tearaway rocker, closely allied to 'Ramrod' or 'Cadillac Ranch'. One can imagine that Springsteen's version differs little. It's archetypal Springsteen from the word 'go'. The first verse alone manages to include references to 'high school', 'the promised land' and 'hamburger stands'. The killer line comes in the second verse: 'First she took his order, then she took his

heart.' It skips along in suitably irreverent vein, until the bridge: 'Oh, but love is bleeding/It's sad but it's true . . .' before swerving into darker territory on the final verse: 'Well, she shot him dead, on a sunny Florida road.' The motive? 'She couldn't stand the way he drove!'

A detour came when Springsteen donated a song, 'Protection', to Donna Summer, which appeared on her eponymous 1982 album. While 'Protection' was not vintage Springsteen, it had its moments: 'Well if you want it, here is my confession/Baby I can't help it, you're my obsession.' He also donated a song to Clarence Clemons for his *Rescue* album, 'Savin' Up', but it was mediocre.

All this activity with different musicians masked a different Springsteen at work. By 1982 he was being hailed as America's premier rock'n'roller. With the E Street Band he had been playing all over the USA and Western Europe to rapturous receptions. But in September, with the release of his next album, he pulled the plugs out and took everybody by surprise. CBS were astounded when they received the tapes of *Nebraska*. Knowing the man's notoriety for studio perfection, it sounded astonishingly like a bootleg – scraps of songs, Springsteen entirely solo, demos for the E Street Band. Anyone expecting a Big Man solo, or any thunderous Mighty Max drumming, was in for a shock. With the E Street Band back in the swamps of Jersey, Bruce Springsteen had been out on the road alone, heading straight for the badlands of the Mid-West. He had spent a lot of time just driving around the country, talking to people, relaxing in the anonymity. In fact, the finished tapes were hand-delivered by Springsteen to CBS after one such long drive.

Nebraska is one of the most iconoclastic albums ever willingly released by a major rock artist. In terms of shock and impact, it is comparable to Dylan's *John Wesley Harding* and Lennon's *Plastic*

The legendary Woody Guthrie, a courageous and outspoken social critic, whose influence can be clearly felt on Nebraska.

Ono Band. Like both of these, it is the sound of an artist baring his soul in public, and doing it in a radically unorthodox manner.

The seeds for the album were sown when Springsteen read Joe Klein's biography of Woody Guthrie, which had inspired him to include Guthrie's 'This Land Is Your Land' at every one of his European shows. The influence went deep. Talking to Marc Didden prior to the release of *Nebraska*, Springsteen said: 'Why do I cover Woody Guthrie? Because that is what is *needed* right now. Everybody is in sackcloth and ashes in my country these days. After Watergate, America just died emotionally. ... Nobody had any hope left. People were so horrified when they learned of the large-scale corruption in the land of the brave and free that they stayed in their houses, scared and numbed ... I sing that song to let people know that America belongs to everybody who lives there: the blacks, Chicanos, Indians, Chinese and the whites. ... It's time that someone took on the reality of the eighties. I'll do my best!'

Half a century before, Woody Guthrie had rambled round the country in the fit of a Depression, writing and commenting on what he saw. The recession of the thirties bit deep, cutting to the heart of the American Dream.

Guthrie was a nomad, a social commentator, a weaver of fairy tales, a folk poet and a political activist. His plaintive voice spoke for the oppressed and dispossessed. While the bankers were evicting entire families, Guthrie wrote this of Pretty Boy Floyd: 'Well, they say he was an outlaw/But I never heard of an outlaw driving families from their homes.' Guthrie was courageous and outspoken, with 'This machine kills fascists' written on his guitar. He

realised that songs and words could be weapons, firing against uncaring governments and 'legalized crooks'. Songs poured out of him – 'Pastures Of Plenty', 'Grand Coulee Dam', 'So Long, It's Been Good To Know Yuh' – but it was 'This Land Is Your Land' that made him public property. Guthrie has been incensed by Irving Berlin's jingoistic 'God Bless America', and wrote the song as a reply, claiming that America was everyone's. At the bottom of the first draft of it he wrote: 'All you can write is what you see.'

The other influence on *Nebraska* was another great figure of American popular music, Hank Williams, the finest artist Country & Western music has yet produced. Williams' songs conveyed a feeling of pain and isolation, with titles like 'I'm So Lonesome I Could Cry' and 'I'll Never Get Out Of This World Alive'. It is no coincidence that Springsteen chose the title of one of his saddest songs, 'Mansion On The Hill', for one of his own songs on *Nebraska*. Long before the release of the album he had told Dave Marsh: 'I love that old country music ... I listened to Hank Williams, I went back and dug up all his first sessions. ... That and the first Johnny Cash record.' (Cash repaid the compliment in 1983 with his *Johnny 99* album, which also included a gripping cover of Springsteen's 'Highway Patrolman', both from *Nebraska*.)

Ironically, *Nebraska* was the album John Hammond had envisaged Springsteen making for his CBS debut ten years before, in the style of Bob Dylan, solo and acoustic. But Springsteen's background was not in folk, and the only element of Dylan's career which had ever impinged on the young Bruce was his controversial electric years of 1965/6. Springsteen's adolescence was a diet of British Beat, R&B, and rock'n'roll. The folk influence had only been apparent on the near-disastrous 'Mary Queen Of Arkansas' from his first album, and the quirky 'Wild Billy's Circus Story' from 1974. Now he seemed to change direction, in a turnabout that was in the opposite direction to Dylan's own. Dylan had horrified the folk purists in 1965 by going electric. In 1982, Springsteen went from rock to acoustic.

Nebraska had not started as a solo album; it just happened that way. Springsteen had written the songs in about two months. He then bought a tape recorder so that he could record demos to play to the band. He told *International Musician and Recording World*: 'I got this little cassette recorder that's supposed to be really good, plugged it in, turned it on, and the first song I did was "Nebraska". I just kinda sat there: you can hear the chair creaking on "Highway Patrolman" in particular. I recorded them in a couple of days. ... I had only four tracks, so I could play the guitar, sing, then I could do two other things. That was it. I mixed it on this little board, an old beat-up Echoplex.'

The tape was taken to the recording studio and was recorded in full band versions, but Springsteen was dissatisfied with the results. The cassette still seemed to sound better. So Springsteen and the record engineer set about the task of making a master out of the home-made demos.

Initially, the album alienated many of his fans, as evinced by the slow sales, but halfway through 1983 it had sold a million copies in the States, and won a number of critics' polls.

The album's critical reception was generally healthy, with many writers surprised by Springsteen's honesty in laying his music so openly on the line. The comparisons with Guthrie and Williams are apparent on the finished album, but there were also echoes of some of the best American rock writers: the Band's Robbie Robertson, Randy Newman and Tom Waits. Robertson (ironically, a Canadian) had proved himself a diligent and sympathetic chronicler of American history with songs like 'The Night They Drove Old Dixie Down' and 'Rocking Chair', and Newman and Waits had a penchant for singling out low-life characters on their albums. The eclectic Ry Cooder had also tackled a project as ambitious as *Nebraska* with his 1972 album, 'Into The Purple Valley', which dwelt on the Depression era through the songs of Guthrie and Sleepy John Estes.

Like Guthrie's and Steinbeck's characters, the people on *Nebraska* are victims, manipulated by faceless bureaucrats and political systems which are beyond their comprehension or control. In conversation with Chet Flippo of *Musician* Springsteen said that it was about the breakdown in spiritual values: 'It was kind of about a spiritual crisis, in which man is left lost. It's like he has nothing left to tie him to society anymore. He's isolated from the government. Isolated from his job. Isolated from his family. And, in something like "Highway Patrolman", isolated from his friends.' It is a record for America under the Reagan administration. But throughout he observes these victims with characteristic sympathy, and recognises that their individuality cannot, will not, be crushed.

Knowing the care that Springsteen attaches to his records, the starkness of this, his sixth album, is symbolic of his desire to convey the topicality and earnestness of the songs. They are hung on the bare frame of a simple guitar and harmonica, so that the lyrics will be paramount. By now, he was confident enough in his lyrical abilities and the inherent strength of his characters to let them stand on their own merits, and *Nebraska*'s strength lies in that starkness. On those ten tracks, there was nothing for the singer to hide behind.

The title track is based on the Charlie Starkweather killings in Nebraska in 1959, events which Terence Malick brilliantly depicted in his 1973 film, *Badlands*. Starkweather and his girlfriend had gone on an orgy of killing in the badlands of Wyoming, and Springsteen contacted Ninette Beaver, who had written a book on the couple, to obtain further background material.

Springsteen's writing has always had a strong cinematic feel, never more so than on the *Nebraska* songs. 'Atlantic City', Springsteen's tale of racketeering on the boardwalk (a bitter distance from the 'Little Eden' of ten years before), obviously had some connection with Louis Malle's 1980 film of the same name. 'Highway Patrolman' refers to the loyalty of friendship so apparent in the films of John Ford. 'Mansion On The Hill' has the atmosphere of a Holywood forties *film noir*, and the home in 'My Father's House' sounds as if it's straight out of *Psycho*! Indeed, so much of the album, starting with the bleak cover shot, is like watching a black and white film. 'Johnny 99' could well have been played by John Garfield or the sullen young Brando. The congregation on 'Reason To Believe' could well be singing 'Shall We Gather At The River?' from any one of a dozen Ford films (and representing the album's darker side, the preacher could well be palyed by Robert Mitchum from Charles Laughton's eerie *Night Of The Hunter*).

Springsteen told *Rolling Stone* in 1978 about the visual aspect of his songs: 'There's no settling down, no fixed action. You pick up on the action, and then at some . . . point . . . the camera pans away,

and whatever happened, that's what happened. The songs I write, they don't have particular beginnings, and they don't have endings. The camera focuses in and then out.' A statement which mirrors Jean Luc Godard's 'All my films have a beginning, a middle and an end – but not necessarily in that order!' That cinematic element in Springsteen's songs is dictated by the artist, zooming in and out on specific scenes, a slice of the action. The original cover for *Darkness On The Edge Of Town* (and which was subsequently used for the 12-inch single of 'Rosalita') was a black and white shot of Springsteen sitting idly outside a gas station at night, caught in the viewfinder for a brief second, before moving on. He may paint in big screen Technicolor, but Springsteen crams his songs with incident and detail to make them intimate.

Also evident on *Nebraska* is the constant, deferential use of the word 'sir'. The characters are resigned to life at the bottom of the ladder, and despite America's being the great democratic paradise, there are still class differences. Even facing death ('Sheriff, when that man pulls the switch sir . . .') all men are not equal. They are the underdogs, the people that the rest of the country (even their own families) wipe their feet on. Robbed of the dignity of labour, crime becomes their only option. These are the 'Dustbowl Ballads of 1982'. 'Johnny 99' could well be a petty criminal, or playing in a rock'n'roll band. But he turns to crime, and in a trial which is a cross between Kafka and Dylan in 'Drifter's Escape', Johnny pours his heart out to 'Mean John Brown'. But to no avail. As Dylan sang on his 1968 song: 'The judge he cast his robe aside, a tear came to his eye/You fail to understand', he said, 'why must you even try?'. 'Atlantic City' is a bitter, dark song, but as on all of Springsteen's best work, there is a residual strand of hope: 'Well I guess that everything dies, baby that's a fact/But maybe everything that dies someday comes back.' 'Highway Patrolman', one of Springsteen's finest songs, has a stately, dignified narrative, which is anguished in its intensity.

Binding the songs is a sense of loyalty, whether it is the loyalty of the killer on the title track to his girlfriend (a spellbinding opening image with the sense of small-town America, depicting the girl 'twirling her baton'), or the loyalty of a son to his father, and his inability to atone for childhood sins, or the loyalty of a man for his brother gone bad. The crisis of duty over filial affection is weighed up, but the consideration that 'man who turns his back on his family just ain't no good' overcomes the guilt of turning a blind eye. But buried even deeper than that sense of loyalty, below even Springsteen's care and concern for the victims, at the core of the album, lies a sense of dignity, a sense of optimism and wonder, that 'at the end of every hard earned day, people find some reason to believe'.

Springsteen's characters seem to have come from somewhere, before being captured in the songs. For one brief, crucial moment, before they drive off, whether it is on the boardwalk, the night time drive down Kingsley, the wreck on the highway, on the Canadian border or in the mansion on the hill. And while the country lumbers on past them, towards an unknown destiny, those characters exist, and have been given a voice.

Springsteen's concerts are tests of strength, where his incredible stamina is taken to the limits in order to entertain his audience for up to 4 hours.

Glory Days

It had been four years since Springsteen's last rock'n'roll album — and four years is a long time in rock'n'roll terms. Four years that begged the question: could Bruce Springsteen still pack a punch, or was he just punching the clock? It was another long wait to the next album, and the advance sounds were not promising. On 10 May 1984 Bruce Springsteen's first new song in 18 months and his first rock'n'roll song in all those years, the single 'Dancing In The Dark' was released. The opening lines were ominous: 'I get up in the evening/And I ain't got nothing to say . . .'. Some of the lines like 'I need a love reaction', were dire. Moreover, 'Dancing In The Dark' was dance-rock, complete with a synthesiser. It even appeared in three additional special 12-inch dance mixes, supervised by New York master mixer Arthur Baker, the man who achieved the impossible by putting the funk into New Order. The new

version stretched the original by emphasising the rhythm, but it seemed little more than a concession to the current fad for alternate mixes. The B-side of all versions, however, was an interesting rarity, 'Pink Cadillac' a Springsteen song which Bette Midler had included in her live shows for a couple of years. It was a pensive, bluesy ballad in the tradition of 'Fire', but it lacked that song's brooding sensuality, and frittered away its potential with regurgitated auto imagery and recycled Biblical references. The single, however, shot up the charts. In the USA it was only kept from the top spot by Prince's 'When Doves Cry'. In the UK it initially only got to number 28, but then, after a BBC special about Springsteen was screened just before Christmas, it started climbing again, rising to number 4, eight months after it was released.

The real meat, however, was not far behind. *Born In The USA*

was released on 4 June in both the UK and the USA. In the UK it shot straight into the album charts at No. 2, showing how well his 1981 tour had established him, while in the States it made top of the charts in three weeks. Within a few months it had sold over 5 million copies worldwide. The reviews were glowing, with critics delighted to find Springsteen back in tandem with the E Street Band, and leaving behind the insularity of *Nebraska*. *Newsweek* welcomed his return as a rock'n'roll hero. *Village Voice* called it his best album to date. *Rolling Stone* proclaimed it 'a classic'. The *Los Angeles Times'* Robert Hilburn (a long-time fan) waxed lyrical: 'John Lennon was wrong when he said no-one has ever improved on the pure rock rejoicing of Jerry Lee Lewis' "Whole Lot Of Shakin' Going On". In terms of sheer exhilaration, Bruce Springsteen's "Born To Run" in 1975 blew "Shakin'" away. Nine years and four albums after "Born To Run", Springsteen continues to blow 'em away!' In Britain, Adam Sweeting of *Melody Maker* had his finger on the pulse when he wrote: 'With successive releases, Springsteen's version of "rock" has moved further and further from any remaining vestiges of what it might feel like to be a delinquent, under-age beer drinker. ... Despite the familiarity of themes and forms, *Born In The USA* makes a stand in the teeth of history and stirs a few unfashionable emotions.'

The actual release of *Born In The USA* was characteristically fraught. Since *The River* in 1980, Springsteen had stockpiled around 100 songs. Often the band had gone into the studio and recorded numbers so new to them that they did not know the chords. In order to keep it fresh there was very little rehearsing. These tracks ranged from rough demos, the most immediate of which became *Nebraska*, to finished full band songs, which became the core of *Born In The USA*. Those songs were endlessly sifted through until the final dozen tracks were selected – ironically, the album's anthem, 'No Surrender', was only included at the very last minute, as a tribute to Miami Steve, who had decided to leave the band.

The second single lifted from *Born In The USA* was 'Cover Me', which included a bonus on the B-side – a live version of Tom Waits' haunting 'Jersey Girl', from his *Heart Attack And Vine* album. Many people felt the song was written for Springsteen, but Waits actually wrote it for his wife, a real Jersey girl. Springsteen had included it in his live shows, and duetted with Waits on the song in Los Angeles in 1981.

Since the release of *Nebraska* in 1982, Springsteen's activities had kept him confined to the studio, recording again with his band. He did return to impromptu live work, though, averaging one appearance a week at various Asbury clubs and bars (including one appearance at an Italian joke-telling contest, where he failed to win the $25 prize!). The bands he jammed with were old favourites, such as Cats On A Smooth Surface, joining them onstage at the Stone Pony in Asbury Park for a version of ZZ Top's 'I'm Bad, I'm Nationwide'. He also appeared regularly with Clarence Clemons, and with Bystander he premiered 'Dancing In The Dark' at Asbury's Club Xanadu in May 1984. Four of Springsteen's songs – 'It's Hard To Be A Saint In The City', 'Adam Raised A Cain', 'She's The One' and 'Streets Of Fire' – were used effectively at this time in John Sayles' film *Baby It's You*, which included a scenic detour in Asbury Park.

Such relative inactivity from Springsteen allowed the E Street

1984 saw a muscular and punchily determined Springsteen, a man of 35 with a vision that was getting even stronger. Born In The U.S.A. *heralded a thundering return to recording and touring.*

Band to pursue their own activities. Max Weinberg finished and published his book on the great rock drummers, *The Big Beat*, early in 1984. Clarence Clemons set up a new band, the Red Bank Rockers, who released their debut album on CBS in late 1983. They attracted great notices for their live appearances, but when the music was captured on vinyl, it lost its spontaneity, and sounded forced and desultory. Miami Steve persevered with his own band, the Disciples of Soul, but while Clemons also continued with the E Street Band, Miami Steve decided to go it alone in early 1984. Springsteen noted the move on 'No Surrender', and it is remembered in 'Bobby Jean'. The split was amicable; as Van Zandt said: 'We were friends long before we played together, we'll be friends forever,' and on the inner sleeve of *Born In The USA* Springsteen bade Little Steven 'a good voyage, my brother', in Italian. Any doubts which may have lingered about the mood of their parting were scotched on 20 August 1984 when Miami Steve joined Bruce on stage at the Meadowlands Arena in New Jersey for a classic version of Dobie Grey's 'Drift Away' and a scorching 'Two Hearts'. Little Steven's second album, *Voice Of America*, was released at the same time as his former boss's, and picked up sympathetic and occasionally glowing reviews, with critics singling

out its overtly human rights sentiments.

Although he had not joined the E Street Band officially until 1975, Steve Van Zandt had been a long-time companion, having been a member of Steel Mill. With such a gap in the ranks, someone very special was required to join as second guitarist. The person chosen was Nils Lofgren, who joined the band, avowedly for a year starting with their 1984 US tour – after borrowing a boxful of bootlegs and live tapes to acquaint himself fully with his new band's style. He and Springsteen had first met in 1969 when they both shared an audition for the Fillmore West, and their paths had crossed several times over the intervening years. Lofgren was a gritty rock'n'roller of the old school, who started life as a precocious 16-year-old guitarist in Chicago before talking his way into Neil Young's backing band and contributing to Young's classic 1970 album *After The Goldrush*. With his own band, Grin, Lofgren then established a devoted cult following. He is also a songwriter, his style veering from the punchy 'I Came To Dance' to the sublime balladry of 'Shine Silently'. His interpretation of the Goffin/King standard 'Goin' Back' emphasised his appreciation of rock history, which must have rated with Springsteen. Following his reunion with Young on the latter's 1983 'Trans' tour, Lofgren played with Springsteen in Asbury Park the Christmas of that year. Springsteen reckoned he had the same musical feelings as Van Zandt: 'We looked at music in the same way and cared about the same things.'

With his band in order, a new album under his belt, even Springsteen could no longer ignore the video boom. After discussions with video aces Godley and Creme, Springsteen eventually chose director Brian de Palma (*Phantom Of The Paradise, Carrie*) to shoot him in his first video performance for 'Dancing In The Dark' in June 1984. His only previous promotion video had been for 'Atlantic City' in 1982, but he did not feature in it. The video showed only views of the town shot from a moving car. He remained opposed in principle to videos, as he believed that his songs were already full of cinematic detail and that visuals introduced an extraneous element. He also feels that the songs work on people's imaginations and that it is up to each individual to see what the song suggests to him, and not to have someone else's vision imposed on him. Nevertheless, he gave way for 'Dancing In The Dark', and was to appreciate that this gave him an audience in pre-teen kids. Moreover, he regarded the video as sufficiently successful to commission John Sayles to shoot another performance video for the 'Born In The USA' single, but the finished product was criticised as Springsteen was clearly miming on it.

Any rumours that this burst of activity was to be Springsteen's swansong were scotched on 29 June 1984, in St Paul, Minnesota, when Bruce Springsteen and the E Street Band kicked off their first tour in three years with a marathon three-and-a-half-hour, 30-song set. Springsteen proved he had coped with the intervening years, and did not compromise a jot in those shows. He had straightened up his diet, kicking his junk food habit, and having chefs prepare large bowls of vegetables for him as soon as he came offstage. He also pumped iron at local health clubs on the road, and the whole band regularly worked out. Raring to get back on the road, Springsteen was fitter, healthier than ever, as he told Debby Miller: 'Jump up and down and scream at the top of your lungs for 20 minutes and see how *you* feel!'

The demand to see Springsteen in concert had not abated during his three-year layoff. In New Jersey the 200,000 tickets for his Meadowlands shows were sold out in one day! In Wisconsin, such was the demand for tickets that 13 July was declared 'Bruce Springsteen Day' by Governor Tony Earl.

The '84 tour included full band versions of the solo songs Springsteen recorded for *Nebraska* – the title track, 'Atlantic City', 'Mansion On The Hill', 'Used Cars' and 'Highway Patrolman', all of which grew in stature when augmented by the discreet band backing. From *Born In The USA*, 'No Surrender', 'Glory Days' and 'Working On The Highway' became integral parts of the set. The evening wrapped up with a swaggering version of the Rolling Stones' 1968 'Street Fighting Man', which Springsteen included because, as he told friends, he just *had* to sing the line: 'So what can a poor boy do/'cept sing for a rock'n'roll band.' Also included were perennial live favourites like 'Born To Run', 'Fire', 'Thunder Road', 'Rosalita' and 'Badlands'. He adeptly juggled around all facets of his recorded career, 1982's 'Used Cars', for example, segued beautifully into 1984's 'My Hometown'; the gloomy 'Downbound Train' from *Born In The USA* led into the sombre 'Atlantic City' from *Nebraska*. Even the sluggish 'Pink Cadillac' came to life in concert, particularly with such laconic Springsteen intros as: 'It seems, according to the Bible, way back when, Eve showed Adam the apple, and Adam took a bite. There's gotta be more to it than that. *Fruit?*'

As well as 'new boy' Nils Lofgren, Springsteen featured another new E Streeter, back-up singer Patti Scialfa, who had worked with Southside Johnny, and whom Springsteen had seen singing in an Asbury bar, where he was enchanted by the 'country feeling' in her voice. The presence of new-comers did not dampen down the spirit of the band on stage: on Halloween Night, which found the E Street Band at the Los Angeles Sports Arena, Springsteen celebrated the date with a suitably hammy intro. He made his entrance lying on a coffin, impervious to the attempts by Clarence Clemons and Patti Scialfa to bring him back to life, until he was given his guitar. Then he was off, bursting into a frantic version of Jerry Lee Lewis' 'High School Confidential'. But there was also a more muted facet to the concerts. At the Takoma Dome in Washington DC on 19 October, for the first time in 11 years he did not play 'Rosalita'. Instead he took at some shows to finishing with the relatively more subdued 'Racing In The Street', highlighting the darker side of his recent albums.

In keeping with his desire to take his music to his real fans, Springsteen's '84 tour reached many places usually ignored by touring bands, including a notable detour to Lincoln, Nebraska. In all the tour was to last 14 months, and was not only to criss-cross the United States, but was to take him for the first time to Australia and the Far East. The Jacksons' 'Victory' tour was launched at the same time as Springsteen's and, although a huge commercial success, suffered notably by comparison. There was howls of protest at a charge of $30 a ticket, plus a minimum order of four, and Bruce would play for nearly three times as long. Critics remained unimpressed by the Jacksons' technological spectacle, but were swayed by the earthy rock'n'roll power of Springsteen's shows. Typical was the comment at the end of the review in the venerable *New York Times*: 'What makes Mr Springsteen such a satisfying harbinger of "the rock and roll future" is not his anticipation of today's trends … but his role as a musician working lovingly within the rock tradition to make serious adult art. That's worth cheering about, just as much as the spellbinding fervour of his actual performances.' After three years away, he had returned to the spotlight, and with shows infused with vigour and integrity, rightly reclaimed his crown as rock music's greatest live performer. The coronation itself was to come later when he was chosen by *Rolling Stone* readers as the Artist of the Year. Although it was the fourth time in six years he had won this accolade, he also scooped five other awards: Album of the Year, Single of the Year ('Dancing in the Dark'), Male Vocalist, Songwriter, and, with the E Street Band, Band of the Year. Only in 1980, when he released *The River*, had he amassed such a total. Clearly for lovers of rock, the tour and the new album were the events of the year.

Significantly, *Born In The USA* was credited only to 'Bruce Springsteen', with no mention of the E Street Band on the label or cover. And that cover! Three years for a shot of Bruce Springsteen's bum! One London paper even speculated that the cap hanging out of his back pocket was a none too subtle gay hallmark.

The inner sleeve included 'Thanks' to scriptwriter/director Paul Schrader (*Taxi Driver, Blue Collar, American Gigolo*). 'Thanks always' to John Hammond Sr who helped bring the wheel full circle: the man who had brought Bruce Springsteen to the world a decade before, and who proved his ears were as acute as ever with his signing and production of the raw Texas blues of Stevie Ray

Bruce is joined on stage by his old friend and ex-E Streeter, 'Miami' Steve Van Zandt.

Vaughan in 1983.

The sound of *Born In The USA* is wholeheartedly, emphatically rock'n'roll – from the classic Springsteen 'Sha-la-laing' of 'Darlington County' to the Creedence-style chooglin' of 'Working On The Highway'. It also sounds surprisingly un-E Street – there is precious little saxophone, the whole band sounds mixed down, the keyboards are sparsely used, – and the record marks the debut of synthesisers on a Springsteen album. The overall impression is of Max's drums driving the songs along, relentlessly propelling them with a force few in rock can match. It is steeped in traditional rock references and influences, and while there are concessions to metronomic pop on songs like 'Dancing In The Dark' and 'Cover Me', Springsteen flouts the current fashions with rock music of such force. The album marks a further development; play it back to back with *Born To Run* and you are aware of the differences – the lyrical sparseness of the later record, the hardhat impact of the songs and their production, the authenticity of the characters and their situations. *Born To Run* is larger than life, *Born In The USA* presents experience at life-size.

Born In The USA is a concept album (although we all breathed a sigh of relief when we thought we'd seen the back of those mutants!). It is a series of songs from a man about to turn 36, trying to come to terms with his age and his vocation in what is, primarily, a young man's game. Four of these songs – 'Born In The USA', 'Working On The Highway', 'Downbound Train' and 'No Surrender' are crucial. They chart the dissipation of idealism, the futility of clinging to what has gone, the exultation of love and partnership, and the acceptance of maturity in the face of diehard teenage dreams. They are, essentially, rock'n'roll dilemmas, which Springsteen tackles head on, because he has lived them, because he is living them. As a background to these themes, Springsteen draws on the rich legacy of American popular music – the plaintive hillbilly blues of Jimmie Rodgers on 'Downbound Train', the Creedence-based, Eddie Cochran rock of 'Working On The Highway', the Spectorish fusion of 'No Surrender', the sly disco rhythms of 'Dancing In The Dark'. He even starts pillaging his own past on the album – 'Darlington Country' resembles the 'up' songs on *The River*. The stately drums which roll in the title track, the first lines of the song, take us straight to the heart of darkness: 'Born down in a dead man's town/First kick I took was when I hit the ground' – Ground down and ensnared from the very moment

of birth. It is a sombre homage to Chuck Berry's 'Back In The USA', the song which eulogised and esteemed the values which Springsteen finds corrupted. Being away, Berry misses the skyscrapers, long highways, drive-ins and corner cafes. Chuck's back from exile, he's missed the hamburgers that 'sizzle on an open grill night and day' and fondly recalls 'the juke box jumping with records'. These are the things that Springsteen would miss, too. But while Berry's 1959 song ends with the triumphant testimonial: 'Anything you want, they got right here in the USA,' all Springsteen finds a quarter of a century on is that 'there's nowhere to run, ain't nowhere to go'. The childhood belief in the American Dream has dissipated; it ends in disillusion and grief.

The title song traces a person's life from birth to his mid-thirties. During his adolescence Springsteen watched the country torn asunder by Vietnam, and his sympathy with the plight of the Vietnam Vets is such that 'Racing In The Street' was inspired by Vet Ron Kovic's book *Born On The 4th Of July*, and he has played a number of Vet benefits. In 'Born In The USA', after the 'hometown jam' of the second verse, the intransigent youth is sent off 'to a foreign land to go and kill and yellow man'. The earlier 'Highway Patrolman' dealt with a similar situation, shipping the brother of the song's narrator to Vietnam in '65. 'Born In The USA' also has two brothers, but both brothers are serving there, now. Moreover the older brother dies at Khe Sahn, the lynchpin of the 1968 Tet Offensive, which proved, indisputably, that America could never win that war. 'They're still there, he's all gone.' And nothing changes, save the finality of one man's death, and its repercussions. On his return home the song's narrator is a spent force – no hero, just an embarrassment. This helps explain the sleeve credit to Paul Schrader, whose *Taxi Driver*, ends with the protagonist, Travis Bickle, shooting into a crowd, his revenge as a Vietnam veteran on a society that has spurned him. Back home, 'the shadow of the penitentiary' nestles next to 'the gas fires of the refinery'. The alternative to death in VietNam is itself pretty bleak. Now, if you're 'Born In The USA', there is none of the climactic optimism of 'Thunder Road' or 'Wreck On The Highway'. Now 'I'm 10 years running down the road/Nowhere to run, ain't nowhere to go.'

'Working On The Highway' is roots rockabilly, slapped bass and jagged guitar. The musical feel is steeped in the fifties, although the lyrics go back to the thirties, to the era of Jimmie Rodgers, 'The Singing Brakeman', flashing by Paul Muni as a fugitive from a chain gang. The London *Guardian* called it 'the best prison rocker since "Jailhouse Rock".' In the song's trial, 'the prosecutor kept the promise ... the judge got mad' recalls the courtroom hysteria of 'Johnny 99'. Despite its exuberant musical punch, the feel of the song is confined, trapped again, whether it's the boredom of working on the two lane blacktop at the beginning, or the confinement of life on the Charlotte Country Road Gang at the end.

'Downbound Train' is the first opportunity to draw breath on the album, a brooding, pensive ballad, bleak and uncompromising. A splintered marriage opens the song, a resigned 'we had it once, we ain't got it anymore'. The motif of the railroad runs throughout the song. Springsteen includes a *Nebraska*-ish tip of the stetson to Hank Williams' tune 'I Heard That Lonesome Whistle', and embraces a tradition which stretches through 'Waiting On A Train', 'Love In Vain' and 'Mystery Train' – C&W, blues and rock, the

BORN IN THE U.S.A. TOUR

BRUCE SPRINGSTEEN AND THE E STREET BAND

grand triumvirate of American popular music. But in the eighties the trains aren't running anymore, and nobody's riding boxcars. There is a sense of emptiness, enforced by the run through the woods at the song's conclusion. In the big, cold house stands an empty bridal bed, which recalls the sense of chilling isolation evoked by 'My Father's House'. A sombre mansion on the hill, once a place of happy, shared memories, it now stands empty and silent.

'No Surrender' is the album's clarion call, with a chorus addressed to the fans: 'Like soldiers in the winter's night with a vow to defend/No retreat, no surrender!' It is Springsteen's statement of intent and faith, to stay true to the power and the glory of rock'n'roll. He is celebrating the rock'n'roll of which Chuck Berry claimed on 'Schooldays' in 1957, 'We learned more from a three-minute record than we ever learned in school'. But by the last verse of 'No Surrender', there's a weary resignation to the inevitability of ageing, something to which you have to surrender. The idealism of the first verse is tarnished in the second, and has gone in the third. Springsteen accepts that the baton has been passed on to a new generation. In lines which deliberately invite comparison with Bob Dylan's idealism of 1963: 'There's a battle outside and it's ragin'/ It'll soon shake your windows and rattle your walls/For the times they are a-changin'.' By 1984 the times have a-changed: Bob Dylan is a 43-year-old conservative evangelist, and Bruce Springsteen (whom many deemed Dylan's successor) is acknowledging: 'There's a war outside still raging/You say it ain't ours anymore to win.' 'No Surrender' ends with – for Springsteen – the crucial line, 'these romantic dreams in my head'. The dreams are not to be poured into any idealised Spanish Johnny or Johnny 99. They are there, but confined to his head, a reaction to what he has witnessed and experienced, but locked away, and only to be savoured alone, like a childhood diary, or a three-minute single bought in adolescence.

The whole last verse conveys, perhaps more successfully than any other song on the album, Springsteen's realisation and recognition of his position: 'I want to sleep beneath peaceful skies in my lover's bed, with a wide open country in my eyes, and these romantic dreams in my head.' The feeling in those lines again evokes the West of John Ford, of domestic contentment in the face of adversity, of idealism contained. Of a whole vast country out there, and all you can do is stand and stare out of your window and contemplate a fraction of that vastness.

The strength of these four songs is that the characters are given a substance and personality, which stops them being mere ciphers. They are drawn from real life and are sympathetically drawn, characters who share the same experiences and environment as Springsteen's audience, with whom they strike a responsive chord.

It is that substance which renders other songs on the album like 'Cover Me', 'Bobby Jean' and 'I'm Going Down' ineffectual. 'Cover Me' is a throwaway, a disco concession, the sort of song Springsteen could write in his sleep, but which he usually has the good sense to farm out to others. When he tries to bolster the song with the lines 'Times are tough now/Just getting tougher,' they come across as merely a sap to the prevalent political/economic

Bruce at Meadowlands, New Jersey in August 1984, with the now familiar headband and a full repertoire of new songs to play.

climate, especially when the writer's only solution to these hard times is to find 'a lover who will come in and cover me', which simply enforces the stereotype of Springsteen as a male chauvinist and ersatz romantic.

Despite its inspiration, 'Bobby Jean' is Springsteen production-line 'remember when ...?' Because he tries too hard, he fails to achieve the wistfulness the song needs. While a line like 'We liked the same music, we liked the same bands, we liked the same clothes' is effective – because those things *are* so important to teenagers – to hear a 35-year-old Springsteen sing 'Now there ain't nobody, nowhere, nohow ever gonna understand me the way you did' is merely embarrassing. It is an embarrassment repeated by the trite lyrics of 'I'm Going Down', an otherwise reliable rocker (despite its beguiling Tex-Mex intro). Beside other songs on the album which are amongst Springsteen's most deliberate, most consumately crafted songs, these come across as weak and clumsy.

However, as well as the four major songs, others songs like the stark and chillingly simple 'I'm On Fire' have great force. It consists of three stabbing verses, pounded by the honed-down chorus. The almost paedophiliac opening lines are sinister ('Hey little girl is your daddy home? Did he go away and leave you all alone? I got a bad desire!') The all-consuming lust and passion is played out against a slyly simple beat which fits the pathological lyrics like a glove. Springsteen imagines a knife 'edgy and dull' cutting 'a six inch valley through the middle of my soul'. It continues with the paranoid 'At night I wake up with the sheets soaking wet and a freight train running through the middle of my head' – it's as if someone gave Norman Bates in *Psycho* a guitar! There are no histrionics, no lyrical legerdemain. As on 'Factory' or 'Wreck On The Highway', it is Springsteen's very restraint which elevates the song, the acts as a powerful argument against those who constantly accuse him of bombast.

Other songs support the main theme of growing older and disillusioned. With 'Glory Days', the initial impression is that Springsteen has succumbed to the unabashed nostalgia he is constantly accused of, but by the time the song has wound its way through three laconic verses, the overall mood is of resignation. The first verse conjures an image of Springsteen sitting down in a bar, revelling in reminiscences over a beer. The baseball hero sounds initially like the hopeful symbol of Joe Di Maggio which Paul Simon drew on 'Mrs Robinson'. But in Springsteen's son you soon realise that all this guy has to keep him going are his memories. In the second verse (and the second broken marriage on the album) there's a wry acceptance of what has been, as tears give way to laughter, but by then it's too late to recapture any of it. By the end of the song, Springsteen himself hopes that when the times comes, he won't be sitting round trying to recapture what has been: 'Just sitting back, trying to recapture/A little of the glory, but time slips away/And leaves you with nothing, mister, but boring stories of glory days.'

That those stories *could* be boring is a revolutionary idea coming from Springsteen. Even by his own standards, he has championed those whose own 'glory days' have long since gone – Gary Bonds, Hank Mizzell, Mitch Ryder. It's almost as if he's asking not be taken as an archivist and revivalist. Having celebrated the optimism and idealism of youth, on 'Glory Days', he reflects from the vantage point of maturity, and castigates the time and effort spent

trying to conjure up what has been. It is the one song which acutely conveys the disillusion and wistfulness Springsteen must feel – a 35-year-old, still plugging on in the business where to live fast, die young and have a good looking corpse seemed to be the ambition! It was as if the ridiculousness of the situation suddenly struck him, as if he remembered Mick Jagger saying he could never envisage himself onstage singing 'Satisfaction' when he was 40.

The problem was not simply one of the passage of time, but the burdens one takes on in getting older. As he told the audience on the opening night of his 1984 tour: 'When I started playing guitar I had a couple of ideas. One was to avoid as much responsibility as possible for the rest of my life. ... Only one idea doesn't work out – the responsibility idea. It seems like when you get older, you realise you can't get that out of the way.'

Born In The USA concludes, somehow inevitably, with 'My Hometown'. The odyssey ends back where it all began, in a black 'that big old Buick' through the cosy, brightly lit streets of your hometown. By the second verse, we're in the turbulence of the mid-sixties. It's 1965, the year of the Watts Riots, and the era of innocence, the time of *American Graffiti*, has passed. Cruising to the heart of Saturday night now involves carrying a shotgun.

The mood of the third verse is chillingly similar to Dylan's 1963 'North Country Blues' – a town dying on its feet, choked by a new depression, beyond the ken of its citizens. Everything's closed down, there's nothing to come home to. As Simon and Garfunkel sang in 1975: 'There's nothing but the dead and dying in my little town.' Even the vestige of pride in the environment has disappeared, the communal memory has given way to desperate individual nostalgia. Now, a 35-year-old man drives his own son around, past 'Main Street's whitewashed windows and vacant stores', round the shell of a town that the boy will never call home. There is talk of packing up and heading south, to some vague promised land. There is nothing here, nothing in the hometown to hold them. Austerity has sunk its claws too deep into the town. . . . It is time to be moving on.

Like the novelist Thomas Wolfe, in whose magnificent *You Can't Go Home Again* Dave Marsh found a suitable coda for *The River*, Springsteen recognises the affinity a writer forges with his country. Wolfe's writing in the thirties bears frequent comparison with Springsteen's attitude to recording: Wolfe could never bear to commit anything to the finality of print, and his editor was driven close to distraction in trying to derive something finite from the mass of manuscripts with which Wolfe presented him – a 5 foot by 2 foot pile of papers, totalling over one million words, constituted one novel! Echoes can be found in the writings themselves: in a letter trying to distil the essence of his work Wolfe wrote:

'The idea . . . is that every man is searching for his father. . . . My conviction is that a native has the whole consciousness of his people and nation in him, that he knows everything about it, every sight, sound and memory of the people. . . . It is not a government, or the Revolutionary War or the Monroe Doctrine, it is the ten million seconds and moments of your life – the shapes you see, the sounds you hear, the food you eat, the colour and texture of the earth you live in.'

This sort of empathy infuses *Darkness On The Edge Of Town*, *The River* and *Nebraska*. It is this sort of intuition which is made quite explicit in 'My Hometown' and the best of the other songs on *Born In The USA*.

Born In The USA is an album about tackling the problems faced by many of the fans, those of growing older, but still being driven and inspired by rock'n'roll. Maybe *Born In The USA* will be the last rock'n'roll album, and Springsteen its last true hero. The album's strength is that it confronts these problems with compassion and honesty, typical of a man who has maintained his integrity and clung to the idealism which separates him from the avarice and compromise of his contemporaries. He has stuck to the standards which Charles Shaar Murray acclaimed in his review of *Born In The USA* in the *New Musical Express*: 'It is very rare to see an artist take a clear cut choice between selling his audience the same old bullshit that he knows they love, and telling them the truth. . . . Springsteen displays the kind of moral and artistic integrity that rock music rarely shows any more.'

The new E Street Band ensemble receive the audience's tributes at Meadowlands, New Jersey, August 1984. The new line-up includes Nils Lofgren, a fine replacement for 'Miami' Steve.

and white, home-movie finale. The song is a beautiful evocation of the cosiness and conformity of small town America, which recalls the opening lines of *Nebraska*. After all the ups and downs, the only place you can return to is where you came from. There you can revel in the pride of environment, of knowing exactly where, why and how everything is, in the only place where it all falls into place. Springsteen has said of the subject of the song: 'It's something you carry with you forever, no matter where you go or what you become. There's a lot of conflicting feelings you have about the place. That's just part of it.'

To begin, you have to go back to being eight years old, with the safe, innocent memory of sitting on your father's lap, and steering

Born To Run

Despite his worldwide success, and his years spent in the public eye, Bruce Springsteen remains an enigmatic character. He uses none of Dylan's capricious role-playing to enhance his charisma, and, unlike the multi-influenced Dylan, his influences are all in music, particularly in the music he enjoyed, instinctively and non-intellectually, as a kid. Apart from Woody Guthrie, as he has often said, it was the rock'n'rollers of the fifties and the British groups of the early sixties that have been his inspiration.

With rock'n'roll, in the end it is its strength, purity, and vigour that count. This is why Springsteen appeals across the spectrum of modern rock – why the 'blue-collar' rocker has also been taken up by the rock intellectuals like Jon Landau, why the overt Americanism of his songs did not get in the way of acceptance in a punk-influenced Britain. So many of the great rock stars have said, like George Harrison of the Beatles, 'We just wanted to play in a rock'n'roll band,' but few have, like Springsteen, achieved this

ambition and stuck to it. It is the excitement of rock that appeals to all who love any form of the music, and Springsteen's great achievement has been to recapture that excitement after the pomposity and vacuity of the early seventies.

This book has tended to concentrate on the lyrics – inevitably because music cannot be captured in print. But the words are but the smaller part of the story. The real strength of rock music is that a collection of lyrics, bound to a tune, highlighted by a heartfelt vocal, with special care taken in the instrumentation and production, can convey a magical power which cannot be found in the cold medium of print. The emotional impact of what is perhaps Springsteen's finest song, 'Independence Day', for example, loses its impact when one simply reads the lyrics. They have to be taken in their intended context – Bruce's poignant reading of the lyrics, the touching interplay between guitar and organ, Clarence's haunting sax break – to be fully appreciated.

This touches upon one of the paradoxes of Springsteen's music. Although his ambition remains just to 'sing in a rock'n'roll band', the songs still have a meaning. In fact, they have to have a meaning. One of the reasons why it takes him so long to produce a record is that Springsteen rejects those songs which when played back do not say anything. But the meaning is not ponderous, it is not forced on the audience or delivered like Holy Writ. For Springsteen, the songs are not his personal property, not philosophies he feels he must impart, but belong almost equally to the audience – they are their songs too. This provides the solution to the paradox. A concert by Bruce Springsteen and the E Street Band is meant to be a good night out, and for those in the audience who just want to sing along a bit, that's fine. But for those who like to be prompted to thought by what they hear, well then they are catered for as well.

The keyword here is community. The concerts are about sharing, about 'breaking down the distance' between the audience and the band. This is not a form of condescension, but is the genuine feeling of a man who comes across as charming and affable, with none of the self-opinion of many in the rock business, who strikes those who stage his shows, like Marlene Anderson, director of the Civic Center in Minneapolis, as being a pleasure to work with, with none of the paranoia and neuroses of so many stars. This sense of community means that there is no flash, no artificial glitter, no lasers at his shows, only music, and to get to them no limousines, no buses overloaded with equipment and effects, but just three or four station wagons. And it is also this sense of community that makes Springsteen so particular about what he delivers to his fans. What other rock star is likely to spend up to four hours doing a detailed sound check from every part of the hall while the band rehearses? Or refuse to play a single night, in a large auditorium, as Springsteen did in Toronto, in favour of playing three nights to only one part of it because he thought that would be more intimate?

Like the songs themselves, Springsteen's long onstage monologues, reminiscing about girls, growing up, music, his father, life and death, are not performances in which the artist tries to dazzle the audience, but are the means of establishing common ground. The tradition stems from Will Rogers and the narrative ballads of folk, blues and country singers. When Springsteen reminisces, he describes feelings and experiences which most of his audience will have shared. So when the songs follow the audience shares in them: 'Independence Day' speaks for every child who failed to communicate with a parent; the exuberance of 'Born To Run' is everybody's.

Springsteen's identification with the people who listen to his music has also manifested itself in a growing politicisation over recent years. Many people were surprised by his appearance at the MUSE concerts in 1979, but he was to follow this up by appearing at a Vietnam Veterans' concert in 1980 and making a speech that was used later in a series of radio advertisements: 'It's like when you're walking down a dark street at night, and out of the corner of your eye, you see somebody getting hurt in a dark alley, but you keep walking because you think it don't have nothing to do with you and you just want to get home. Vietnam turned this whole country into that dark street, and unless we can walk down those dark alleys and look into the eyes of those men and women, we are never gonna get home!'

He also participated in the American music business's fund-raising record for victims of the Ethiopian famine, 'We Are The World', in February 1985. 'USA For Africa', as the group was called, also included Bob Dylan, Stevie Wonder, Lionel Richie, Paul Simon, Smokey Robinson, Ray Charles and Billy Joel.

His involvement in politics has since grown beyond interest in only those causes that appeal to his own generation. Halfway through the 1984 American tour in Pittsburgh, Springsteen was approached by an ex-steelworker, who asked him to read some information onstage about food banks and help for the unemployed. Since then, Springsteen has made an effort to contact similar organisations in every city he has played, and in concert will make a point of plugging local food banks and unions. In Poughkeepsie in November 1984, he told the crowd about the Old-Timers Steelworkers Foundation Food Bank, and collected $1,300. He donated $20,000 himself to the organisation.

As he told *Rolling Stone* in December 1984, the growing politicisation 'seems to be an inevitable progression of what our band has been doing, of the idea that we got into this for – that idea being the urge to make people think a bit as well as be entertained, to change the world a little bit'.

Showing his usual sensitivity, President Reagan claimed allegiance with Springsteen during his 1984 campaign. When in New Jersey, he quoted Springsteen's songs as conveying a 'message of hope' similar to his own! Springsteen rightly saw this as a crass bit of political manipulation and told an audience shortly after hearing of the President's remarks: 'I've heard the President of the USA liked my records. . . . I don't think he's been listening to this one lately' before launching into a blistering 'Johnny 99'.

The sense of identification and involvement with the audience would not exist if the feeling of community was not already there with, and amongst, the band. They have known each other a long time, and most of them have played together for years. There is a pronounced empathy and trust between them. Danny Federici dances behind his banks of keyboards; 'Mighty' Max Weinberg crouches behind his kit, tiny in relation to the sound he produces; Garry Tallent, in the tradition of great rock bassists, stands immovable, providing the rhythm; Steve Van Zandt used to prowl the stage, like a gunfighter looking for a shoot out; 'Professor' Roy Bittan studiously sticks to his piano. Then there's 'The King of the World! The Master of the Universe!! The Duke of Paducah!!! – Spotlight on the Big Man!' Bruce and Clarence Clemons onstage are a great partnership; whether it's the Abbott and Costello clowning which accompanies 'Fire', or the sprinting climax to 'Thunder Road', it's pantomime rock'n'roll. It is fast and fun but the music is never forgotten for the antics.

The proof of the trust between the band members can be found in their repertoire. At the drop of a hat, they can conjure up any spectre from rock's 30-year history. Van Zandt remembered Springsteen announcing 'Midnight Hour' as an encore once. They hadn't played it in five years, but as soon as the band swung into it, they were off and running. It is that sort of innate understanding – and comprehensive appreciation of music – that has enabled the E Street Band to become established as the best live rock'n'roll band.

Springsteen has frequently been compared to Robert de Niro,

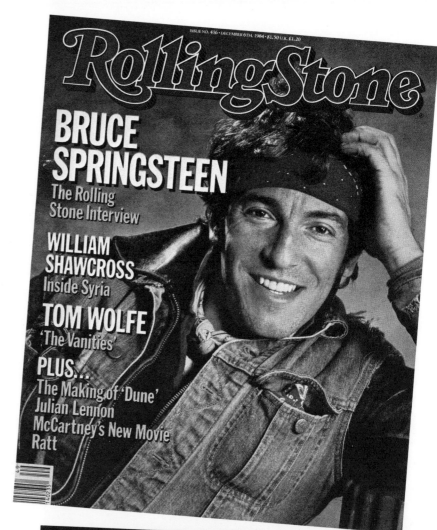

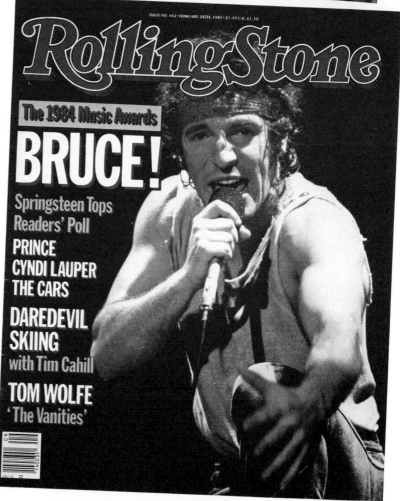

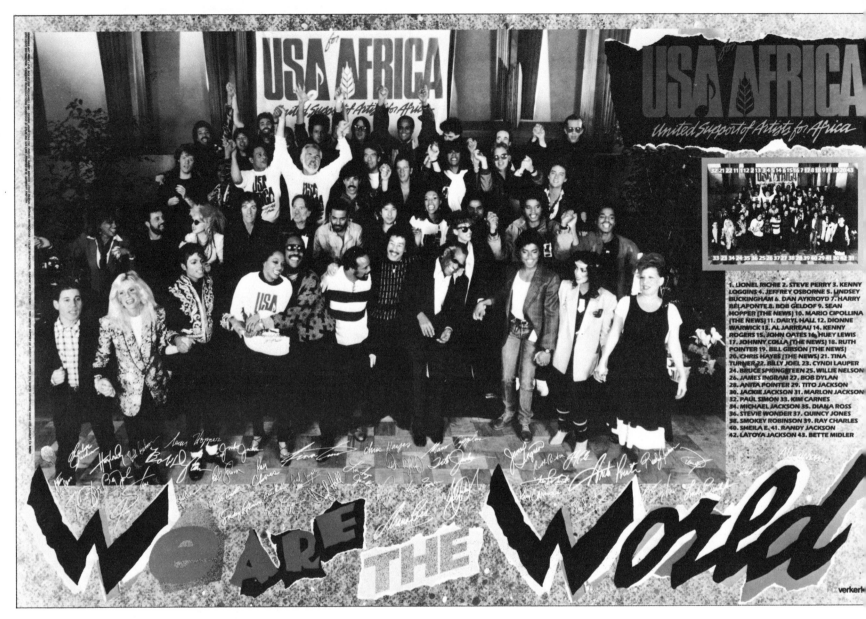

USA for AFRICA — United Support of Artists for Africa

1. LIONEL RICHIE 2. STEVE PERRY 3. KENNY LOGGINS 4. JEFFREY OSBORNE 5. LINDSEY BUCKINGHAM 6. DAN AYKROYD 7. HARRY BELAFONTE 8. BOB GELDOF 9. SEAN HOPPER [THE NEWS] 10. MARIO CIPOLLINA [THE NEWS] 11. DARYL HALL 12. DIONNE WARWICK 13. AL JARREAU 14. KENNY ROGERS 15. JOHN OATES 16. HUEY LEWIS 17. JOHNNY COLLA [THE NEWS] 18. RUTH POINTER 19. BILL GIBSON [THE NEWS] 20. CHRIS HAYES [THE NEWS] 21. TINA TURNER 22. BILLY JOEL 23. CYNDI LAUPER 24. BRUCE SPRINGSTEEN 25. WILLIE NELSON 26. JAMES INGRAM 27. BOB DYLAN 28. ANITA POINTER 29. TITO JACKSON 30. JACKIE JACKSON 31. MARLON JACKSON 32. PAUL SIMON 33. KIM CARNES 34. MICHAEL JACKSON 35. DIANA ROSS 36. STEVIE WONDER 37. QUINCY JONES 38. SMOKEY ROBINSON 39. RAY CHARLES 40. SHEILA E. 41. RANDY JACKSON 42. LATOYA JACKSON 43. BETTE MIDLER

WE ARE THE World

verkerke

who like Springsteen, shows total dedication to his work. But there are other cinematic parallels. Dave Marsh singled out the outlaw code as a parallel to Springsteen's concern with loyalty, but in fact the parallel works with other aspects of the Western, especially the films of John Ford. The search theme of *Born To Run* is an echo of John Wayne's quest in *The Searchers*, and it is more than coincidence that made Ford film John Steinbeck's *Grapes Of Wrath*, vividly capturing the despair of Depression-ridden America in the thirties, the feeling of which was to so haunt Springsteen on *Nebraska* in 1982.

Many of Ford's classic Westerns highlight that sense of community, of trust, of plaintive hillside funerals singing 'Shall We Gather At The River' or exuberant community dances. They are tiny figures in an enormous landscape. But Ford's vision, like Springsteen's, changed as he grew older. Springsteen recognised this in 1981: 'John Ford had a dance scene in every one of his movies, and a fool would say that they were all the same. But for him those dance scenes were only a means towards something. . . .

When John Ford grew older, his dance scenes grew more bitter and they always said more about how he saw people.'

In a typically enigmatic fashion, the world heard of Springsteen's marriage only days before the event in 13 May 1985. Bruce and 25-year-old actress Julianne Phillips met backstage in 1984 and tied the knot near the bride's home in Lake Oswego, Oregon. This event certainly reinforces his sense of family, despite recent comments that he did not feel ready for marriage. Although now a millionaire, money genuinely seems to be unimportant to him. And the communal feelings in performance vanish after a concert, when his favourite way of winding down is to go home and eat on his own, then go for a solitary walk in the small hours. But the paradoxes pale into insignificance when one listens to the music, for that is the only real document.

From the primitive Hammond demos of 1972 to the assured superstar of 1985, it has been a long and fruitful journey. To stay static is to moulder, to start dying, little by little, piece by piece. Whatever is the future of rock'n'roll we can be sure that Springsteen will remain loyal to its essence, yet deliver many surprises.

The Bruce Files

All Those Years

(*Career Milestones And Stage, Radio, And TV Appearances*)

1965

NEW JERSEY THE WOODHAVEN SWIM CLUB
Bruce's first professional gig with The Castiles. The band split $35 five ways, with manager Tex Vinyard receiving ten per cent. Glenn Miller's 'In The Mood', rearranged by Bruce, closes the set. Hostels, high schools, roller rinks, teen clubs, drive-ins and a Shoprite supermarket provide venues for the band's infrequent gigs. Bruce sings on two numbers – Them's 'Mystic Eyes' and the Who's 'My Generation'.

1966
MAY
22 **BRICKTOWN, NEW JERSEY RECORDING STUDIO, BRICK MALL SHOPPING CENTRE**
Tex Vinyard and The Castiles pay $50 for one hour of studio time. The result is an unreleased single: 'That's What You Get'/'Baby I', written by Springsteen and George Theiss. Acetates still exist.

DEC/JAN
67 **NEW YORK CITY THE CAFE WHA**
The band play 29 sets.
The Castiles' reputation and musical development blossoms. Settled into a regular five-piece line-up, they appear at the Elks Club (where Bruce first plays 'Twist And Shout'), the Hubabaloo Club and the Sea and Surf in Sea Bright, New Jersey. With glossy promotional photographs and sporting new stage uniforms they compete in local battle-of-the-bands contests against older, more established celebrities — and claim the top prizes. Late in the year, stage props and smoke bombs join the repertoire.

1967

The band must decide between college and music. Bruce leaves St Rose of Lima high school and, late in the year, the group splits. Bruce forms other local bands and jams with the Source, led by Steve Van Zandt.

1968

ASBURY PARK, NEW JERSEY THE UPSTAGE CLUB
Bruce, now at Ocean County College, begins to hang out here and over the next 18 months he will meet and 'learn his trade' with a host of now legendary Asbury musicians. He eventually puts together his new band, Earth, managed by Rick Stachner. They're heavy rockers who will shortly be re-named Child.

1969
JUNE
1 **RICHMOND, VIRGINIA MONROE PARK**

JULY
15 **ASBURY PARK, NEW JERSEY PANDEMONIUM**

AUGUST
29 **SEA BRIGHT, NEW JERSEY OCEANSIDE SURF CLUB**

SEPTEMBER
19/20 RICHMOND, VIRGINIA THE CENTRE

NOVEMBER
1   RICHMOND, VIRGINIA VCU GYM
Child, formed in the summer and managed by Francis Duffy, consists of Bruce, Vini Lopez and Danny Federici but will soon include Vini Roslyn, late of Motif, on bass. To avoid confusion with another local band, Child become Steel Mill and are now managed by Carl 'Tinker' West. Bruce leaves college but remains in Freehold, New Jersey when his parents, Douglas and Adele, and sisters, Ginny and Pamela, leave for San Mateo, California. He avoids the draft by claiming mental instability. This winter, Steel Mill head for California and play their first gig at Esalen.

1970
JANUARY
13 SAN FRANCISCO THE MATRIX
Songs include 'Satin Doll', 'American Tune' and 'Look To The River'. Philip Elwood writes a highly favourable review in the *San Francisco Examiner*.

FEBRUARY
12/14 SAN FRANCISCO THE MATRIX
The band open for Boz Scaggs.

22 SAN FRANCISCO THE FILLMORE RECORD STUDIOS
At Bill Graham's Recording Studio, Steel Mill record a demo tape which includes 'Goin' Back To Georgia', 'The Train Song' and 'He's Guilty (Send That Boy To Jail)'. They refuse a recording contract.

27/28 RICHMOND, VIRGINIA THE CENTRE

MAY
4   LONG BRANCH, NEW JERSEY MONMOUTH COLLEGE
Songs include 'He's Guilty' and 'Run, Shaker Life'.

16 RICHMOND, VIRGINIA VCU GYM
Songs include 'Resurrection' and 'Come On' (a Steel Mill original).

JUNE
21 ATLANTIC HIGHLANDS, NEW JERSEY CLEARWATER SWIM CLUB

JULY
17/18 ASBURY PARK, NEW JERSEY SUNSHINE INN

27 ASBURY PARK, NEW JERSEY THE UPSTAGE

AUGUST
8   LONG BRANCH, NEW JERSEY THE BEACHCOMBER

SEPTEMBER
11 ATLANTIC HIGHLANDS, NEW JERSEY CLEARWATER SWIM CLUB

NOVEMBER
2   RICHMOND, VIRGINIA UNIVERSITY OF RICHMOND
An interesting set which includes Dylan's 'It's All Over Now, Baby Blue', 'Not Fade Away', 'Got My Mojo Working' and an early work-out of 'When You Dance' which will later appear on Southside Johnny's 1977 album, *This Time It's For Real*.

20 RICHMOND, VIRGINIA THE CENTRE
During 1970, the band are a regular opening act for various name singers and bands in the San Francisco area. Other venues played this year include the 7th and Marshall Street Parking Deck and the String Factory in Richmond, Virginia; the Ocean City Ice Palace in Bricktown, New Jersey and the Student Prince in Asbury Park, New Jersey. They also play in Ocean Grove and West End, New Jersey and it is here, during March, that Steve Van Zandt replaces Vini Roslyn on bass.

1971
JANUARY
18 NEW YORK THE SCENE
An 80-minute set which includes 'I Can't Take It', 'Oh Mama Why' and the Rolling Stones' 'Honky Tonk Woman' segued into 'Dancing In The Street'.

22/23 ASBURY PARK, NEW JERSEY THE UPSTAGE CLUB
Billed as the last Steel Mill concerts but, according to Vini Lopez, 'one or two' gigs take place subsequently.

MAY
14 ASBURY PARK, NEW JERSEY THE SUNSHINE INN
Featuring Dr Zoom and the Sonic Boom, the band formed by Bruce after the demise of Steel Mill. They spend most of their short life in rehearsal and, with a nucleus consisting of Springsteen, Lopez, Van Zandt, David Sancious and Garry Tallent, the line-up fluctuates between five and 30 members. No song titles are confirmed from this era.

15 UNION, NEW JERSEY NEWARK STATE UNIVERSITY
Dr Zoom and the Sonic Boom.

JULY
10 ASBURY PARK, NEW JERSEY BROOKDALE COMMUNITY COLLEGE
The Bruce Springsteen Band, following closely in the footsteps of Dr Zoom and again featuring a fluctuating line-up based on the same five-person nucleus. The band includes a horn section and Delores Holmes and Francine Daniels on backing vocals.

DECEMBER
17 NEW BRUNSWICK, NEW JERSEY RUTGERS UNIVERSITY
The Bruce Springsteen Band.
Other gigs during 1971 are at the VCU Gym and the Mosque in Richmond, Virginia; Rutgers University in New Brunswick, New Jersey (including 'Jambalaya', 'Dance, Dance, Dance', 'My Baby's Natural Magic' and 'You Mean So Much To Me'); the Sunshine Inn, Asbury Park, New Jersey ('When You Dance' features Bruce on lead vocals) and at least four gigs at the Student Prince, Asbury Park, one of which features Southside Johnny singing lead on 'Ain't That Peculiar' and playing harp throughout.

1972
FEBRUARY
RICHMOND, VIRGINIA THE BACK DOOR
One of the final Bruce Springsteen Band gigs. The songs ('When You Dance', 'Cowboys Of The Sea', 'I Just Can't Change' and 'The Band's Just Boppin' The Blues') all indicate Bruce's current musical direction.

MAY
2   NEW YORK CBS BUILDING
A 15-minute audition at 11a.m. with John Hammond of CBS turns into a two-hour session. The appointment has been arranged by Mike Appel of the Wes Farrell songwriting organisation after he and Jim Cretecos are introduced to Bruce by Carl 'Tinker' West in late 1971. This introduction has resulted in Appel becoming Bruce's manager and signing him to his production company, Laurel Canyon Music Ltd, and Cretecos signing him to the music publishing company, Sioux City Music Ltd in March 1972. Later, this one-year contract with four one-year options will nearly wreck Bruce's career.

NEW YORK THE GASLIGHT CLUB
An impressed John Hammond has persuaded Sam Hood, proprietor of the club, to book Bruce for this evening.

Give Summer A Good Start See the "CHILD" Direct From an Engagement With James Cotton, plus "BROTHER DUCK" at Monroe Park, 1pm. Sunday June 1st. FREE FREE!!

At Fort Horne', 'Street Queen', 'Southern Son', 'No Need', 'If I Were The Priest', 'Vibes Man', 'Cowboys Of The Sea', 'The Song', 'Song Of The Orphans', 'Tokyo', 'Circus Song', 'Arabian Night' and 'She's Leaving'. The tape is sent to various music publishers and surfaces in London in late 1972. Judging by the content and superior studio quality, it's likely to have been recorded after the Hammond demos.

1973
JANUARY
3/5 BRYN MAWR, PENNSYLVANIA THE MAIN POINT
The start of a short series of nightly shows with two or three sets per night. Bruce is now doing 40-minute sets.

5 *Greetings from Asbury Park N.J.* is released in the U.S. (COL. KC. 31903).

8/10 BOSTON, MASSACHUSETTS PAUL'S MALL
The start of another series of nightly gigs with two or three sets apiece.

16 VILLANOVA, PENNSYLVANIA VILLANOVA UNIVERSITY
Rumoured only 25 people attend this gig!

24 CHICAGO, ILLINOIS THE QUIET KNIGHT

31/4 FEB
NEW YORK, N.Y. MAX'S KANSAS CITY
Five nights, three sets per night. Bruce opens these sets acoustically with 'Mary, Queen of Arkansas', 'The Bishop Dance' and 'Circus Song'. The first set on the opening night includes the above three songs plus 'Spirit In The Night', 'Does This Bus Stop At 82nd Street?' and 'Thundercrack'.

FEBRUARY
10 ASBURY PARK, NEW JERSEY STUDENT PRINCE

11 SOUTH ORANGE, NEW JERSEY SETON HALL UNIVERSITY

16 LONG BRANCH, NEW JERSEY MONMOUTH COLLEGE

23 'Blinded By The Light'/'The Angel' is released in the U.S. (COL. 4 45850).

MARCH
9 *Greetings from Asbury Park N.J.* is released in the U.K. (CBS 65480).

12 BOSTON, MASSACHUSETTS OLIVERS

APRIL
13 VILLANOVA, PENNSYLVANIA VILLANOVA UNIVERSITY

23 HARTFORD, CONNECTICUT SHABOO

24 BRYN MAWR, PENNSYLVANIA THE MAIN POINT
'New York City Song', 'Circus Song', 'Spirit In The Night', 'Does This Bus Stop At 82nd Street?', 'Hey Santa Ana', 'Tokyo' and 'Thundercrack' are later broadcast on WMMR.

MAY
1 LOS ANGELES, CALIFORNIA AHMANSON THEATRE

3 NEW YORK CBS STUDIOS
With Hammond, further impressed after the live performance, at the controls while Jane Boutwell writes a feature on him for the *New Yorker*, Bruce, accompanying himself on the piano and acoustic guitar, records 14 takes in two hours. Songs include 'Mary, Queen Of Arkansas' (two takes), 'It's Hard To Be A Saint In The City', 'If I Were The Priest', 'Southern Son', 'Jazz Musician' (two takes), 'Growin' Up', 'Two Hearts In True Waltz Time', 'Arabian Night', 'Street Queen', 'The Angel', 'Cowboys Of The Sea' and 'Does This Bus Stop At 82nd Street?'.

JUNE
9 Bruce signs a recording contract with CBS and starts to assemble a band to record his first album. Rehearsals take place at Point Pleasant and the basic tracks are recorded at 914 Sound Studios, Blauvelt, New York in eight or nine days. Bruce adds a few more songs, remixes some of the vocals and, by early September, the record is complete. Bruce, Danny Federici, Clarence Clemons, Garry Tallent and Vini Lopez (later to be known as the E Street Band) are ready to tour.

AUGUST
NEW YORK MAX'S KANSAS CITY
Songs include 'Mary Queen of Arkansas', 'Spirit In The Night', 'Song Of The Orphans' and 'The Bishop Dance'. This last number is recorded and, on 30 August, is played on the King Biscuit Flower Hour: the band's first ever exposure on radio.

DECEMBER
NEW YORK KENNY'S CASTAWAYS
Songs include 'Circus Song', 'Song Of The Orphans', 'Blinded By The Light', 'Growin' Up' and 'For You'.

7 NEW YORK PRISON CONCERT
Invited by the Prisoners' Liaison Committee, the band play on the anniversary of Pearl Harbor. Other gigs played this year are on 12 November at York, Pennsylvania (one of the earliest with the new four-piece band), 29 December at Dayton, Ohio and 30 December at Columbus, Ohio.
Also during 1972, Bruce records a demo tape which includes 'Marie', 'Henry Boy', 'Visitation

The CBS 'Week of Music' convention at which Bruce performs five or six songs including 'Blinded By The Light', an encore of 'Twist And Shout' and 'Circus Song' and 'Thundercrack' are used for a CBS promo video. A live version of 'Circus Song' will be released on the CBS Playback series in June. Reports suggest that Bruce is not the most popular performer at the convention.

11 'Spirit In The Night'/'For You' is released in the U.S. (COL. 4–45864).

26/28 WASHINGTON D.C. CHILDE HAROLD

31 RICHMOND, VIRGINIA ALFA STUDIOS
A six-song acoustic session is recorded by WGOE Radio prior to the evening concert with Chicago. Bruce, Danny, Garry and Clarence start with Duke Ellington's 'Satin Doll'. Also performed are 'Growin' Up' and 'You Mean So Much To Me'.
At the Coliseum, a four-song, 45-minute set includes the first known version of 'Secret To The Blues'.

JUNE
1 HAMPTON, VIRGINIA COLISEUM

2 BETHESDA, MARYLAND WHFS RADIO STUDIOS
A five song acoustic set is recorded. 'Satin Doll', the first number, is followed by 'Mary, Queen Of Arkansas' and 'Growin' Up'.
This evening, Bruce appears at the Civic Centre, Baltimore, Maryland.

3 NEW HAVEN, CONNECTICUT ARENA

6 PHILADELPHIA, PENNSYLVANIA THE SPECTRUM
Bruce is booed by the Philly audience!

8/9 BOSTON, MASSACHUSETTS GARDENS

10 SPRINGFIELD, MASSACHUSETTS CIVIC CENTRE

14/15 NEW YORK, N.Y. MADISON SQUARE GARDEN
Bruce's first show here and the last on the Chicago tour. He will not return for five years.

22/24 SEASIDE HEIGHTS, NEW JERSEY FAT CITY
David Sancious joins the band.

JULY
5/9 BRYN MAWR, PENNSYLVANIA THE MAIN POINT

18/23 NEW YORK, N.Y. MAX'S KANSAS CITY
Two to three sets per night. A seven-song set includes the first known versions of '4th Of July, Asbury Park (Sandy)', 'Something You Got' and 'Zero And Blind Terry'.

31 ROSLYN, NEW YORK MY FATHER'S PLACE
A 60-minute radio broadcast on WLIR with the first known version of 'It's Hard To Be A Saint in the City' plus six other songs.

AUGUST
1/2, 4 ASBURY PARK, NEW JERSEY CONVENTION CENTRE

This man puts more thoughts, more ideas and images into one song than most people put into an album.

Some silicone sister with her manager's mister told me I got what it takes.
She said I'll turn you on sonny, to something strong if you play that song with the funky break.
And go-cart Mozart was checkin' out the weather chart to see if it was safe to go outside.
And little Early-Pearly came by in her curly-wurly and asked me if I needed a ride.
— "Blinded by the Light", Bruce Springsteen

"There hasn't been an album like this in ages. There are individual lines worth entire records. The record rocks, then glides, then rocks again. Bruce Springsteen sings with a freshness and urgency that I haven't heard since I was rocked by 'Like a Rolling Stone.'"
— Peter Knobler, Crawdaddy

And some new-mown chaperone was standin' in the corner all alone watchin' the young girls dance.
And some fresh-sown moonstone was messin' with his frozen zone to remind him of the feeling of romance.
— "Blinded by the Light", Bruce Springsteen

"Debut LP instantly establishes artist as one of our most brilliant singer-songwriters. A completely original vision and a work of genius!"
— Record World, Cover Review

Oh, some hazard from Harvard was skunked on beer playin' backyard bombadier.
Yes and Scotland Yard was trying hard, they sent some dude with a calling card.
He said, "Do what you like, but don't do it here!"
— "Blinded by the Light", Bruce Springsteen

"You know the kid is good when you wake up and you're singing his songs."
— Peter Knobler, Crawdaddy

Music: Springsteen preview

Bruce Springsteen At Childe Harold May 26 - 28, 1973.

Bruce Springsteen's Memorial weekend appearance at Childe Harold created quite a scene in the Watergate shaken Capitol. The house was packed by the time he walked on each night with people crammed in each other's laps.

If John Prine comes over as American rural Dylan Thomas, Springsteen is a latter day Allen Ginsberg and more particularly the Ginsberg of "Howl", with its high pressure, crazily juxtaposed rushes of poetic imagery. He writes lyrics that remind you of Bob Dylan's "Bringing It All Back Home" and he sometimes sounds like a curious cross between Van Morrison's upbeat enthusiasm and the down home funkiness of Robbie Robertson of the Band. Just for good measure, he swipes licks from everybody who was being influenced by Dylan at the time [...] to the

Bruce Springsteen

attitude. His present band is solid and consists of saxophone, bass, organ-piano, piano, drums and even tuba (Note: at present there are a deplorable number of unemployed tuba players in the U.S.)

His first set was impressive and consisted primarily of new material from an upcoming [...] Columbia release, fea [...] debut

album, **Greetings from Asbury Park, N.J.** (Columbia KC 31903). His music is fraught with urban experience and has an attractively driving infectiousness about it, particularly the uptempo numbers.

Bruce Springsteen will be touring the country this summer with Chicago and will appear at the Baltimore Civic Center on June 2nd.

By Bob Goald

14   CHERRY HILL, NEW JERSEY ERLTON LOUNGE

16   EAST PATERSON, NEW JERSEY MR D'S

20/26 BOSTON, MASSACHUSETTS OLIVERS

31/2   SEASIDE HEIGHTS, NEW JERSEY FAT Sept   CITY

SEPTEMBER

6   FRANKLIN, MASSACHUSETTS DEAN JUNIOR COLLEGE

7   UNIVERSITY PARK, PENNSYLVANIA PENN STATE UNIVERSITY

8   PITTSBURG, PENNSYLVANIA UNIVERSITY OF PITTSBURGH

11   *The Wild, The Innocent And The E Street Shuffle* is released in U.S. (COL. KC. 32432).

14/16 SYRACUSE, NEW YORK JABBERWOCKY CLUB

22   MIAMI BEACH, FLORIDA JAI ALAI FRONTON

28   HAMPDEN-SYDNEY, VIRGINIA HAMPDEN-SYDNEY COLLEGE

29   WAYNESBURG, VIRGINIA WAYNESBURG COLLEGE

30   STONY BROOK, NEW YORK STATE UNIVERSITY OF NEW YORK

OCTOBER

6   VILLANOVA, PENNSYLVANIA UNIVERSITY OF VILLANOVA

13   WASHINGTON D.C. KENNEDY CENTRE

15/16 BOSTON, MASSACHUSETTS OLIVERS

20   RINDGE, NEW HAMPSHIRE FRANKLIN PIERCE COLLEGE

26   GENEVA, NEW YORK HOBART COLLEGE

29/31 BRYN MAWR, PENNSYLVANIA THE MAIN POINT
The last night features the first known versions of 'The E Street Shuffle', (Al Tellone guests on the baritone sax) and 'Lost In The Flood'.

NOVEMBER
3   HOULTON, MAINE RICKLER COLLEGE

6/10   NEW YORK, N.Y. MAX'S KANSAS CITY
Roy Bittan, while playing with Niki Aukema's band, appears on the same bill and meets Bruce for the first time.

11   TRENTON, NEW JERSEY TRENTON STATE COLLEGE

14/16 ROSLYN, NEW YORK MY FATHER'S PLACE

17   MANAYUNK, PENNSYLVANIA ROXY THEATRE

DECEMBER
1   HAMDEN. CONNECTICUT QUINNIPIAC COLLEGE

6/8   WASHINGTON D.C. CHILDE HAROLD

14   NEW HAVEN, CONNECTICUT PINE CREST

15   GARDEN CITY, NEW YORK NASSAU COMMUNITY COLLEGE

16   HARTFORD, CONNECTICUT SHABOO

17/18 ASBURY PARK, NEW JERSEY STUDENT PRINCE
Bruce's final appearance at this early haunt.

20   PROVIDENCE, RHODE ISLAND ROGER WILLIAMS COLLEGE

21/22 CHERRY HILL, NEW JERSEY ERLTON LOUNGE

27/30 BRYN MAWR, PENNSYLVANIA THE MAIN POINT
Early in 1973 at the 914 Sound Studios, Blauvelt, New York, Bruce, Danny, Garry, Clarence and Vini record *The Fever*, a Laurel Canyon Music Publishing demo.
On 14 February, Bruce and the band back Chuck Berry in Richmond, Virginia and on the 28th they play the first of three West Coast gigs in Stockton, California.
On 2 March they play Berkeley, California; 3,

Santa Monica, California; 5, Denver, Colorado; 7, Seattle, Washington; 8, Portland, Oregon; 18, Kingston, Rhode Island; 23 Providence, Rhode Island; 24, Niagara, New York; 29, Kutztown, Pennsylvania.
On 1 April they appear in New Brunswick, New Jersey; 7, Norfolk, Pennsylvania; 11, Atlanta, Georgia; 18, Lincroft, New Jersey; 27, Athens, Ohio; 28, College Park, Maryland.
On 5 May they play Providence, Rhode Island; 6, Amherst, Massachusetts; 11, Columbus, Ohio; 12, Niagara, New York; 30, Fayetteville, North Carolina.
At Binghampton, New York on 12 June they play a 45-minute set which features the first known versions of 'Over The Hills Of St Croix' (later re-worked as 'Zero And Blind Terry'), 'Seaside Bar Song' and Bruce's version of 'Take Me Out To The Ball Game'.
Mid-July to late August is spent recording their second album.
On 25 November they play Amherst, Massachusetts and 30 November, Richmond, Virginia.

1974
JANUARY
5   BOSTON, MASSACHUSETTS JOE'S PLACE
Songs include the first known live performances of 'Kitty's Back', 'Let The Four Winds Blow', and 'Rosalita'.

12   PARSIPPANY, NEW JERSEY JOINT IN THE WOODS
Featuring the only known versions of 'Ring Of Fire' and '634-5789'.

19   KENT, OHIO KENT STATE UNIVERSITY
Opened for Black Oak Arkansas.

25   RICHMOND, VIRGINIA MOSQUE
Eight-song set. 'Rosalita' now established as the closing song before encores for every show.

26   NORFOLK, VIRGINIA CHRYSLER THEATRE

FEBRUARY
1   CLEVELAND, OHIO ALLEN THEATRE

2   SPRINGFIELD, MASSACHUSETTS SPRINGFIELD COLLEGE

Brucie's back in town

BRUCE SPRINGSTEEN

special guest Goose Creek Symphony

Mosque Fri. Jan. 25 8pm $4/4.50/5.

7/9   **ATLANTA, GEORGIA POOR RICHARD'S**

12   **LEXINGTON, KENTUCKY UNIVERSITY OF KENTUCKY**

15   **TOLEDO, OHIO UNIVERSITY OF TOLEDO**

17   **COLUMBUS, OHIO THE AGORA**

18   **CLEVELAND, OHIO THE AGORA**
Vini Lopez plays his last show with the band.

22   *The Wild, The Innocent And The E Street Shuffle* is released in U.K. (CBS 65780).

23   **COOKSTOWN, NEW JERSEY SATELLITE LOUNGE**
Ernest 'Boom' Carter, a friend of David Sancious, joins the band for his first appearance.

24/25   **BRYN MAWR, PENNSYLVANIA THE MAIN POINT**

MARCH
  NEW BRUNSWICK, NEW JERSEY STATE THEATRE
Cancelled due to illness.

2   **PARSIPANNY, NEW JERSEY JOINT IN THE WOODS**
Cancelled due to illness.

3/4   **WASHINGTON D.C. GASTON HALL, GEORGETOWN UNIVERSITY**
First night broadcast live on WGTB. A 90-minute set with ten songs. The second night included the first known performance of 'Incident On 57th Street'.

7/11   **HOUSTON, TEXAS LIBERTY HALL**
Five nights including a nine-song radio broadcast on the 9th, for KILT station. The final night's show, a 13-song, 100-minute set, includes the first known versions of three songs: 'The Fever', 'Give Me That Wine' (a spoken/sung song with vocals by Clarence Clemons) and a new song, probably titled 'She's So Fine'. A further KILT radio broadcast on the 8th featured acoustic versions of 'Satin Doll' and 'Something You Got'.

15/16   **AUSTIN, TEXAS ARMADILLO WORLD H.Q.**
Reviewed by *Rolling Stone* magazine, show includes 'N.Y.C. Serenade' (the opening number), 'Let The Four Winds Blow' and 'Twist And Shout'.

18/21   **DALLAS, TEXAS MOTHER BLUES**

24   **PHOENIX, ARIZONA CELEBRITY THEATRE**
David Sancious reportedly rates this to be one of the best ever gigs!

APRIL
5   **CHESTER, PENNSYLVANIA WIDENER COLLEGE**

6   **PEMBERTON, NEW JERSEY BURLINGTON COUNTY COLLEGE**

7   **SOUTH ORANGE, NEW JERSEY SETON HALL UNIVERSITY**

9   **BOSTON, MASSACHUSETTS WBCN STUDIOS**
The band, minus Ernest, perform six numbers acoustically for a radio broadcast. The 45-minute session closes with 'Rosalita'.

9/11   **CAMBRIDGE, MASSACHUSETTS CHARLIE'S BAR**
Outside the venue, the band meet Jon Landau for the first time. Songs include 'N.Y.C. Serenade' and 'Let The Four Winds Blow'.

13   **RICHMOND, VIRGINIA COLISEUM**

18   **W. LONG BRANCH, NEW JERSEY MONMOUTH COLLEGE**

19   **NEW BRUNSWICK, NEW JERSEY STATE THEATRE**

20   **COLLEGEVILLE, PENNSYLVANIA URSINUS COLLEGE**

26   **PROVIDENCE, RHODE ISLAND BROWN'S UNIVERSITY**

27   **STORRS, CONNECTICUT UNIVERSITY OF CONNECTICUT**

28   **SWARTHMORE, PENNSYLVANIA SWARTHMORE COLLEGE**

29   **ALLENTOWN, PENNSYLVANIA ROXY THEATRE**

MAY
4   **UPPER MONTCLAIR, NEW JERSEY MONTCLAIR STATE COLLEGE**

5   **KENT, OHIO KENT STATE UNIVERSITY**

6   **NEWTOWN, PENNSYLVANIA BUCKS COUNTY COMMUNITY COLLEGE**

9   **CAMBRIDGE, MASSACHUSETTS HARVARD SQUARE THEATRE**
Opening for Bonnie Raitt, Bruce performs the first known version of 'I Sold My Heart To The Junkman' and 'Born to Run' for the first time. The show that inspires Jon Landau of *The Real Paper* to write an infamous review in his column, 'Loose Ends', on 22 May.

10   **PROVIDENCE, RHODE ISLAND PALACE THEATRE**

11   **RUTHERFORD, NEW JERSEY FAIRLEIGH DICKENSON UNIVERSITY**

12   **GLASSBORO, NEW JERSEY GLASSBORO STATE COLLEGE**

14   **GREENVILLE, TENNESSEE TUSCULUM COLLEGE**

24   **TRENTON, NEW JERSEY WAR MEMORIAL**

25   **RADNOR, PENNSYLVANIA ARCHBISHOP HIGH SCHOOL**

28/29   **BRYN MAWR, PENNSYLVANIA MAIN POINT**

31   **COLUMBUS, OHIO THE AGORA**

JUNE
1   **KENT, OHIO KENT STATE UNIVERSITY**

2   **TOLEDO, OHIO UNIVERSITY OF TOLEDO**

3   **CLEVELAND, OHIO THE AGORA**
60-minute radio broadcast on WMNS. Seven

MAY 28 & 29 BRUCE SPRINGSTEEN

MAY 23-27 · BUZZY LINHART
MAY 30-JUNE 2 · DOC WATSON
plus DICK FELLER
JUNE 4 & 5 · JIMMY BUFFETT
JUNE 6-9 · LORI LIEBERMAN
JUNE 13-16 · MICHAEL COONEY
JUNE 27-30 · MURRAY McLAUCHLAN
JULY 18-21 · HALL & OATES

ADVANCE TICKETS ON SALE FOR
ALL SHOWS

TICKET AGENCIES
MAD'S RECORDS · ARDMORE
LAMPOST RECORDS · BRYN MAWR
HOBBY HUT · WOODBURY NJ
CENTRAL CITY · 1422 CHESTNUT
BAG & BAGGAGE · WILMINGTON
TRAVEL MART · CASTOR-MAGEE

COFFEE CONCERTS
BEST LOCAL TALENT MONDAYS 8 P.M.
HOOT & AUDITIONS
4th SUNDAY of MONTH · 1-6 P.M.

SHOW TIMES
8 & 10 P.M. TUE, WED, THUR & SUN
8, 10 & 11:30 FRI & SAT · 8 P.M. MON

LA5- 3375

874 LANCASTER AVE. · BRYN MAWR

---

songs including the first known versions of 'You Never Can Tell' and 'I'm Ready'. The old Fats Domino song is sequenced into the final encore, 'Let The Four Winds Blow'.

14 ARLINGTON, TEXAS TEXAS HALL

15 AUSTIN, TEXAS ARMADILLO WORLD H.Q.

16 HOUSTON, TEXAS MUSIC HALL

19 KANSAS CITY, MISSOURI COWTOWN BALLROOM

26/30 MEMPHIS, TENNESSEE LA FAYETTES

JULY
5 ST LOUIS, MISSOURI AMBASSADOR THEATRE

12/14 NEW YORK, N.Y. THE BOTTOM LINE
Shows include the debut of 'Jungleland' plus 'Then She Kissed Me' and 'No Money Down'.

82

---

16 NEWARK, DELAWARE STONE BALLROOM

19 SEDALIA, MISSOURI OUT DOOR SHOW

25 SANTA MONICA, CALIFORNIA CIVIC CENTRE
Opened for Dr John with a 45-minute set. Encored with 'New York City Serenade'.

27 PHOENIX, ARIZONA CELEBRITY THEATRE

28 TUCSON, ARIZONA RACEWAY

AUGUST
3 NEW YORK, N.Y. SCHAEFER MUSIC FESTIVAL, CENTRAL PARK
Opened for Anne Murray, who was reportedly met with loud booing and chants of 'We Want Bruce'.

9 LENOX, MASSACHUSETTS TANGLEWOOD MUSIC FESTIVAL

10 PORTCHESTER, N.Y. CAPITOL THEATRE

12 BOSTON, MASSACHUSETTS PERFORMANCE CENTRE

14 RED BANK, NEW JERSEY CARLTON THEATRE
David Sancious and Ernest 'Boom' Carter play their last gig as members of the E Street Band. Two weeks previously, David and Ernest had

---

been in the 914 Sound Studios, Blauvelt, New York to record a track for Bruce's next album. Its title: 'Born To Run'.

SEPTEMBER
8 ASBURY PARK, NEW JERSEY STONE PONY
The Blackberry Booze Band finish their set and Bruce, Vini Lopez and Garry Tallent join Southside Johnny onstage for several oldies including 'Twist And Shout'.

18/19 BRYN MAWR, PENNSYLVANIA MAIN POINT
Max, Roy and Suki make their live debuts with the E Street Band. The opening song is 'Incident On 57th Street'.

20 PHILADELPHIA, PENNSYLVANIA TOWER THEATRE

21 ONEONTA, NEW YORK STATE UNIVERSITY

22 UNION, NEW JERSEY KEAN COLLEGE

OCTOBER
4 NEW YORK, N.Y. AVERY FISHER (PHILHARMONIC) HALL
A 15-song set that includes the first known versions of 'A Love So Fine', 'Cupid' and 'She's The One', ends with the front of the stage collapsing after the second encore, 'Quarter To Three'.

5 READING, PENNSYLVANIA ALLBRIGHT COLLEGE

6 WORCESTER, MASSACHUSETTS CLARK UNIVERSITY

11 GAITHERSBURG, MARYLAND SHADY GROVE MUSIC FAIR

12 PRINCETON, NEW JERSEY ALEXANDER HALL, PRINCETON UNIVERSITY
The band perform two sets. The late show features 13 songs, all of them Bruce's own compositions.

8 CORPUS CHRISTI, TEXAS RITZ THEATRE

9 HOUSTON, TEXAS MUSIC HALL

10 DALLAS, TEXAS SPORTATORIUM

16 WASHINGTON D.C. GASTON HALL, GEORGETOWN UNIVERSITY

21 BLACKWOOD, NEW JERSEY CAMDEN COMMUNITY COLLEGE

22 WEST CHESTER, PENNSYLVANIA WIDENER COLLEGE

23 SALEM, MASSACHUSETTS SALEM STATE COLLEGE
'Growin' Up' is brought into a 12-song set for the first time since January 1974.

29/30 TRENTON, NEW JERSEY WAR MEMORIAL BUILDING
The 15-song set includes the debut of Dylan's 'I Want You' with a hauntingly beautiful violin backing by Suki Lahav. 'Wear My Ring Around Your Neck' is part of a four-song encore.

DECEMBER

6 NEW BRUNSWICK, NEW JERSEY STATE THEATRE
15 songs plus an instrumental included in the encores.

7 GENEVA, NEW YORK HOBART COLLEGE

8 BURLINGTON, VERMONT UNIVERSITY OF VERMONT
This 15-song set is typical of those from this period. Songs include 'Incident On 57th Street'; 'Spirit In The Night'; 'Does This Bus Stop At 82nd Street?'; 'I Want You'; 'Growin' Up'; 'The E Street Shuffle'; It's Hard To Be A Saint In The City'; 'Jungleland'; 'Kitty's Back'; 'New York City Serenade'; 'Rosalita (Come Out Tonight)'; '4th Of July, Asbury Park (Sandy)'; 'A Love So Fine'; 'Wear My Ring Around Your Neck'; 'Quarter To Three'.

25 PHILADELPHIA, PENNSYLVANIA WMMR RADIO BROADCAST
Prerecorded Christmas message from Bruce. Other shows this year are on 13 June in Oklahoma City; 26 July in San Diego, California; 13 August in Wilmington, Delaware; 15 November in Eaton, Pennsylvania; and 17 November in Charlottesville, Virginia.
In August 1974 an advert is placed in the *Village Voice* for a drummer, pianist, violinist and trumpet player. Auditions take place at Studio Instrumental Rentals, 54th Street, New York City and from over 40 applicants, three are finally chosen: Roy Bittan on piano, Max Weinberg on drums and recording engineer Louis Lahav's wife, Suki, on violin. In October, the new line-up record 'A Love So Fine' at the 914 Sound Studios. It will never be released.

1975
FEBRUARY
5 BRYN MAWR, PENNSYLVANIA MAIN POINT
A benefit concert broadcast on WMMR for the club that has played host to Bruce on numerous occasions. This 18-song show debuts 'Mountain Of Love', 'Back In The U.S.A.' and an early rendition of a new song, 'Thunder Road'.

18 PASSAIC, NEW JERSEY CAPITOL THEATRE
A 13-song set features the debut of 'Spanish Harlem'.

19 SCHENECTADY, NEW YORK UNION COLLEGE
'Lost In The Flood' is added to the previous night's songs.

20 CARLISLE, PENNSYLVANIA DICKENSON COLLEGE

25 HANOVER, NEW HAMPSHIRE DARTMOUTH COLLEGE

26 SPRINGFIELD, MASSACHUSETTS SPRINGFIELD COLLEGE

27 MILLESVILLE, PENNSYLVANIA STATE COLLEGE

29 BOSTON, MASSACHUSETTS MUSIC HALL
'Cupid' is played for the last time in a 13-song set.

NOVEMBER
1/2 PHILADELPHIA, PENNSYLVANIA TOWER THEATRE

3 PHILADELPHIA, PENNSYLVANIA WMMR RADIO BROADCAST
Interview with DJ Ed Sciaky. The 40-minute broadcast includes the demo tape of 'The Fever' and a pre-lease tape of 'Born To Run'.

6/7 AUSTIN, TEXAS ARMADILLO WORLD HEADQUARTERS
Bruce believed to have had at least one of these shows filmed.

6/7 WEST CHESTER, PENNSYLVANIA WIDENER COLLEGE

18 CLEVELAND, OHIO JOHN CARROLL UNIVERSITY

19 UNIVERSITY PARK, PENNSYLVANIA PENN STATE UNIVERSITY

20 PITTSBURGH, PENNSYLVANIA UNIVERSITY OF PITTSBURGH

23 WESTBURY, NEW YORK WESTBURY MUSIC FAIR
At the afternoon soundcheck, Bruce tries out a couple of songs, 'Soothe Me' and 'Needles And Pins', but they won't be played this evening or appear at any concert in the future.

MARCH
1 SYRACUSE, NEW YORK SYRACUSE UNIVERSITY

2 PLATTSBURGH, PENNSYLVANIA STATE UNIVERSITY OF NEW YORK

7 BALTIMORE, MARYLAND PAINTERS MILL MUSIC FAIR

8/9 WASHINGTON D.C. CONSTITUTION HALL
The final live show with Suki Lahav who has given such a distinct flavour to the sound of the E Street Band. Dylan's 'I Want You', to which Suki has added so much, is played for the last time.

NEPTUNE, NEW JERSEY
Bruce and the E Street Band (with Suki) resume rehearsals for the recording of the third album. At Jon Landau's suggestion, studio sessions are

SPRINGSTEEN!

"Born to Run," "The Wild, the Innocent & the E Street Shuffle" and "Greetings From Asbury Park." All on Columbia Records and Tapes.

Available At your favorite record store.

switched from the 914 Sound Studios, Blauvelt, New York to the Record Plant Studios, New York City. The next five months, according to Bruce, are 'the worst experience of my life'. With hindsight, the problems are as nothing compared to the making of his fourth album.

APRIL

15   NEW YORK, N.Y. RADIO BROADCAST
Arranged by John Hammond and originally taped in 1974, this 30-minute interview with Father Bill Ayers, a Catholic priest who had a regular programme called *On This Rock*, was Bruce's first radio interview.

JULY

20   PROVIDENCE, RHODE ISLAND PALACE THEATRE
Miami Steve Van Zandt debuts with the E Street Band. Introduced for the first time in this 15-song set are 'Tenth Avenue Freeze-Out' and 'Sha La La'.

22   GENEVA, N.Y. GENEVA THEATRE
The afternoon soundcheck features three songs never before performed live, 'You Really Got Me', 'Soothe Me' and Solomon Burke's classic 'Cry To Me'. The evening concert is a 15-song set.

23   LENOX, MASSACHUSETTS MUSIC INN
Clarence is called on to perform 'Give Me That Wine' in a 16-song set which includes an instrumental.

25/26 KUTZTOWN, PENNSYLVANIA KEYSTONE HALL, KUTZTOWN STATE COLLEGE
Two nights featuring the regular 15 or 16-song sets and the first known version of 'Carol'.

28/29 WASHINGTON D.C. CARTER BARON AMPHITHEATRE
Two 15-song sets that include regular favourites like 'Kitty's Back', 'The E Street Shuffle' and 'New York City Serenade'.

29   BETHESDA, MARYLAND WHFS RADIO BROADCAST
Bruce and Clarence drop in on an unsure and unprepared DJ who asks, amongst other things, if Suki's still playing the glockenspiel! Clarence tells him he's the synthesizer player in an hilarious 15-minute interview.

AUGUST

1   RICHMOND, VIRGINIA MOSQUE
'Up On The Roof' debuts in a 16-song set.

2   NORFOLK, VIRGINIA CHRYSLER THEATRE

8   AKRON, OHIO CIVIC THEATRE
20-song concert which features the live debuts of 'Backstreets' and 'Havin' A Party' plus 'Up On The Roof', 'Carol' and 'Then She Kissed Me'.

9   PITTSBURGH, PENNSYLVANIA SYRIA MOSQUE

10   CANTON, OHIO CIVIC THEATRE
Last live version of 'New York City Serenade'.

13/17 NEW YORK, N.Y. BOTTOM LINE
These five nights, with two shows per night, herald Bruce's emergence from a cult figure to an internationally acclaimed artiste. CBS and the press surround these gigs with an incredible amount of publicity, even though Bruce's third album is not yet released. A slow 'Thunder Road' opens the first show and 'When You Walk In The Room' is debuted.
The early show on the second night debuts 'Night' and is a 13-song set.
On the third night, the 14-song early show is broadcast live on WNEW and includes a brief backstage chat with Bruce. This Friday morning, a review by leading rock critic, John Rockwell, makes the front page of the *New York Times*.
The fourth night debuts 'It's Gonna Work Out Fine' in a 16-song set which includes five other cover versions and four songs from the yet-to-be-released *Born To Run* LP.
The early show on the last night features a 15-song set and concludes a series of gigs which are reputed to be the most talked-about since Dylan's 1966 Albert Hall show.

21/23 ATLANTA, GEORGIA ELECTRIC BALLROOM

**25   *Born To Run* (COL. PC 33793) is released in the U.S.

**29   'Born To Run'/'Meeting Across The River' (COL. 3-10209) is released in the U.S.

SEPTEMBER

6   NEW ORLEANS, LOUISIANA PERFORMING ARTS CENTRE
Boz Scaggs joins Bruce onstage for 'Twist And Shout', the final encore of a 17-song set. Bruce records a 40-minute interview with Mike Timms for broadcast in Sweden.

7   NEW ORLEANS, LOUISIANA YA YA LOUNGE

The E Street Band perform at Lee Dorsey's club where they attempt to lure him onstage to perform his old hits.

11   ARLINGTON, TEXAS TEXAS HALL

12   AUSTIN, TEXAS MUNICIPAL AUDITORIUM
15-song set.

13/14 HOUSTON, TEXAS MUSIC HALL
Debut of 'Pretty Flamingo' and the band's first known version of 'Lucille'. Also included in the middle break of 'Kitty's Back' is a one-off performance of Stevie Wonder's 'Nothing's Too Good For My Baby'.

16   DALLAS, TEXAS TARRANT COUNTY CONVENTION CENTRE
15-song set.

17   OKLAHOMA CITY, OKLAHOMA MUSIC HALL

**19   'Born To Run'/'Meeting Across The River' (CBS 3661) is released in U.K.

20   GRINNELL, IOWA GRINNELL UNIVERSITY

21   MINNEAPOLIS, MINNESOTA TYRONE GUTHRIE THEATRE
'Backstreets' returns to this 15-song set and from now on becomes a regular part of the live act.

23   ANN ARBOR, MICHIGAN HILL AUDITORIUM, UNIVERSITY OF MICHIGAN
Bruce celebrates his 26th birthday with an 18-song set that debuts a five-song medley: 'Devil With The Blue Dress', 'Good Golly Miss Molly', 'C.C. Rider', 'Jenny Take A Ride' and (for one time only) 'Back In The U.S.A.'.

25   CHICAGO, ILLINOIS AUDITORIUM
A 20-minute colour 8mm film, shot without permission by a member of the audience, shows some of the earliest known footage of Bruce, complete with beard and black leather jacket.

26   IOWA CITY, IOWA UNIVERSITY OF IOWA

27   ST LOUIS, MISSOURI AMBASSADOR THEATRE

28   KANSAS CITY, MISSOURI MEMORIAL HALL
Rumoured that Bruce's first visit is marked with a version of Wilbert Harrison's 'Kansas City'.

30   OMAHA, NEBRASKA UNIVERSITY OF NEBRASKA

OCTOBER

2   MILWAUKEE, WISCONSIN UPTOWN THEATRE
The show opens with a live debut of 'Meeting Across The River'. After six more songs, a bomb scare postpones the concert until midnight, when Bruce and the E Street Band returned to an ecstatic crowd with the debut of 'Little Queenie', complete with impromptu lyrics about the 'mad bomber'. The second half of the show is illegally filmed by a member of the audience.

4   DETROIT, MICHIGAN MICHIGAN PALACE
'Ain't Too Proud To Beg' is performed for the

first time in a show that also includes the 'Devil With The Blue Dress' medley, 'Little Queenie' and thirteen other songs.

10 *Born To Run* (CBS 69170) is released in U.K.

11 **RED BANK, NEW JERSEY CARLTON THEATRE**
At the late show David Sancious joins Bruce onstage for an encore, 'Carol'.

16/19 LOS ANGELES, CALIFORNIA ROXY
Bruce opens a four-night residency in front of a star-studded audience including Robert De Niro, Warren Beatty, Tom Waits, Jack Nicholson and Carly Simon (who apparently walks out after the second number).
Broadcast live on KEST, the early show on the second night features the debut of 'Goin' Back'. During a 14-song set at the early show on the third night, Bruce dedicates 'Carol' to audience member Carole King. The late show includes 'Pretty Flamingo' and the medley.
On the final night, Bruce's West Coast appearances gain the influential support of *Los Angeles Times* rock critic, Robert Hilburn, who gives him ecstatic press coverage.

20 **LOS ANGELES, CALIFORNIA GOLD STAR STUDIOS**
Bruce and Miami Steve meet up with Phil Spector while he's producing the Dion LP, *Born To Be With You*.

25 **PORTLAND, OREGON PARAMOUNT THEATRE**

26 **SEATTLE, WASHINGTON PARAMOUNT THEATRE**
'For You' returns to the set for the first time since February 1975.

29 **SACRAMENTO, CALIFORNIA MEMORIAL AUDITORIUM**

30 **OAKLAND, CALIFORNIA PARAMOUNT THEATRE**

NOVEMBER

1 **SANTA BARBARA, CALIFORNIA UNIVERSITY OF CALIFORNIA**

3/4/6 PHOENIX, ARIZONA ARIZONA STATE UNIVERSITY
'Twist And Shout' ends a 13-song plus medley set on the last night.

9 **TAMPA, FLORIDA JAI ALAI PAVILION**
12 songs plus medley.

11 **MIAMI, FLORIDA JAI ALAI PAVILION**
The final concert before a short European tour and Bruce and the band deliver a 14-song plus medley set.

18 **LONDON, ENGLAND HAMMERSMITH ODEON**
Dismayed by the overblown CBS hype he's met with, Bruce has ripped down posters proclaiming 'Finally The World Is Ready For Bruce Springsteen'. Bruce considers the show, a 15-song plus medley set, to be a total failure. The critics agree and are quick to denounce the U.S. singer as no more than a second or even third-rate Dylan.

21 **STOCKHOLM, SWEDEN KONSERTHUSET**
A 14-song plus medley set.

23 **AMSTERDAM, HOLLAND R.A.I. BUILDING**
A successful 14-song plus medley show. Both Bruce and the audience are happy.

24 **LONDON, ENGLAND HAMMERSMITH ODEON**
It's unlikely Bruce would have agreed to return to England so soon after the experience he and the band went through at the first show. However, promoter Harvey Goldsmith books Bruce for a second show due to initial ticket demand and he returns, albeit reluctantly, to a three hour show with nine encores, the longest he's ever done. He nervously opens with 'Thunder Road', and after 21 songs, including a frantic 'Devil With The Blue Dress' medley, an exhausted Bruce is carried off-stage by the E

Street Band. BBC TV cameras are present at the London gig, but no footage has ever been released. 'When You Walk In The Room' and 'Little Queenie' are played for the final time.

DECEMBER

2/3 **BOSTON, MASSACHUSETTS MUSIC HALL**
Both concerts feature 17-song plus medley sets and the first show sees the live debuts of 'Santa Claus Is Comin' To Town' and 'Party Lights'.

5/6 **WASHINGTON D.C. McDONOUGH GYM, GEORGETOWN UNIVERSITY**
17-song plus medley sets on both nights.

6 **WASHINGTON D.C.**
Bruce is interviewed by a local radio station D.J. A Christmas message from Bruce is broadcast separately.

SPRINGSTEEN
BUCKNELL UNIVERSITY
DAVIS GYM 8:30 P.M.
WEDNESDAY DEC. 10TH

$6.50 General Admission
Doors Open 7:30

TICKETS ON SALE AT:

Jack Lashays
Home Entertainment Center
Orchard Park Plaza
Shamokin Dam, Pa.

The Stereo House
905 Penn St.
Williamsport, Pa.

The Center by M—L
Independence St.
Shamokin, Pa.

Shotgun Boogy
Market St.
Sunbury, Pa.

Record Bar
East College Ave.
State College, Pa.

Bloomsburg State College
Information Desk Student Union
Bloomsburg, Pa.

The Stereo House
Rt. 15
Lewisburg, Pa.

Bucknell University
University Center
2nd Floor Information Desk
Lewisburg, Pa.

Produced by the
Bucknell Concert Committee

No Smoking
No Liquor
No Blankets
in Davis Gym

For Information
Call 717-524-3480

---

10 LEWISBURG, PENNSYLVANIA BUCKNELL UNIVERSITY

11 SOUTH ORANGE, NEW JERSEY SETON HALL UNIVERSITY
Last performance of 'Party Lights' in a 20-song plus medley set.

12 GREENVALE, NEW YORK C.W. POST COLLEGE
Debut of 'It's My Life' in a 17-song plus medley set that features the version of 'Santa Claus Is Comin' To Town' released in 1981 on the charity album *In Harmony 2*.
'Tenth Avenue Freeze-Out'/'She's The One' (COL. 3–10274) is released in the U.S.

16 OSWEGO, NEW YORK STATE UNIVERSITY OF NEW YORK
16-song plus medley set.

17 BUFFALO, NEW YORK KLEINHAUS MUSIC HALL

19 MONTREAL, CANADA PLACE DES ARTES
The start of Bruce's first short tour of Canada.

20 OTTAWA, CANADA NATIONAL ARTS CENTRE

21 TORONTO, CANADA SENECA COLLEGE
16-song plus medley set ends the three-day visit to Canada.
In Bethesda, Maryland, the pre-recorded Christmas message is transmitted by a WHFS radio D.J.

27/28 PHILADELPHIA, PENNSYLVANIA TOWER THEATRE

30/31 The first night features a rare performance of 'Back In The U.S.A.' in a 17-song plus medley set.
On the second night, 'Sha La La' is played for the last time.
Bruce slows down 'Tenth Avenue Freeze-Out' on the third night to a ballad tempo in an 18-song plus medley set that also features 'Mountain Of Love', 'It's Gonna Work Out Fine' and the last ever performance of 'Wear My Ring Around Your Neck'.
A great New Year's Eve concert on the 31st again features the down-tempo 'Tenth Avenue Freeze-Out' as well as last ever performances of 'Mountain Of Love' and 'Does This Bus Stop At 82nd Street?'.
In September 1975, Bruce is invited on stage at Main Point, Bryn Mawr, Pennsylvania to perform acoustic versions of 'Thunder Road' and 'Born To Run' at a six-night free benefit for the club given by Jackson Browne, accompanied by David Lindley.
8,9,11 and 12 of October are scheduled for gigs at Memphis, Nashville, Shreveport and La Fayette but are later cancelled.
On 27 October, both *Time* and *Newsweek* feature Bruce on their front covers.
A general guide to two typical 1975 shows, before and after the release of *Born to Run*:
Pre *Born to Run* at the Mosque, Richmond, Virginia, 1 August 1975.
'Incident On 57th Street'; 'Tenth Avenue Freeze-Out'; 'Spirit In The Night'; 'The E Street Shuffle'; 'It's Hard To Be A Saint In The City'; 'She's The One'; ('Born to Run'); 'Thunder Road'; 'Growin' Up'; 'Up On The Road'; 'Kitty's Back'; 'New York City Serenade'; 'Roslita (Come Out Tonight)'; '4th Of July, Asbury Park (Sandy)'; 'A Love So Fine'; 'Carol'; 'Quarter To Three'.
Post *Born to Run* in Oswego, New York, 16 December 1975. 'Thunder Road'; 'Tenth Avenue Freeze-Out'; 'Spirit In The Night'; 'Lost in the Flood'; 'She's The One'; 'Born To Run'; 'Pretty Flamingo'; 'It's Hard To Be A Saint In The City'; 'Backstreets'; 'Kitty's Back'; 'Jungleland'; 'Rosalita (Come Out Tonight)'; '4th Of July, Asbury Park (Sandy)'; 'Santa Claus Is Comin' To Town'; 'Devil With The Blue Dress' medley; 'For You'; 'Quarter To Three'.

1976
FEBRUARY
6 'Tenth Avenue Freeze-Out'/'She's The One' (CBS 3940) is released in U.K.

MARCH
21 ASBURY PARK, NEW JERSEY STONE PONY
In a rehearsal for the forthcoming tour, Bruce and the E Street Band go through most of the *Born To Run* songs plus 'Raise Your Hand' in front of an invited audience of 300.

25 COLUMBIA, SOUTH CAROLINA TOWNSHIP AUDITORIUM

26 ATLANTA, GEORGIA FOX THEATRE

28 DURHAM, NORTH CAROLINA DUKE UNIVERSITY

29 CHARLOTTE, NORTH CAROLINA OVEN'S AUDITORIUM

APRIL
1 ATHENS, OHIO UNIVERSITY OF OHIO

2 LOUISVILLE, KENTUCKY McALLY THEATRE

4 EAST LANSING, MICHIGAN MICHIGAN STATE UNIVERSITY
Show includes a new song, 'Frankie'. Also played are 'Raise Your Hand' and a rare performance of 'Meeting Across The River' in a 17-song plus medley set.

5 COLUMBUS, OHIO OHIO THEATRE

7/8 CLEVELAND, OHIO ALLEN THEATRE
Featuring 'Frankie' and a rare performance of 'Blinded By The Light'.

9 HAMILTON, NEW YORK COLGATE UNIVERSITY
Last known performance of 'Blinded By The Light' in an 18-song plus medley set.

BRUCE SPRINGSTEEN
in CONCERT

PAUL MELLON ARTS CENTER
Saturday - April 10, 1976
8 P.M.
$6.00

10 WALLINGFORD, CONNECTICUT PAUL MELLON ARTS CENTRE, CHOATE SCHOOL
Free benefit concert played at the request of John Hammond.

12 JOHNSTOWN, PENNSYLVANIA MEMORIAL AUDITORIUM

13 UNIVERSITY PARK, PENNSYLVANIA RECREATION HALL, PENN STATE UNIVERSITY
Max's 24th birthday is celebrated with an 18-song plus medley set.

15 PITTSBURGH, PENNSYLVANIA SYRIA MOSQUE

16 MEADVILLE, PENNSYLVANIA ALLEGHENY COLLEGE

17 ROCHESTER, NEW YORK UNIVERSITY OF ROCHESTER

20 JOHNSON CITY, TENNESSEE FREEDOM HALL

21 KNOXVILLE, TENNESSEE AUDITORIUM

22 BLACKSBURG, VIRGINIA BURRUS AUDITORIUM, VIRGINIA POLYTECHNIC
Last known version of 'Frankie'.

24 BOONE, NORTH CAROLINA APPALACHIAN STATE UNIVERSITY

26   CHATTANOOGA, TENNESSEE TIVOLI THEATRE

28   NASHVILLE, TENNESSEE GRAND OL' OPRY

29   MEMPHIS, TENNESSEE ELLIS AUDITORIUM
Eddie Floyd joins Bruce onstage for three songs, 'Raise Your Hand', 'Yum Yum I Want Some' and 'Knock On Wood', in a 16-song plus medley set. After the show, Bruce tries to see Elvis Presley but his somewhat unconventional method of gaining entry to Graceland by scaling the wall is thwarted by guards. Bruce never gets to meet Elvis.

30   BIRMINGHAM, ALABAMA MUNICIPAL AUDITORIUM

MAY
3   LITTLE ROCK, ARKANSAS ROBINSON AUDITORIUM

4   JACKSON, MISSISSIPPI MUNICIPAL AUDITORIUM

6   SHREVEPORT, LOUISIANA MUNICIPAL AUDITORIUM

8   BATON ROUGE, LOUISIANA ASSEMBLY CENTRE

9/10   MOBILE, ALABAMA MUNICIPAL AUDITORIUM
Jon Landau's 28th birthday is celebrated on the 10th, with a set that includes 'Quarter To Three'.

11   AUBURN, ALABAMA AUBURN UNIVERSITY

13   NEW ORLEANS, LOUISIANA MUNICIPAL AUDITORIUM
The end of the official tour.

27   WEST POINT, NEW YORK EISENHOWER HALL, U.S. MILITARY ACADEMY
Invited by the Dialectic Society, Bruce and the E Street Band deliver a set that's typical of the first tour of 1976: 'Night'; 'Tenth Avenue Freeze-Out'; 'Spirit In The Night'; 'It's My Life'; 'Thunder Road'; 'She's The One'; 'Born To Run'; 'Pretty Flamingo'; 'Growin' Up'; 'It's Hard To Be A Saint In The City'; 'Backstreets'; 'Jungleland'; 'Rosalita (Come Out Tonight)'; Raise Your Hand'; '4th Of July, Asbury Park (Sandy)'; 'Devil With The Blue Dress' medley.

30   ASBURY PARK, NEW JERSEY STONE PONY
Bruce joins Southside Johnny and the Asbury Jukes onstage for one song, 'Havin' A Party', broadcast by WMMR radio. Southside's debut LP is filmed at this gig and features cameo appearances by Bruce, various members of the E Street Band and Dave Marsh.

AUGUST
1/3   RED BANK, NEW JERSEY MONMOUTH
5/7   ARTS CENTRE (formerly the CARLTON THEATRE)
On the 1st, debuts of 'Rendezvous', 'Something In The Night' and two oldies, 'She's Sure The Girl I Love' and 'You Can't Sit Down' feature in a 16-song set.
The 2nd, 3rd, 5th and 6th are all 15-song sets and on the 3rd is the debut of a song allegedly

written that day and reckoned to be Bruce's finest unreleased song – 'The Promise'.
The 7th features a 17-song set and, as on the five previous nights, Bruce and the E Street Band are joined by the Jukes horn section.

21   WATERBURY, CONNECTICUT PALACE THEATRE
A 15-song set. The Miami Horns – Rick Gazda, Earl Gardner, Bob Malach, Bill Zacagni and Louis Parente – feature on three songs.

SEPTEMBER
4   ASBURY PARK, NEW JERSEY STONE PONY
Bruce joins Southside Johnny onstage for back-up vocals on one song, 'Havin' A Party'.

26   PHOENIX, ARIZONA VETERANS MEMORIAL COLISEUM
The second short tour of 1976 begins with a 16-song set. The Miami Horns are featured at all 23 gigs.

29/30   SANTA MONICA, CALIFORNIA CIVIC CENTRE
15-song set on the 29th includes the second performance of 'The Promise'. From now on it will become a regular encore. The 30th features a 16-song set and after the gig, Bruce and Miami Steve go to Los Angeles and join Dion onstage at the Roxy for one song, 'A Teenager In Love'. Max, Danny and Garry are in the audience but do not play.

OCTOBER
2   OAKLAND, CALIFORNIA PARAMOUNT THEATRE

3   SANTA CLARA, CALIFORNIA SANTA CLARA UNIVERSITY

5   SANTA BARBARA, CALIFORNIA COUNTY BOWL
15-song set.

9   SOUTH BEND, INDIANA NOTRE DAME UNIVERSITY
15-song set.

10   OXFORD, OHIO MIAMI UNIVERSITY
15-song set.

12   NEW BRUNSWICK, NEW JERSEY RUTGERS GYM, RUTGERS UNIVERSITY
16-song set.

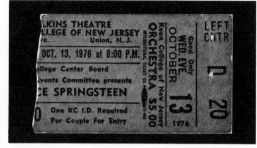

13   UNION, NEW JERSEY WILKINS THEATRE, KEAN COLLEGE
16-song set.

16   WILLIAMSBURG, VIRGINIA WILLIAM AND MARY UNIVERSITY
16-song set.

17/18   WASHINGTON D.C. GEORGETOWN UNIVERSITY
15-song set on the 18th.

25   PHILADELPHIA, PENNSYLVANIA THE SPECTRUM
17-songs, including the first known performance of 'A Fine, Fine Girl'. Bruce's first headlined gig at a large venue.

26   PHILADELPHIA, PENNSYLVANIA WMMR RADIO
A five-minute phone interview with Ed Sciaky.

27   PHILADELPHIA, PENNSYLVANIA THE SPECTRUM
A 17-song set featuring a rare performance of 'Incident On 57th Street'. Ed Sciaky had told radio listeners the previous day that Bruce no longer plays it!

28/30   NEW YORK, N.Y. PALLADIUM
All three nights feature 17-song sets. On the second night, Gary U.S. Bonds joins Bruce for the first encore, 'Quarter To Three'. On the third night, Patti Smith joins Bruce for 'Rosalita'.

NOVEMBER
2/4   NEW YORK, N.Y. PALLADIUM
The first night features a 17-song set, typical of the second short tour of 1976: 'Night'; 'Rendezvous'; 'Spirit In The Night'; 'It's My Life'; 'Thunder Road'; 'She's The One'; 'Something In The Night'; 'Backstreets'; 'Growin' Up'; 'Tenth Avenue Freeze-Out'*; 'Jungleland'; 'Rosalita (Come Out Tonight)'; 'The Promise'; 'A Fine, Fine Girl'*; 'Raise Your Hand'*; '4th of July, Asbury Park (Sandy)'; 'Born To Run'. (* with the Miami Horns.)
A shorter 15-song set on the second night premieres 'Mona'. The introduction to 'Rosalita' features the Beach Boys 'Be True To Your School'.
On the third night, Ronnie Spector appears onstage for a three-song Ronettes medley with Bruce. The show features 19 songs, including the debut of 'We Gotta Get Outta This Place', and is later broadcast on WCOZ in Boston.

BRUCE SPRINGSTEEN AND THE E STREET BAND

Sunday
March 20, 1977
8 p.m.

Providence
College
Alumni
Hall

All Seats Reserved
$7.00 & $7.50
Available at:
Ladd's
Roth's
Beacon Shop
Midland Records (Midland Mall)
Brown, R.I.C., P.C.

Presented By
The
BANZINI
BROS.
and the P.C. B.O.G.

Photo: David Gahr
Graphics: Umeda Design

6   NEW YORK, N.Y. WNEW RADIO
A 60-minute interview with Richard Neer.

16   'Born To Run'/'Spirit In The Night' is released in the U.S. in Columbia's 'Hall of Fame' series (13 33323).

26   NEW YORK, N.Y. BOTTOM LINE
Bruce joins Patti Smith on piano for seven songs. In the late show, he joins her once more for four songs on piano and one on guitar.

In 1976, Bruce takes part in legal proceedings which nearly wreck his career.
On 14 May Mike Appel's Laurel Canyon Productions sends Bruce a royalty and earnings statement for $67,000. This is the first account since Bruce signed for Mike on a car bonnet in a darkened car park in March 1972. During this time, it will later be argued, Bruce earned in excess of $2 million! Bruce begins to sever his links with Mike.
1 June is the date Bruce originally planned to start recording his fourth album, but it will be exactly one year before work begins.
On 2 July Bruce receives a letter from Mike Appel stating that, under the terms of his contract, he cannot record with Jon Landau as producer. On the 27th, Bruce files suit against Appel for fraud and mismanagement but on the 29th, Appel files a counter suit against Bruce and at the first court hearing on 9 August Judge Arnold Fein awards an injunction against recording with Jon Landau. However on 1 August, Mike Appel is refused a request for a civil order to stop the forthcoming Monmouth Arts Centre concerts.
The second hearing of the Appel vs Springsteen court case is on 15 September. Bruce's request for the recording ban to be lifted is not upheld.
On 18 November, Bruce's lawyer submits an affidavit to the court asking for the federal and state issues in the case to be linked to the civil actions for one trial.
On 8 December Bruce submits a second

affidavit, asking for permission to record an album with Landau producing, on condition that the tapes be placed in the custody of the court until legal matters are resolved. This is later refused.

1977
FEBRUARY
7   ALBANY, NEW YORK PALACE THEATRE

8   ROCHESTER, NEW YORK AUDITORIUM THEATRE
16-song set featuring the first known version of 'Action In The Streets'.

9   BUFFALO, NEW YORK KLEINHAUS AUDITORIUM

10   UTTICA, NEW YORK MEMORIAL AUDITORIUM

12   OTTAWA, CANADA CIVIC CENTRE

13   TORONTO, CANADA MAPLE LEAF GARDENS CONCERT BOWL
A typical set from the first half of the short two-month tour: 'Night'; 'Rendezvous'; 'Spirit In The Night'; 'It's My Life'; 'Thunder Road'; 'Mona'; 'She's The One'; 'Tenth Avenue Freeze-out'*; 'Something In The Night'; 'Growin' Up'; 'Action In The Streets'*; 'Backstreets'; 'Jungleland'; 'Rosalita (Come Out Tonight)'*; 'Raise Your Hand'*; 'Born To Run'. (* are with the addition of the Miami Horns.)

15   DETROIT, MICHIGAN MASONIC TEMPLE AUDITORIUM
Only performance of the 'Devil With The Blue Dress' medley on the 1977 tour.

16   COLUMBUS, OHIO VETERANS AUDITORIUM

17   CLEVELAND, OHIO RICHFIELD COLISEUM
Ronnie Spector and Flo and Eddie join Bruce

onstage for a three-song Ronettes medley plus the Billy Joel song 'Say Goodbye To Hollywood' in an 18-song set.

19   ST PAUL, MINNESOTA CIVIC CENTRE
14-song set, illegally filmed by a member of the audience.

20   MADISON, WISCONSIN DANE COUNTY COLISEUM

22   MILWAUKEE, WISCONSIN ARENA AUDITORIUM

23   CHICAGO, ILLINOIS AUDITORIUM THEATRE
'The Promise' included in a 15-song set.

25   LA FAYETTE, INDIANA PURDUE UNIVERSITY

26   INDIANAPOLIS, INDIANA CONVENTION CENTRE

27   CINCINNATTI, OHIO RIVERFRONT COLISEUM

28   ST LOUIS, MISSOURI FOX THEATRE
14-song set ends with 'Quarter To Three'.

MARCH
2   ATLANTA, GEORGIA CIVIC CENTRE

4   JACKSONVILLE, FLORIDA AUDITORIUM
14-song set.

5   ORLANDO, FLORIDA JAI ALAI FRONTON
'4th Of July, Asbury Park (Sandy)' is played for the first time since the beginning of the tour.

6   MIAMI, FLORIDA JAI ALAI FRONTON

10   TOLEDO, OHIO SPORTS ARENA
Live debut of 'Don't Look Back' in a 15-song set that also includes 'Growin' Up'.

11   LA TROBE, PENNSYLVANIA ST VINCENTS COLLEGE

13   BALTIMORE, MARYLAND TOWSON STATE COLLEGE
14-song set.

14   POUGHKEEPSIE, NEW YORK MID-HUDSON CIVIC CENTRE
14-song set.

15   BINGHAMPTON, NEW YORK COMMUNITY ARENA
14-song set.

18   NEW HAVEN, CONNECTICUT MEMORIAL COLISEUM
14-song set.

19   LEWISTON, MAINE CENTRAL MAINE YOUTH CENTRE

20   PROVIDENCE, RHODE ISLAND ALUMNI HALL, PROVIDENCE COLLEGE

22/25 BOSTON, MASSACHUSETTS MUSIC HALL
Bruce delivers four devastating sets. The first night's 16-song set includes 'You Can't Sit Down' brought back for the first time since September 1976.

JUNE

1 NEW YORK, N.Y. ATLANTIC STUDIOS
Bruce, the E Street Band and Jon Landau begin work on the *Darkness On The Edge Of Town* sessions. It's the first time since July 1975 that Bruce can record his own songs.

SEPTEMBER

4 ASBURY PARK, NEW JERSEY STONE PONY
Bruce joins the Shots, a local New Jersey band, onstage and plays guitar on two songs: 'Further On Up The Road' and 'Funky Broadway'.

13 ASBURY PARK, NEW JERSEY STONE PONY
At a benefit show for the club, Bruce joins Southside Johnny and the Asbury Jukes for a shared vocal on two songs: 'I Don't Want To Go Home' and 'Havin' A Party'. The E Street Band follow (minus Steve Van Zandt) for 'Thunder Road', 'Mona', 'She's The One' and 'Born To Run'.

OCTOBER

13 ASBURY PARK, NEW JERSEY STONE PONY
Bruce joins Southside Johnny and the Asbury Jukes onstage with guitar and back-up vocals on four songs including 'Down In The Valley' and 'Let The Good Times Roll'. He sings lead vocals on 'Carol'.

NOVEMBER

5 NEW YORK, N.Y. WNEW RADIO
Bruce rings DJ Richard Neer from the Record Plant Studios for a ten-minute interview.

DECEMBER

2 NEW YORK, N.Y. LOEB STUDENT CENTRE, NEW YORK UNIVERSITY
Bruce joins Robert Gordon and Link Wray onstage for a shared vocal on 'Heartbreak Hotel'.

30 NEW YORK, N.Y. CBGB's
Bruce joins Patti Smith for shared vocals in his first public performance of 'Because The Night'.

31 PASSAIC, NEW JERSEY CAPITOL THEATRE
Bruce and the E Street Band leave their seats in the audience for the following songs at Southside Johnny and the Asbury Jukes' New Year's Eve radio broadcast on WNEW. 'Havin' A Party', 'I Don't Want To Go Home' and 'Higher And Higher' feature Bruce on back-up and shared vocals with Southside and the Asbury Jukes. The full E Street Band take the stage for 'Little Latin Lupe Lu', 'You Can't Sit Down' (all broadcast on WNEW), 'Backstreets' (which features the makings of a new song, 'Drive All Night', in the introduction), 'Born To Run' and 'Quarter To Three'. Filmed by the theatre video crew. Bruce is very much the worse for drink but still manages a great performance.
On 22 March 1977, Bruce's and Mike Appel's legal wrangle takes a turn for the better when Bruce's motion to submit an amended answer to Mike's complaintive is agreed by the court.
On 28 May, they agree to settle out of court. The 15-month ordeal is over.
In November, the *Darkness On The Edge Of Town* recording sessions are switched from the Atlantic Studios to the Record Plant Studios, New York.

On the second night, 'Incident On 57th Street' is included in a 16-song set which also includes the debut of 'Little Latin Lupe Lu'.
The third night features the debut of Jackie Wilson's 'Higher And Higher' in an 18-song set. 'It's Hard To Be A Saint In The City' is played for the first time since May 1976.
The fourth night is reputed to be one of Bruce's finest shows ever and includes 'Night'; 'Don't Look Back'; 'Spirit In The Night'; 'Incident On 57th Street'; 'Thunder Road'; 'Mona'; 'She's The One'; 'Tenth Avenue Freeze-Out'*; 'Action In The Streets'*; 'It's Hard To Be A Saint In The City'; 'Backstreets'; 'Jungleland'; 'Rosalita (Come Out Tonight)'; 'Born To Run'; 'Quarter To Three'*; 'Little Latin Lupe Lu'*; 'You Can't Sit Down'*; 'Higher and Higher'*. (* with the Miami Horns, who take part in the whole tour.)

APRIL

17 ASBURY PARK, NEW JERSEY STONE PONY
Bruce joins Southside Johnny and the Asbury Jukes onstage with lead vocals on 'The Fever' and shared vocals with Johnny on 'I Don't Want To Go Home' and 'You Mean So Much To Me'.

MAY

12/13 RED BANK, NEW JERSEY MONMOUTH ARTS CENTRE

Southside Johnny and the Asbury Jukes' scheduled 'homecoming' shows (with Ronnie Spector and Miami Steve already announced as special guests) are in danger of being cancelled due to the singer's illness. Miami Steve saves the day. After making a few phone calls he announces that 'Everything will be all right' and, consequently, show 1 on the 12th and shows 2 and 3 on the 13th provide a unique record of 'The Asbury All Stars Revue'. The shows go as follows:
At all three, Bruce plays guitar and sings back-up vocals for Miami Steve and the Asbury Jukes on 'This Time It's For Real', 'Got to Get You Off My Mind', 'Without Love' and 'She Got Me Where She Wants Me'.
Without Bruce, Ronnie Spector and the E Street Band play four numbers and Miami Steve and the Asbury Jukes play four (three at shows 2 and 3).
Backed by the Asbury Jukes, Bruce features on lead vocals on 'The Fever', shared vocals with Miami Steve on 'I Don't Want To Go Home', 'Havin' A Party' and, at show 3 only, 'Amen' and sings a duet with Ronnie Spector on 'You Mean So Much To Me'.
With the E Street Band, Bruce sings 'Thunder Road', 'Rendezvous', 'Backstreets' and 'Born To Run' at show 1; 'Thunder Road' at show 2 and 'Higher And Higher' at show 3.

1978
MAY
**19 ASBURY PARK, NEW
JERSEY PARAMOUNT THEATRE**
Rehearsal for tour.

23 BUFFALO, NEW YORK SHEA THEATRE
First night of the tour and Bruce plays all of the
unreleased new LP except 'Factory'. A
permanent feature of the shows is a 15/20
minute interval. The second half opens with the
debut of 'Paradise By The Sea' and 'Fire' with
the E Street Band in a 23-song set.

24 ALBANY, NEW YORK PALACE THEATRE
All Bruce originals, apart from 'Mona' in a
21-song set.

**26/27 PHILADELPHIA,
PENNSYLVANIA SPECTRUM**
Both shows consist of 23-song sets, including
the first 1978 performances of 'Jungleland' and
'It's Hard To Be A Saint In The City'.

29/31 BOSTON, MASSACHUSETTS MUSIC HALL
22 and 23-song sets. 'Because The Night'
makes its live debut with the E Street Band on
the 30th. 'Quarter To Three' is played for the first
time in 1978 on the final night.

JUNE
**1 ANNAPOLIS, MARYLAND U.S. NAVAL
ACADEMY**

2 *Darkness On The Edge Of Town* is released
worldwide (COL. PC 35318 U.S. and CBS
86061–U.K.)

**3 UNIONDALE, NEW YORK NASSAU
COLISEUM**
'4th Of July, Asbury Park (Sandy)' is played for
the first time on the 1978 tour in a 23-song set.

5 TOLEDO, OHIO SPORTS ARENA

**6 INDIANAPOLIS, INDIANA CONVENTION
CENTRE**

**8 MADISON, WISCONSIN DANE COUNTY
COLISEUM**

9 'Prove It All Night'/'Factory' is released
worldwide (COL. 3–10763–U.S. and CBS
6424–U.K.

9 MILWAUKEE, WISCONSIN ARENA
'Darkness On The Edge Of Town' appears
regularly in the live shows from here on.

10 BLOOMINGTON, MINNESOTA ARENA

13 IOWA CITY, IOWA UNIVERSITY OF IOWA

14 OMAHA, NEBRASKA MUSIC HALL
A 22-song set, typical of those from the first 2
months of the tour: 'Badlands'; 'Night'; 'Spirit In
The Night'; 'Darkness On The Edge Of Town';
'For You'; 'The Promised Land'; 'Prove It All
Night'; 'Racing In The Street'; 'Thunder Road';
'Jungleland' – Intermission – 'Paradise By The
Sea'; 'Fire'; 'Adam Raised A Cain'; 'Mona';
'She's The One'; 'Growin' Up'; 'Backstreets';
'Rosalita (Come Out Tonight)'; 'The Promise';
'Born To Run'; 'Tenth Avenue Freeze-Out';
'Quarter To Three'.

16 KANSAS CITY, MISSOURI MUNICIPAL AUDITORIUM

17 ST LOUIS, MISSOURI KIEL OPERA HOUSE

20 DENVER, COLORADO RED ROCKS
Rare outside gig.

24 PORTLAND, OREGON PARAMOUNT THEATRE

25 SEATTLE, WASHINGTON ARENA
Five encores performed, including 'I Fought The Law'.

26 VANCOUVER, CANADA QUEEN ELIZABETH THEATRE

29 SAN JOSE, CALIFORNIA PERFORMING ARTS CENTRE

30 BERKELEY, CALIFORNIA COMMUNITY AUDITORIUM

JULY

1 BERKELEY, CALIFORNIA COMMUNITY AUDITORIUM
Two songs from this concert, 'Paradise By The Sea' and 'Prove It All Night' make up an unreleased 12″ promotion-only disc (AS 480). The officially recorded tape of these two songs is later broadcast on 9 July.

4 LOS ANGELES, CALIFORNIA KMET RADIO
60-minute interview with Mary Turner.

5 LOS ANGELES, CALIFORNIA FORUM
22-song set, filmed in part by KABC TV.

5 LOS ANGELES, CALIFORNIA EYE WITNESS NEWS KABC TV
Backstage at the Forum, J. J. Jackson interviews Bruce for a ten-minute spot, broadcast 7 July, that will mark Bruce's first TV appearance.

6 LOS ANGELES, CALIFORNIA SUNDANCE CLUB, CALABASSA ROAD
Bruce joins an unknown band from Oklahoma for several oldies.

7 LOS ANGELES, CALIFORNIA ROXY
Broadcast live on KMET. An amazing three-hour, 26-song set that debuts 'Rave On', 'Point Blank' and 'Independence Day'. 'Heartbreak Hotel' is played for the first time with the E Street Band. 'Twist and Shout' is performed for the first time since April 1976.

8 PHOENIX, ARIZONA MEMORIAL COLISEUM
Five songs filmed by a professional crew for promotion use including 'Rosalita'.

9 SAN DIEGO, CALIFORNIA KBFH RADIO
A 90-minute interview with DJ Dave Herman, also broadcast on WNEW, includes the premieres of 'Paradise By The Sea' and 'Prove It All Night'.

9 SAN DIEGO, CALIFORNIA SPORTS ARENA
This 25-song set debuts 'Not Fade Away' and 'Gloria' into the 'She's The One' build-up.

12 DALLAS, TEXAS CONVENTION CENTRE

BRUCE:
The Myth Just Keeps On Coming

By TONY PARSONS

Pix JOE STEVENS

GREETINGS from the New Jersey shoreline's omnipresent leisure industry of endless beaches, broadwalks, amusement parks, souvenir arcades, piers, clubs, pubs, bars and sideshow booths . . . greetings from small town life in Asbury Park. N.J.

Our story begins circa the early '60s. At a strict Catholic school, a strange, solitary boy of eleven has been caught skipping lessons. His punishment is being placed in a class of six year olds.

His arms and legs feel too long for his body as he sits at the dinky table and chair built for a mere mite. Stared at by the room full of curious Catholic ankle-biters — immobile, embarrassed Gulliver — he grins self-consciously, his face burning.

The Sister of Mercy's voice breaks the silence.

"Let's show this young man," she intones, her eyes never leaving the boy, "what we do to children who smile in this class."

One of the six year olds stands up and walks over to where the big kid is sitting. Their eyes are level. Then the small child pulls back his fist and, with all the force he can muster from the spirit of the Holy Mother Mary, rams it home into the older boy's face.

"Very good," smiles the Sister.

Stunned with shock, shame and pain, the boy clutches his face, fighting back the tears.

"There's a dark cloud rising from the desert floor/I packed my bags and I'm heading straight into the storm/Gonna be a twister to blow everything down/That ain't got the faith to stand its ground/Blow away the dreams that tear you apart. Blow away the dreams that break your heart/Blow away the lies that leave you nothing but lost and brokenhearted/The dogs on mainstreet howl 'cause they understand/If I could take one moment into my hands/Mister, I ain't a boy/No, I'm a man/And I believe in a Promised Land."

● Continues over

---

14   **SAN ANTONIO, TEXAS MEMORIAL AUDITORIUM**
'The Fever' is played for the first time since 1974.

15   **HOUSTON, TEXAS KILT RADIO**
A 15-minute interview with DJ Ed Beauchamp.

15   **HOUSTON, TEXAS COLISEUM**
'The Promise' played for the last time in a 23-song set that also includes 'The Fever'.

16   **NEW ORLEANS, LOUISIANA AUDITORIUM**

18   **JACKSON, MISSISSIPPI CIVIC CENTRE**

19   **MEMPHIS, TENNESSEE ELLIS AUDITORIUM**

21   'Badlands'/'Something In The Night' (CBS 6532) released in the U.K.

21   **NASHVILLE, TENNESSEE MUNICIPAL AUDITORIUM**

Debut of 'Factory', the last of the *Darkness On The Edge Of Town* songs to be performed live.

28   **MIAMI, FLORIDA JAI ALAI FRONTON**
Debut of 'Summertime Blues' in a 23-song set that also includes 'Heartbreak Hotel' and 'I Fought The Law'.

29   **ST PETERSBURG, FLORIDA BAY FRONT CENTRE**
Debuts of 'Oh Boy' and 'Around And Around'.

31   **COLUMBIA, SOUTH CAROLINA AUDITORIUM**

AUGUST

1   **CHARLESTON, SOUTH CAROLINA MUNICIPAL AUDITORIUM**

2   **CHARLOTTE, NORTH CAROLINA COLISEUM**

4   **CHARLESTON, WEST VIRGINIA CIVIC CENTRE**

5   **LOUISVILLE, KENTUCKY LOUISVILLE GARDENS**
Debuts of 'Sweet Little Sixteen' and a new song, 'Sherry Darling'.

7   **KALAMAZOO, MICHIGAN WINGS AUDITORIUM**

9   **CLEVELAND, OHIO AGORA THEATRE**
Benefit concert, broadcast live, for radio WMMS tenth anniversary. The three-hour, 24-song set includes 'Fire', 'Sherry Darling' and 'Twist and Shout'.

10   **ROCHESTER, NEW YORK MEMORIAL AUDITORIUM**
'Sweet Little Sixteen' opens the second half of a 22-song set.

12   **AUGUSTA, MAINE CIVIC CENTRE**

14   'Badlands'/'Streets Of Fire' is released in U.S. (COL. 3-10801).

14   **HAMPTON, VIRGINIA COLISEUM**
Debut of 'Highschool Confidential', the opening number in a 22-song set.

15   **LARGO, MARYLAND CAPITAL CENTRE**
23-song set filmed for the huge screen backdrop above the stage area.

18   **PHILADELPHIA, PENNSYLVANIA SPECTRUM**
Gary Busey, star of 'The Buddy Holly Story', joins Bruce for lead vocals on 'Rave On' and backup vocals on 'Quarter To Three'. The 24-song set also includes a rare performance of 'The Fever'.

18   **PHILADELPHIA, PENNSYLVANIA WIOQ RADIO**
Backstage interview with DJ Ed Sciaky broadcast on the 19th.

19   **PHILADELPHIA, PENNSYLVANIA SPECTRUM**
24-song set opens with 'Good Rockin' Tonight', played for the first time. The second half opens with 'Rave On' (with Gary Busey), 'The Fever',

'Sweet Little Sixteen' and 'Sherry Darling'.

21   NEW YORK, N.Y. WABC TV
A ten-minute interview with J. Siegal.

21/23 NEW YORK, N.Y. MADISON SQUARE GARDEN
Bruce returns triumphantly to the venue he had last played as support to Chicago in 1973. The three sold-out gigs are laced with numerous cover versions and unrecorded new songs. The final 26-song set is marked by an appearance by Bruce's mother, demanding a final encore from her son.

25   NEW HAVEN, CONNECTICUT VETERANS MEMORIAL COLISEUM
25-song set. 'It's Gonna Work Out Fine' is performed for the first time since December 1975. A backstage interview with Bob Harris of The Old Grey Whistle Test is recorded by the BBC and will be broadcast on 27 March 1979.

25   NEW HAVEN, CONNECTICUT TOAD'S PLACE
Bruce and Clarence join Beaver Brown onstage at 2 a.m. for a performance of 'Rosalita (Come Out Tonight)', 'Double Shot Of My Baby's Love' and 'You Can't Sit Down'.

26   PROVIDENCE, RHODE ISLAND WBZ TV
15-minute interview with Robin Young.

26   PROVIDENCE, RHODE ISLAND CIVIC CENTRE
A typical mid-tour concert: 'Summertime Blues'; 'Badlands'; 'Streets Of Fire'; 'Spirit In The Night'; 'Darkness On The Edge Of Town'; 'Heartbreak Hotel'; 'Factory'; 'The Promised Land'; 'Prove It All Night'; 'Racing In The Street'; 'Thunder Road'; 'Jungleland' – Intermission – 'Paradise By The Sea'; 'For You'; 'Sherry Darling'; '4th Of July, Asbury Park (Sandy)'; 'Candy's Room'; 'Not Fade Away'; 'Gloria'; 'She's The One'; 'Growin' Up'; 'Backstreets'; 'Rosalita (Come Out Tonight)'; 'Born To Run'; 'Because The Night'; 'Quarter To Three'.

28/29 PITTSBURG, PENNSYLVANIA STANLEY THEATRE

30   CLEVELAND, OHIO RICHFIELD COLISEUM

31   CLEVELAND, OHIO AGORA
Bruce joins Southside Johnny and the Asbury Jukes onstage for three songs, filmed by a TV crew. 'The Fever', 'Havin' A Party' and 'I Don't Want To Go Home'.

SEPTEMBER

1   DETROIT, MICHIGAN MASONIC TEMPLE
Bob Dylan's 'Chimes Of Freedom' is played for the one and only time in a 24-song set, also including the last performance of 'Lost In The Flood'.

3   SAGINAW, MICHIGAN CIVIC CENTRE
Debut of '(I Don't Want To) Hang Up My Rock'n'Roll Shoes' in what is reckoned to be one of the finest sets from 1978.

5   COLUMBUS, OHIO VETERANS AUDITORIUM

6   CHICAGO, ILLINOIS UPTOWN THEATRE
Illegally filmed, in part.

9   SOUTH BEND, ILLINOIS NOTRE DAME UNIVERSITY
E Street Band debut of 'Double Shot Of My Baby's Love' and 'Louie Louie'.

BOSS RADIO

WNEW-FM proudly presents
Bruce Springsteen live
from the Capitol Theater in Passaic, New Jersey,
Tuesday, September 19th.

Catch the event of the year airing
from 9 P.M. to 12 Midnight (approximate).

Bruce Springsteen's
"Darkness On
The Edge Of Town,"

Bruce
Springsteen
Darkness
On The Edge
Of Town

including:
Prove It All Night
Badlands
Racing In
The Street
The Promised
Land
Adam Raised
A Cain

CAMPUS CRAVINGS '78
HIGH SCHOOL CONFIDENTIALS — AND MORE!

CRAWDADDY

OCTOBER 1978 $1.25

BRUCE SPRINGSTEEN
HEART OF DARKNESS
BY PETER KNOBLER

NICK NOLTE: THIS
TIME IT'S FOR REAL

TV'S "GALACTICA":
THE FORCE OR FARCE?

---

10   CINCINNATTI, OHIO RIVERFRONT COLISEUM

12   SYRACUSE, NEW YORK WAR MEMORIAL

13   SPRINGFIELD, MASSACHUSETTS CIVIC CENTRE

15   NEW YORK, N.Y. PALLADIUM
Last performance of 'Adam Raised A Cain' and 'Something In The Night' in a 23-song set that opens with 'Darkness On The Edge Of Town'. 'Kitty's Back' is also played for the first time since December 1975.

15   NEW YORK, N.Y. WPLJ RADIO
15-minute interview with Carol Miller, backstage at the Palladium.

16   NEW YORK, N.Y. PALLADIUM
'Point Blank' and 'Independence Day' become a regular part of the live shows from here on. 'Incident On 57th Street' and the 'Devil With The Blue Dress' medley played for the first time in 1978.

16   NEW YORK, N.Y. WHEW RADIO
Bruce is joined backstage by the E Street Band for a 15-minute interview with DJ Vin Scelsa. It will be broadcast during the interval of the live Passaic, New Jersey show on the 19th.

17   NEW YORK, N.Y. PALLADIUM
'Meeting Across The River' brought back into the set for the first time since April 1976.

19/21 PASSAIC, NEW JERSEY CAPITOL THEATRE
Broadcast live on WNEW. An outstanding performance from Bruce and the E Street Band. Backstage, Felipe Luciano of WNBC TV interviews Bruce for the 'News Centre Four' programme. On the 20th, 'Santa Claus Is Comin' To Town' is performed for the first time in 1978 in a 21-song plus medley set. 'It's My Life' is played for the final time. On the 21st, 'Kitty's Back' is performed for the final time in a 24-song set. All the Passaic shows are filmed in black and white by members of the club's staff.

25   BOSTON, MASSACHUSETTS BOSTON GARDENS

26   BOSTON, MASSACHUSETTS WBCN RADIO
40-minute interview with station DJ.

29   BIRMINGHAM, ALABAMA BOUTWELL AUDITORIUM
'Paradise By The Sea', played for the final time, opens the second half.

30   ATLANTA, GEORGIA FOX THEATRE
A three-hour set, broadcast live on WINZ. A 24-song plus medley set. The instrumental, 'Night Train', opens the second half.

OCTOBER
27   'The Promised Land'/'Streets Of Fire' (CBS 6720) is released in U.K.

NOVEMBER
1   PRINCETON, NEW JERSEY JADWIN GYM, PRINCETON UNIVERSITY
Debut of a new song, 'The Ties That Bind', in a 22-song set.

95

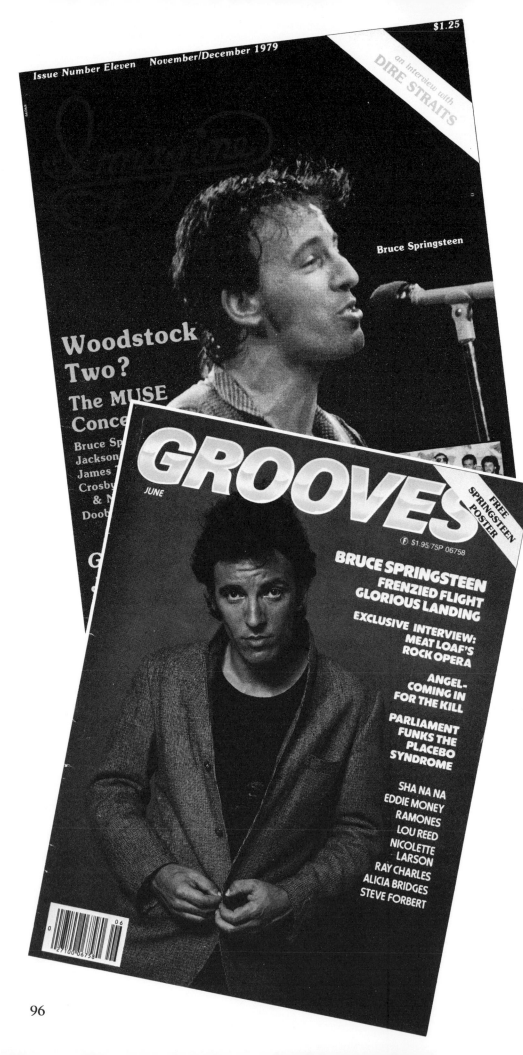

5 BATON ROUGE, LOUISIANA LOUISIANA STATE UNIVERSITY

7 AUSTIN, TEXAS UNIVERSITY OF TEXAS

8 HOUSTON, TEXAS SUMMIT
For the first time 'The Preacher's Daughter' is segued into the 'She's The One' build up in a 27-song plus medley set that includes 'It's Hard To Be A Saint In The City', 'The Fever' and 'You Can't Sit Down', performed before an ecstatic audience.

9 DALLAS, TEXAS CONVENTION CENTRE
'Good Rockin' Tonight' and 'Heartbreak Hotel' included in a 25-song plus medley set.

11 BOULDER, COLORADO UNIVERSITY OF COLORADO

13 TUCSON, ARIZONA COMMUNITY CENTRE ARENA

13 TUCSON, ARIZONA KSAN RADIO
Ten-minute interview recorded, to be broadcast during the interval of the live concert from the Winterland on 15 December.

15/16 SAN FRANCISCO, CALIFORNIA WINTERLAND
On the 15th, the three-and-a-half-hour concert is broadcast live by KSAN. Show features 'The Fever', 'Mona', 'The Preacher's Daughter', 'Fire' and 'Raise Your Hand'.
On the 16th, 'Rendezvous' is performed for the first time since May 1977 in a 26-song plus medley set.

19 PORTLAND, OREGAN PARAMOUNT THEATRE
A typical two-and-a-half-hour set from the latter part of the seven month tour: 'Good Rockin' Tonight'; 'Badlands'; 'Streets Of Fire'; 'Spirit In The Night'; 'Rendezvous'; 'Darkness On The Edge Of Town'; 'Independence Day'; 'The Promised Land'; 'Prove It All Night'; 'Racing In The Street'; 'Thunder Road'; 'Jungleland' – Intermission – 'The Ties That Bind'; 'Santa Claus Is Comin' To Town'; 'Rave On'; 'Fire'; 'Candy's Room'; 'Because The Night'; 'Point Blank'; 'Mona'; 'The Preacher's Daughter'; 'She's The One'; 'Backstreets'; 'Rosalita (Come Out Tonight)'; 'Born To Run'; 'Devil With The Blue Dress' medley; 'Tenth Avenue Freeze-Out'; 'Quarter To Three'.

20 SEATTLE, WASHINGTON SEATTLE ARENA
'Pretty Flamingo' is played for the first time since May 1976. Six encores, including 'Rave On', 'Quarter To Three' and 'Twist And Shout'.

27/28 PITTSBURG, PENNSYLVANIA STANLEY THEATRE
Debut of a new song, 'Ramrod', opens the show on the 28th.

30 DETROIT, MICHIGAN COBO HALL

31 CLEVELAND, OHIO RICHFIELD COLISEUM
This New Year's Eve concert features an incredible three-hour 29-song plus medley set. 'Pretty Flamingo' is played for the final time but celebrations are marred by an audience-thrown firecracker exploding by Bruce's face. He tells the culprit in no uncertain terms what he thinks of such behaviour.

In addition to the 1978 concerts already listed, the band play La Crosse, Wisconsin on 12 June; Salt Lake City, Utah on 22 June and Santa Barbara, California on 3 July.

In July they are booked to play four shows which are later cancelled: Birmingham, Alabama on the 22nd; Atlanta, Georgia on the 23rd; Jacksonville, Florida on the 25th; and Lakeland, Florida on the 26th.

In New York in August 1978, WNEW TV broadcast a previously filmed interview and concert footage on the news programme, 'PM Magazine'.

In October, Bruce joins the Knack onstage for two songs, 'Mona' and 'Not Fade Away', at the Troubador in Los Angeles, California.

1979
JANUARY
1   CLEVELAND, OHIO RICHFIELD COLISEUM
The final night of an incredible 118-date tour. The Rolling Stones' 'The Last Time' is performed to mark the event. Also played tonight for the final time are 'Meeting Across The River', 'The Fever', 'The Preacher's Daughter' and 'Streets Of Fire' in a 32-song plus medley set.

FEBRUARY
9   U.S. premiere of *Heroes of Rock'n'Roll*, the ABC two-hour documentary featuring Bruce's 'Rosalita' recorded live in Phoenix, 8 July 1978.

23   'Born to Run'/'Meeting Across the River' re-released in U.K. (CBS 7077).

MARCH
27   UNITED KINGDOM BBC TV
First U.K. TV exposure. 20 minutes of Bruce and the E Street Band on 'The Old Grey Whistle Test' showing live footage of 'Rosalita' from Phoenix, 8 July 1978, and the interview with Bob Harris backstage at the Veterans Memorial Coliseum, 25 August 1978.

APRIL
13/15 ASBURY PARK, NEW JERSEY THE FAST LANE
On the 13th, Bruce guests with local band Beaver Brown. On the 15th he joins them for four songs: 'You Can't Sit Down', 'Havin A Party', 'Ain't That A Shame' and 'Rosalita'.

MAY
7   ASBURY PARK, NEW JERSEY PARAMOUNT THEATRE
Bruce joins Robert Gordon for 'Fire' and 'Heartbreak Hotel'.

JUNE
3   LOS ANGELES, CALIFORINA THE WHISKEY
At the private wedding reception of tour lighting director Mark Brickman and June Rudley, Bruce, with members of the E Street Band, Rickie Lee Jones and Boz Scaggs, jams on various songs including 'Thunder Road', 'It's Gonna Work Out Fine', 'Fire' and 'Mother In Law', amongst others.

SEPTEMBER
21/22 NEW YORK, N.Y. MADISON SQUARE GARDEN
The band headline the two final nights of the

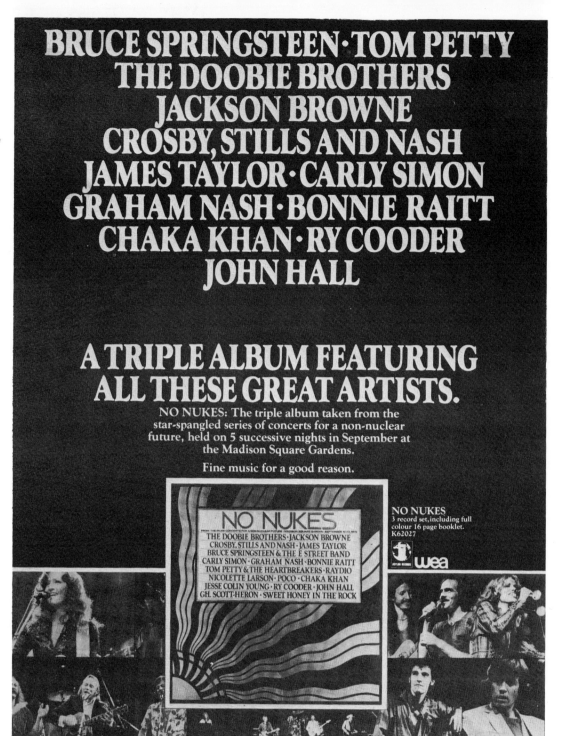

BRUCE SPRINGSTEEN · TOM PETTY
THE DOOBIE BROTHERS
JACKSON BROWNE
CROSBY, STILLS AND NASH
JAMES TAYLOR · CARLY SIMON
GRAHAM NASH · BONNIE RAITT
CHAKA KHAN · RY COODER
JOHN HALL

A TRIPLE ALBUM FEATURING ALL THESE GREAT ARTISTS.

NO NUKES: The triple album taken from the star-spangled series of concerts for a non-nuclear future, held on 5 successive nights in September at the Madison Square Gardens.

Fine music for a good reason.

NO NUKES
3 record set, including full colour 16 page booklet.
K62027

NO NUKES
FROM THE MUSE CONCERTS FOR A NON-NUCLEAR FUTURE · MADISON SQUARE GARDEN · SEPTEMBER 19-23, 1979
THE DOOBIE BROTHERS · JACKSON BROWNE
CROSBY, STILLS AND NASH · JAMES TAYLOR
BRUCE SPRINGSTEEN & THE E STREET BAND
CARLY SIMON · GRAHAM NASH · BONNIE RAITT
TOM PETTY & THE HEARTBREAKERS · RAYDIO
NICOLETTE LARSON · POCO · CHAKA KHAN
JESSE COLIN YOUNG · RY COODER · JOHN HALL
G.H. SCOTT-HERON · SWEET HONEY IN THE ROCK

M.U.S.E (Musicians United for Safe Energy) concerts. On the 21st, a 12-song, 90-minute set debuts 'The River' and a shared duet with Jackson Browne on 'Stay'. 'Stay' and the 'Devil with the Blue Dress' medley are later released on the *No Nukes* LP. On the 22nd, the band play 11 songs, three of which appear in the 'No Nukes' film: 'Thunder Road', 'The River' and an edited 'Quarter to Three'. Jackson Browne again duets on 'Stay', with Tom Petty and Rosemary Butler. Bruce's ex-girlfriend, photographer Lynn Goldsmith, takes shots without premission and Bruce hauls her out of the crowd.

OCTOBER
5/6 ASBURY PARK, NEW JERSEY THE FAST LANE

On the 5th, Bruce guests on three songs at the Beaver Brown gig: 'Rosalita', 'Ain't That A Shame' and 'Twist And Shout'. On the 6th, Beaver Brown are joined onstage by Bruce, Ellen Shipley, Vini Lopez and Dave Marsh for two songs: 'Rosalita' and 'Twist And Shout'.

In April 1979, sessions begin at the Power Station Studios, New York for *The River* album. In June, Bruce sues for infringement of copyright on 35 songs when the FBI seize 12 tons of bootleg records (predominantly live Springsteen material) and recording equipment in California.

In December, the No Nukes LP is released on Asylum (U.S. ML 801 U.K. K 62027). *Bruce Springsteen*, a boxed set of the first three LPs, is released in the U.K. (CBS 66353).

ROLLING STONE'S 1980 ROCK & ROLL AWARDS

READERS' POLL

The Fifth Annual ROLLING STONE Readers' Poll drew almost 3000 ballots, with Bruce Springsteen emerging the big winner. In fact, Springsteen carried almost every category in which he competed: Artist of the Year, Best Album, Best Single, Male Vocalist and Songwriter. Of note was Springsteen's margins of victory; the guy just walked away with the cake. As Artist of the Year, for example, he outdistanced Pink Floyd by more than four to one. Bruce's group, the E Street Band, beat out the Rolling Stones for best band, and the Boss' coproducer, Jon Landau, took the producer slot. Even Bruce's sidekick, saxophonist Clarence Clemons, put in a respectable showing, being edged out by Jeff Beck as best instrumentalist.

The overwhelming favorite for Best New Artist were the Pretenders, with leader Chrissie Hynde making a strong second-place showing as the top female vocalist—first place went to Pat Benatar. Stevie Wonder jumped from his fourth-place spot last year to 1980's best soul artist. Meanwhile, George Benson placed third in this category and also emerged as the top jazz artist. Willie Nelson took country-artist honors. In fact, along with WMMS-FM of Cleveland, the best radio station, Willie was the only one of last year's winners to retain his crown.

"Rock Memorabilia" is a new addition to the awards. With the exception of the worst hit, the contributions were culled from 'The Book of Rock Lists', by Dave Marsh and Kevin Stein, which will be published in the fall of 1981.*

*A Dell Trade Paperback © Dave Marsh and Kevin Stein

Runners-up are listed in descending order.

ARTIST OF THE YEAR
Bruce Springsteen

Pink Floyd
The Clash
The Rolling Stones
Queen

BAND OF THE YEAR
E Street Band

The Rolling Stones
The Clash
Pink Floyd
The Who

BEST ALBUM
Bruce Springsteen: *The River*

Pink Floyd: *The Wall*
The Clash: *London Calling*
Pete Townshend: *Empty Glass*
AC/DC: *Back in Black*
The Rolling Stones: *Emotional Rescue*

The Clash: frontmen Joe Strummer (left) and Mick Jones

BEST NEW ARTIST
The Pretenders

Christopher Cross
Pat Benatar
Rossington Collins Band
The Vapors

BEST SINGLE
Bruce Springsteen: "Hungry Heart"

Queen: "Another One Bites the Dust"
Blondie: "Call Me"
Doobie Brothers: "Real Love"
The Vapors: "Turning Japanese"

FEMALE VOCALIST
Pat Benatar

Chrissie Hynde
Linda Ronstadt
Deborah Harry
Ann Wilson

MALE VOCALIST
Bruce Springsteen

Jackson Browne
Billy Joel
Bob Seger
Mick Jagger

SONGWRITER
Bruce Springsteen

Pete Townshend
Jackson Browne
Elvis Costello
Billy Joel

PRODUCER
Jon Landau

Nick Lowe
Brian Eno
Phil Ramone
Ted Templeman

Springsteen at home in New Jersey; Bruce had a good year, with a chart-topping LP and record-breaking tour.

1980
MARCH
1 ASBURY PARK, NEW JERSEY STONE PONY
Bruce guests with the David Johanssen Band.

5 A *Rolling Stone* readers' poll places Bruce and the E Street Band in 1st place in all but one of the eligible sections. Jeff Beck wins the instrumental category and Clarence is placed 2nd.

OCTOBER
3 ANN ARBOR, MICHIGAN CHRYSLER ARENA
For the first time, 'Born To Run' opens the 26-song set which includes 11 songs from the unreleased new album, *The River*. Seven of these appear for the first time: 'Wreck On The Highway'; 'Stolen Car'; 'Jackson Cage'; 'Out In The Street'; 'I Wanna Marry You'; 'Cadillac Ranch' and 'Crush On You'. Bob Seger joins Bruce for a spur-of-the-moment encore of 'Thunder Road', the second time tonight the song has been played.

4 CINCINNATTI, OHIO RIVERFRONT COLISEUM
'The Ties That Bind' and 'Independence Day' make their 1980 debuts in a 27-song set.

6 CLEVELAND, OHIO RICHFIELD COLISEUM
Debut of 'Two Hearts' in a 27-song set.

7 CLEVELAND, OHIO RICHFIELD COLISEUM
Debut of 'You Can Look' in a 28-song set.

9 DETROIT, MICHIGAN COBO HALL
In this 27-song, set, 'I Hear A Train' joins the medley and becomes a regular addition from here on.

10/11 CHICAGO, ILLINOIS UPTOWN THEATRE
29-song set. In the five-song medley this time is a part song believed to be titled 'Gee Wiz I'm In Love Again'. The debut of 'Here She Comes' on the 11th is the intro to 'I Wanna Marry You' in a 32-song set which also includes 'Good Rockin, Tonight' and 'Raise Your Hand'.
The River is released in U.S. (COL. PC2 36854).

13 ST PAUL, MINNESOTA CIVIC CENTRE
Illegally filmed by an audience member, this is a typical concert from the early part of the tour: 'Born To Run'; 'Prove It All Night'; 'Tenth Avenue Freeze-Out'; 'Darkness On The Edge Of Town'; 'Independence Day'; 'Factory'; 'Jackson Cage'; 'The Promised Land'; 'Out In The Street'; 'Racing In The Street'; 'The River'; 'Badlands'; 'Thunder Road' – Intermission – 'Cadillac Ranch'; 'Fire'; 'Sherry Darling'; 'Here She Comes'; 'I Wanna Marry You'; 'For You'; 'The Ties That Bind'; 'Wreck On The Highway'; 'Point Blank'; 'Crush On You'; 'Ramrod'; 'You Can Look'; 'Because The Night'; 'Stolen Car'; 'Backstreets'; 'Rosalita'; 'Jungleland'; 'Devil With The Blue Dress' medley (five songs).

14 MILWAUKEE, WISCONSIN ARENA
Debut of the classic Wilson Pickett song, 'In The Midnight Hour', included in this 30-song set.

17 ST LOUIS, MISSOURI KIEL OPERA HOUSE
29-song set.
The River is released in the U.K. (CBS 88510).

18 ST LOUIS, MISSOURI KIEL OPERA HOUSE
A 29-song set debuts 'Hungry Heart', 'Drive All Night' and 'I'm A Rocker'. Once again, 'Good Rockin' Tonight' opens the second set.
'Hungry Heart'/'Held Up Without A Gun' is released in U.S. (COL. 11–11391).

20 DENVER, COLORADO McNICHOLLS ARENA
29-song set. It is in Denver that Bruce, during a visit to the movies (Woody Allen's *Stardust Memories*), is recognised by a fan, and after the film goes back to his house.

23 SEATTLE, WASHINGTON OLD TIMER'S CAFE
Bruce joins The Lost Highway Band onstage for several oldies including 'Route 66' and 'In The Midnight Hour'.

24 SEATTLE, WASHINGTON ARENA
30-song set.

25 PORTLAND, OREGON COLISEUM
Under the smouldering eye of Mount St Helens, the one and only performance of 'On Top Of Old Smokey'. 30-song set.

27 OAKLAND, CALIFORNIA COLISEUM
31-song set.

28 OAKLAND, CALIFORNIA COLISEUM
'Good Rockin' Tonight' opens a 32-song set.

30 LOS ANGELES, CALIFORNIA SPORTS ARENA
31-song set. As with all the L.A. shows this week, Bruce makes an onstage appeal to try and squash the sale of high-priced black market tickets.

31 LOS ANGELES, CALIFORNIA TV BROADCAST
Ten-minute interview with J. J. Jackson.

BRUCE SPRINGSTEEN

SPORTS ARENA LOS ANGELES, CA
OCTOBER 30, 1980

AFTER SHOW ONLY

14 HOUSTON, TEXAS THE SUMMIT
30-song set including 'In The Midnight Hour'.

15 HOUSTON, TEXAS THE SUMMIT
31-song set.
The River reaches No. 1 in the U.S. charts.

20 ROSEMONT, ILLINOIS THE HORIZON
30-song set.

23/24 LARGO, MARYLAND CAPITAL CENTRE
29-song set on the 24th when 'Lonesome Train' is included in the 'Devil With A Blue Dress' medley for the first time. Both nights at the Capital Centre are filmed for a huge backdrop screen designed to give the audience maximum viewing advantage.

27/28 NEW YORK, N.Y. MADISON SQUARE GARDEN
The first night's 32-song set is followed by an amazing 34-song set featuring 'Open All Night' segued into 'Ramrod', '4th Of July, Asbury Park (Sandy)' played for the first time since December 1978 and a one and only performance of 'Mystery Train' included in the six-song medley. At least one of the gigs is illegally filmed, in part.

30 PITTSBURG, PENNSYLVANIA CIVIC CENTRE
32-song set

DECEMBER
1 PITTSBURG, PENNSYLVANIA CIVIC CENTRE
'For You' is played for the first time since January 1979 in a 31-song set.

2 ROCHESTER, NEW YORK WAR MEMORIAL
32-song set includes '4th Of July, Asbury Park (Sandy)' and 'For You'.

4 BUFFALO, NEW YORK WAR MEMORIAL
'I Fought The Law' and 'Santa Claus Is Comin' To Town' played for the first time in 1980. 'Lonesome Train' included in a six-part medley. 'Sherry Darling' is filmed and used for TV news. The 35-song set made one the longest shows of the tour.

6/8 PHILADELPHIA,
9 PENNSLYVANIA SPECTRUM
'Uptight (Everthing's Alright)' included in the medley in a 34-song set on the 6th. 'I'm Ready' is included in a six-part medley on the 8th. Bruce finishes the 35-song set and is told of the tragic murder of John Lennon. A shaken Bruce opens the set on the 9th with a spoken tribute to John Lennon and closes the 34-song set with a moving version of 'Twist And Shout'. Also included tonight is the first 1980 performance of 'Rendezvous'.

31 LOS ANGELES, CALIFORNIA SPORTS ARENA
Halloween night – Bruce is carried onstage in a coffin and opens the 31-song set with 'Haunted House'. Also debuted tonight are 'The Price You Pay' and 'Out Of Limits', the instrumental that opens the second half. 'No Money Down' is used as an intro to 'Cadillac Ranch' for the first time.
'Hungry Heart'/'Held Up Without A Gun' is released in U.K. (CBS 9309).

NOVEMBER
1 LOS ANGELES, CALIFORNIA SPORTS ARENA
Debut of 'Fade Away', the last of the *River* songs to be performed live. Changed lyrics to one verse of 'Price You Pay'. Jackson Browne joins Bruce for one of the encores, 'Sweet Little Sixteen'.
The River peaks at No. 2 in the U.K. charts.

3 LOS ANGELES, CALIFORNIA SPORTS ARENA
30-song set.

5 TEMPE, ARIZONA ARIZONA STATE UNIVERSITY
34-song set, illegally filmed by a member of the audience, including 18 songs from *The River*.

8 DALLAS, TEXAS REUNION AUDITORIUM
30-song set, including an instrumental debut of 'Yellow Rose Of Texas'.

9 AUSTIN, TEXAS UNIVERSITY OF TEXAS
33 songs, including the debut of 'Waltz Across Texas', and 'Yellow Rose Of Texas' again.

11 BATON ROUGE, LOUISIANA LOUISIANA STATE UNIVERSITY
29-song set.

AFTER SHOW ONLY

11 PROVIDENCE, RHODE ISLAND CIVIC CENTRE
33-song set illegally filmed by a member of the audience.

12 HARTFORD, CONNECTICUT VETERANS MEMORIAL COLISEUM
33-song set.

15/16 BOSTON, MASSACHUSETTS BOSTON GARDENS
The first night's 33-song set is followed by a blistering 35-song set, including the last performance of 'Crush On You' and a rare version of 'Spirit In The Night', last performed in January 1979.

18/19 NEW YORK, N.Y. MADISON SQUARE GARDENS
Debut of 'Who'll Stop The Rain?' in the first night's 35-song set. A huge public outcry preceded the shows at the Garden, due to thousands of tickets going 'missing' and then being sold on the black market. Bruce hires a private detective to try and find the culprits.

RON DELSENER PROUDLY ANNOUNCES

BRUCE SPRINGSTEEN
&
THE E STREET BAND

NOVEMBER 27, 28 & DECEMBER 18, 19—8 PM

ALL SEATS RESERVED $12.50, 10.50. Available by mail only! (Limit 4 per person.) Fill in coupon and send to SPRINGSTEEN, GENERAL P.O. Box 59, NYC 10116. Send only certified check or money order payable to: Madison Square Garden Center (Do not send cash or personal check). Enclose a stamped self-addressed envelope plus $1.00 for handling (per order). Orders will be accepted by mail only. Do not drop off envelopes at Madison Square Garden. Specify preference for November or December dates. For additional information call (212) 564-5153.

ALLOW FOUR WEEKS FOR PROCESSING.

SPRINGSTEEN, GENERAL P.O. BOX 59, NEW YORK, N.Y. 10116

INDICATE PREFERENCE FOR: NOVEMBER ☐ DECEMBER ☐
(CHECK ONE)
NUMBER OF TICKETS @ $ _____ = $ _____
(LIMIT 4 PER PERSON)
HANDLING CHARGE + $ 1.00
TOTAL AMT. CERT. CHECK OR MONEY ORDER $ _____
NAME _____
ADDRESS _____ STATE _____ ZIP _____
CITY _____
DAY TELEPHONE NUMBER _____
NO ORDERS WILL BE ACCEPTED POST MARKED BEFORE OCTOBER 1

madison square garden
Pennsylvania Plaza 7th Ave 31st to 33rd Sts

28/29, UNIONDALE, NEW YORK NASSAU
31 COLISEUM

Debut of 'Merry Christmas Baby' and 'This Land Is Your Land' on the 28th. Flo and Eddie join Bruce onstage for back-up vocals on 'Hungry Heart' in a 33-song set. On the 29th, 'Incident On 57th Street' is performed for the final time in a 35-song set that opens with 'Night', last used in July 1978. On the 31st there is a one and only performance of 'Held Up Without A Gun' in an epic four-hour, 38 song New Year's Eve show

that is the longest set yet played by Bruce Please note that the 'Devil With The Blue Dress' medley, played at every concert on the 132–date tour (which covers 12 months and 13 different countries), consists of 'Devil With The Blue Dress', 'Good Golly Miss Molly', 'C.C. Rider', 'Jenny Take A Ride' and 'I Hear A Train' unless otherwise stated. The medley has been counted as one song in the totals.
In January 1980, Dave Marsh's biography of Bruce, *Born To Run*, becomes the first rock book to enter the *New York Times* bestseller list.

In LA in the summer, Bruce joins Jackson Browne onstage at the Forum for 'Sweet Little Sixteen' and 'Stay'.
Warner Brothers' 'No Nukes' film, produced and directed by Julian Schlossberg and Danny Goldberg and featuring 20 minutes of Bruce and the band playing 'Thunder Road', 'The River' and an edited version of 'Quarter To Three', is released in the U.S. in August.
In September, rehearsals for the forthcoming tour, filmed at Bruce's request, take place at a large, barn-type building in Pennsylvania.

WPLJ Radio Welcomes
BRUCE SPRINGSTEEN
The River Tour 1980
Madison Square Garden
Nov 27, 28
Dec 18, 19

BRUCE SPRINGSTEEN

AFTER SHOW ONLY
DECEMBER 19, 1980
MADISON SQUARE GARDENS, NY

1981

JANUARY

20/21 TORONTO, CANADA MAPLE LEAF GARDENS
Two 32-song sets.

23 MONTREAL, CANADA FORUM
31-song set, illegally filmed by a member of the audience.

24 OTTAWA, CANADA CIVIC CENTRE
Bruce's short tour of Canada ends with a 31-song set which includes 'I Fought The Law'.

26 SOUTH BEND, INDIANA NOTRE DAME UNIVERSITY
'Double Shot Of My Baby's Love' and 'Louie Louie' (as always in South Bend) included in the 32-song set.

28 ST LOUIS, MISSOURI CHECKERDOME
James Brown's 'I Feel Good (I Got You)' included in a six-part medley. The 29-song set includes the last performance of 'Night'.

29 AMES, IOWA HILTON COLISEUM
'I Feel Good (I Got You)' again included in the medley.

FEBRUARY

1 St PAUL, MINNESOTA CIVIC CENTRE

2 MADISON, WISCONSIN DANE COUNTY COLISEUM
30-song set ends with 'Twist And Shout'.

3 'Fade Away'/'Be True' is released in U.S. (Columbia 11-11431)

5 KANSAS CITY, MISSOURI KEMPER ARENA
First known version of 'Kansas City' in a 29-song set.

7 CHAMPAIGN, ILLINOIS UNIVERSITY OF ILLINOIS
30-song set with 'Twist And Shout' again closing the show.

9 INDIANAPOLIS, INDIANA MARKET SQUARE ARENA
Rescheduled for March 5 due to Bruce's bout of exhaustion and illness.

10 LEXINGTON, KENTUCKY RUPP ARENA
Rescheduled due to Bruce's illness.

12 MOBILE, ALABAMA MUNICIPAL AUDITORIUM
28-song set

13 STARKVILLE, MISSOURI STATE UNIVERSITY
28-song set

15/16 LAKELAND, FLORIDA CIVIC CENTRE
On the second night Bruce is back on top form. 'Highschool Confidential' and 'Good Rockin' Tonight' are both included in a six-song medley. 28 and 30-song sets respectively

18 JACKSONVILLE, FLORIDA CIVIC CENTRE
'Highschool Confidential' included in a five-song medley. 27-song set.

20 HOLLYWOOD, FLORIDA SPORTATORIUM
27-song set with rare performances of both 'The Price You Pay' and 'Fade Away'. ('Sherry Darling'/'Be True' is released in U.K. CBS 9568.

22 COLUMBIA, SOUTH CAROLINA CAROLINA COLISEUM
'Highschool Confidential' included in the six-song medley. 28-song set.

23 ATLANTA, GEORGIA THE OMNI
28-song set.

25 MEMPHIS, TENNESSEE MID-SOUTH COLISEUM

26 NASHVILLE, TENNESSEE MUNICIPAL AUDITORIUM

28 GREENSBORO, NORTH CAROLINA COLISEUM
27-song set.

MARCH

2 HAMPTON, VIRGINIA HAMPTON ROADS COLISEUM
'Ramrod' opens the second half of a 28-song set.

4 LEXINGTON, KENTUCKY RUPP ARENA

5 INDIANAPOLIS, INDIANA MARKET SQUARE ARENA
30-song set includes the final performance of 'Fade Away'.

13 Capital Radio in London announces the postponement of the U.K. tour, due to start in five days time in Brighton. Full credit to Harvey Goldsmith of the hastily rearranged U.K. tour dates that will now follow the rest of the European shows.

26 'No Nukes' film premiered in the U.K. at three cinemas in London.

26 *Born To Run*, the Dave Marsh biography of Bruce is published in the U.K.

APRIL

7 HAMBURG, W. GERMANY CONGRESS CENTRUM
Debut of 'Rockin' All Over The World' in a 24-song set that, oddly, does not include 'This Land Is Your Land'.

8 BERLIN, E. GERMANY I.C.C. HALLE
'Factory' opens a 27-song set that includes 'Twist And Shout'.

11 ZURICH, SWITZERLAND HALLEN STADION
Identical set to the Berlin show but without the final encore of 'Twist And Shout'.

14 FRANKFURT, W. GERMANY FESTHALLE
26-song set with 'Point Blank' replacing 'Wreck On The Highway' from the previous show.

16 MUNICH, W. GERMANY OLYMPIA HALLE
'The Ties That Bind' makes it's European debut in a 25-song set.

18 PARIS, FRANCE PALAIS DES SPORTS
Debut of 'Can't Help Falling In Love' and the first European performance of 'Candy's Room' in a 27-song set

SPECIAL ANNOUNCEMENT

Bruce Springsteen Tour has been postponed.

Rescheduled dates are as shown below. **Keep your ticket** and turn up only on the rescheduled night. Refunds can be obtained by returning your ticket to point of purchase by 5th April 1981.

Venue	Old Date	New Date
Brighton Centre	March 17 valid for	**May 26**
Wembley Arena	March 19 valid for	**May 29**
Wembley Arena	March 20 valid for	**May 30**
Manchester Apollo	March 23 valid for	**May 13**
Manchester Apollo	March 24 valid for	**May 14**
Birmingham N.E.C.	March 27 valid for	**June 7**
Birmingham N.E.C.	March 28 valid for	**June 8**
Edinburgh Playhouse	March 30 valid for	**May 16**
Newcastle City Hall	March 31 valid for	**May 11**
Wembley Arena	April 2 valid for	**June 1**
Wembley Arena	April 3 valid for	**June 2**
Wembley Arena	April 4 valid for	**June 4**

19 PARIS, FRANCE PALAIS DES SPORTS
Reputed to be one of the best European shows. Opening the 28-song set is a new arrangement of Elvis's 'Follow That Dream' performed for the first time. 'Highschool Confidential' is included in the medley and is followed by a full version of another debut song, 'Sweet Soul Music'.

21 BARCELONA, SPAIN PALACIO DE DEPORTES
'Because The Night' is played for the first time in Europe. 26-song set.

24 LYON, FRANCE PALAIS DES SPORTS
26-song set. A 30-minute audience tape is illegally broadcast by a DJ on France Inter radio.

26 BRUSSELS, BELGIUM VORST NATIONAAL
'Follow That Dream' opens this 27-song set with a guest appearance by Flo and Eddie on back-up vocals on 'Hungry Heart'. European debut of 'Stolen Car'.

28/29 ROTTERDAM, HOLLAND AHOY SPORTSPALAIS
The first night's 27-song set is followed by a 28-song set that debuts 'Run Through The Jungle' and the European debut of 'I'm A Rocker'.

29 HOLLAND RADIO BROADCAST
Miami Steve is interviewed by phone in a ten-minute chat with local station DJ.

MAY

1 COPENHAGEN, DENMARK FORUM
Bruce's one and only guest ppearance in Europe is with a Danish band called Malurt. He joins them onstage for a strangely slowed-down version of 'Hungry Heart'.

2 COPENHAGEN, DENMARK BRONDBYHALLEN
The latter European dates are best typified by the following 30-song set: 'Follow That Dream'; 'Prove It All Night'; 'Out In The Street'; 'The Ties That Bind'; 'Darkness On The Edge Of Town'; 'Independence Day'; 'Factory'; 'Who'll Stop The Rain'?; 'Two Hearts'; 'The Promised Land'; 'This Land Is Your Land'; 'The River'; 'Badlands'; 'Thunder Road' – Intermission – 'Cadillac Ranch'; 'Sherry Darling'; 'Hungry Heart'; 'Because The Night'; 'You Can Look'; 'Fire'; 'Wreck On The Highway'; 'Point Blank'; 'Backstreets'; 'Candy's Room'; 'Ramrod'; 'Rosalita'; 'Born To Run'; 'Devil With The Blue Dress' medley; 'I'm A Rocker'; 'Rockin' All Over The World'.

3 GOTHENBURG, DENMARK SCANDINAVIUM
28-song set. John Fogerty's 'Run Through The Jungle' opens the show for the second time. 'The River'/'Indenpendence Day' is released in U.K. (CBS A 1179).

5 DRAMMEN, NORWAY DRAMMENSHALLEN
28-song set.

7/8 STOCKHOLM, SWEDEN JOHNANNESHOV ICE STADIUM
27-song set with 'Highschool Confidential' included in a six-song medley.
The 2nd night is reputed to be one of the best of all the European shows, with a 31-song set including 'Highschool Confidential' and 'Land Of A Thousand Dances' in a six-song medley. 'Run Through The Jungle' is performed for the last time. 'The Price You Pay' is played for the first time in Europe. 'Twist And Shout' rounds off a superb two-and-a-half-hour set.

11 NEWCASTLE, ENGLAND NEWCASTLE CITY HALL
After nearly six years, Bruce's long-awaited return to the U.K. opens with an impressive 28-song set at the smallest venue he's played since the Roxy, L.A. in July 1978.

13 MANCHESTER, ENGLAND APOLLO THEATRE
Debut of 'Johnny Bye Bye' in a 27-song set that includes 'The Price You Pay' but falls to include 'Thunder Road'.

14 MANCHESTER, ENGLAND APOLLO THEATRE

A short 24-song set. Bruce is in poor voice which gives cause for concern that so soon after the illness that caused the initial postponement of the U.K. shows.

16/17 EDINBURGH, SCOTLAND PLAYHOUSE THEATRE
A 24-song set on the first night, followed by a 26-song show. Bruce's back on form.

20 STAFFORD, ENGLAND NEW BINGLEY HALL
This venue often used for cattle shows, with its notoriously poor acoustics and seating, is transformed by Bruce's 27-song show.

26/27 BRIGHTON, ENGLAND CONFERENCE CENTRE
The first night's 26-song set is played before a rowdy and enthusiastic crowd who rush the front of the stage area.
On the 27th Bruce delivers a superb 26-song set that includes the first European performance of 'Jungleland' and Bruce's 'spotlight on the big man' routine during 'Rosalita'. Final appearance of 'The Price You Pay'.

29/30 LONDON, ENGLAND WEMBLEY ARENA
On the 29th, a self-confessed nervous and apprehensive Bruce finally dispels the bad memories of the last London experience with an ecstatically received 29-song set including the debut of 'Trapped'.
The European debut on the 30th of 'Jackson Cage' in a 28-song set also includes the only U.K. performance of 'Twist And Shout'.

NO NUKES

EXPERIENCE THE MOVIE

JACKSON BROWNE · CROSBY, STILLS AND NASH
DOOBIE BROTHERS · JOHN HALL · GRAHAM NASH
BONNIE RAITT · GIL SCOTT-HERON · CARLY SIMON
BRUCE SPRINGSTEEN · JAMES TAYLOR · JESSE COLIN YOUNG
"NO NUKES"
PRODUCED BY JULIAN SCHLOSSBERG · DANNY GOLDBERG
DIRECTED BY JULIAN SCHLOSSBERG · DANNY GOLDBERG · ANTHONY POTENZA

"NO NUKES" CONCERT ALBUM ON ASYLUM RECORDS AND TAPES

DISTRIBUTED BY WARNER BROS.   A Warner Communications Company
© 1980 Warner Bros. All Rights Reserved

DOLBY STEREO

JUNE

'The River' 'Born To Run'/'Rosalita (Come Out Tonight)' is released in the U.K. to coincide with the tour (CBS A13 1179).

1/2   LONDON, ENGLAND WEMBLEY ARENA
Debut of 'Shake' as part of the five-song medley in a 27-song set on the 1st. Link Wray joins Bruce onstage on the 2nd for 'I Fought The Law' in a fine 27-song set.

4/5   Another 27-song set on the 4th is followed on the 5th by 'Jole Blon' debuted in a fine 32-song farewell to London that also includes 'I Fought The Law', 'Here She Comes', 'I Wanna Marry You' and 'Can't Help Falling In Love With You'.

7/8   BIRMINGHAM, ENGLAND NATIONAL EXHIBITION CENTRE ARENA
On the 7th, Pete Townshend joins Bruce for 'Born To Run' and an incredible eight-song medley. 'Drive All Night' makes its European debut.
Bruce bids farewell to Europe on the 8th with a 30-song set. Throughout the whole of the European tour, only 'Rosalita' is performed from the first two albums. Bruce signs off with 'Rockin' All Over The World'.

14   LOS ANGELES, CALIFORNIA HOLLYWOOD BOWL'
At 'Survival Sunday', an anti-nuclear benefit filmed for the TV news, Bruce sings 'This Land Is Your Land', an acoustic version of 'The Promised Land' (with Jackson Browne), 'Jole Blon' (with Gary U.S. Bonds), 'Hungry Heart' and a massed-choir version of 'Brother John Is Gone' with numerous M.U.S.E. regulars including Bonnie Raitt, Stephen Stills and Graham Nash.

15   SAN FRANCISCO, CALIFORNIA OLD WALDORF
Bruce joins Gary U.S. Bonds onstage for three songs, 'Jole Blon', 'This Little Girl' and 'Quarter To Three'.

JULY

2/3   EAST RUTHERFORD, NEW JERSEY BYRNE
5/6   MEADOWLANDS ARENA
8/9   Bruce opens the new arena with a 29 'homecoming' set, opening with 'Born To Run' for the last time, that debuts the excellent Tom Waits song, 'Jersey Girl' and features 'I Don't Want To Go Home' with lead vocals by Miami Steve.
On the 3rd, Gary U.S. Bonds joins Bruce onstage for 'Jole Blon' and 'This Little Girl' in a 28-song set.
A 28-song set on the 5th includes 'Jersey Girl',

For The Sportsman and First Nighter

action

Spectrum

BULK RATE
U.S. POSTAGE
PAID
Permit No. 148
Philadelphia, Pa.

THIRD CLASS MAIL

VOL.14—NO.14   JUNE/JULY, 1981   Circulation 50,000   PRICE 60c

Bruce Springsteen

July 13,15,16,18,19

SOLD OUT!

BRUCE SPRINGSTEEN SUMMER TOUR 81 AFTER SHOW ONLY

BYRNE MEADOWLANDS ARENA

JULY 2, 1981

'Trapped' and '4th Of July, Asbury Park (Sandy)'.

The 6th features a typical set from the latter part of the world tour: 'Thunder Road'; 'Prove It All Night'; 'Tenth Avenue Freeze-Out'; 'Darkness On The Edge Of Town'; 'Follow That Dream'; 'Independence Day'; 'Trapped'; 'Two Hearts'; 'The Promised Land'; 'The River'; 'This Land Is Your Land'; 'Who'll Stop The Rain?'; 'Badlands'; 'Out In The Street' – Intermission – 'Hungry Heart'; 'You Can Look'; 'Cadillac Ranch'; 'Sherry Darling'; 'Jole Blon'; 'Johnny Bye Bye'; 'Racing In The Street'; 'Ramrod'; 'Rosalita (Come Out Tonight)'; 'I Don't Want To Go Home' (Miami Steve on lead vocals); 'Jungleland'; 'Born To Run'; 'Devil With The Blue Dress' medley (seven songs including the debut of 'Sock It To Me Baby'); 'Twist And Shout'.

A 27-song set on the 8th has an eight-part medley including 'Land Of A Thousand Dances', 'Sock It To Me Baby', 'Sweet Soul Music' and Shake'.

At the 28-song set on the 9th, Gary U.S. Bonds again joins Bruce for 'Jole Blon' and 'The Little Girl'.

11   RED BANK, NEW JERSEY   BIG MAN'S WEST

The opening night of Clarence Clemons' new nightclub, and Bruce jumps up onstage for six songs: 'Ramrod', 'Around And Around', 'Summertime Blues', 'Jole Blon' (with Gary U.S. Bonds), 'You Can't Sit Down' and 'Cadillac Ranch'. He's illegally filmed by a member of the audience.

13   PHILADELPHIA,
15/16   PENNSYLVANIA   SPECTRUM
18/19   A 27-song on the 13th and 26-song sets on the 15th and 18th. On the 15th, 'Tenth Avenue Freeze-Out' opens the second half and 'You Can't Sit Down' replaces 'Sock It To Me Baby' in a nine-song medley.

The 16th and 19th are 25-song sets which on the 19th includes 'For You', 'I Fought The Law', '4th Of July, Asbury Park (Sandy)' and 'Growin' Up'.

29/30   CLEVELAND, OHIO   RICHFIELD COLISEUM

Southside Johnny joins Bruce on both nights for a duet on 'I Don't Want To Go Home' in 29 and 28-song sets respectively.

4/5, 7   LARGO, MARYLAND   CAPITAL CENTRE

At the final night's performance, 'Tenth Avenue Freeze-Out' opens the second half in a 27-song set that also includes 'Summertime Blues', 'Twist And Shout' and '4th Of July, Asbury Park (Sandy)'.

AUGUST

6 WASHINGTON, D.C. BAYOU CLUB
Bruce, Garry and Clarence join ex-Steel Mill member Robbin Thompson for an eight-minute version of 'Carol'.

11/12 DETROIT, MICHIGAN JOE LOUIS ARENA
A 29-song set on the first night is followed by a 27-song set with Mitch Ryder joining Bruce onstage for a four-song 'Devil With The Blue Dress' medley.

16/17 DENVER, COLORADO RED ROCKS
Torrential rain on the final night and Bruce opens the 28-song set with 'Who'll Stop The Rain'? The second half is opened by a one and only performance of 'Sea Cruise'.

**20/21 LOS ANGELES, CALIFORNIA SPORTS
23/24 ARENA
27/28**
On the first of six nights a benefit show for the Vietnam Veteran's is preceded by a short, heartfelt speech by Bruce. A 29-song set features a one and only performance of 'Ballad Of Easy Rider'.
On the 21st 'For You' opens the second half of a 26-song set.
On the 23rd, 'Summertime Blues' opens a 28-song set with rare performances of 'Rave On' and 'Stolen Car'.
On the 24th, Tom Waits joins Bruce onstage for a duet on his own composition, 'Jersey Girl', in a 28-song set.
'Twist And Shout' preceded by a nine-part medley, closes a 27-song set on the 27th.
A 29-song set on the 28th debuts 'Proud Mary' and a one and only performance of 'Deportee (Plane Crash At Los Gatos)'. 'Quarter To Three' is played for the first time since September 1979.

SEPTEMBER

2 SAN DIEGO, CALIFORNIA SPORTS ARENA
'Jackson Cage' and 'Growin' Up' are performed in a long, 30-song set.

5 PASSADENA, CALIFORNIA PERKIN'S COW PALACE
Bruce joins the Pretenders onstage for a vocal duet with Chrissie Hynde on 'Higher And Higher'.

**8/10
11 ROSEMONT, ILLINOIS HORIZON**
Superb performance on the 8th of '4th Of July, Asbury Park (Sandy)', 'Point Blank' and 'Candy's Room' in a 26-song set.
'Mona' and 'She's The One' return on the 10th for a one-off performance – their first since 1 January 1979. 'I Fought The Law' and 'Wreck On The Highway' are also performed. The 28-song set debuts 'Mony Mony' in a six-part medley.
On the 11th 'It's Hard To Be A Saint In The City' gets it's first airing since 1 January 1979 in a 28-song set, marked by the final performances of 'I Wanna Marry You' and 'Drive All Night'.

13/14 CINCINNATTI, OHIO RIVERFRONT COLISEUM
The 1980–81 The River tour has taken in 13 countries, lasted for 12 months and included 139 shows. The 27-song set on the 13th opens with 'Out In The Street' and fittingly, the final night's 29-song set opens with 'Rockin' All Over The World' and includes 'It's Hard To Be A Saint

In The City', 'Proud Mary' and an encore of 'Quarter To Three'. This is Miami Steve's final live E Street Band performance.

DECEMBER

10 In Harmony 2 is released. (U.S., COL. BFC 37643 U.K., CBS 85451) This 'Various Artists' album includes one Bruce offering: the version of 'Santa Claus Is Coming To Town' recorded at C.W. Post College, Greenvale, New York back in December 1975. It becomes the fourth live song to be released by Bruce.

1982
JANUARY

3/4 HOLMDEL, NEW JERSEY
Bruce records some demos at his New Jersey home. They will later be released as the solo Nebraska LP.

5 ASBURY PARK, NEW JERSEY STONE PONY
Bruce performs 'Midnight Hour' and 'Jole Blon' with Lord Gunner.

12 NEW JERSEY ROYAL MANOR NORTH
Bruce performs 'Lucille' and 'Carol' with Nils Lofgren.

FEBRUARY

20 RED BANK, NEW JERSEY BIG MAN'S WEST
'Ain't That A Shame', 'Money' and 'You Can't Sit Down' with Beaver Brown.

APRIL

**9/11, RED BANK, NEW JERSEY BIG MAN'S
16 WEST**
'Twist And Shout' with Beaver Brown on the 9th. 'Lucille', 'Jersey Girl', 'Jole Blon' and 'Twist And Shout' with Beaver Brown on the 10th. 'Long Tall Sally', 'Rockin' All Over The World', 'Proud Mary' and 'Carol' with John Eddie and the Front Street Runners on the 11th. 'Tenth Avenue Freeze-Out' with C.C. and the Red Bank Rockers on the 16th.

MAY

25 ASBURY PARK, NEW JERSEY STONE PONY
Bruce performs with Cats on a Smooth Surface.

2 ASBURY PARK, NEW JERSEY STONE PONY
Bruce performs with Cats on a Smooth Surface.

8 ASBURY PARK, NEW JERSEY FAST LANE
'Jole Blon', 'Jersey Girl', 'Lucille' and 'Around And Around' with Beaver Brown.

16 RED BANK, NEW JERSEY BIG MAN'S WEST
'Tenth Avenue Freeze-Out' with C.C. and the Red Bank Rockers.

23 ASBURY PARK, NEW JERSEY FAST LANE
Bruce performs with Cats on a Smooth Surface.

29 RED BANK, NEW JERSEY BIG MAN'S WEST
'Little Latin Lupe Lu', 'Summertime Blues', 'Around And Around' and 'Highschool Confidential' with Beaver Brown. Southside Johnny also guests.

JUNE

6 ASBURY PARK, NEW JERSEY STONE PONY
Bruce performs with Cats On A Smooth Surface.

12 NEW YORK, N.Y. CENTRAL PARK
Bruce joins Jackson Browne onstage at the 'Rally for Disarmament' outdoor festival for the backing vocals of Browne's 'Running On Empty' and an acoustic version of 'Promised Land', performed as a duet with Bruce on guitar. Joan Baez, Gary U.S. Bonds and James Taylor also perform. The concert attracts over 500,000 people and is televised on cable TV.
The same evening, Bruce guests with Sonny Kenn at Big Man's West, Red Bank, New Jersey on 'Route 66', 'Walking The Dog' and 'Carol'.
Gary U.S. Bonds' On The Line LP is released.

13, 20 ASBURY PARK, NEW JERSEY STONE PONY
'Lucille' and 'Heartbreak Hotel' on the 13th and six songs including 'Let's Go', 'Sweet Little Sixteen' and 'Around And Around' on the 20th with Cats On A Smooth Surface.

26/27 RED BANK, NEW JERSEY BIG MAN'S WEST
'Lucille' with Bill Chinook on the 26th and 'Tenth Avenue Freeze-Out' with C.C. and the Red Bank Rockers on the 27th.
At the Stone Pony, Asbury Park this evening, Bruce sings six songs with Cats On A Smooth Surface, including the debut of 'From Small Things, Big Things One Day Come'.

JULY

17 RED BANK, NEW JERSEY BIG MAN'S WEST
'Mony Mony', 'Shout', 'Johnny Bye Bye' and 'Shake' with the Iron City Houserockers.

18 NEW YORK, N.Y. PEPPERMINT LOUNGE
Live debut of Little Steven and the Disciples of Soul. Filmed for video release as a companion to the LP, Men Without Women.

And Shout' with Beaver Brown on the 6th.
Six songs with Beaver Brown on the 7th,
including 'From Small Things . . .', 'Lucille' and
'Do You Wanna Dance'.

**8, 15   ASBURY PARK, NEW JERSEY STONE
PONY**
Eight songs with Cats On A Smooth Surface on
the 8th, including a version of 'Lucille' that
debuts part of a new song, 'On The Prowl', in the
middle break.
    On the 15th Bruce sings a 'Devil With The
Blue Dress' medley at the Cats On A Smooth
Surface gig, including 'Shake' and 'Sweet Soul
Music'. A further six songs include 'You Can
Look', 'From Small Things . . .', 'Around And
Around' and 'Havin' A Party'.

**31   ASBURY PARK, NEW JERSEY JOHN
JOHN'S CLUB**
Bruce performs with Cats On A Smooth Surface.

SEPTEMBER
**4, 18   RED BANK, NEW JERSEY. BIG MAN'S
WEST**
'From Small Things . . .', 'Let's Go' and 'Lucille'
with Beaver Brown on the 4th. At the Dave
Edmunds gig on the 18th Bruce shares vocals
on 'From Small Things . . .', 'Lucille' and 'Carol',
and contributes guitar and backing vocals to
'Johnny B Goode', 'Let's Talk About Us' and
'Bama Lama Bama Loo'.

**23   RED BANK, NEW JERSEY MONMOUTH
COUNTY FAIR**
'Long Tall Sally' and 'Twist And Shout' with
Sonny Kenn.
At the Fast Lane, Asbury Park, Bruce sings three
songs with the Stray Cats at their evening gig:
'Twenty Flight Rock', 'Be Bop A Lula' and 'Long
Tall Sally'.

**25   ASBURY PARK, NEW JERSEY STONE
PONY**
Eight songs with Cats On A Smooth Surface,
including 'Ramrod', 'Let's Go', 'From Small
Things . . .' and 'The Wanderer'.

**31   RED BANK, NEW JERSEY BIG MAN'S
WEST**
Five songs with Sonny Keen, including 'Sweet
Little Sixteen', 'Rip It Up' and 'Sweet Little Rock
'n' Roller'.

AUGUST
**1   ASBURY PARK, NEW JERSEY STONE
PONY**
Six songs with Cats On A Smooth Surface,
including 'Come On Over To My Place', 'Let's
Go' and 'Twist And Shout'.

**6/7   RED BANK, NEW JERSEY BIG MAN'S
WEST**
'Ready Teddy', 'Lucille', 'Jersey Girl' and 'Twist

19 **ASBURY PARK, NEW JERSEY STONE PONY**
Twelve songs with Cats On A Smooth Surface, including 'Come On Over To My Place', 'Havin' A Party', 'Wooly Bully', 'Louie Louie' and 'High Heeled Sneakers'.

20 *Nebraska* is released in the U.S. (COL. TC 38358).

21 **NEW YORK, N.Y. PEPPERMINT LOUNGE**
Bruce guests with Dave Edmunds on 'From Small Things, Big Things One Day Come'.

24 *Nebraska* is released in the U.K. (CBS 25100).

25 **ASBURY PARK, NEW JERSEY STONE PONY**
Five songs with Cats On A Smooth Surface, including 'Come On Over To My Place', 'From Small Things . . .' and 'Twist And Shout'.

29 **WESTWOOD, NEW JERSEY ON BROADWAY**
Bruce joins Billy Rancher and the Unreal Gods onstage for one song.

30 'Atlantic City'/'Mansion On the Hill' is released in the U.K. (CBS A2794).

OCTOBER
3 **ASBURY PARK, NEW JERSEY STONE PONY**
14 songs with Cats On A Smooth Surface, including 'Let's Go', 'Do You Wanna Dance', 'Wooly Bully', 'Rock Baby Rock', 'Louie Louie', a complete version of the new 'On The Prowl' and an electric version of 'Open All Night'.

16 Little Steven and the Disciples Of Soul appear on the German TV show, 'Rockpalast' and their *Men Without Women* LP is released in the U.K.

18 **LONDON, ENGLAND MARQUEE**
Little Steven and the Disciples of Soul's U.K. debut.

NOVEMBER
20 'Open All Night'/'The Big Payback' is released in the U.K. (CBS A2969).

27 **LOS ANGELES, CALIFORNIA CLUB LINGERIE**
Bruce is believed to have joined local LA band Jimmy and the Mustangs, onstage.

DECEMBER
3 **PALO ALTO, CALIFORNIA THE KEY STONE**
Bruce, who has brought his mother to see a C.C. and the Red Bank Rockers gig, jumps up onstage for two songs: 'Lucille' and 'From Small Things . . .'.

22 World premiere of 'Atlantic City' promo video on MTV cable TV. The low-budget black-and-white film shows clips of Atlantic City viewed from the inside of a car. Bruce is not featured.

31 **NEW YORK, N.Y. HARKNESS HOUSE BALLET SCHOOL**
The wedding reception for Steve Van Zandt and his bride Maureen Santoro. The wedding itself featured Percy Sledge singing 'When A Man Loves A Woman' as the couple walked down the

aisle, and the Reverend Richard Penniman (Little Richard) performed the ceremony. The guest list includes best man Bruce, Southside Johnny, Gary U.S. Bonds, the E Street Band and former and present members of the Asbury Jukes. Music is supplied by Lester Chambers and the Chamber Brothers who are joined by Bruce and various Asbury cohorts on 'Save The Last Dance For Me', 'Jole Blon', 'Hungry Heart' and 'Twist And Shout'. The happy couple depart in a horse-drawn carriage. At Steve's request a video was made of the wedding.
On November 20, *Greetings From Asbury Park N.J.* is re-released in the U.K. with a new catalogue number (CBS 32210).

1983
JANUARY
8 **RED BANK, NEW JERSEY BIG MAN'S WEST**
Bruce, Max, Garry and Clarence join old friends Larson for two songs, 'Rockin' All Over The World' and 'Lucille'. This is the final night that Big Man's West will open. Health and Safety regulations, cash problems and the inevitable rip offs finally force Clarence to shut up shop for good.

FEBRUARY
5 **BUFFALO, NEW YORK UNIVERSITY OF BUFFALO**
Little Steven and the Disciples Of Soul kick off a one-month, 15-date tour of the U.S.

APRIL
13 **BRUSSELS, BELGIUM**
Little Steven and the Disciples Of Soul arrive in Europe for a 20-date tour (including eight U.K. gigs). First stop is at the ICP Studios to record 'Rock'n'Roll Rebel' for a future release.

14 **ANTWERP, BELGIUM HOF TER LO**
Little Steven and the Disciples Of Soul begin their European shows.

24, 27 **ASBURY PARK, NEW JERSEY STONE PONY**
Bruce joins the Cats (formerly Cats On A Smooth Surface) for four songs: 'From Small Things, Big Things One Day Come', 'Around And Around', 'Lucille' and 'Twist And Shout'. The Cats, led by Bobby Bandiera, have by now split into two factions, with former members Harry Filkin, Peter Schulle and Joel Krause teaming up with Eddie Inglewski and Mike Bovenzi to form the Diamonds, who made their debut opening for Little Steven at Big Man's West, December 16 and 17 1982.
On the 27th Bruce joins the Diamonds onstage for two songs: 'Lucille' and 'Long Tall Sally'.

MAY
13 **CANNES, FRANCE PALM BEACH CASINO**
Little Steven and the Disciples Of Soul conclude their first major tour of Europe with a free concert after attending the European premiere of their film, 'Men Without Women', at the Cannes film festival.

30 **SAN BERNADINO, CALIFORNIA US FESTIVAL**
Little Steven opens the Monday show at 9:30 a.m. Bruce was offered a reputed $1 million to appear solo but declined.

JUNE
18 **ASBURY PARK, NEW JERSEY STONE PONY**
Bruce joins the Diamonds onstage for three songs: 'Around And Around', 'Lucille' and 'Twist And Shout'.

24 **LOS ANGELES, CALIFORNIA FOX MOVIE THEATRE**
'Men Without Women' opens for a one-week stint. A general release is hoped for, but a home video release (EMI TVE/TXE 90 1289) is scheduled for late 1983 but has yet to be distributed.

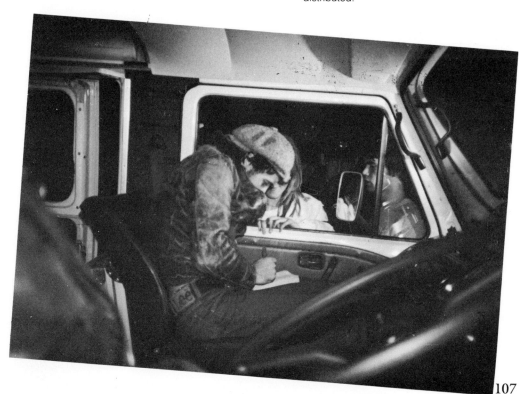

ABDICATING THE ROCK 'N' ROLL PEDESTAL:
BRUCE SPRINGSTEEN GETS DOWN
BY DON McLEESE

You can hide 'ne...
        covers
And study your...
Make crosses...
        lovers
Throw rose...
Waste you...
        in va...
For a...
        the...
Well...

Wat
Springste...
kan, kan
Springstee...
alleen!

ONE MAN'S MASTERPIECE

17

KING AND COUNTRY

At a time when both American political parties are fighting to see which can most reclaim the flag and its attendant values as its own, how odd to see a rock 'n' roller predate them. Bruce Springsteen, as evidenced by 'Born In The USA's' introspective, even homey slice-of-American-life sagas, has created a curious but very real rock audience that might unknowingly have more in common with Cotton Mather than with Judas Priest, with Woody Guthrie than with Prince. Springsteen's shows, his music and his attitudes share with his audiences a sort of New Puritanism, a sense of quasi-religious manifest destiny, and a fundamentalist acceptance of life and its troubles, along with the faith that true belief will bring a better way. When Springsteen ends his shows with a cry to 'let freedom ring — that's what we're here for, even if we have to fight for it every day', there are no scoffers in his rock 'n' roll flock, only true believers.

Springsteen has the power and the touch. In many ways, he resembles the television evangelists riding the crest of a rebirth of religious fervor in America. Unlike Jerry Falwell, though, Springsteen's message is that true salvation lies in a rock 'n' roll way of life. Articulating that way is not easy; it seems to be an intuitive way of knowledge. How unusual it is to hear 20,000 people cheer a performer's rap on what's wrong with your street and your town [...]

call it, but I know that most of my records after 'Born To Run' were somehow a reaction to that album. To my own experience of it, which was really wild, it was really a big moment in my life.

Now 'Born To Run' the song means a lot more to me than it did then. I can sing it tonight and feel like it breathes in all those extra years. It's been like — I wrote it ten years ago now. But it still feels really real. Very real, for me. It's one of the most emotional moments of the night. I can see all of those people and that song to them is like — that's their song, man. It's almost as much the audience's as it is mine. I like it when the lights are up because you can see so much from people's faces. That's what it's about. But I like doing the old songs now, because I really feel they let the years in, they don't feel limiting. Like, I hear part of 'Nebraska' in 'Born To Run' now.

Is 'Born To [...] [...] about, as it suggested [...] rock 'n' roll [...]

It was kind [...] learning [...] which I [...] 'Darkness [...] Car' and [...] kind of [...] the [...] know, [...] heroic [...] ryday, [...] Glory [...] me [...] to [...] Neb [...] dy [...] ce [...] at [...]

JULY

10 ASBURY PARK, NEW JERSEY STONE PONY
Bruce guests with the Cats for five songs: 'Keep A Knockin'', 'Around And Around', 'Wooly Bully', 'Little Latin Lupe Lu' and 'Twist And Shout'.

16 NEPTUNE, NEW JERSEY HEADLINER
Bruce joins local band, Midnite Thunder, for several songs including 'Lucille', 'Sweet Little Sixteen', 'Louie Louie', 'Woolly Bully' and 'Twist And Shout'.

AUGUST

2 NEW YORK, N.Y. MADISON SQUARE GARDEN
Bruce joins good friend Jackson Browne on guitar and shared vocals for the encores: 'Stay', 'Sweet Little Sixteen' and 'Running On Empty'. Jackson had previously dedicated a new song, appropriately called 'For A Rocker', to 'the Boss'.

14 ASBURY PARK, NEW JERSEY STONE PONY
Bruce joins the Cats for six songs: 'Ready Teddy', 'Around And Around', 'Jersey Girl', 'Lucille', 'Twist And Shout' and a first-time performance of Jimmy Reed's 'Ain't That Lovin' You Baby'.

19 GELEEN, HOLLAND DE HANENHOF
Little Steven and the Disciples Of Soul, now minus La Bamba's Mambomen (the four or five-piece horn section) start a short eight-date tour of Europe. The current line-up: Steve, Jean Beauvior, Monti Ellison, Dino Danelli, Pee Wee Weber and Zoe Yanakis.

19 LONG BRANCH, NEW JERSEY BRIGHTON BAR
Good friend John Eddie and the Front Street Runners are joined by Bruce for five songs at one of the smallest venues he's ever played:

'Blue Suede Shoes', 'Rockin' All Over The World', 'Ain't That Lovin' You Baby', 'Jersey Girl' and 'Carol'.

28 READING, ENGLAND THAMESIDE ARENA
Little Steven's short European tour culminates at the 23rd and last-ever National Rock Festival, 'Reading Rock 1983'. Thin Lizzy top the bill. The Disciples Of Soul become the last American act ever to appear at Reading.

SEPTEMBER

23 LONDON, ENGLAND BBC RADIO
Disciples Of Soul appearance at the Reading Festival are aired on the BBC's 'In concert' programme: 'Resurrection Shuffle'/'Money To The Rescue' (CBS A 3803) Clarence Clemons and the Red Bank Rockers' single is released in the U.K.

NOVEMBER

6 ASBURY PARK, NEW JERSEY STONE PONY
Bruce joins the Cats onstage for a 45-minute guest apparance. Amongst the nine songs is a first-ever performance of the Rolling Stones' 'It's All Over Now'.

11 *Rescue*, Clarence Clemons and the Red Bank Rockers' first LP, is released and their single consisting of two Springsteen compositions (COL. BFC 38033 U.S., CBS 25699 U.K.). 'Savin' Up'/'Summer On Signal Hill' (CBS A 3928) is released in the U.K.

DECEMBER

28 RED BANK, NEW JERSEY MONMOUTH ARTS CENTRE
Nils Lofgren and numerous Asbury musicians play throughout the evening at a benefit show billed as 'La Bamba's Holiday Hurrah'. Bruce arrives in the evening for 'From Small Things, Big Things One Day Come', 'Santa Claus Is Comin' To Town' and 'Twist And Shout'.

31 ASBURY PARK, NEW JERSEY STONE PONY
Bruce attends a Beaver Brown and John Eddie and the Front Street Runners show but doesn't play. After the set, Bruce hosts a New Year's Eve party at his home.

1984
JANUARY

8 ASBURY PARK, NEW JERSEY STONE PONY
Sunday night's 'joke telling' contest is livened up when Bruce saunters onstage to tell an Italian joke. He doesn't win the $25 first prize but later redeems himself with two songs with the Cats: 'Lucille' and 'Carol'. the current Cats line-up is Bobby Bandiera, Glenn Burtrick, Fran Smith, Ray Anderson and Mike Bovenzi. Bruce's 'Blinded By The Light' appears on track one, side one of *CBS Showcase* (CBS XPC 4003), a various artists, promotion only cassette, released in August 1983 throughout the U.K. in W. H. Smith stores' record departments to promote the CBS 'Nice Price' LP range.
In September, Bruce records basic tracks at the Hit Factory Studios, New York. He is unhappy with the 40 songs he'd had mixed in LA in October 1982.

14 NEW BRUNSWICK, NEW JERSEY PATRIX
Bruce makes a surprise appearance with John Eddie and the Front Street Runners for 'Rockin' All Over The World', 'Aint Too Proud To Beg', 'Boom Boom', 'Proud Mary', 'Twist And Shout' and 'Hang On Sloopy'. An interesting set with two of the songs making their debut in Bruce's repertoire.

MARCH

25 ASBURY PARK, NEW JERSEY STONE PONY
Debut of the ZZ Top song 'I'm Bad, I'm Nationwide' and 'Lucille' with the Cats.

APRIL

2 STOCKHOLM, SWEDEN
Clarence Clemons and the Red Bank Rockers begin a five-date tour of Sweden, Norway and

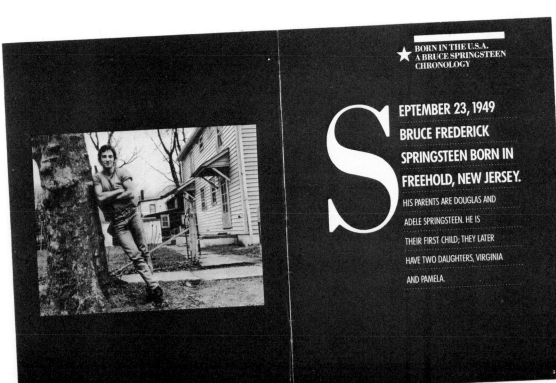

BORN IN THE U.S.A.
A BRUCE SPRINGSTEEN
CHRONOLOGY

SEPTEMBER 23, 1949 BRUCE FREDERICK SPRINGSTEEN BORN IN FREEHOLD, NEW JERSEY. HIS PARENTS ARE DOUGLAS AND ADELE SPRINGSTEEN. HE IS THEIR FIRST CHILD; THEY LATER HAVE TWO DAUGHTERS, VIRGINIA AND PAMELA.

Denmark with a live TV appearance. The current line up of the band is Clarence, J. T. Bowen vocals, Lloyd Landesman keyboards, Hugh McDonald bass/guitar, Dennis Amoruso piano/brass and Wells Kelly drums.

8 ASBURY PARK, NEW JERSEY STONE PONY
'Proud Mary', 'I'm Bad, I'm Nationwide', 'Lucille' and the debut of 'Dirty Water' performed with the Cats.

13 PHILADELPHIA, PENNSYLVANIA RIPLEY MUSIC HALL
Bruce guests with Clarence Clemons and the Red Bank Rockers for 'Fire' and 'Rockin' All Over The World'.

21 MOUNT IVY, NEW YORK EXPO
Four songs with Clarence Clemons and the Red Bank Rockers including the Beatles' 'A Hard Day's Night'.

22 ASBURY PARK, NEW JERSEY STONE PONY
'I'm Bad, I'm Nationwide', 'Little Latin Lupe Lu' and 'Jersey Girl' performed with the Cats.

MAY
11 'Dancing In The Dark'/'Pink Cadillac' is released in U.S. (COL. 38–04463)

19 ASBURY PARK, NEW JERSEY STONE PONY

Bruce joins Clarence Clemons and the Red Bank Rockers for 'Fire', 'In The Midnight Hour', 'Lucille' and 'Twist And Shout'.

26 ASBURY PARK, NEW JERSEY XANADU
Live debut of the new single 'Dancing In The Dark' with local band Bystander.

JUNE
1 ASBURY PARK, NEW JERSEY STONE PONY
John Eddie and the Front Street Runners are joined by Bruce for 'I'm Bad, I'm Nationwide', 'Proud Mary', 'Carol' and 'Bright Lights, Big City'.

4 *Born In The U.S.A.* is released worldwide. (U.S. COL. QU 38653, U.K. CBS 86304).

8 ASBURY PARK, NEW JERSEY STONE PONY
Bruce and the E Street Band, including new member Nils Lofgren, make a surprise 2 a.m. appearance. 'Thunder Road', 'Out In The Street', 'Prove It All Night', 'Glory Days', 'The River', 'Darlington County', 'Dancing In The Dark', 'The Promised Land', 'My Home Town', 'Born In The U.S.A.', 'Badlands' and 'Born To Run'.

10 ASBURY PARK, NEW JERSEY STONE PONY
Bruce and Nils Lofgren join the Cats for 'Gloria', 'Boom Boom', 'We Gotta Get Outta This Place',

'The Last Time' and 'Rockin' All Over The World'.

21 LANCASTER, PENNSYLVANIA VILLAGE
Bruce and the E Street Band play a final warm-up before the major tour, 'Out In The Street', 'Prove It All Night', 'Glory Days', 'Hungry Heart', 'Dancing In The Dark' and 'Rosalita (Come Out Tonight)'.

28 ST PAUL, MINNESOTA CIVIC CENTRE
The 'Dancing In The Dark' video directed by Brian De Palma is filmed in front of 200 extras. After completion, Bruce and the E Street Band perform the 'Devil With The Blue Dress' medley.

29 ST PAUL, MINNESOTA CIVIC CENTRE
Opening night of the tour and Bruce staggers everyone with a 31-song plus medley set that includes eight songs from *Born In The U.S.A.* and five from *Nebraska*. Debuted were 'Johnny 99', 'Atlantic City', 'Mansion On The Hill', 'No Surrender', 'Used Cars', 'Highway Patrolman', 'I'm On Fire', 'Working On The Highway', 'Bobby Jean' and the Rolling Stones' 'Street Fighting Man'. 'Dancing In The Dark' is performed twice due to Brian De Palma's completion of the video. Patti Scialfa makes her E Street Band debut.

JULY
1/2 ST PAUL, MINNESOTA CIVIC CENTRE
Debuted on the 1st, 'Reasons To Believe', 'Nebraska' and 'Pink Cadillac'. 'Open All Night' gets its first full E Street Band airing in a 31-song plus medley set. On the 2nd, 'Downbound Train' and 'Cover Me' debuted in a 28-song set that closes with 'Twist And Shout'.

5/6 CINCINNATTI, OHIO RIVERFRONT COLISEUM

8/9 CLEVELAND, OHIO RICHFIELD COLISEUM

12/13 EAST TROY, WISCONSIN ALPINE VALLEY MUSIC THEATRE
Bruce's first open air show of the tour debuts a new song called 'Man At The Top' in a 26-song plus medley set. 'Twist And Shout' closes the second night's 27-song set.

15, 17/18 ROSEMONT, ILLINOIS HORIZON

21 MONTREAL, CANADA FORUM
29-song plus medley set that includes 'Tenth Avenue Freeze-Out' and the debut of 'Do You Love Me' segued into 'Twist And Shout'.

23/24, 26 TORONTO, CANADA NATIONAL EXHIBITION GRANDSTAND
Three 27-song plus medley sets that includes 'Trapped' on the 24th. The final night saw 'Who'll Stop The Rain?' and a rare performance of 'Ramrod'. 'Dancing In The Dark' video premiered on MTV on the 25th.

27 SARATOGA SPRINGS, NEW YORK PERFORMING ARTS CENTRE
'Who'll Stop The Rain?' performed at the sound check of a 28-song medley set.

30/31 DETROIT, MICHIGAN JOE LOUIS ARENA
'Travelin' Band' debuted into the medley. 'Cover Me'/'Jersey Girl' is released in the U.S.A. (COL. 38–04561)

AUGUST

1   DETROIT, MICHIGAN JOE LOUIS ARENA

5/6   EAST RUTHERFORD, NEW JERSEY BYRNE
8/9   MEADOWLANDS ARENA
11/12 Ten sell-out shows that culminate on the final
16/17 night with a guest appearance by ex-E Street
19/20 Band member Little Steven who joins in for 'Two
Hearts' and 'Drift Away'. The encores are aided
by the Miami Horns. Throughout the three and a
half hour shows, averaging 29–30 songs per
night, were numerous highlights, including on
the 17th the live debut of 'Goin' Down'. Guest
appearances by J. T. Bowen for shared vocals
on the 9th on 'Woman's Got The Power'; on the
11th John Entwistle played bass on 'Twist And
Shout' and on the 12th Southside Johnny

shared vocals on the same song. On the 6th and
the 13th a TV interview with presenter Barbara
Howard is broadcast on 'Entertainment Tonight'.

**22   ASBURY PARK, NEW JERSEY STONE
PONY**
Bruce guests with La Bamba's Hubcaps for
'Travelin' Band' and 'I'm Bad, I'm Nationwide'.

**23   LONG BRANCH, NEW JERSEY BRIGHTON
BAR**
Bruce guests with an all-girl group called Mama
Tried for 'Twist And Shout'.

25/26 LARGO, MARYLAND CAPITAL CENTRE
28/29 Live debut of 'Be True' on the 26th. From the
first leg of the tour a fairly typical set would be –
'Born In The U.S.A.'/'Out In The Street'/'Spirit
In The Night'/'Atlantic City'/'Independence
Day'/'Reason To Believe' (with changed
lyrics)/'Prove It All Night'/'Darlington
County'/'Glory Days'/'The Promised Land'/'The
River'/'Trapped'/'Badlands'/'Thunder Road'
Intermission 'Cadillac Ranch'/'Hungry
Heart'/'Dancing In The Dark'/'Sherry
Darling'/'Follow That Dream'/'Because The
Night'/'Cover Me'/'Growin' Up'/'Bobby
Jean'/'Racing In The Street'/'Rosalita' Encores
'Jungleland'/'Born To Run'/'Devil With The Blue
Dress' medley including 'Travelin' Band'/'Twist
And Shout'/'Do You Love Me?'.

SEPTEMBER

**3   ASBURY PARK, NEW JERSEY STONE
PONY**
John Eddie and the Front Street Runners are
joined by Bruce.

**4/5   WORCHESTER, MASSACHUSETTS CIVIC
AUDITORIUM**

7/8   HARTFORD, CONNECTICUT CIVIC CENTRE
Bruce opens with 'Rave On' in honour of Buddy
Holly's birthdate on the 7th.

11/12, PHILADELPHIA,
14/15, PENNSYLVANIA SPECTRUM
17/18 'I'm Bad, I'm Nationwide' is performed for the
first time with the E Street Band. On the 12th,
CBS 'Nightly News' feature a five minute TV
interview with Bruce.

20   PITTSBURGH, PENNSYLVANIA DECADE
Bruce jumps onstage with a local band for
'Wooly Bully' and 'Lucille'.

**21/22 PITTSBURGH, PENNSYLVANIA CIVIC
ARENA**

**23   TUPELO, MISSISSIPPI NATIONAL PUBLIC
RADIO**
A 15 minute birthday profile where Bruce refers
to President Ronald Reagan's recent remarks
about him at a campaign rally in Hammonton,
New Jersey.

**24/25 BUFFALO, NEW YORK MEMORIAL
AUDITORIUM**
Bruce and the new band wind up the first leg of
the tour with 29 and 30-song plus medley sets
that feature on the 24th 'Trapped', 'State
Trooper' and 'Downbound Train', and on the
25th 'Point Blank', 'Candy's Room' and 'Santa
Claus Is Comin' To Town'. 'Cover Me'/'Jersey
Girl' is released in the U.K. on the 24th. (CBS A
4662)

30   LONDON, ENGLAND CAPITAL RADIO
An interview with Bruce by Roger Scott,
recorded in Hartford, Connecticut on September
8 1984 is broadcast on Capital Radio.

OCTOBER

**15   VANCOUVER, BRITISH COLUMBIA
PACIFIC COLISEUM**

17/19 TACOMA, WASHINGTON TACOMA DOME
The second night's show, originally scheduled
for the 18th but postponed due to illness, saw an
unprecedented 'Rosalita' dropped from the set
for the first time in over 10 years! 'Born To Run'
closes the second half and the 33-song plus
medley, four and a half hour show ends with
'Santa Claus Is Comin' To Town'.

21/22 OAKLAND, CALIFORNIA COLISEUM
Debut of 'Shut Out The Light' in the second
night's 32-song plus medley set, that also
features a rare performance of 'Stolen Car'. On
the 21st MTV broadcast a one-hour 'Sunday
Special' on Bruce that includes live footage from
Meadowlands.

25/26, LOS ANGELES, CALIFORNIA SPORTS
28/29 ARENA
31 'Cover Me' and 'Dancing In The Dark' open the
second half of each night's show. The first
night's 32-song plus medley set is followed on
the 26th by a 31-song plus medley set with
'Rosalita' in the encores. On the 28th a 29-song
plus medley set and on the 29th 'Night' and
'Candy's Room' are included in the 26-song
plus medley set. Finally on the 31st, Halloween
night, Bruce lies motionless on a table in the
centre of the stage, shrouded by smoke and
eerie music. He narrates a story of a 'Dr
Frankensteen' who cannot be woken from his
trance – 'they tried music' (a ghetto blaster plays
'Louie Louie'), 'they tried sex' (Patti dressed in a
nurse's uniform) but nothing stirs him, until at
last the Big Man brings him his guitar and Bruce
jumps up for 'Highschool Confidential'. They
also perform in the 32-song plus medley set 'I
Fought The Law', 'Trapped' with 'Hungry Heart'
and 'Sherry Darling'. On the 30th, BBC TV's
'Whistle Test' features a 20 minute preview of
the forthcoming one hour 'Born In The U.S.A.'
special.

NOVEMBER

**2/4   LOS ANGELES, CALIFORNIA SPORTS
ARENA**
A 30-song plus medley set is performed on the
2nd. The final night is typical of the second leg of
the tour now that 'Rosalita' is no longer a
standard inclusion. 'Born In The U.S.A.'/'Prove
It All Night'/'Out In The Street'/'Atlantic
City'/'Johnny 99'/'Reason To
Believe'/'Nebraska'/'Johnny Bye
Bye'/'Darlington County'/'Glory Days'/'The
Promised Land'/'Shut Out The Light'/'My
Hometown'/'Badlands'/'Thunder Road' Interval
'Cover Me'/'Dancing In The Dark'/'Cadillac
Ranch'/'No Surrender' (dedicated to Peter
Bogdanovich, producer of *Mask*)/'Because The
Night'/'I'm On Fire'/'Pink Cadillac'/'Bobby
Jean'/'Racing In The Street' Encores
'Jungleland'/'Born To Run'/'Devil With The Blue
Dress' medley/'Twist And Shout' (with 'Sweet
Soul Music' and 'Do You Love Me?')/'Santa
Claus Is Comin' To Town'. The Video for the
'Born In The U.S.A.' single, directed by John
Sayles, is filmed on the 4th.

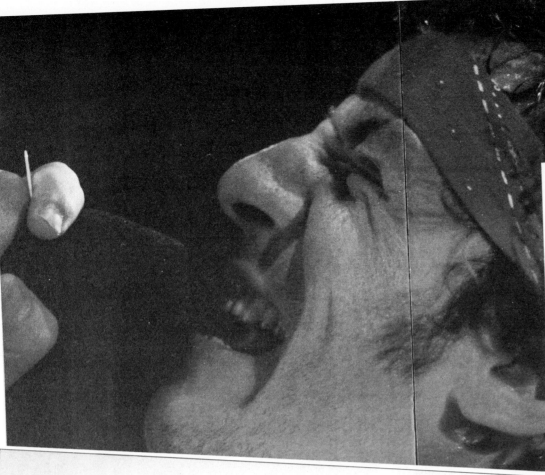

BRUCE SPRINGSTEEN

S EATTLE WAS THE MARKET, BUT TACOMA WAS Bruce Springsteen's kind of town. He and the E Street Band had flown in from Vancouver on the second leg of their *Born in the U.S.A.* tour, and immediately everybody got sick. Something in the air. "The Tacoma aroma," locals call it, a lung-raking stench of noxious lumber-milling fumes and other foul industrial emissions that imparted a green-gilled tinge to most members of the Springsteen tour party and made Bruce himself sick to his stomach. Nevertheless, his first, sold-out show at the 25,000-seat Tacoma Dome went on as scheduled. Bruce is nothing if not a trouper.

He could have played the Kingdome in Seattle, thirty miles away, where the air is clear and the ambiance more upscale. But the smaller Tacoma Dome has better acoustics, and anyway, Springsteen – although he's something of an upscale guy himself these days – maintains a well-known interest in the embattled world of the working class. Tacoma, in its bilious way, was perfect.

He really was sick, though – white as a sheet when he took the stage and wiped out for sure when he left it four hours later. But he never let it show. He kicked off with a booming, boot-stomping "Born in the U.S.A." and then descended into several songs from his starkly brilliant *Nebraska* album, keeping the audience with him all the way. He's got his raps down on this tour, talking about "powerlessness" at one point and, at another, "blind faith – whether it's in your girlfriend or the government." "This is 1984," he tells the howling crowds, "and people seem to be searchin' for something." In Tacoma, before counting off the haunting "My Hometown," he delivered an extended plug for a community-action group called Washington Fair Share, which recently helped force the cleanup of an illegal landfill and is working to overturn Governor

John Spellman's veto of a "right to know" law that would require local industries to inform employees of all toxic chemicals they're being exposed to on the job. "They think that people should come before profit, and the community before the corporation," Bruce announced. And then added, pointedly, "This is your hometown."

This is world-class rock & roll, all right, but something more besides. And in 1984, Bruce Springsteen has become something decidedly more than just another rock star with an album to flog. He is a national presence, his charisma co-opted by as unlikely an adherent as Ronald Reagan – even as Springsteen himself pokes relentlessly through the withered and waterless cultural underbrush of the president's new American Eden. In pursuit of what can only be called his dream, Springsteen has been tenacious: dropping out of Ocean County College in his native New Jersey in 1968 to take his unlikely chances as a songwriting rock & roller and stubbornly waiting out a devastating, yearlong legal dispute with his then manager, Mike Appel, that prevented him from recording for nearly a year in the mid-Seventies. After selling 2 million copies of his 1980 double album, *The River*, he followed it up with *Nebraska*, a striking, guitar-and-voice meditation on various kinds of pain and craziness in the American hinterlands, and then followed *that* up with *Born in the U.S.A.*, which treats some of the same themes within a full-bore band context and has suddenly become his biggest album to date.

As the tour progressed, Springsteen sat down for interviews in Oakland, California – where he plugged the Berkeley Emergency Food Project – and in Los Angeles, where he maintains a house in the Hollywood Hills. Asked how he keeps his tightly structured stage show fresh down to the last mock-rambling anecdote, he said, "It's a matter of: Are you

By Kurt Loder

THE WINNERS

Readers' Poll

Cyndi Lauper: a solo success

Tina: a stunning comeback

Readers say Horn's hot.

Artist of the Year:
BRUCE SPRINGSTEEN
Prince 2961
Cyndi Lauper 2532
Michael Jackson 171
Huey Lewis 153

Male Vocalist:
BRUCE SPRINGSTEEN 2113
Prince 1121
David Bowie 364
Lionel Richie 341
Billy Idol 250

Female Vocalist:
TINA TURNER 1931
Cyndi Lauper 1727
Madonna 1144
Pat Benatar 644
Christine Kerr (Hynde) 553

Band of the Year:
BRUCE SPRINGSTEEN AND THE E STREET BAND
Van Halen 992
ZZ Top 727
The Cars 606
U2 545
Prince 501

Producer:
TREVOR HORN 750
Prince 621
Quincy Jones 477
Bruce Springsteen 318
Ted Templeman 288

Country Artist:
KENNY ROGERS 1234
Willie Nelson 712
Alabama 614
Ricky Skaggs 273
Dolly Parton 242

New Artist:
CYNDI LAUPER 1810
Madonna 1106
Julian Lennon 591
Frankie Goes to
Hollywood 386
Ratt 341

Soul-R&B Artist:
PRINCE 1325
Lionel Richie 1106
Tina Turner 924
Stevie Wonder 348
James Brown and Afrika
Bambaataa 197

Songwriter:
BRUCE SPRINGSTEEN 1863
Prince 1121
Lionel Richie 553
Van Halen 295
Christine Kerr 243

Reggae Artist:
UB40 1499
Eddy Grant 1128
Bob Marley 787
Peter Tosh 326
Jimmy Cliff 159

Jazz Artist:
HERBIE HANCOCK 1030
Wynton Marsalis 954
Pat Metheny 386
Al Jarreau 333
Chuck Mangione 144

Video:
"YOU MIGHT THINK"
– The Cars 946
"Hot for Teacher"
– Van Halen 515
"Legs" – ZZ Top 379
"Blue Jean" – David Bowie 541
"When Doves Cry"
– Prince 288

Radio Station:
WMMS, Cleveland 1447
WDVE, Pittsburgh 598
WBCN, Boston 485
KZEW, Dallas 348
WNEW, New York 250

Album of the Year:
'BORN IN THE U.S.A.'
– Bruce Springsteen 2358
Purple Rain – Prince 1756
1984 – Van Halen 373
Sports – Huey Lewis and the
News 276
Eliminator – ZZ Top 163

Single of the Year:
"DANCING IN THE DARK"
– Bruce Springsteen 923
"When Doves Cry"
– Prince 765
"Jump" – Van Halen 439
"Let's Go Crazy" – Prince 409
"Born in the U.S.A."
– Bruce Springsteen 379

Bruce says thanks.

England's UB40: the year's best reggae band

Critics' Poll

Los Lobos: one of the critics' favorite bands

Artist of the Year:
PRINCE
Bruce Springsteen
Tina Turner

Band of the Year:
LOS LOBOS
BRUCE SPRINGSTEEN AND THE E STREET BAND
(Tie)
Van Halen
R.E.M.
Eight Tied for Fifth Place

New Artist:
LOS LOBOS
The Bangles
Cyndi Lauper
Del Fuegos
The Del-Lords

Male Vocalist:
PRINCE
Bruce Springsteen
Paul Young
Morrissey

Country Artist:
JOHN ANDERSON
Ricky Skaggs
George Strait
Reba McEntire
Five Tied for Fifth Place

Female Vocalist:
TINA TURNER
Cyndi Lauper
Christine Kerr (Hynde)
Madonna

Songwriter:
BRUCE SPRINGSTEEN
Prince
Christine Kerr
Lou Reed
Laurie Anderson

Producer:
TREVOR HORN
Prince
Arthur Baker
Bill Laswell
Two Tied for Fifth Place

Soul-R&B Artist:
PRINCE
Tina Turner
Afrika Bambaataa
James Brown
Run-D.M.C.

Reggae Artist:
UB40
Black Uhuru
Yellowman
Six Tied for Fourth Place

Jazz Artist:
HERBIE HANCOCK BOBBY McFERRIN WYNTON MARSALIS (Tie)
Four Tied for Fourth Place

Video:
"TWO TRIBES"
– Frankie Goes to Hollywood
"Girls Just Want to Have
Fun" – Cyndi Lauper
"Close (To the Edit)" – Art of
Noise
"Jump" – Van Halen
Seven Tied for Fifth Place

Album of the Year:
'BORN IN THE U.S.A.'
– Bruce Springsteen
Purple Rain – Prince
Private Dancer – Tina Turner
How Will the Wolf Survive?
– Los Lobos
Learning to Crawl – The
Pretenders

Prince was hot.

Single of the Year:
"WHAT'S LOVE GOT TO DO WITH IT"
– Tina Turner
"Jump" – Van Halen
"When Doves Cry" – Prince
"Dancing in the Dark"
– Bruce Springsteen
"Pride (In the Name of Love)"
– U2

EDITOR'S NOTE: *The following twenty-three writers took part in this poll: Vince Aletti, Debby Bull, Christopher Connelly, Sally Cragin, David Fricke, Deborah Frost, Mikal Gilmore, Merle Ginsberg, Michael Goldberg, James Henke, Lisa Henricksen, Stephen Holden, Kurt Loder, Kristine McKenna, Joyce Millman, Chris Morris, Robert Palmer, Jon Pareles, Steve Pond, Parke Puterbaugh, Fred Schruers, Don Shewey and Ken Tucker.*

Jazzbo McFerrin

SPRINGSTEEN MINDERS FIGHT AIRPORT 'MOB'

BOSSY!

EXCLUSIVE PICTURE!

THE BOSS MEE...

ROCK 'N' ROLL FEVER THEN 12 HOURS IN BED

THE BOSS!

AND THE FANS GO WILD

King of the rock castle

Thunder Road came to Co Meath at the weekend when Bruce Springsteen, now the most vital force in rock, started his European tour. Phil Shaw reports.

Fans pack showground for Springsteen

BY GRAHAM REILLY

THE MAN WHO PUTS THE ROCK INTO ROLL

When Bruce Springsteen starts his sell-out tour this week, the fans will go wild over the man who's sold 50 million records and is the rockstars' favourite rockstar. Simon Kinnersley reports.

"I've always lived my life night by night"

' The veterans of Vietnam are the nation's forgotten people '

' If the price of fame is that you have to be isolated from the people you write for, that's too high a price to pay '

BOSS'S BRIDE!

EXCLUSIVE PICTURES OF SUPERSTAR BRUCE SPRINGSTEEN'S MODEL

MARATHON MAN . . . Bruce's stage show is one long rave-up

● THE BOSS — International pop superstar Bruce Springsteen—begins his invasion of Europe with a brand new face in his entourage. Her name is Julianne—and she's the new Mrs. Springsteen.
● THE news of their wedding shocked female fans through-out America. But Julianne could be facing a few surprises herself.
● SHE'LL have to get used to sharing her man with his millions of devoted admirers, who can't get enough of the dedicated rock king.

POP STAR SPECIAL

Love at last for Bruce, the King of Rock

From Terry Willows in Los Angeles

THE BOSS has taken a wife. Secretly and suddenly, to give the rock 'n' roll world its hottest gossip for years.

After all, whoever would have believed that Bruce Springsteen could ever get hitched?

The rocker who's a no-holds-barred hero in biker boots, tight faded jeans, and red headband, always vowed he'd never wed.

But at 35, Bruce has finally taken the plunge and married model and actress Julianne Phillips in a secretive midnight ceremony at a lakeside church near Portland, Oregon.

MEET THE BOSS'S WIFE

BEAUTY AND THE BEAT . . . lovely Julianne won the heart of the world's No. 1 rocker and turned him from a loner to a lover

LOVE-STRUCK BOSS TO RUN NO MORE

By MARIANNE GOLDSTEIN

POP STAR SURPRISE WEDDING

★ ROCK IDOL Bruce Springsteen fooled photographers yesterday by getting married in a secret ceremony . . . at midnight

★ The 35 year old bachelor was due to wed beautiful actress Julianne Phillips tomorrow.

★ But after the news leaked out, furious Springsteen brought forward the ceremony in Julianne's home town of Lake Oswego, Oregon.

★ Only close family were present. The bride's brother, William, said: "Everybody feared that Wednesday's wedding would turn into a circus."

Julianne . . . jumped the gun over news

BRIDE FOR 'THE BOSS'

From IVOR KEY in New York

Bride-to-be Julianne: Never far from Bruce's side

BRUCE SAYS MEET MY BRIDE-TO-BE

By SUN REPORTER

Stepping out . . . Bruce and Julianne on a night out together.

Bruce: He's smitten

Picture by BARBARA KINNEY

TODAY Meet the Boss's bride

— First real look at Bruce Springsteen's model wife — Centre Pages

THE BOSS ALL SET TO WED!

HE'LL be wed in the USA . . . Rock star Bruce Springsteen is ready to tie the knot with his long-time girlfriend model Julianne Phillips (right). The pair will wed next week in Oregon. For all the details see Page 7.

THE REAL THING! Julianne and Bruce

ROMANCING IN THE DARK

Bruce weds in midnight hour

By Jeannie Williams and Maggie Martin
USA TODAY

Bruce Springsteen said "I do" loud and clear, and kissed his bride, Julianne Phillips, who wore a borrowed, high-neck lace gown and cried afterward.

And so rock's most eligible bachelor wed in traditional style in Lake Oswego, Ore.

The newlyweds, who met last September, are in seclusion amid reports of a week-end reception in Los Angeles.

"Isn't this wonderful!" Springsteen told Michael C. Phillips, one of the bride's four brothers, after the ceremony at Our Lady of the Lake church in the Portland suburb.

PHILLIPS: She and husband Bruce are in seclusion.

men, along with the singer's manager, Jon Landau.

Springsteen, 35, and actress/model Phillips, 25, each walked down the aisle with their parents — Douglas and Adele Springsteen, and William and Ann Phillips.

The only unorthodox elements of the wedding — Catholic, but with no Mass — were the time, 12:15 a.m. Monday, and the 50 guests' rendezvous in a high school parking lot before driving to the church, where lights were dimmed.

Originally set for Wednesday, the date was changed after a weekend with reporters and fans camped outside the Phillips' home and the church. "It was a beautiful ceremony, but it was a little like a Robert Ludlum spy novel," said Phillips family friend Barbara Block. Said the bride's dad, "We're very proud. They're a wonderful couple."

The bride's attendants were Pam Springsteen, one of Bruce's two sisters; her own sister, Mary Lepschat; and best friend, Ann Stuckey Bickford, whose gown she borrowed. Springsteen wore a navy suit and the couple exchanged gold wedding bands set with diamonds.

● Elusive Bruce, 2D

5 'Born In The U.S.A.'/'Shut Out The Light' is released in the U.S. (COL. 38–04680)

8 **TEMPE, ARIZONA ARIZONA STATE UNIVERSITY**

11/12 **DENVER, COLORADO McNICHOLLS ARENA**

15 **ST LOUIS, MISSOURI ST LOUIS ARENA**

16 **AMES, IOWA STATE UNIVERSITY**
Debut of 'Sugarland'.

18 **LINCOLN, NEBRASKA STATE UNIVERSITY**

19 **KANSAS CITY, MISSOURI KEMPER ARENA**

21 **OKLAHOMA CITY, OKLAHOMA ARENA**

23 **AUSTIN, TEXAS ERWIN SPECIAL EVENTS CENTRE**

25/26 **DALLAS, TEXAS REUNION ARENA**

29/30 **HOUSTON, TEXAS SUMMIT**

DECEMBER
1 **BILOXI, MISSISSIPPI CIVIC CENTRE**

2 **BATON ROUGE, LOUISIANA LOUISIANA STATE UNIVERSITY**

6 **BIRMINGHAM, ALABAMA JEFFERSON CIVIC CENTRE COLISEUM**

7 **TALLAHASSEE, FLORIDA SPORTATORIUM**
Debut of 'Tallahassee Lassie'.

9 **MURFREESBORO, TENNESSEE ARENA**

11 **LEXINGTON, KENTUCKY RUPP ARENA**

13/14 **MEMPHIS, TENNESSEE MID SOUTH COLISEUM**
Little Steven guests on the encores, which included 'Two Hearts', 'Drift Away' and the debut of Chuck Berry's 'Memphis, Tennessee'. A 20 minute interview by Steve Wood is recorded on the 13th for French cable TV 'Les Enfants Du Rock',.which also includes live footage of 'Born In The U.S.A.'.

16/17 **ATLANTA, GEORGIA OMNI ARENA**

1985
JANUARY
4/5 **HAMPTON, VIRGINIA COLISEUM**

7/8 **INDIANAPOLIS, INDIANA MARKET SQUARE ARENA**

10 **LOUISVILLE, KENTUCKY FREEDOM HALL**

13 **COLUMBIA, SOUTH CAROLINA COLISEUM**

15/16 **CHARLOTTE, NORTH CAROLINA COLISEUM**

17 **GREENSBORO, NORTH CAROLINA RHINOCEROS CLUB**
Bruce guests with the Del Fuegos for 'Hang On Sloopy' and 'Stand By Me'.

18/19 **GREENSBORO, NORTH CAROLINA COLISEUM**

23/24 **PROVIDENCE, RHODE ISLAND CIVIC ARENA**

26/27 **SYRACUSE, NEW YORK CARRIER DOME**

28/29 **LOS ANGELES, CALIFORNIA GOLD STAR STUDIOS**
Bruce flies in to LA to take part in the recording sessions of 'We Are The World', the benefit record for the starving millions in Ethiopia. Also in the all-star line up are Bob Dylan, Stevie Wonder, Diana Ross and Michael Jackson.

FEBRUARY
4 'I'm On Fire'/'Johnny Bye Bye' is released in the U.S. (COL. 38–04772).

26 **LOS ANGELES, CALIFORNIA SHRINE AUDITORIUM**
Bruce attends the 27th annual Grammy Awards Ceremony and receives his first ever Grammy for the best male vocalist on 'Dancing In The Dark'.

28 **ROLLING STONE MAGAZINE'S NINTH ANNUAL POLL**

Bruce and the E Street Band scoop an unprecedented nine awards at *Rolling Stone's* annual poll. These include Album of the Year, Single of the Year, Songwriter and Artist of the Year.

MARCH
21, **SYDNEY, AUSTRALIA SYDNEY**
23/24 **ENTERTAINMENTS CENTRE**
27/28 Bruce opens his first ever concerts in Australia with a 28-song plus medley set. On the 22 March Bruce and Nils join Neil Young onstage for a version of 'Down By The River'.

31 **BRISBANE, AUSTRALIA QE2 STADIUM**

APRIL
3/4 **MELBOURNE, AUSTRALIA**
SHOWGROUNDS

10/11 **TOKYO, JAPAN YOYOGI OLYMPIC POOL**
13,
15/16

19 **KYOTO, JAPAN FURITSU-TAIIKUKAN**

21/22 **OSAKA, JAPAN OSAKA-JYO HALL**

MAY
13 Bruce marries model Julianne Phillips in a

secret ceremony at midnight, at Our Lady Of The Lake Catholic church, Lake Oswego, Portland Oregon. The best man and ushers were Little Steven, Jon Landau and Clarence Clemons.

22 'Glory Days'/'Stand On It' released in the U.S. (COL. 38–04924).

JUNE
1 **DUBLIN, EIRE SLANE CASTLE**
Bruce opens his European tour with a 27-song set in front of 65,000 people.

3 'I'm On Fire'/'Born In The U.S.A.' released in the U.K. (CBS A 6342).

BRUCE SPRINGSTEEN

AND THE E STREET BAND

In concert – no support
ST JAMES PARK NEWCASTLE
WEDNESDAY 5TH JUNE
£14.00 inc. VAT
Gates open at 4pm

Do not bring **alcohol**, bottles, cans, or tape recorders. No overnight camping. Ticket holders consent to the filming and sound recording of themselves as members of the audience.

4/5 NEWCASTLE, ENGLAND ST JAMES PARK

8/9 GOTHENBURG, SWEDEN, ULLEVI STADIUM

12/13 ROTTERDAM, HOLLAND DE KUIP
FEYENOORD STADIUM

15 BOCHUM, WEST GERMANY

16 FRANKFURT, WEST GERMANY

18/19 MUNICH, WEST GERMANY

21 MILAN, ITALY

23 MONTPELLIER, FRANCE STADE RICHTER

25 ST ETIENNE, FRANCE STADE GEOFFROY
GUICHARD

29/30 PARIS, FRANCE STADE DE COLOMBES

JULY
3/4 LONDON, ENGLAND WEMBLEY STADIUM
6

7 LEEDS, ENGLAND ROUNDHAY PARK

WEMBLEY STADIUM

Harvey Goldsmith Entertainments
proudly presents

Bruce Springsteen
The E Street Band
3/7/85

THIS PORTION TO
BE GIVEN UP AT
TURNSTILES

C

**BRUCE SPRINGSTEEN
& THE E STREET BAND**

In concert: No support

WED., 3 JULY, 1985
GATES OPEN AT 4.00 p.m.
Concert starts approx. 6 p.m.

No ticket genuine unless it carries the Wembley
Lion superimposed on the Towers.

Price £14.50 incl. VAT

TURNSTILES

C

6049

6049

TO BE GIVEN UP   TO BE RETAINED

ISSUED SUBJECT TO THE
CONDITIONS ON BACK

The new single from "Darkness on The Edge of Town". On Columbia Records and Tapes.

Photo: Eric Meola

Exclusive Selling Agent for
the United States and Canada
WARNER BROS. PUBLICATIONS INC.
75 Rockefeller Plaza • New York, N.Y. 10019

$1.50
in U.S.A.

Cool Rockin' Daddy

(*The Springsteen Songbook*)

Bruce Springsteen is a remarkable composer and lyricist, and has been a prolific songwriter since the earliest days. Amazingly, all of the songs listed here are Springsteen compositions and the list stands as a testimony to the incredible output Springsteen has generated in his career to date.

'Action In The Street'
Debuted and performed throughout the short 1977 tour, no studio version known.

'Adam Raised A Cain'
Released on the *Darkness On The Edge Of Town* LP

1978. Made its live debut at the Shea Theatre, Buffalo, New York on 23 May 1978 and was last performed at the Palladium, New York City, 15 September 1978. It was also used in the 1983 film soundtrack of *Baby, It's You.*

'A Gun In Every Home'
Unreleased out-take from the *Born In The U.S.A.* recording sessions.

'All I Need'
Recorded by Gary U.S. Bonds in 1982 for the *On The Line* LP. Bruce co-produced, played guitar and sang

back-up vocals on all his songs featured on the record.

'A Love So Fine'
Original song, often confused with the Chiffons, single of the same name. Recorded in October 1974 at the 914 Sound Studios, Blauvelt, New York. Performed live from October 1974 to August 1975. Unreleased out-take from *Born To Run*.

'All I Want To Do Is Dance'
One known performance at the Back Door, Richmond, Virginia in February 1972 with the Bruce Springsteen Band.

Band but never released in this form. A black and white video, not featuring Bruce, was premiered on MTV, 22 December 1982. Performed live throughout the 1984–85 tour since its debut at the Civic Centre, St Paul, Minnesota on 29 June 1984.

'Baby I'
Co-written with fellow Castile George Theiss and recorded by the band at the Brickmall Shopping Centre recording studios, Bricktown, New Jersey, 22 May 1966. Unreleased, but the acetate still exists. The song title comes from Bruce's nickname in the Castiles.

'Backstreets'
Released on the *Born To Run* LP in August 1975. One known out-take from these sessions even featured strings in the backing. It has been a constant part of the live shows ever since its debut at the Civic Theatre, Akron, Ohio, on 8 August 1975. Also released as the B side of the obscure Japanese 'Born To Run' single and in fragment form on the *Pitman Family Of Music* compilation LP given to employees of CBS in 1980.

'Badlands'
Released on *Darkness On The Edge Of Town* in 1978 and as a single in most parts of the world. Made its live debut on the opening night of the 1978 tour and has remained a constant part of every tour since. Also released on the promotion only LP *As Requested Around The World*.

'Ballad Of The Self Loading Pistol'

Known only from a Laurel Canyon music lyric sheet, *circa* 1973.

'The Band's Just Boppin' The Blues'
Performed in concert with the Bruce Springsteen Band from late 1971 to 1972. It later evolved into 'Secret To The Blues', performed in 1973.

'Because The Night'
Top-five hit for Patti Smith who, after hearing Bruce's first take, co-wrote it with Bruce to suit her style. Originally recorded at the Atlantic Studios, New York City, between July and November 1977. A further three studio versions were recorded by Bruce at the Record Plant, New York City, for the *Darkness On The Edge Of Town* LP and again in 1979–80 for *The River*, but were never released. Since its debut with the E Street Band at the Music Hall, Boston, Massachusetts, on 30 May 1978, it has been performed at frequent intervals on all the tours. The song has also been recorded by Starsound and performed live by Marianne Faithfull.

'Be True'
Released in February 1981 as the B side of 'Fade Away' in the U.S. and 'Sherry Darling' in the U.K. and the rest of Europe. It wasn't until 26 August 1984 that it made its live debut at the Capital Centre, Largo, Maryland. Also issued on the U.S. promotion only 12" (AS 928). One studio out-take known.

'The Big Payback'
Unreleased in the U.S. It was the B side of the European single 'Open All Night'. Recorded at the same time as the *Nebraska* album.

'All Night Long (Breakout)'
Darkness On The Edge Of Town out-take that was to evolve into two different songs, 'Prove It All Night' and 'Badlands'. Unreleased.

'American Tune'
Steel Mill song known from press review of a gig at the Matrix, San Francisco, California, in January 1970. The song is described as a 'political-military observation' of the U.S.A.

'(Fucked Up) Amplifier Blues'
A slow blues 'protest' song from Bruce's Steel Mill days, *circa* 1969.

'Angelyne'
Recorded by Gary U.S. Bonds on the *On The Line* LP, released in 1982. As with a lot of the songs for this album, it sounds as though it was written especially for Gary.

'The Angel'
Recorded for the John Hammond demo tape, 3 May 1972. This dirge was once described by Bruce as his most sophisticated song. Released on *Greetings From Asbury Park N.J.* in 1973 with session man Richard Davis featured on bass, it was also the B side of the first U.S. single. Never performed live.

'Arabian Nights'
Recorded on 3 May 1972 for the John Hammond demo tape and also for the music publishing demo tape of original songs sent out for other artistes to hear and consider recording.

'Atlantic City'
Released on the *Nebraska* LP. As with all the songs on the album, it was recorded at Bruce's rented home in Holmdel, New Jersey, between the 3rd and 4th of January 1982. It was later re-recorded with the E Street

120

'Bishop Dance'
Performed live as one of the opening numbers of Bruce's shows from late 1972 to 1973. Bruce's very first radio broadcast for King Biscuit Flour Hour on 30 August 1972 featured a live version of this song from Max's Kansas City, New York City.

'Black Sun A Rising'
Steel Mill song *circa* 1970.

'Black Widow Spider (Mary Louise Watson)'
Bruce first performed this song with Steel Mill. He later included it in concerts with the Bruce Springsteen Band in 1971. It has a driving beat similar to 'She's The One'.

'Blinded By The Light'
Released on *Greetings From Asbury Park N.J.* in 1973. It was the first single release in the U.S. A rare Spanish single (CBS 5121) formed the only European single from the debut LP. More recently it was issued on the promotion only *The Last American Hero* and *Bruce Springsteen Sampler* LPs and the European cassette only releases *Storia E Musica* and *Showcase*. Bruce performed it live from 1973 to 1976. It was recorded by Allan Clarke, and Manfred Mann's Earth Band who had a U.S. number one with it in 1976. It has also been recorded by James Last.

'Bobby Jean'
Released on *Born In the U.S.A* in 1984. Preceded on the album by 'No Surrender', they are both thought to be Bruce's way of tribute to ex-E Street Band member and close friend Steven Van Zandt. Debuted live at the Civic Centre, St Paul, Minnesota, 29 June 1984.

'Born In The U.S.A.'
Title track of Bruce's seventh album, also released as a single and on 12" with 3 mixes by Arthur Baker. A promotion video was made by John Sayles, filmed in the Los Angeles Sports Arena, California, 4 November 1984. It was also issued on the promotion only 12" discs COL. AS 1957 and COL. AS 1959. Debuted live at the Stone Pony, Asbury Park, New Jersey, 8 June 1984.

'Born To Run'
Initally sent out in tape form to certain U.S. disc jockeys in October 1974 to test its chart potential, it was released in August 1975 as the title track of Bruce's third album. It was also released as a single worldwide and on numerous promotion only releases including *The Heavyweights, The Front Runners, Il Ciocco, As Requested Around The World* and *The Last American Hero*. It made its live debut at the Harvard Square Theatre, Cambridge, Massachusetts on 9 May 1974 and has been a constant part of Bruce's stage show since February 1975. Recorded by Allan Clarke, the MBAs, Joe Piscopo and Frankie Goes To Hollywood.

'Bottle Of Red Wine'
Performed with the Bruce Springsteen Band in 1971, and possibly co-written with others. Vini Lopez took lead vocals.

'Cadillac Ranch'
Released on *The River* in 1980 and as a single in the U.K. and South Africa. Also issued on the promotion only LPs *As Requested Around The World* and *Bruce Springsteen Sampler*. Debuted live at the Crisler

Arena, Ann Arbor, Michigan on 3 October 1980 and has since become a regular part of the opening of the second half of the 1980–81 and 1984–85 tours. It has been performed live by both Warren Zevon and Gary U.S. Bonds.

'Candy's Boy'
Medium paced out-take recorded for *Darkness On The Edge Of Town*. Unreleased.

'Candy's Room'
Released on *Darkness On The Edge Of Town* in 1978 and also on the promotion only *Bruce Springsteen Sampler*, It also appears as the B side of 'Badlands' on a rare Dutch pressing (CBS 6678). Performed constantly throughout the 1978, 1980–81 tours and occasionally in 1984–85.

'Change It (Revolution)'
Steel Mill song, with slightly optimistic lyric and drug references, *circa* 1971.

'Chasing A Chevrolet'
Rumoured out-take from the *Born In The U.S.A.* recording sessions.

'Cindy'
Out-take from *The River* sessions, at the Power Station, New York City, 1979–80. A medium paced song about an unrequited love. Unreleased.

'Circus Song'
Released on the promotion only Playback series (AS 52). Recorded at the Ahmanson Theatre, Los Angeles, California on 1 May 1973, during the CBS convention 'Week of Music'. It is, so far, the only original Bruce Springsteen song to be issued from a live concert. The song was also recorded for the music publishing demo tape in 1972. It later evolved into 'Wild Billy's Circus Story'.

'City At Night'
Slow scenario sung by Bruce in a tired, late night/early morning style of voice that perfectly suited the lyric. You can almost feel the rain on the taxi cab windscreen that Bruce narrates the song from. Unreleased *Darkness On The Edge Of Town* out-take.

'Club Soul City'
Recorded by Gary U.S. Bonds for the 1982 release *On The Line*.

'Come On'
Steel Mill song with a heavy Kinks style guitar riff, *circa* 1970.

'Coming Home'
Uncertain title for a song performed with the Bruce Springsteen Band *circa* 1971.

'Cover Me'
Released on *Born In the U.S.A.* and as a single in most parts of the world (along with the 12″ remixes by Arthur Baker). Made its live debut at the Civic Centre, St. Paul, Minnesota on 2 July 1984.

'Cowboys Of The Sea'
Performed live with the Bruce Springsteen Band in 1972. It was recorded for the John Hammond demo tape at Columbia Studios in New York City on 3 May 1972, and again for the music publishing demo tape.

'Crown Liquor'
Known only from a press report, from around the time of Child and Steel Mill. Possibly it was not an original song.

'Crush On You'
Released on *The River* in 1980. An infrequent part of the live show, it was last performed at the Gardens, Boston, Massachusetts on 16 December 1980. One studio out-take is known.

'Daddy Sing Me A Cradle Song'
Better than the title suggests, this Steel Mill song from 1970 concerns a girlfriend/groupie remembered for her repeated requests for a favourite song.

'Dance Dance Dance'
Bruce Springsteen Band tune *circa* 1971.

'Dance On Little Angel'
Performed live in late 1972 and early 1973. Some of the lyrics were later used in '4th Of July, Asbury Park (Sandy)'.

'Dancing In The Dark'
Released on the *Born In The U.S.A.* LP and the U.S. promotion only 12″ (COL. AS 1862) this song has been Bruce's biggest selling single both in the U.S. and U.K. A promotion video, directed by Brian De Palma was shot at the Civic Centre, St. Paul, Minnesota on 28/29 June 1984 and premiered on MTV 25 July 1984. It was remixed by Arthur Baker for 12″ release. It made its live debut at the Xanadu Club, Asbury Park, New Jersey on 26 May 1984. Recently recorded by U.S. group Big Daddy, with some success.

'Darkness Darkness'
Instrumental performed with the Bruce Springsteen Band, *circa* 1971. Bruce played numerous instrumentals during his time with Child, Steel Mill and the Bruce Springsteen Band but this one seems to have been the more favoured; it's a little like Booker T and the M.G.'s 'Green Onions' played at 78 rpm!

'Darkness On The Edge Of Town'
Title song of Bruce's fourth album. Debuted live at the Shea Theatre, Buffalo, New York on 23 May 1978 and a regular part of the live shows ever since. One studio out-take is known, a slightly more up-tempo version.

'Darlington County'
Released on *Born In The U.S.A.* in 1984. The song really comes alive in concert where it usually precedes 'Glory Days' and the two songs form a common bond if only for their contradictory points of view. Debuted live at the Stone Pony, Asbury Park, New Jersey on 8 June 1984.

'Do It With A Feeling'
Heavy metal Steel Mill dirge that takes a long time to say very little, *circa* 1970.

'Don't Back Down'
A short one minute demo version is known, possibly recorded at Bruce's New Jersey home in 1982. The demo is likely to have evolved into the later release 'I'm Goin' Down' in 1984.

'Don't Look Back'
Included on the first acetate copies of *Darkness On The Edge Of Town* (take number 3, recorded 1 March 1978) but left off the final release. It is an earthy rocker with strong lyrics that would not have looked out of place on the album. Performed live on the last half of the 1977 tour.

'Fade Away'
Released on *The River* LP in 1980 and as a single in most parts of the world (except Europe), and also issued on the promotion only 12″ (AS 928). It made its live debut at the Sports Arena, Los Angeles, California on 1 November 1980, but has made few appearances since.

'The Fever'
Unreleased Laurel Canyon Music publishing demo, recorded in 1973 at the 914 Sound Studios, Blauvelt, New York with Danny, Garry, Clarence and Vini Lopez. The first known live performance was at the Liberty Hall, Houston, Texas on 11 March 1974, but the song remained out of the live shows from mid-1974 until its surprise resurrection at the Spectrum in Philadelphia, Pennsylvania on 18 August 1978. Several other performances followed throughout 1978 up until its last airing at the Richfield Coliseum, Cleveland, Ohio on 1 January 1979. Recorded by Dean Ford, Alan Rich, Southside Johnny and the Asbury Jukes and the Pointer Sisters.

'Fire'
Outstanding in live performance with Bruce and Clarence hamming it up onstage. Never released on record by Bruce, although he did play piano on the Robert Gordon release. Studio out-takes known from the *Darkness On The Edge Of Town* sessions, possibly re-recorded and considered for *The River* in 1980. Also recorded by Shakin' Stevens, Starsound and the Pointer Sisters (who had a U.S. number two hit with it in 1978). Live versions have been performed by Cher, Ronnie Milsap, Robin Williams and Clarence Clemons and The Red Bank Rockers. Bruce originally wrote the song for Elvis Presley to whom he sent a demo copy only weeks before his untimely death on 16 August 1977.

'Follow That Dream'
Performed on the 1984–85 tour. Bruce wrote new lyrics

'Don't Lose Heart'
Written for Stevie Nicks and recorded by her for release on her 1985 LP.

'Don't Say No'
Echoey rocker with a Duane Eddy style guitar twang throughout this *Darkness On The Edge Of Town* out-take.

'Don't You Want To Be An Outlaw?'
Performed live with the Bruce Springsteen Band, *circa* 1971.

'Downbound Train'
Released on the *Born In The U.S.A.* album in 1984. It made its live debut at the Civic Centre, St. Paul, Minnesota on 2 July 1984 and has been played at infrequent intervals throughout the 1984–85 tour.

'Down By The River'
Unreleased out-take from *The River* sessions. A busy rocker with a nice sax solo by Clarence comes to an abrupt end when Bruce shouts out 'This song should be one verse'.

'Down To Mexico'
Good Bruce Springsteen Band tune with sparse lyric, consisting mainly of the title being repeated over a great David Sancious organ riff.

'Drive All Night'
Originally recorded for *Darkness On The Edge Of Town* in 1978, it was released on *The River* in 1980. One

superb out-take known. Debuted live at the Kiel Opera House, St. Louis, Missouri on 18 October 1980, it made its final appearance at the National Exhibition Centre in Birmingham, England on 7 June 1981. This was also the only European performance of the song.

'Endless Night'
Superb out-take from *The River* LP. Lyrically it picks up from where 'Candy's Room' leaves off . . . "The other day, you had the look of a modern girl" pleads Bruce to his young lady of the night. Great jangling guitar break, the song would have been a natural for Southside Johnny to cover.

'The E Street Shuffle'
Released on Bruce's second album in 1973. On stage it was introduced with a rap about meeting 'The Big Man', but sadly the last performance of this song was back in December 1975. Also released as the B side of a rare German single (CBS 3512), the song has been performed live and recorded by Bette Midler.

'Factory'
The last of the *Darkness On The Edge Of Town* LP songs to be performed in concert, at the Nashville Auditorium in Tennessee on 21 July 1978. Bruce consistently used it on the 1980–81 tour, usually with a tense narrative about his father preceding the song. One known out-take from the Record Plant, New York City, featured a violin mixed to the fore. Recorded by the Arizona Smoke Revue and the Flying Pickets, both covers are in acappela versions. The song has been performed live by Eric Burdon.

CANDY'S ROOM
No.3 Summer/Autumn 1981

INCLUDES FREE POSTER (LIMITED EDITION)

LATEST US NEWS ASBURY PARK VISIT

SPECIAL TOUR EDITION

PIC BY G.NAGLE

and added an arrangement that left little, if any, of the Elvis Presley song of the same name that he'd covered in 1981.

'For You'
Released on *Greetings From Asbury Park N.J.* It was Bruce's talking-pace live versions in 1974–75 that really made the song stand out. Also recorded by Greg Kihn, Duesenberg, Manfred Mann's Earth Band and a Swedish version ('Till Dei') by Janne Anderson.

'4th Of July, Asbury Park (Sandy)'
Released on Bruce's second LP in 1973; a firm favourite with fans both on record and in concert. First known performance about July 1973 (when David Sancious joined the band) and a regular inclusion on every tour up until the 1984–85 shows. Also released on the Dutch *Rockwork* LP in an edited form and a rare German single (CBS 3512). Recorded by the Hollies and Swedish singer Ulf Lundell in an adapted version called 'Sanna'.

'Frankie'
First known live version dates from April 1976, but has not been performed live since. Originally recorded for the *Darkness On The Edge Of Town* sessions and then again in 1983–84 for the *Born In The U.S.A.* LP, but has never been released.

'From Small Things, Big Things One Day Come'
Bruce played the song acoustically to Dave Edmunds backstage at Wembley Arena in June 1981. Dave Edmunds liked it and was duly sent a demo tape by Bruce. Dave Edmunds recorded it for the *D.E.7th* LP in 1982. Bruce has often performed the song around the bar joints of New Jersey during 1982 and 1983. Bruce's demo version was played twice (in part) on U.K. radio in 1981.

'Garden State Parkway Blues'
A Steel Mill song concerning a lousy job and lack of money.

'Glory Days'
Released on the *Born In The U.S.A* LP in 1984. Live in concert the song is one of the highlights, with an introduction rap about Bruce's early teens. Debuted live at the Stone Pony, Asbury Park, New Jersey on 8 June 1984. One known out-take featured an extra verse.

'Goin' Back To Georgia'
An obvious favourite of Steel Mill fans, and one of Bruce's best performances from that era, with powerful vocals and a strong arrangement. Recorded at Bill Graham's Fillmore Records Studios in San Francisco, California in February 1970 but never released.

'Growin' Up'
First recorded for the John Hammond demo in May 1972; released on the first LP in 1973. Live versions really came to life in 1978 and again in 1984 with the inclusion of various fantasy introductions. Also recorded by Alvin Stardust, Heroes and Any Trouble. David Bowie is believed to have recorded a version that has yet to surface.

'Hearts Of Stone'
Recorded for the *Darkness On The Edge Of Town* LP, this superb song was given to Southside Johnny for his 1978 album of the same name. Also recorded by Helen Schneider in 1981.

'Held Up Without A Gun'
Released as the B side of 'Hungry Heart' in most parts of the world in 1980. Performed live just once, at the Nassau Coliseum on 31 December 1980. Originally scheduled (and included as such on CBS press releases) for inclusion on *The River*.

'Henry Boy'
A strange song that in some ways mirrors 'Growin' Up', but told in the third person rather than the first. Recorded for the music publishing demo tape in 1972.

'He's Guilty (Send That Boy To Jail)'
A Steel Mill song that was a regular part of their live show. Recorded at Bill Graham's Fillmore Records Studios in San Francisco, California, February 1970.

'Here She Comes'
Used as an introduction to 'I Wanna Marry You' in concert.

'Hey Santa Ana'
Written in 1973 and recorded for *The Wild, The Innocent And The E Street Shuffle* LP, but never released. Sometimes mistakenly referred to as 'Contessa', it contains some classic lines and paints a vivid scenario. Performed live during 1973.

'Highway Patrolman'
Released on the *Nebraska* LP in 1982. A tale of two brothers, and how their love is tried and tested by their being on opposite sides of the law. Debuted live at the Civic Centre, St Paul, Minnesota on 29 June 1984. Also recorded by Johnny Cash.

'Hold On (To What You Got)'
Written for the Gary U.S. Bonds album *On The Line*. As with the other six songs Bruce wrote for the album, he is featured on guitar and back-up vocals.

'Hungry Heart'
Released on *The River* in 1980. It became Bruce's first top five single in the U.S, and reached number 44 in the U.K. Also issued on the promotion only *Rocktagon, As Requested Around The World* and *Hitline '80*. First performed live at the Kiel Opera House, St Louis, Missouri on 18 October 1980. A brief segment of the song appears in the film *Risky Business*. Instrumental version recorded by Andy Hamilton. Performed live by Darlene Love.

'I Am A Doctor'
This country-sounding Steel Mill song from 1970 has a slightly pretentious lyric, but all the same, it shows the diversity and promise that the band were capable of.

'I Can't Take It'
Steel Mill song about 1971.

'The Iceman'
Traumatic song with a slow eerie piano/bass introduction that builds into one of the most taut and compelling performances by Bruce, both lyrically and vocally. Recorded for the *Darkness On The Edge Of Town* LP but never released.

'If I Was The Priest'
Played at the initial John Hammond audition on 2 May 1972, it was recorded for the demo tape the next day. A further version was recorded for the music publisher's demo tape which was heard and recorded by Allan Clarke in 1973 (the first cover version).

'I Get Mad'
Bridged into the middle break of 'She's The One' on a few occasions in November and December 1978. Influenced by Bo Diddley's 'Say Man'.

'I Hear A Train'
Inspired by no *one* song in particular, Bruce's lyric is based around classic train songs like 'Mystery Train', 'Lonesome Train' and Muddy Waters' 'Two Trains Running'. All are similar, but none quite the same. The song is usually followed in the 'Devil With The Blue Dress' medley with Bruce rocking through his interpretation of Chuck Berry's 'All Aboard', reeling through a list of the towns he'd played and culminating with that night's venue.

'I Just Can't Change'
Steel Mill ballad with a typical boy/girl lyric, about 1970.

'I'm A Rocker'
Released on *The River* LP in 1980. Strong organ riff and beat make it a popular choice for the live shows, but lyrically it is not one of Bruce's strongest songs.

'I'm Going Back'
Frantic rocker recorded for *The River* sessions. A wailing sax underpins a driving beat with a really wicked vocal and harmonica fade-out by Bruce. Unreleased.

'I'm Goin' Down'
Released on the *Born In the U.S.A.* LP in 1984. Made a long-awaited debut at the Byrne Meadowlands Arena, East Rutherford, New Jersey on 17 August 1984. Bruce introduced the song with a rap about a boy/girl relationship that takes itself for granted.

'I'm On Fire'
Released on the *Born In The U.S.A.* LP in 1984. Debuted in concert at the Civic Centre, St. Paul, Minnesota on 29 June 1984, and performed at frequent intervals throughout the 1984–85 tour.

'Incident On 57th Street'

Released on Bruce's second album in 1973. Made its live debut at the Main Point, Bryn Mawr, Pennslyvania on 18 September 1974. The line-up included new E Street Band members Roy Bittan, Max Weinberg and Suki Lahav (whose violin playing added a dimension to the song that has never been equalled). Last performed at the Nassau Coliseum, Uniondale, New York on 29 December 1980.

'Independence Day'

Originally recorded for the *Darkness On The Edge Of Town* LP in 1978, Bruce called it the flip side to 'Adam Raised A Cain', but it didn't make the final selection. Debuted live at the Roxy, Los Angeles, California in July 1978 and performed frequently throughout that year. Released on *The River* in 1980 and played on all but a handful of dates on the 1980–81 world tour. In 1984–85 it made rare but effective appearances.

'I Remember'

Brooding Steel Mill song about a broken love affair, about 1970–71.

'It's Hard To Be A Saint In The City'

First song Bruce sang at the audition with John Hammond on 2 May 1972. It was recorded the next day for the Columbia/John Hammond demo tape. Released on the *Greetings From Asbury Park N.J.* LP in 1973. Performed in concert from 1973 up until 1981. David Bowie is believed to have recorded an (as yet) unreleased version.

'I Wanna Be Where The Bands Are'

Upbeat out-take from *The River* recording sessions. As the title suggests, it's a joyous celebration of a song, with the E Street Band at full tilt.

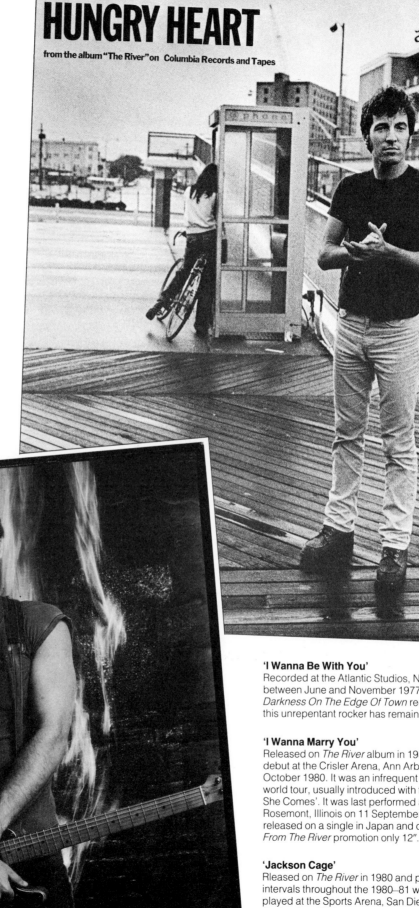

'I Wanna Be With You'

Recorded at the Atlantic Studios, New York City, between June and November 1977 for the initial *Darkness On The Edge Of Town* recording sessions, this unrepentant rocker has remained unreleased.

'I Wanna Marry You'

Released on *The River* album in 1980, it made its live debut at the Crisler Arena, Ann Arbour, Michigan on 3 October 1980. It was an infrequent part of the 1980–81 world tour, usually introduced with the song/rap 'Here She Comes'. It was last performed at the Horizon, Rosemont, Illinois on 11 September 1981. Also released on a single in Japan and on the *Killer Tracks From The River* promotion only 12″.

'Jackson Cage'

Rleased on *The River* in 1980 and played at infrequent intervals throughout the 1980–81 world tour. It was last played at the Sports Arena, San Diego, California on 2 September 1981.

'Jambalaya (It's All Over)'
Bruce performed this song with the Bruce Springsteen Band (and possibly before that, with Dr Zoom and the Sonic Boom). Despite the obvious Hank Williams title similarity, this was a full blooded show stopper of a song, with the girl back-up singers featured to the fore.

'Janey Needs A Shooter'
Bruce's original version of this song, recorded for *Darkness On The Edge Of Town* in 1978, is totally different to the Warren Zevon collaboration 'Jeannie Needs A Shooter'. Bruce's version has a power chord back beat and fiery vocal that even Steel Mill would have been proud of. Originally written in 1973.

'Jazz Musician'
Recorded in two takes for the John Hammond demo tape, 3 May 1972. The song, about the seamy side of a struggling musician's life in New York City, contains a couple of lines that turned up in 'Tenth Avenue Freeze-Out'.

'Jeannie, I Want To Thank You'
Steel Mill song, *circa* 1969–70.

'Jeannie Needs A Shooter'
Co-written with Warren Zevon, the song came about after Warren, intrigued by the title of the original, asked if he could record it. Bruce told him to put his own words to it, and Warren brought back the new lyric and together they finished up with the version released on the *Bad Luck Streak In A Dancing School* LP in 1980.

'Johnny Bye Bye'
Sad song concerning the effect of Elvis Presley's death that owes more than a passing debt to a Chuck Berry original, 'Bye Bye Johnny' (with the first two lines of the song being identical). Bruce obviously likes those two lines, as they had earlier been used in the song 'Lets Go Tonight'. Debuted live at the Apollo Theatre, Manchester, England, on 13 May 1981. In 1984–85 Bruce altered the lyric and tempo of the song for live shows.

'Johnny 99'
Released on the *Nebraska* LP in 1982. Debuted live at the Civic Centre, St Paul, Minnesota on 29 June 1984. Recorded by Johnny Cash as the title song of his 1983 LP.

'Jungleland'
Released on the *Born To Run* LP in 1975. Originally performed live as far back as July 1974, when it had an altogether more jazzy feel and unpolished lyric. Also released on the promotion only *Last American Hero* and the *Storia E Musica*. Bruce worked long and hard to get the end result; Suki Lahav was used for backing vocals but left off the final mix, although it was her (uncredited) violin playing that underpinned the whole song. Performed live by Billy Joel.

'Key To The Highway'
Bruce Springsteen Band number from 1971.

'Kitty's Back'
Written in January 1973 and released on Bruce's second LP. It owed much to the fine organ solo by David Sancious. Live performances showcased the E Street Band's versatility, stretching the song out to unbound limits, up until its last performance at the Capitol Theatre, Passaic, New Jersey on 21 September 1978. One instrumental studio out-take known.

'Last Night In Tulsa'
Bruce Springsteen Band song about a final night in

prison, longing to get home to see his girl. A medium-paced blues about 1971.

'Lets Go Tonight'
Darkness On The Edge Of Town out-take, recorded at the Record Plant, New York City between November 1977 and May 1978. The song later evolved into 'Johnny Bye Bye'.

'Like A Stranger'
Complex lyric concerning a girlfriend who knows him too well and Bruce wishing he could become a little more unpredictable. A medium-paced Bruce Springsteen Band song that, like a lot of the 1971 material, picks up for a long, hard finale.

'Linda Let Me Be The One'
Recorded for the *Born To Run* sessions at New York's Record Plant studios between October 1974 and August 1975. Unreleased.

'Little Girl So Fine'
Co-written with Steve Van Zandt for Southside Johnny and released on the *This Time It's For Real* LP in 1977.

'Livin' Rock'n'Roll'
Performed with the Bruce Springsteen Band about 1971.

'Look To The River'
Lyrically strong ballad from the Steel Mill era, about 1970.

'Loose End'
Unreleased out-take from *The River* recording sessions at the Power Station, New York City, from May 1979 to October 1980. Good lyric concerning the breakup of a relationship, with jangling guitar backing and sax solo.

'Lost In The Flood'
Released on Bruce's debut LP *Greetings From Asbury Park N.J.* in 1973. A fairly regular inclusion in the live shows up until the end of 1975, it made a rare (and final) appearance at the Masonic Temple Auditorium, Detroit, Michigan on 1 September 1978.

'Love Is A Crazy Thing'
Bruce Springsteen Band ballad with a fast chorus, extolling the virtues of a girlfriend about 1972.

'Love On The Wrong Side Of Town'
Co-written with Steve Van Zandt for the second Southside Johnny and the Asbury Jukes LP *This Time It's For Real*, 1977.

'Love's On The Line'
Strongest song on the Gary U.S. Bonds album *On The Line*, released in 1982. No studio or live performance by Bruce is known.

'Magic Kind Of Loving'
Short, sharp Bruce Springsteen Band song from 1972 with great Keith Richards – style guitar.

'Make Up Your Mind'
Medium-paced Bruce Springsteen Band song about a

two-timing girlfriend, about 1971–72.

'Man At The Top'
Debuted live at the Music Theatre, Alpine Valley, East Troy, Wisconsin on 12 July 1984, where Bruce introduced it as a song for election year. Possibly recorded for the *Born In The U.S.A.* LP but, as yet, unreleased.

'Mansion On The Hill'
Released on the *Nebraska* LP in 1982, and also as the B side of 'Atlantic City' in most parts of the world. Debuted live at the Civic Centre, St Paul, Minnesota on 29 June 1984.

'Marie'
Recorded for the music publishing demo tape in 1972. The strange, uneven lyrics are possibly the reason no one took a chance on recording it.

'Mary Lou'
Unreleased out-take from *The River* LP, the lyrics were to evolve into the later released song 'Be True'.

'Mary, Queen Of Arkansas'
First recorded in two takes for the John Hammond demo tape. A similar version, featuring Bruce on vocals, guitar and muted harmonica, was released on *Greetings From Asbury Park N.J.* in 1973. Performed live from 1972 to early 1974.

'Meeting Across The River'
Recorded in a couple of takes and released on the *Born To Run* LP in 1975. Making its live debut at the Uptown Theatre, Milwaukee in October 1975, it put in a few rare appearances on the 1978 tour and was last played at the Richfield Coliseum, Cleveland, Ohio on 1 January 1979.

'Mistress Annie'
Performed by the Bruce Springsteen Band in 1971.

'Murder Incorporated'
Scorching rocker that almost made it onto the *Born In The U.S.A* LP. Bruce expounds that from hometown homicides to worldwide terrorism 'Everywhere you look it's just Murder Incorporated'.

'My Baby's Natural Magic'
Bruce Springsteen Band song from 1971 strongly influenced by Smokey Robinson's 'Tracks Of My Tears'.

'My Home Town'
Released on the *Born In The U.S.A.* LP in 1984. Debuted live at the Stone Pony, Asbury Park, New Jersey on 8 June 1984 and performed constantly throughout the 1984–85 tour.

'My Love Won't Let You Down'
Out-take from the *Born In The U.S.A.* recording sessions, a gritty rocker as yet unreleased.

'Nebraska'
Title track of Bruce's sixth album, inspired by Malik's film *Badlands*. Debuted live at the Civic Centre, St Paul, Minnesota on 1 July 1984.

'New York City Serenade'
Bruce's longest song, released on the second LP in 1973. One of the highlights of live shows from 1973 to its last performance at the Allen Theatre, Cleveland, Ohio, on 10 August 1975. Also issued on the promotion only *Last American Hero, From Asbury Park N.J.*

'New York City Song'
Evolved from the 1972 song 'Vibes Man' and performed live up until the summer of 1973, by which time it had evolved into the more stylish 'New York City Serenade'.

'Nothing Can Stop Me Now'
Furious-paced Bruce Springsteen Band song that featured inspired backing vocals by Francine Daniels and Delores Holmes. A Van Morrison influence prevails throughout this soul-type number. Possibly played by the preceding band, Dr Zoom and the Sonic Boom.

'No Need'
Traumatic love song, recorded in 1972 for the music publishing demo.

'No Surrender'
Dedicated in a live performance to ex-E Street Band member Little Steven, where it was slowed down to become an emotional ballad. Released on the *Born In The U.S.A.* LP in 1984.

'Night'
Released on the *Born To Run* LP in 1975. From its first known live performance at the Bottom Line, New York City on 14 August 1975 it became a regular part of the live act, opening most of the 1976 and 1977 shows, and has made the occasional appearance on every tour since.

'Oh Mama Why'
Steel Mill song featuring a shared vocal with Steve Van Zandt, about 1971.

'On The Boulevard'
Known from a soundcheck at the Spectrum, Philadelphia, Pennsylvania on 17 September 1984.

'On The Prowl'
Frantic rocker with a self mocking humorous lyric, debuted at the Stone Pony, Asbury Park, New Jersey on 8 August 1982, when it was mixed into the middle break of 'Lucille'. A complete version (again performed with Cats On A Smooth Surface) was played at the Stone Pony on 3 October 1982. So far unreleased.

'Open All Night'
Debuted (in part) at Madison Square Garden, New York on 28 November 1980. The song was finally released on *Nebraska* in 1982 and also as a single in most parts of the world. A full version of the song was performed with Cats On A Smooth Surface at the Stone Pony on 3 October 1982.

'Out In The Street'
This song was released on *The River* LP in 1980, but it is in concert where it works best. Perfomed constantly throughout the 1980–81 world tour and then during the 1984–85 tour but with Patti Scialfa featured on the chorus to outstanding effect.

'Out Of Work'
Written for the Gary U.S. Bonds 1982 album *On The Line*. Full credit to Gary's performance in taking this rather bland lyric to number 21 in the U.S. singles chart, July 1982.

'Outside Lookin' In'
Unreleased angry rocker from the *Darkness On The Edge Of Town* recording sessions at the Atlantic Studios in New York City between June and November 1977. Lyrically it could well be about Bruce's legal wrangle with ex-manager Mike Appel.

'Over The Hills Of St Croix'
One known performance at Binghampton, New York on 12 June 1973. The same tune and part of the lyric, evolved into the better known 'Zero And Blind Terry' later that same year.

'Paradise By The Sea'
This instrumental opened the second half of Bruce's concerts from May to mid-September, 1978. A live version from Berkeley, California on 1 July 1978, was sent out in tape form to selected radio stations. The same take was originally scheduled for release as a promotion only 12″ (AS 480) but never issued. The tune was originally used in the melody of the song 'A Love So Fine'.

'Pink Cadillac'
Originally recorded for the *Nebraska* LP, it made a remarkable transformation into a near rockabilly tune for release as the B side of 'Dancing In The Dark' in May 1984. Also released on the promotion only 12″ (AS 1957). Debuted live at the Civic Centre, St Paul, Minnesota on 1 July 1984, and performed frequently throughout the 1984–85 tour, usually with a rap about Adam and Eve preceding the song.

'Point Blank'
Debuted live at the Roxy, Los Angeles, California on 7 July 1978, and finally released on *The River* in 1980. The 1978 live versions had an even more personal lyric (built around a girl friend's drug addiction) that was sheer desolation. Performed frequently throughout the 1980–81 world tour and occasionally in 1984–85.

'The Preacher's Daughter'
Recorded for the *Darkness On The Edge Of Town* LP, it was debuted live (in part) at the Summit, Houston, Texas on 8 December 1978 when Bruce segued the 'Go Billy Go' verse into 'Mona' and 'She's The One'. As yet, this excellent song remains unreleased.

'The Price You Pay'
Released on *The River* in 1980. This song has seldom been performed live, a notable exception being at a concert at the Sports Arena, Los Angeles, California on 1 November 1980 when, for the first time, Bruce changed the lyrics to a recorded song, altering the middle verse. It was last performed at the Conference Centre, Brighton, England on 27 May 1981. Also recorded by Emmylou Harris.

'The Promise'
Debuted at the Monmouth Arts Centre, Red Bank, New Jersey on 3 August 1976 and played at regular intervals throughout the 1976, 1977 and (the first third of) the 1978 tours, up until its final performance at the Coliseum, Houston, Texas on 15 July 1978. Recorded for *Darkness On The Edge Of Town* but, as yet, unreleased.

'The Promised Land'
Released on *Darkness On The Edge Of Town* in 1978. Debuted live at the Shea Theatre, Buffalo, New York on 23 May 1978 and a constant part of the live shows ever since. In 1981 and again in 1982 Bruce guested with Jackson Browne at anti-nuclear rallies for an acoustic duet of the song. Also released as a single in the U.K.

'Protection'
Recorded by Donna Summer for her album *Donna Summer*, 1982. Bruce is credited with the guitar solo and can also be heard on the fade out vocals. A studio version by Bruce is believed to have been recorded.

'Prove It All Night'
Released on *Darkness On The Edge Of Town* in 1978, this song has become a stalwart of the live shows since its debut on the opening night of the 1978 tour. It has been played at almost every concert since, usually with a scorching guitar introduction. Also released on the promotion only LPs *Bruce Springsteen Sampler*, *Especial FM* and *As Requested Around The World*.

'Racing In The Street'
Released on *Darkness On The Edge Of Town* in 1978, and a constant part of Bruce's live concerts. In 1984 it replaced 'Rosalita' as the closing number to the second half. One superb out-take is known. Also recorded by Paul Haan, Emmylou Harris, Paul Rallt and Roger Taylor.

'Ramrod'
Made its live debut as far back as 28 December 1978 at the Stanley Theatre, Pittsburgh, Pennsylvania. It was first recorded at the *Darkness On The Edge Of Town* recording sessions in 1978 and was eventually re-recorded and released on *The River* in 1980.

'Reason To Believe'
Released on the *Nebraska* LP in 1982. Debuted live at the Civic Centre, St Paul, Minnesota on 1 July 1984 and performed at regular intervals throughout the 1984–85 tour, where it underwent a change of lyrics.

'Rendezvous'
Unreleased out-take recorded at the *Darkness On The Edge Of Town* sessions at the Atlantic Studios in New York City between June and November 1977. Performed live throughout the second short tour of 1976 and the earlier part of the 1977 tour, since then it

has turned up on odd nights during 1978 and the 1980–81 tours. Recorded by Greg Kihn and Gary U.S. Bonds.

'Restless Nights'
Out-take from *The River* recording sessions.

'Resurrection'
Well-known Steel Mill song with anti-religious lyrics. Live versions *circa* 1970 lasted as long as fifteen to twenty minutes.

'Rickie Wants A Man (Of Her Own)'
Unreleased out-take from *The River* recording sessions, 1980. Good bouncy beat, lyrically it concerns female adolescence.

'The River'
Title track of Bruce's fifth LP, which was recorded at New York's Power Station Studios between May 1979 and September 1980. Made its live debut at Madison Square Garden, New York on 21 September 1979 and was included in every show of the 1980–81 world tour, and on regular intervals throughout the 1984–85 tour. Also released on the promotion only *As Requested Around The World*, *Bruce Springsteen Sampler* and *Killer Cuts From The River*, as a single in most parts of the world and featured in the film *No Nukes*.

'Rosalita (Come Out Tonight)'
Released on Bruce's second LP in 1973 and also on the promotion only *Last American Hero*, *Nice Price Sampler*, *As Requested Around The World*, *Bruce Springsteen Sampler*, *Playback (AS 66)*, the DJ-Only EP *(AE7 1088)* and the Italian cassette *Storia E Musica*. It has been performed live at every concert as the show closer from late 1973 until 19 October 1984 at the Tacoma Dome, Tacoma, Washington, when it was surprisingly dropped. Since then it has made occasional appearances throughout the 1984–85 tour. It is well-known from the live video recorded at Phoenix, Arizona on 8 July 1978.

'Roulette'
Superb song concerning the events at Three Mile Island and the dangers of the misuse of nuclear power. As yet, unreleased and never performed live. Recorded for *The River* sessions at Power Station, New York between May 1979 and September 1980. One of Bruce's best songs.

'Savin' Up'
Recorded by Clarence Clemons and the Red Bank Rockers on their debut LP *Rescue* in 1983. Bruce is featured on guitar and backing vocals. In concert, the song reached new heights where it took on a gospel feel.

'Seaside Bar Song'
Unreleased out-take from *The Wild, The Innocent And The E Street Shuffle* LP. Sometimes incorrectly referred to as 'Get Your Wheels And Roll' or 'The Beat Song'. Tremendous swirling organ underpins the song; some of the lyrics later turn up on 'Born To Run'. Performed live in 1973. Recorded by French band Little Bob Story.

'Secret To The Blues'
This evolved from the 1972 Bruce Springsteen Band song 'The Band's Just Boppin' The Blues'; same tune, different lyrics. Performed live in 1973.

'Sherry Darling'
Debuted live at the Gardens, Louisville, Kentucky on 5 August 1978, it made several more appearances throughout the 1978 tour. Originally recorded for

Darkness On The Edge Of Town, it was eventually released on *The River* in 1980 and as a single throughout Europe in 1981. Also released on the promotion only *As Requested Around The World*.

'She's A Woman'
Short sharp rocker from the Bruce Springsteen Band, about 1971.

'She's Leaving'
Performed live with the Bruce Springsteen Band in 1971–72 and recorded for the music publishing demo tape in 1972.

'She's So Fine (Ride On Sweet William)'
One known live performance at the Liberty Hall, Houston, Texas, 11 March 1974.

'She's The One'
Released on *Born To Run* in 1975. The original live and first studio versions had a more aggressive lyric. Issued worldwide as the B side of 'Tenth Avenue Freeze-Out' and on the promotion only *Last American Hero*. Recorded by a U.K. all-girl group called Rhonda with a slight lyric change (to 'He's The One'). Performed constantly since its first known performance at the Avery Fisher Hall, New York on 4 October 1974, until the 1980–81 tour, when it made a rare (and last) performance at the Rosemont Horizon, Illinois on 10 September 1981.

'Shut Out The Light'
Released on the B side of the single 'Born In The U.S.A.' and on the promotion only 12″ (AS 1957). Debuted live at the Coliseum, Oakland, California on 22 October 1984. Inspired by the Ron Kovic book *Born On The 4th Of July*.

'Shuttered Window'
Rumoured to be an out-take from the *Born In The U.S.A.* recording sessions.

'Sister Theresa'
Steel Mill song performed live in 1970. Bruce's profane lyrics are set to an untypical acoustic guitar and gentle flute backing.

'Something's Gotta Break'
Steel Mill song that starts off gloomily but picks up to a fast, heavy beat, about 1970.

'Something In The Night'
Debuted live at the Monmouth Arts Centre, Red Bank, New Jersey on 1 August 1976 with different lyrics to what was eventually released on the 1978 LP *Darkness On The Edge Of Town*. Last performed at the Palladium, New York City on 15 September 1978.

'The Song'
Recorded for the music publishing demo in 1972.

'Song Of The Orphans'
Performed live in 1972 and 1973 as part of the acoustic opening set. Recorded for the music publishing demo tape in 1972. Imagery abounds in a song that would not have looked out of place on the first LP.

'Southern Son'
Recorded for the John Hammond demo tape on 3 May 1972 and again for the music publishing demo later that same year.

'Spanish Eyes'
Unreleased out-take from the *Darkness On The Edge Of Town* LP, recorded at the Record Plant, New York City between November 1977 and May 1978. The song

bears a strong resemblence to Them's 'Here Comes The Night'.

'Spirit In The Night'
Released on the first LP in 1973, also on the promotion only LPs *Last American Hero* and the *Bruce Springsteen Sampler*. Single releases are rare, collectable items, the second U.S. single being the hardest to find. The song was a constant part of the live shows up to 1979, but had made few appearances in 1980 and 1984–85. Recorded by Manfred Mann's Earth Band who had a top 40 hit with it in 1977.

'State Trooper'
Released on the *Nebraska* LP in 1982.

'Stolen Car'
Superb atmosphere built around Danny Federici's keyboard playing; released on *The River* in 1980. One remarkable out-take known with different lyrics. Performed at irregular intervals throughout the 1980–81 and 1984–85 tours.

'Street Queen'
Recorded for the John Hammond demo tape on 3 May 1972 and for the music publishing demo tape later that same year. The lyrics are full of sexual innuendo. Rumoured to have been considered for inclusion on the first album at one time, but still unreleased.

'Streets Of Fire'
Released on the *Darkness On The Edge Of Town* LP in 1978. Performed infrequently throughout the 1978 tour and last played at the Richfield Coliseum, Cleveland, Ohio on 1 January 1979. Recorded by a band called Dick Tool Company for their LP *Emo Omu*.

'Sugerland'
Nebraska-style song concerning the plight of the farmer and his stance against low grain prices, harsh conditions, the weather and trying to keep family unity. Debuted live in Ames, Iowa on 16 November 1984. As yet, unreleased.

'Summer On Signal Hill'
Released by Clarence Clemons and the Red Bank Rockers on a single-only release in 1983. This instrumental was produced by Bruce, who also featured on guitar.

'Sure Can Feel The Pain'
Performed with the Bruce Springsteen Band in 1971.

'Sweet Melinda'
A short Steel Mill song in the style of Bob Dylan's 'Rainy Day Women 12 & 35'.

'Take Them As They Come'
Unreleased out-take from *The River* sessions with a guitar backing reminiscent of early Searchers hits.

'Talk To Me'
Recorded by Southside Johnny and the Asbury Jukes for the excellent *Hearts Of Stone* LP in 1978. No studio or live versions known by Bruce.

'Talking About My Baby'
Bruce Springsteen Band song, about 1971.

'Tell Me Mama, Why It's So Hard'
Bruce Springsteen Band with a solid organ backing from David Sancious, about 1971.

'Temporary Out Of Order'
A Steel Mill heavy metal rocker concerning Bruce's (fictional?) juvenile problems.

'Tenth Avenue Freeze-Out'
Released on *Born To Run* in 1975; also included on the promotion only *Last American Hero* and the Italian cassette *Storia E Musica*. A constant part of the live act since its debut at the Palace Theatre, Providence, Rhode Island on 20 July 1975. On two occasions in December 1975 at the Tower, Philadelphia, Pennsylvania, Bruce slowed the song down for a version that didn't really work. Released as a single worldwide, the most collectable of these being the Japanese picture sleeve. Recorded by a Baltimore band called 1/2 Japanese.

'That's What You Get'
Unreleased Castiles single, co-written with lead singer George Theiss and recorded at the Brickmall Shopping Centre recording studio, Bricktown, New Jersey on 22 May 1966.

'This Hard Land'
Unreleased out-take from the *Born In The U.S.A* LP, rated by Max Weinberg as one of Bruce's finest songs. It is very much in the *Nebraska* vein, with his brother Frank this time on the same side of the law, as they search for lost cattle down by the Rio Grande.

'This Little Girl'
Recorded by Gary U.S. Bonds for the 1981 LP *Dedication*. Bruce can clearly be heard on back-up vocals and guitar. Performed in concert with Gary U.S. Bonds.

'Thundercrack'
Performed live throughout 1973 and the early part of 1974, it preceded 'Rosalita' as the closing number of the show. It was recorded for the second LP in late 1973 but was never released. Often incorrectly referred to as 'Angel From The Inner Lake-Heart Of A Ballerina'. The lyrics revolve around the dance floor antics of a young lady.

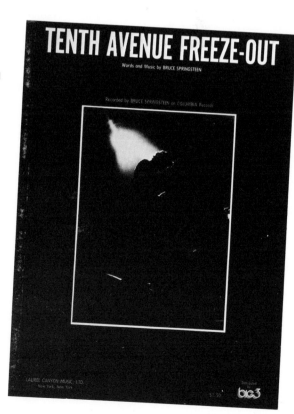

THUNDER ROAD

Vol. 2, No. 2
#4

Summer 1979
$1.25

'Thunder Road'
A classic Bruce, released on the *Born To Run* LP in 1975. An out-take from these sessions features a superb acoustic version. First performed at the Main Point, Bryn Mawr, Pennsylvania on 5 February 1975 with formative lyrics. Also released on the promotion only *Last American Hero, Mastersound Highlights* and the *Bruce Springsteen Sampler*. Performed at almost every concert since the epic gigs at New York's Bottom Line in August 1975, sometimes to great effect as a slow, very theatrical, opening number with just Roy Bittan's piano and harmonica backing. Also featured in the *No Nukes* movie.

'Tokyo'
Recorded for the music publishing demo tape in 1972. Performed live up to the early part of 1973. Sometimes incorrectly referred to as 'And The Band Played'.

'Tonight'
Studio out-take possibly recorded for the *Darkness On The Edge Of Town* LP.

'The Ties That Bind'
Debuted live at Princeton University, Princeton, New Jersey on 1 November 1978 and eventually released on *The River* in 1980. An Austrian 7″ promotion flexi-disc contained a segmented live version.

'The Train Song'
A weird country rock tale that chugs along nicely, recorded for the Bill Graham Fillmore Records Studios in San Francisco, California in February 1970. Regularly included in live Steel Mill shows, about 1970.

'Trapped Again'
Co-written with Southside Johnny and Miami Steve for the Southside Johnny and the Asbury Jukes LP *Hearts Of Stone* in 1978.

'Two Hearts'
Released on *The River* in 1980. Debuted live at the Richfield Coliseum, Cleveland, Ohio on 6 October 1980 and played constantly throughout the 1980–81 world tour. In 1984–85 it returned to the set on two occasions when ex-E Street Band member Steve Van Zandt guested with the band in East Rutherford, New Jersey and Memphis, Tennessee.

'Two Hearts In True Waltz Time'
Recorded for the John Hammond demo tape, 3 May 1972.

'Used Cars'
Released on the *Nebraska* LP in 1982. Debuted live at the Civic Centre, St Paul, Minnesota on 29 June 1984 and performed regularly throughout the 1984–85 tour, usually preceded with a rap about the week-end drive with his mom, dad and sister.

'Vibes Man'
Recorded for the music publishing demo tape in 1972, the song evolved via 'New York City Song' into the classic 'New York City Serenade' in 1973.

'Visitation At Fort Horne'
Recorded for the music publishing demo tape in 1972, and at one time considered for release on the first LP. Believed to have been included on early acetate copies, only to be replaced by 'It's Hard To Be A Saint In The City'.

'Walking In The Street'
Recorded for the *Born To Run* LP but, as yet, unreleased. Sometimes referred to as 'Lovers In The Cold'.

'The War Is Over'
Lengthy Steel Mill song from 1970.

'The Way'
Unreleased ballad from the *Darkness On The Edge Of Town* LP, recorded at the Record Plant, New York City between November 1977 and May 1978. Rich deep vocal from Bruce and nice sax solo in the middle break, courtesy of 'The Big Man'.

THUNDER ROAD $1.50

'We'll All Man The Guns'
Steel Mill song concerning a young man's apprehensive, though patriotic feelings about getting drafted into the army. Possibly inspired by the Byrds 'Draft Morning'.

'When You Dance'
Originally written by Bruce for the Bruce Springsteen Band in 1972, it was later revived in conjunction with Steve Van Zandt for an up-to-date version recorded by Southside Johnny and the Asbury Jukes on their *This Time It's For Real* LP, released in 1977.

'Whispers And Screams'
Rumoured out-take from the *Born In the U.S.A.* recording sessions.

'Why'd You Do That?'
Fast rocker from the Steel Mill band *circa* 1970.

'Wild Billy's Circus Story'
Released on the second album in 1973. Performed in concert in 1973–74 when Bruce used to open his sets with various acoustic numbers. Its last known performance was at a live broadcast for WBCN in Boston, Massachusetts on 9 April 1974.

'Wild Kisses'
Studio out-take, possibly recorded for the *Darkness On The Edge Of Town* LP.

'The Wind And the Rain'
Well-known Steel Mill song about lost summer love that featured some fine Jimi Hendrix/B. B. King style guitar.

'Working On The Highway'
Released on the *Born In The U.S.A.* LP in 1984. Made its live debut at the Civic Centre, St Paul, Minnesota on 29 June 1984.

'Wreck On The Highway'
Written in one night and recorded in three or four takes for release on *The River* in 1980. Debuted live at the Crisler Arena, Ann Arbor, Michigan on 3 October 1980. A regular part of the 1980–81 tour, it made infrequent appearances in 1984–85. Also released as the B side of the U.K. single 'Cadillac Ranch' and the rare South African single 'Hungry Heart'.

'You Can Look (But You Better Not Touch)'
Released on *The River* in 1980. One known out-take featured the song done in true rockabilly style.

'You Mean So Much To Me'
Originally written and performed with the Bruce Springsteen Band in 1971 with Delores Holmes and Francine Daniels on background vocals. Bruce honed up the lyrics in 1973 for the occasional live performance. In 1976 it was recorded by Southside Johnny and the Asbury Jukes with Ronnie Spector on a vocal duet for the *I Don't Want To Go Home* LP. Last performed by Bruce at the Monmouth Arts Centre, Red Bank, New Jersey in May 1977.

'Your Love'
Recorded by Gary U.S. Bonds for the 1981 release *Dedication*.

'You Sure Can Dance'
Bruce Springsteen Band song from 1971–72. Plenty of improvised playing set to a token lyric.

'Zero And Blind Terry'
Unreleased out-take from *The Wild, The Innocent And The E Street Shuffle*. Performed live from July 1973 to the early part of 1974.

Fire On The Fingertips

(Bootleg Singles, EPs and Albums)

'Because The Night' and **'Racing In The Street'/'Because The Night'** and **'The Promise'** – (WNYC RADIO)
Source: Out-takes from the Record Plant Studios in New York City, recorded between June 1977 and May 1978.
Cover: Excellent black and white sleeve.
Sound: Excellent/good.
Remarks: In three different colour vinyls – black, red and clear. Credited to Bruce Springsteen. Second version of 'Because The Night' features Patti Smith on lead vocals.

'Because The Night'/'Santa Claus Is Comin' To Town' – (TEST RECORDS)
Source: Side one – out-take from the Record Plant, New York City, recorded between June 1977 and May 1978. Side two – C.W. Post College, Greenvale, New York, 12 December 1975.

Cover: Plain white sleeve.
Sound: Fair/good.
Remarks: Coloured vinyl. Credited to 'The Jersey Devil'.

'Because The Night'/'Santa Claus'
'Rendezvous'/'The Fever'
Remarks: Re-packaged as a double 45. See under original entries for further comment.

'Devil With The Blue Dress Medley'/'Point Blank' – (FIRST RECORDS)
Source: The Capitol Theatre, Passaic, New Jersey, 19 September 1978 (WNEW radio broadcast).
Cover: Plain white sleeve.
Sound: Good/very good.
Remarks: Black vinyl. No credit.

'The Fever'/'Higher And Higher' – (Picture logo only)

Source: Side one – studio demo from 1973. Side two features a shared vocal with Southside Johnny from a WNEW radio broadcast of a concert at The Capitol Theatre, Passaic, New Jersey, 31 December 1977.
Cover: Black and white photo.
Sound: Very good.
Remarks: Coloured vinyl. No credits.

File Under Bruce Springsteen – PICTURE DISC
Side one: 'Bishop Dance'
Side two: 'Prove It All Night'
Source: Side one: – Max's Kansas City, N.Y.C., August 1972. Side two: – Community Auditorium, Berkeley, California, 1 July 1978.
Cover: Mock-up file with insert.
Sound: Good.
Remarks: 12″ black and white picture disc, housed in a file to give the impression of being the test pressing.

Bruce
Springsteen
Outside
The Seven-Eleven
Store

'Fire'/'Paradise By The Sea'
Source: Side one – WMEW radio broadcast from The Capitol Theatre, Passaic, New Jersey, 19 September 1978. Side two – The Roxy, Los Angeles, California, 7 July 1978.
Cover: Black and white photo.
Sound: Very good.
Remarks: Black vinyl. Credited to Bruce Springsteen.

'Fire'/'Raise Your Hand' – (FIRST RECORDS)
Source: The Capitol Theatre, Passaic, New Jersey, 19 September 1978 (WNEW radio broadcast).
Cover: Plain white sleeve.
Sound: Fair.
Remarks: Black vinyl. Rarest of all the singles.

'Johnny Bye Bye'/'Follow That Dream' – (IBDB – 007)
Source: National Exhibition Centre, Birmingham, England, 8 June 1981.
Cover: Black and white insert.
Sound: Fair/good.
Remarks: Black vinyl. Credited to 'Baltimore Jack and the Jackson Cage All Stars'.

'Little Latin Lupe Lu'/'You Can't Sit Down'
Source: The Capitol Theatre, Passaic, New Jersey, 31 December 1977 (WNEW radio broadcast).
Cover: Black and white photo.
Sound: Very good.
Remarks: Recorded at a Southside Johnny New Year's Eve concert. Bruce and the E Street Band took the stage for these two songs plus three others (not broadcast). Coloured vinyl. No credits.

Picture Disc – (92444)
Remarks: Released with up to 12 different black and white picture faces; the actual songs on the disc are by Elvis Presley, tracing his film career.

'Point Blank'/'Rendezvous' and **'We Gotta Get Outta This Place'**
Source: Side one is from the Fox Theatre, Atlanta, Georgia, 30 September 1978 (WINZ radio broadcast). Side two is from the Palladium, New York City, 4 November 1976.
Cover: Black and white photo.
Sound: Excellent/fair.
Remarks: Coloured vinyl. No credit.

'The Promise'/'Because The Night' – (TEST RECORDS)
Source: Side one – unknown 1976 concert. Side two – out-take from the Record Plant, recorded between June 1977 and May 1978.
Cover: Plain white sleeve.
Sound: Good/fair.
Remarks: Pressed on both black and yellow vinyl. No credits.

'Ramrod'/'Spanish Eyes' – (JERSEY RECORDS)
Source: Out-takes from The Power Station Studios, New York, 1978.
Cover: Plain white sleeve.
Sound: Fair/good.
Remarks: Only available with the bootleg album *Still On The Edge*.

'Rendezvous'/'The Fever' – (BRUCE RECORDS)
Source: Side one – The Palladium, New York, 4 November 1976. Side two – studio demo from 1973.
Cover: Plain white sleeve.
Sound: Good.
Remarks: Black vinyl. Credited to 'The Jersey Devil'.

'Rendezvous' and **'Santa Claus Is Comin' To Town'/'The Fever'** – (BRUCE RECORDS)
Source: Track one – The Palladium, New York City, 4 November 1976. Track two – C.W. Post College, Greenvale, New York, 12 December 1975. Track three – studio demo from 1973.
Cover: Plain white sleeve.
Sound: Very good.
Remarks: Coloured vinyl. Credited to 'The Jersey Devil'.

The River That Talks – (SCORPIO RECORDS)
Record One: 'Roulette'/'You Can Look (But You Better Not Touch)'
Record Two: 'Restless Nights'/'Cindy'
Source: Out-takes from *The River* sessions, recorded at The Power Station Studios, New York City, between May 1979 and September 1980.
Cover: Deluxe colour gatefold.
Sound: Very good/excellent.
Remarks: Superb cover with lyrics on the inside and great picture labels. Pressed in a limited numbered edition on black vinyl and a further very limited edition on red. A labour of love.

Side One – Fever   *Side Two* – Higher & Higher

'Rockin' All Over The World'/'Twist And Shout' – (RAVEN RECORDS)
Source: Side one – Festhalle, Frankfurt, 14 April 1981. Side two – I.C.C., Berlin, 8 April 1981.
Cover: Plain white sleeve.
Sound: Fair.
Remarks: Available only with the bootleg album *The Boss Hits The Badlands*. Black vinyl.

'Santa Claus Is Comin' To Town'/'Night Train' and **'Heartbreak Hotel'**
Source: Tracks one and two – The Fox Theatre, Atlanta, Georgia, 30 September 1978 (WINZ radio broadcast). Track three – The Roxy, Los Angeles, California, 7 July 1978 (KMET radio broadcast).
Cover: Black and white photo.
Sound: Very good/good.
Remarks: Pressed on black and coloured vinyl. Credited to Bruce Springsteen.

'Santa Claus Is Comin' To Town'/'Rendezvous' and **'The Fever'** – (Picture disc)
Remarks: A 7″ featuring a black and white photo of Bruce and Clarence. Only fifteen copies are believed to have been pressed.

'She's The One'/'Thunder Road' – (WINNER RECORDS)
Source: Out-takes from the Record Plant, New York City, 1974–75.
Cover: Black and white photo.
Sound: Good/excellent.
Remarks: Superb acoustic version of 'Thunder Road'. Coloured vinyl. Credited to 'B.S. and E Street Band'.

'Sherry Darling'/'Independence Day'
Source: Side one – The Agora Ballroom, Cleveland, Ohio, 9 August 1978 (WMNS radio broadcast). Side two – The Capitol Theatre, Passaic, New Jersey, 19 September 1978 (WNEW radio broadcast).
Cover: Black and white photo.
Sound: Good/very good.
Remarks: Coloured vinyl. No credit.

'Summertime Blues'/'Sweet Little Sixteen'
Source: Side one – The Agora Ballroom, Cleveland, Ohio, 9 August 1978. WMNS radio broadcast. Side two – Madison Square Garden, New York City, 21 August 1978.
Cover: Black and white photo.
Sound: Good/fair.

Remarks: Coloured vinyl. Credited to Bruce Springsteen.

'Trapped'/'Jole Blon' – (IBDB)
Source: National Exhibition Centre, Birmingham, England, 8 June 1981.
Cover: Black and white photo.
Sound: Fair/good.
Remarks: Black vinyl. Credited to 'Baltimore Jack and the Jackson Cage All Stars'.

'We Gotta Get Outta This Place'/'Action In The Streets' – (TOASTED RECORDS)
Source: Side one –The Palladium, New York City, 4 November 1976. Side two –The Music Hall, Boston, Massachusetts, 25 March 1977.
Cover: Plain white sleeve.
Sound: Good.
Remarks: Available only with the bootleg album *New York Palladium 1976*. Pressed on orange vinyl.

Acoustic Radio Jam – (PHORPHORA RECORDS)
Side one: 'Satin Doll'/'Does This Bus Stop At 82nd Street?'/'I Fought The Law'/'Growin' Up'/'Wild Billy's Circus Song'.
Side two: '4th Of July, Asbury Park (Sandy)'/'Rosalita'.
Source: WBCN Studios, Boston, Massachusetts, 9 April 1974. Radio broadcast.
Cover: Deluxe black and white.
Sound: Very good.
Remarks: 'I Fought The Law' is not a complete song, but just a brief snatch of the chorus. 'Does This Bus Stop At 82nd Street?' incorrectly listed as 'Mary Queen Of Hearts', 'Satin Doll' incorrectly listed as 'A Jazzy Tune'. As the album title suggests, all songs are acoustic versions.

Action In The Streets – (SCORPIO RECORDS)
Side one: 'Night'/'Don't Look Back'/'Action In The Streets'/'Quarter To Three'.
Side two: 'It's Hard To Be A Saint In The City'/'Little Latin Lupe Lu'/'You Can't Sit Down'/'Higher And Higher'.
Source: The Music Hall, Boston, Massachusetts, 25 March 1977.
Cover: Deluxe black and white.
Sound: Very good.
Remarks: Numbered edition pressed on black vinyl.

Action In The Streets – PICTURE DISC
Remarks: Picture disc pressed from the original plates (Scorpio Records).

The Agora Show Part One – (BS 2000)
Side one: 'Summertime Blues'/'Badlands'/'Spirit In The Night'/'Darkness On The Edge Of Town'/'Factory'.
Side two: 'The Promised Land'/'Racing In The Street'/'Thunder Road'.
Side three: 'Jungleland'/'Prove It All Night'.
Side four: 'Fire'/'Sherry Darling'/'Not Fade Away' . . . 'Gloria' . . . 'She's The One'.
Source: The Agora Ballroom, Cleveland, Ohio, 9 August 1978 (WMNS radio broadcast).
Cover: Colour insert.
Sound: Very good.
Remarks: 'Factory' is not listed on the cover, and 'Spirit In The Night' is listed as 'Wild Billy's Circus Story'. Black vinyl. Copied on Modern Jazz Records EGF 1200.

The Agora Show Part Two – (BS 4000)
Side one: 'Growin' Up'/'Backstreets'.
Side two: 'Rosalita'/'4th Of July, Asbury Park (Sandy)'.
Side three: 'Born To Run'/'Because The Night'/'Raise Your Hand'/'Twist And Shout'.
Side four: 'Little Latin Lupe Lu'/'You Can't Sit Down'/'Fire'/'Raise Your Hand'.
Source: Sides one, two and three – the Agora, Cleveland, Ohio, 9 August 1978 (WMNS radio broadcast). Side four, tracks one and two – The Capitol Theatre, Passaic, New Jersey, 31 December 1977. Side four, tracks three and four – The Capitol Theatre, Passaic, New Jersey, 19 September 1978 (WNEW radio broadcast).
Cover: Colour insert.
Sound: Very good.
Remarks: Incorrect cover listings list 'Rosalita' as 'The Ties That Bind', and fail to mention 'Raise Your Hand' and 'Twist And Shout'. Side four is copied from two bootleg EPs. Copied on Modern Jazz Records EGF 1200.

Ain't Nobody Here From Billboard Tonight – (HAR 160)
Side one: 'Thunder Road'/'Tenth Avenue Freeze Out'/'Spirit In The Night'/'Pretty Flamingo'.
Side two: 'She's The One'/'Born To Run'/'4th of July, Asbury Park (Sandy)'/'Backstreets'.
Side three: 'Kitty's Back'/'Jungleland'.
Side four: 'Rosalita'/'Goin' Back'/'Devil With The Blue Dress' medley.
Source: The Roxy Theatre, Los Angeles, 17 October 1975 (KEST radio broadcast).
Cover: Black and white insert.
Sound: Good.

ALL THOSE YEARS   BRUCE SPRINGSTEEN

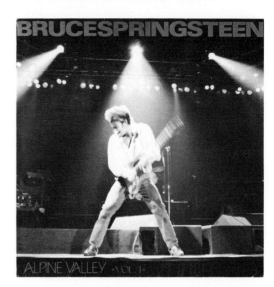

Remarks: Copied on Impossible Records (IMP 1105) on coloured and black vinyls and also on Opportunity Records on black vinyl.

All Those Years – (SR 111–1102)
Side one: 'Oh Mama Why'/'Change It'.
Side two: 'Dancing In The Street' . . . 'Honky Tonk Women'/'I Can't Take It'.
Side three: 'Song Of The Orphans' (Max's Kansas City, N.Y., August 1972)/'Zero And Blind Terry' (Max's Kansas City, N.Y., July 1973)/'You Mean So Much To Me' (My Fathers Place, Roslyn, N.Y., 31 July 1973).
Side four: 'New York City Serenade'/'4th Of July, Asbury Park (Sandy)'/'Something You Got'.
Side five: 'Mary Queen Of Arkansas'/'The Fever'/'The E Street Shuffle'.
Side six: 'She's So Fine (Ride On Sweet William)'/'Thundercrack'.
Side seven: 'Jungleland' (Bottom Line, N.Y.C., 12 July 1974)/'Give Me That Wine' (Liberty Hall, Houston, Texas, 11 March 1974)/'Spanish Harlem' (Schenectady, N.Y., 19 October 1974).
Side eight: 'I Sold My Heart To The Junkman' (Harvard Square Theatre, Cambridge, Mass., 9 May 1974)/'Tokyo' (Agora, Cleveland, Ohio, 3 June 1974)/'Lost In The Flood' (Union College, Schenectady, N.Y., 19 October 1974).
Side nine: 'Kitty's Back'/'Sha La La'.
Side ten: 'Little Queenie'/'Mountain Of Love'/'Wear My Ring Around Your Neck'/'Thunder Road'.
Side eleven: 'Frankie'/'Growin' Up'/'It's Hard To Be A Saint In The City'/'Blinded By The Light'.
Side twelve: 'Jungleland' (Mobile, Ala., 10 May 1976)/'Tenth Avenue Freeze-Out'/'Spirit In The Night'.
Side thirteen: 'Backstreets'/'Action In The Streets'.
Side fourteen: 'Night'/'Rendezvous'/'Incident On 57th. Street' (Music Hall, Boston, Mass., 25 March 1977).
Side fifteen: 'The Promise' (Berkeley, Cal., 1 July 1978)/'For You' (Cleveland, Ohio, 1 January 1979)/'Don't Look Back' (Studio out-take 1978)/'(I Can't Get No) Satisfaction'/'Heart Full Of Soul' (Rehearsals for 1978 tour).
Side sixteen: 'Good Rockin' Tonight' (Portland, Ore., 18 December 1978)/'Because The Night' (Berkeley, Cal., 1 July 1978)/'Paradise By The Sea' (Cleveland, Ohio, 9 August 1978)/'Adam Raised A Cain' (Berkeley, Cal., 30 June 1978).

133

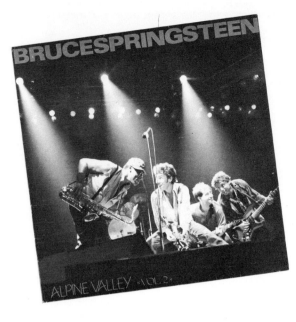

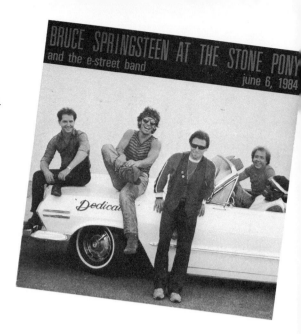

Side seventeen: 'Wreck On The Highway'/'Cadillac Ranch'/'Fire'/'The Promised Land'/'Darkness On The Edge Of Town'.

Side eighteen: 'The River'/'Out In The Street'/'I'm A Rocker' (Wembley, England, 29 May 1981)/'Run Through The Jungle' (Rotterdam, Holland, 29 April 1981)/'Can't Help Falling In Love' (Paris, France, 19 April 1981).

Side nineteen: 'Follow That Dream'/'Johnny Bye Bye'/'Jersey Girl'/'I Don't Want To Go Home'.

Side twenty: 'Come On Over To My Place'/'Around And Around'/'Lucille'... 'On The Prowl'/'Twist And Shout'/'From Small Things, Big Things One Day Come' (with Dave Edmunds, Big Man's West, Red Bank, N.J., 18 September 1982).

Source: Unless otherwise noted . . . sides one and two – the Scene, N.Y., 18 January 1971. Side four – Max's Kansas City, N.Y., 18–23 July 1973. Sides five and six – Liberty Hall, Houston, Tex., 11 March 1974. Side nine and side ten track one – Uptown Theatre, Milwaukee, Wisc., 2 October 1975. Side ten tracks two to four – Tower Theatre, Upper Darby, Pa., 30 December 1975. Sides eleven and twelve – Allen Theatre, Cleveland, Ohio, 7 April 1976. Side thirteen and side fourteen tracks one and two – Jai Alai Fronton, Orlando, Flo., 5 March 1977. Side seventeen and side eighteen tracks one and two – 1980 tour rehearsal. Side nineteen – Bryne Meadowlands Arena, East Rutherford, N.J., 2 July 1981. Side twenty tracks one to five – Stone Pony, Asbury Park, N.J., 8 August 1982 (with Cats On A Smooth Surface).

Cover: Deluxe colour box set.

Sound: Overall, very good to excellent.

Remarks: Limited numbered edition that includes a superb twenty four page booklet featuring unpublished colour photos, rare song lyrics, track list details and E Street Band personnel. All ten albums pressed on black vinyl with title labels and printed inner sleeves. The thoughtful choice of songs and all round excellence of sound, packaging and production makes this the ultimate in bootlegging.

All Those Years – (PICTURE DISC)

Remarks: Limited numbered edition featuring the IO LP set in colour picture disc form, plus a bonus 7" one sided single of 'Wild Kisses' on red vinyl. Packaged in a deluxe red box.

Alpine Valley Volume I – (SPACEMATIC RECORDS)

Side one: 'Thunder Road'/'Out In The Street'/'Prove It All Night'/'Darkness On The Edge Of Town'.

Side two: 'Johnny 99'/'Nebraska'/'Darlington County'/'Glory Days'.

Side three: 'The Promised Land'/'Used Cars'/'The River'/'Born In The U.S.A.'.

Side four: 'Badlands'/'Cadillac Ranch'/'Hungry Heart'/'Dancing In The Dark'/'Sherry Darling'.

Source: The Music Theatre, Alpine Valley, East Troy, Wisconsin, 13 July 1984.

Cover: Deluxe colour.

Sound: Excellent.

Remarks: Superb textured sleeve and production.

Alpine Valley Volume II – (SPACEMATIC RECORDS)

Side one: 'No Surrender'/'Pink Cadillac'/'Fire'/'Bobby Jean'.

Side two: 'Racing In The Streets'/'Rosalita (Come Out Tonight)'.

Side three: 'Jungleland'/'Born To Run'/'Street Fighting Man'.

Side four: 'Twist And Shout'/'Highway Patrolman'/'I'm On Fire'/'Working On The Highway'.

Source: The Music Theatre, Alpine Valley, East Troy, Wisconsin, 13 July 1984. Except side four, tracks 2, 3 and 4 Civic Centre, St. Paul, Minnesota, 29 June 1984.

Cover: Deluxe colour.

Sound: Excellent, apart from the St. Paul Minnesota, 29 June 1984 songs, which are fair.

Remarks: Excellent all round quality and production.

As Requested Around The World Live – (RFC 110)

Side one: 'Who'll Stop The Rain?'/'Two Hearts'/'The Promised Land'/'The River'.

Side two: 'Fire'/'Stolen Car'/'Jazz Musician'/'Does This Bus Stop At 82nd Street?'.

Side three: 'Sherry Darling'/'Independence Day'/'The Fever'/'Higher And Higher'.

Side four: 'Born To Run'/'Devil With The Blue Dress' medley/'Rockin' All Over The World'.

Source: Side one; side two, tracks one and two; side four – Stockholm, 7 May 1981. Side two, tracks three and four – John Hammond demo tapes, 3 May 1972. Side three, track one – The Agora, Cleveland, Ohio, 9 August 1978. Side three, track two – Passaic, New Jersey, 19 September 1978. Side three, tracks three and four – Passaic, New Jersey, 31 December 1977.

Cover: Blue insert.

Sound: Good/very good.

Remarks: Pressed on red vinyl. Cover track listings inaccurate on almost all the dates and venues. All songs are copied from previously pressed bootleg albums and EPs, re-pressed on black vinyl.

At The Stone Pony – (RIOJA RECORDS SP 84)

Side one: 'Glory Days'/'The River'/'Darlington County'/'Dancing In The Dark'/'The Promised Land'.

Side two: 'My Hometown'/'Born In The U.S.A.'/'Badlands'/'Born To Run'.

Source: Stone Pony, Asbury Park, New Jersey, 8 June 1984.

Cover: Deluxe colour.

Sound: Good.

Remarks: Nils Lofgren makes his debut with the E Street Band at a warm-up for the forthcoming 1984–85 tour.

Atlanta Georgia 1975 – (NONE)

Side one: 'Kitty's Back'.

Side two: 'Rosalita'/'4th Of July, Asbury Park (Sandy)'/'Twist And Shout'.

Side three: 'E Street Shuffle'.

Side four: 'She's The One'/'Born To Run'/'Then She Kissed Me'.

Source: The Electric Ballroom, Atlanta, Georgia, 21 August 1975.

Cover: Deluxe black and white.

Sound: Good.

Remarks: Black vinyl.

Because The Night – (ZOOT RECORDS Z–331)

Side one: 'Fire'/'Candy's Room'/'Because The Night'/'Backstreets'.

Side two: 'The Ties That Bind'/'Born To Run'/'Racing In The Street'/'Santa Claus Is Comin' To Town'.

Source: Winterland, San Francisco, California, 15 December 1978 (KSAN radio broadcast).

Cover: Deluxe black and white.

Sound: Very good.

Remarks: Black vinyl.

Blinded By Life – (C 4776)

Side one: 'Frankie'/'Backstreets'/'Growin' Up'.

Side two: 'It's Hard To Be A Saint In The City'/'Blinded By The Light'/'Jungleland'.

Side three: 'Rosalita (Come Out Tonight)'/'4th Of July, Asbury Park (Sandy)'.

Side four: 'Devil With The Blue Dress' medley/'Quarter To Three'.

THE BOSS

HITS THE

DON'T LOOK BACK bruce springsteen Collectors Items 1974-1980

Source: Allen Theatre, Cleveland, Ohio, 7 April 1976.
Cover: Deluxe black and white.
Sound: Very good.
Remarks: Several of the songs are incomplete versions.

Born In Cincinnati – (84 BSOH)
Side one: 'Out In The Street'/'Prove It All Night'/'Johnny 99'/'Atlantic City'.
Side two: 'Darlington County'/'Glory Days'/'The Promised Land'/'Highway Patrolman'.
Side three: 'Born In The U.S.A.'/'Badlands'/'Cadillac Ranch'/'Hungry Heart'.
Side four: 'Used Cars'/'Pink Cadillac'.
Side five: 'Racing In The Streets'/'Rosalita (Come Out Tonight)'.
Side six: 'Street Fighting Man'/'Devil With The Blue Dress' medley.
Side seven: 'The River'/'My Hometown'/'Dancing In The Dark'.
Side eight: 'Sherry Darling'/'Bobby Jean'/'Jungleland'/'Born To Run'.
Source: Riverfront Coliseum, Cincinnati, Ohio, 6 July 1984.
Cover: Red, white and blue insert.
Sound: Very good.
Remarks: Cover lists songs in the wrong order and 'Highway Patrolman' as 'Frankie'.

Born To Be The Boss – (HOLSTEN TEAM RECORDS HOT–3)
Side one: 'Born To Run'/'Prove It All Night'/'Out In The Street'/'Follow That Dream'/'Darkness On The Edge Of Town'.
Side two: 'Independence Day'/'Johnny Bye Bye'/'Two Hearts'/'Who'll Stop The Rain?'/'This Land Is Your Land'.
Side three: 'The River'/'I Fought The Law'/'Badlands'/'Thunder Road'.
Side four: 'Hungry Heart'/'You Can Look'/'Cadillac Ranch'/'Sherry Darling'/'Jole Blon'/'Fire'.
Side five: 'Because The Night'/'I Wanna Marry You'/'Point Blank'/'Candy's Room'.
Side six: 'Ramrod'/'Rosalita (Come Out Tonight)'/'I'm A Rocker'.
Side seven: 'Jungleland'/'Can't Help Falling In Love'/'Devil With The Blue Dress' medley including 'Shake' and 'Sweet Soul Music'.
Side eight: Blank.
Source: Wembley Arena, London, England, 5 June 1981.
Cover: Deluxe colour gatefold.
Sound: Very good.
Remarks: Superb all round production and

packaging. Pressed on black vinyl with picture labels.

Boss Ahoy
Remarks: Sides three and four of *Nassau* re-packaged in shoddy sleeve. No track listing on cover. Black vinyl.

The Boss At His Best – (BLACK AND WHITE RECORDS BWR 8301)
Side one: 'Higher And Higher'/'Jackson Cage'/'Two Hearts'/'Fade Away'.
Side two: 'Merry Christmas Baby'/'Racing In The Street'/'The River'/'Prove It All Night'.
Source: Side one, track one – Music Hall, Boston, Massachusetts, 25 March 1977. Side one tracks two and three and side two, tracks two, three and four were all recorded during the first half of a concert at Seattle, Washington, 24 October 1980. Side one, track four and side two, track one recorded at Nassau Coliseum, Uniondale, New York, 31 December 1980.
Cover: Deluxe black and white.
Sound: Very good/good.

The Boss Hits The Badlands – (RAVEN RECORDS RV–8122)
Side one: 'Factory'/'Prove It All Night'/'Out In The Street'/'Tenth Avenue Freeze Out'/'Darkness On The Edge Of Town'.
Side two: 'Independence Day'/'Who'll Stop The Rain?'/'Two Hearts'/'The Promised Land'/'This Land Is Your Land'.
Side three: 'The River'/'Thunder Road'/'Cadillac Ranch'/'Sherry Darling'/'Hungry Heart'.
Side four: 'Fire'/'You Can Look'/'Point Blank'/'Ramrod'.
Extra single: 'Rockin' All Over The World'/'Twist And Shout'.
Source: Festhalle, Frankfurt, 14 April 1981; 'Twist And Shout' – Berlin, 8 April 1981.
Cover: Deluxe black and white. Original covers misspelt as 'Bandlands' (sic).
Sound: Fair/poor.
Remarks: Re-pressed on coloured vinyl with different cover.

The Boss Hits The Sixties – (HOLSTEN TEAM RECORDS)
Side one: 'Little Queenie'/'Around And Around'.
Side two: 'The Last Time'/'Carol'.
Side three: 'Double Shot Of My Baby's Love'/'Louie Louie'.
Side four: 'Sha La La'/'I Don't Wanna Hang Up My Rock'n'Roll Shoes'.
Source: Side one, track one – Detroit, Michigan, 4 October 1975; track two – St Petersburg,

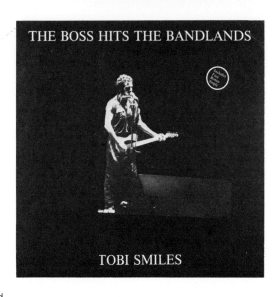

THE BOSS HITS THE BANDLANDS

TOBI SMILES

29 July 1978. Side two, track one – Cleveland, Ohio, 1 January 1979; track two – Akron, Ohio, 8 August 1975. Side three – South Bend, Indiana, 9 September 1978. Side four, track one – Hammersmith Odeon, London, 24 November 1975; track two – Saginaw, 3 September 1978.
Cover: Superb colour gatefold.
Sound: Good/very good.
Remarks: Numbered limited edition. All sides play at 45 r.p.m. Black vinyl with great picture labels.

The Boss In Boston – (SPARROW PRODUCTIONS A–C–3L)
Side one: 'Born To Run'/'Out In The Street'/'Tenth Avenue Freeze Out'.
Side two: 'Darkness On The Edge Of Town'/'The Price You Pay'/'Independence Day'/'Two Hearts'.
Side three: 'Prove It All Night'/'The Promised Land'/'Racing In The Street'.
Side four: 'The River'/'Badlands'/'Thunder Road'.
Source: The Garden, Boston, Massachusetts, 15 December 1980 (cover states 1981).
Cover: Black and white insert.
Sound: Poor/fair.
Remarks: First half of Bruce's concert at The Garden.

The Boss Is Back – (RECORD MAN 913)
Side one: 'Tenth Avenue Freeze Out'/'Spirit In The Night'/'Then She Kissed Me'/'Growin' Up'/'It's Hard To Be A Saint In The City'.
Side two: 'E Street Shuffle'/'Every Time You Walk In The Room'/'She's The One'.
Side three: 'Born To Run'/'Kitty's Back'.
Side four: 'Thunder Road'/'Rosalita'/'4th Of July, Asbury Park (Sandy)'/'Quarter To Three'.
Source: Copy of *Live* (CORAL RECORDS)
Cover: Deluxe colour.
Sound: Good.

The Boss Of E Street – (BMC 5155)
Side one: 'Fire'/'Sherry Darling'/'Not Fade Away' . . . 'She's The One'.
Side two: 'Rendezvous'/'High School Confidential'/'Pretty Flamingo'/'The Ties That Bind'.
Source: Side one – Madison Square Garden, New York City, 23 August 1978. Side two, track one – The Palladium, New York City, 4 November 1976; track two – Madison Square Garden, New York City, 23 August 1978; track three – The Roxy, Los Angeles, California, 17 October 1975; track four – Winterland, San Francisco, California, 15 December 1978.

Cover: Deluxe black and white.
Sound: Very good.
Remarks: Pressed on black vinyl.

The Boss Of The Boardwalk – (BIG BOSS MAN 100)
Side one: 'Jazz Musician'/'Mary Queen Of Arkansas'/'It's Hard To Be A Saint In The City'/'Two Hearts In True Waltz Time'/'Does This Bus Stop At 82nd Street?'
Side two: 'If I Were The Priest'/'Growin' Up'/'Arabian Nights'/'Street Queen'.
Source: John Hammond demo tapes, 3 May 1972.
Cover: Black and white insert.
Sound: Good.
Remarks: Numbered edition pressed on black vinyl. Re-pressed with a different insert, un-numbered.

The Boss Was Here – (FLYING HORSE RECORDS FC 021)
Side one: 'Summertime Blues'/'Spirit In The Night'/'Because The Night'/'Ramrod'.
Side two: 'The River'/'Independence Day'/'Who'll Stop The Rain?'
Side three: 'She's The One'/'Raise Your Hand'/'Darkness On The Edge Of Town'.
Side four: 'Can't Help Falling In Love'/'Born To Run'/'Devil With The Blue Dress' medley/'Twist And Shout'.
Source: Side one, tracks one, two and three; side three; side four, track four – WMMS radio broadcast of the Cleveland Agora benefit show, 9 August 1978. All other tracks – Paris, 18 April 1981.
Cover: Deluxe black and white gatefold.
Sound: Very good/good.
Remarks: Pressed on black vinyl. Live debut of 'Can't Help Falling In Love', introduced by Bruce as one of his favourite Elvis songs.

Box O' Rocks – (HAR 160, HAR 164, HAR 147)
Side one: 'Circus Song'/'New York Song'/'Spirit In The Night'/'Hey Santa Ana'.
Side two: 'Tokyo'/'Thundercrack'/'Thunder Road'.
Side three: 'Thunder Road'/'Tenth Avenue Freeze Out'/'Spirit In The Night'/'Pretty Flamingo'.
Side four: 'She's The One'/'Born To Run'/'4th Of July, Asbury Park (Sandy)'/'Backstreets'.
Side five: 'Kitty's Back'/'Jungleland'.
Side six: 'Rosalita'/'Goin' Back'/'Devil With The Blue Dress' medley.
Side seven: 'It's Hard To Be A Saint In The City'/'E Street Shuffle'.
Side eight: 'New York City Serenade'/'Lost In The Flood'.

Side nine: 'For You'/'Night'/'Tenth Avenue Freeze Out'/'Does This Bus Stop At 82nd Street?'/'You Never Can Tell'.
Side ten: 'Wear My Ring Around Your Neck'/'It's My Life'/'Sha La La'/'Santa Claus Is Comin' To Town'/'It's Gonna Work Out Fine'/'Up On The Roof'.
Source: Sides one and two a re-issue of *Jersey Devil*; sides three, four, five and six a re-issue of *Aint No One Here From Billboard Tonight*; sides seven, eight, nine, ten and eleven a re-issue of *Hot Coals From The Fiery Furnace*. See under relevant entries for details.
Cover: Box with insert.
Sound: Varies from poor to very good. (see under relevant entries).
Remarks: Original copies on coloured vinyl with black stripe. Later re-pressing on coloured vinyl (two blue, two yellow and one red).

Box O' Rocks – (QUICK Q RECORDS)
Remarks: 1980/81 copy of above. All records on black vinyl. Different black and white insert.

Bring Him Back Alive – (S)
Side one: 'The E Street Shuffle'/'For You'.
Side two: '4th Of July, Asbury Park (Sandy)'/'Kitty's Back'.
Source: Allen Theatre, Cleveland, Ohio, 10 August 1975.
Cover: Deluxe black and white.
Sound: Good.
Remarks: Limited numbered edition on black and red vinyls.

Bruce Juice – (NO LABEL)
Side one: 'The Ties That Bind'/'Who'll Stop The Rain?'/'Two Hearts'/'Cadillac Ranch'/'Because The Night'.
Side two: 'Backstreets'/'Devil With The Blue Dress' medley/'Rockin' All Over The World'.
Source: Palacie de Deportes, Barcelona, 21 April 1981.
Cover: Black and white insert.
Sound: Fair.
Remarks: Same record as *El Boos En Barcelona*.

Bruce Juice – (PICTURE DISC)
Remarks: Picture disc of the above. Same track listing.

Bruce Springsteen Live 1981 – (B 17 2 82)
Side one: 'Run Through The Jungle'/'Prove It All Night'/'The Ties That Bind'/'Tenth Avenue Freeze Out'/'Rockin' All Over The World'.
Side two: 'Backstreets'/'Candy's Room'/'Ramrod'/'Rosalita'.
Side three: 'Prove It All Night'/'Out In The Street'/'Tenth Avenue Freeze Out'/'Darkness On The Edge Of Town'.
Side four: 'Backstreets'/'Candy's Room'/'Ramrod'.
Side five: 'Candy's Room'/'Ramrod'/'Rosalita'.
Side six: 'Born To Run'/'Devil With The Blue Dress' medley.
Source: Sides one and two (except 'Rockin' All Over The World') – Isstadion, Stockholm, 8 May 1981. All other tracks – Stockholm, 7 May 1981.
Cover: Box with insert.
Sound: Very good.
Remarks: Confusing song sequence, and the same versions of 'Candy's Room' and 'Ramrod' are duplicated on sides four and five. Copied from the full Stockholm concert albums *Teardrops On The City* and *Follow That Dream*.

Bruce Springsteen 78 – (AUDIFON ACR 61)
Side one: 'Badlands'/'Streets Of Fire'/'Independence Day'/'The Promised Land'.
Side two: 'Racing In The Street'/'Thunder Road'/'Meeting Across The River'/'Because The Night'.
Side three: 'Kitty's Back'/'Not Fade Away' . . . 'She's The One'.
Side four: 'Backstreets'/'Rosalita'.
Source: The Capitol Theatre, Passaic, New Jersey, 19 September 1978 (WNEW radio broadcast).
Cover: Deluxe colour.
Sound: Very good.
Remarks: Cover states incorrectly that the concert is from Cincinnatti, 1978. Black vinyl.

Bruce Springsteen And His Disciples Live In Ahoy 1981 – (B.S.R RECORDS RD 121)
Side one: 'Follow That Dream'/'Prove It All Night'/'Out In The Street'/'The Ties That Bind'/'Darkness On The Edge Of Town'.
Side two: 'Independence Day'/'Who'll Stop The Rain?'/'Two Hearts'/'The Promised Land'.

137

Source: The Ahoy, Rotterdam, 28 April 1981.
Cover: Deluxe black and white.
Sound: Good/fair.

By The River – (BS 1000)
Side one: 'Roulette'/'Take Them As They Come'/'Cindy'/'Loose Ends'/'Rickie Wants A Man'.
Side two: 'Circus Song'/'Fire'/'Raise Your Hand'/'Point Blank'/'Hungry Heart'.
Source: Side one – studio out-takes, Power Station Studios, May 1979 to September 1980. Side two, track one – Ahmanson Theatre, Los Angeles, California, May 1973; tracks two, three and four – Capitol Theatre, 19 September 1978; track five – The Forum, Copenhagen (with Danish band Malurt), 1 May 1981.
Cover: Deluxe black and white.
Sound: Very good/excellent.
Remarks: First 100 pressed on blue vinyl, of which the first 25 came with a numbered 44-page lyric book of all B.S. songs.

By The River – (MOD 1012)
Remarks: Copy of the above; identical track listing, but with a black and white insert instead of the deluxe sleeve. Black vinyl.

Christmas Songs For All The Good Boys – (PICTURE DISC)
Side one: 'Santa Claus Is Comin' To Town'/'Merry Christmas Baby'/'In The Midnight Hour'/'Auld Lang Syne'.
Side two: 'On Top Of Old Smokey'/'I'm A Rocker'/'Sweet Little Sixteen'/'No Money Down'/'Cadillac Ranch'.
Source: Side one tracks 2, 3, 4 and side two track 5 Nassau Coliseum, Uniondale, New York, 31 December 1980. side two track 1 Portland, Oregon, 25 October 1980, track 3 Louisville, Kentucky, 8 May 1978, track 4 Bottom Line, New York City, 13 July 1974. Side one track 1 and side two track 2 unknown live 1980.
Disc: Great full colour picture.
Sound: Fair.
Remarks: Limited edition.

Clarence Clemons And The Red Bank Rockers – (FC 002)
Side one: 'Working Man'/'634 5789'/'Philadelphia Special'/'I'll Be There'/'Backdoor Key'.
Side two: 'Sweet Soul Music'/'I Can't Turn You

Loose'/'September 23rd'/'Nobody Is My Soul'/'Everybody Needs A Star'.
Source: The Chestnut Cabaret, Philadelphia, Pennsylvania, 28 January 1982.
Cover: Deluxe black and white.
Sound: Fair to good.
Remarks: Limited numbered edition.

Criminals And Artists – (GO 100)
Side one: 'Rosalita' (instrumental)/'Kitty's Back'/'Thunder Road'/'4th Of July, Asbury Park (Sandy)' (instrumental).
Side two: 'Walking In The Street'/'She's The One'/'A Love So Fine' (instrumental)/'Born To Run'/'Thunder Road'/'Jungleland' (part).
Source: Inferior copy of E Ticket.
Cover: Black and white cartoon insert.
Sound: Poor.
Remarks: Cover states the contents to be a 'rare jam' with Southside Johnny in 1978. Black vinyl.

Cry Me A River (BS)
Side one: 'Tenth Avenue Freeze Out'/'Rendezvous'/'Jungleland'/'Thunder Road'.
Side two: 'Night'/'Spirit In Th Night'/'She's The One'.
Source: Copy of Live in Philadelphia.
Cover: Black and white insert.
Sound: Good.
Remarks: Available on both coloured and black vinyl.

Cult Of Personality
Remarks: Worthless home-made re-packaging of The Boss In Boston with black and white insert cover.

Dancing In The U.S.A (NEUROTIC RECORDS)
Side one: 'Born In The U.S.A.'/'Out In The Street'/'Prove It All Night'/'Atlantic City'.
Side two: 'Used Cars'/'My Hometown'/'Thunder Road'/'Dancing In The Dark'.
Side three: 'Hungry Heart'/'Cadillac Ranch'/'Nebraska'/'Rosalita'.
Side four: 'Jungleland'/'Born To Run'/'Street Fighting Man'/'Twist And Shout'.
Source: Civic Centre, St Paul, Minnesota, 2 July 1984.
Cover: Deluxe colour.
Sound: Fair.

Dead Trousers (S–20)
Remarks: Worthless home-made re-packaging of sides 1–2 of the Stockholm Tapes in a new deluxe black and white cover.

The Demo Tapes (D1 D2)
Side one: 'Street Queen'/'Southern Son'/'Henry Boy'/'If I Were The Priest'/'Vibes Man'.
Side two: 'Song Of The Orphans'/'She's Leaving'/'The Song'/'Arabian Nights'/'Cowboys Of The Sea'.
Source: Music publishing demos; 'Southern Son' and 'Henry Boy' are definitely from Laurel

Canyon – possibly the others are too. Circa 1972, unknown studio(s).
Cover: Deluxe black and white.
Sound: Excellent.
Remarks: Original pressing was numbered. Re-pressings have come on blue vinyl with a blue sleeve, and on blue and yellow vinyl with a green sleeve. Not to be confused with the John Hammond demos.

The Devil In Disguise – (WHITE KNIGHT WK 274)
Side one: 'Rosalita'/'Kitty's Back'/'Thunder Road'/'4th Of July, Asbury Park (Sandy)'.
Side two: 'Walking In The Street'/'She's The One'/'A Love So Fine'/'Born To Run'/'Thunder Road'/'Jungleland' (part).
Source: Copy of E Ticket. See under relevant entry.
Cover: Deluxe colour.
Sound: Very good.
Remarks: Black vinyl.

Do I Have To Say His Name? – (DEVIL RECORD COMPANY 81918)
Side one: 'The Promise'/'Candy's Room'/'Spanish Eyes'/'Racing In The Street'.
Side two: 'Because The Night'/'Fire'/'Candy's Room'/'Jersey Girl'/'Southern Son'/'Cowboys Of The Sea'.
Source: Side one and the first three tracks on side two are out-takes from the Record Plant Studios, New York City, 1977–78. Side two, track four – Meadowlands, July 1981. Side two, tracks five and six are John Hammond demo tapes, 3 May 1972.
Cover: Deluxe colour.
Sound: Very good.
Remarks: Original pressings on black vinyl; later issued on red vinyl in a limited numbered edition. Superb colour photos from the M.U.S.E shows, 1979. Also know as The Jersey Devil Hits Again.

Do You Love Me? (STONED PONY PRODUCTIONS SR 10)
Side one: 'Born In The U.S.A.'/'Prove It All Night'/'Out In The Street'/'Atlantic City'.
Side two: 'Open All Night'/'Nebraska'/'Cover Me'/'Darlington County'.
Side three: 'Glory Days'/'The Promised Land'/'Johnny Bye Bye'/'The River'.
Side four: 'Badlands'/'Thunder Road'/'Hungry Heart'/'Dancing In The Dark'.
Side five: 'Cadillac Ranch'/'Sherry Darling'/'No Surrender'/'My Hometown'.

Side six: 'Pink Cadillac'/'Fire'/'Bobby Jean'/'Backstreets'.

Side seven: 'Rosalita'/'Jungleland'.

Side eight: 'I'm A Rocker'/'Devil With The Blue Dress' medley including 'Travelin' Band'/'Twist And Shout'/'Do You Love Me?'.

Source: Byrne Meadowlands Arena, East Rutherford, New Jersey, 16 August 1984.

Cover: Deluxe colour gatefold.

Sound: Very good.

Remarks: Superb cover and all round production.

Don't Look Back (PUD P 4234)

Side one: 'Roulette'/'Don't Look Back'/'Tenth Avenue Freeze Out'/'Rosalita'.

Side two: 'The Way'/'Santa Claus Is Comin' To Town'/'The Fever'/'The Promise'.

Source: Side one, track three – The Spectrum, Philadelphia, Pennsylvania, 1976 (slow version); track four – WBCN studios, Boston, 9 April 1974. Side two, track two – C.W. Post College, Greenvale, New York, 12 December 1975; track three – duet with Southside Johnny, possibly from The Stone Pony, Asbury Park, New Jersey, 17 April 1977; track four – unknown live recording, 1978. Remaining songs are studio out-takes, 1977–79.

Cover: Deluxe black and white photos with black lettering.

Sound: Good/excellent.

Remarks: Second pressing has blue border on cover. Extremely rare in its original form. A further limited pressing came on gold/yellow vinyl. Also known as *Collectors Items 1974–1980*.

Don't Look Back (PICTURE DISC)

Remarks: Identical track listing as above.

El Boos En Barcelona (MACARONI RECORDS)

Side one: 'The Ties That Bind'/'Who'll Stop The Rain?'/'Two Hearts'/'Cadillac Ranch'/'Because The Night'.

Side two: 'Backstreets'/'Devil With The Blue Dress' medley/'Rockin' All Over The World'.

Source: Palicio de Deportes, Barcelona, 21 April 1981.

Cover: Deluxe colour.

Sound: Fair.

Remarks: Limited numbered edition on black vinyl. Cover has a written dedication signed by Bruce. Same record as *Bruce Juice*.

E Ticket – (ESB 75–002)

Side one: 'Rosalita' (instrumental)/'Kitty's Back'/'Thunder Road'/'4th Of July, Asbury Park (Sandy)' (instrumental).

Side two: 'Walking In The Street'/'She's The One'/'A Love So Fine' (instrumental)/'Born To Run'/'Thunder Road'/'Jungleland' (part).

Source: Side one, tracks one, two and four – 914 Studios, Blauvelt, New York. All other songs – Record Plant, New York City. Recorded between October 1974 and August 1975.

Cover: Deluxe black and white photo of Bruce sitting outside a gas station. Believed to have been second choice as cover for the *Darkness* . . . . . LP. Excellent all round design.

Sound: Excellent.

Remarks: Rated as one of the best unofficial albums ever. Black vinyl. Has been copied with same track listing and cover (label unknown).

BRUCE SPRINGSTEEN

Follow that dream

E Ticket – PICTURE DISC
Remarks: Identical track listing to above; great picture, but with expected poorer sound.

Fire – (W9)
Side one: 'The Fever'/'Point Blank'.
Side two: 'Because The Night'/'Mona . . .'/'The Preacher's Daughter'/'She's The One'.
Side three: 'Fire'/'Candy's Room'/'Badlands'/'Streets Of Fire'.
Side four: 'The Promised Land'/'The Ties That Bind'/'Santa Claus Is Comin' To Town'.
Source: Winterland, San Francisco, California, 15 December 1978 (KSAN radio broadcast).
Cover: Red and yellow insert.
Sound: Good/very good.
Remarks: Pressed on 'Fire Wax' (yellow/orange vinyl with red spots).

Fire On The Fingertips – (U.K. 4)
Side one: 'Guns Of Kid Cole'/'Mama Knows 'Rithmatic, Knows How To Take A Fall'/'Get Your Wheels And Roll'.
Side two: 'Kid Called Zero'/'Angel From The Inner Lake – Ballerina'.
Source: Side one, tracks one and three – 914 Studios, Blaufelt, New York City, 1973;

track two – radio broadcast from Max's Kansas City, New York City, 30 August 1972. Side two, track one – 914 Studios, 1973; track two – unknown live, 1973.
Cover: Deluxe red and black photo.
Sound: Very good/excellent.
Remarks: Titles listed incorrectly – should read as follows . . .
Side one: 'Hey Santa Ana'/'Bishop Dance'/'Seaside Bar Song'.
Side two: 'Zero And Blind Terry'/'Thundercrack'. First issued on red vinyl, later copies on black or grey vinyl. One re-issue had a 12" insert cover.

Fire On The Fingertips – PICTURE DISC
Remarks: Superb red and black vinyl. Identical track listing to above.

Flat Top And Pin Drop – (SODD 006)
Side one: 'Thunder Road'/'Tenth Avenue Freeze Out'/'Spirit In The Night'/'Pretty Flamingo'.

Side two: 'She's The One'/'Born To Run'/'4th Of July, Asbury Park (Sandy)'/'Backstreets'.
Side three: 'Kitty's Back'/'Jungleland'.
Side four: 'Rosalita'/'Goin' Back'/'Devil With The Blue Dress' medley.
Source: Copy of *Aint No One Here From Billboard Tonight* (HAR 160).
Cover: Black and white insert.
Sound: Very good.

Follow That Dream – (BS)
Side one: 'Follow That Dream'/'Prove It All Night'/'Out In The Street'/'Tenth Avenue Freeze Out'/'Darkness On The Edge Of Town'/'Independence Day'.
Side two: 'Who'll Stop The Rain?'/'Two Hearts'/'The Promised Land'/'This Land Is Your Land'/'The River'.
Side three: 'Badlands'/'Thunder Road'/'Cadillac Ranch'/'Sherry Darling'/'Hungry Heart'.
Side four: 'Fire'/'You Can Look'/'Stolen Car'/'Racing In The Street'.
Side five: 'Backstreets'/'Candy's Room'/'Ramrod'/'Rosalita'.
Side six: 'Born To Run'/'Devil With The Blue Dress' medley (includes 'High School Confidential')/'Rockin' All Over The World'.
Source: Isstadion, Stockholm, 7 May 1981.
Cover: Deluxe colour gatefold. Opens out to a 24" by 12" photo of Bruce and Clarence.
Sound: Excellent.
Remarks: Superb all-round production. First pressing on black vinyl with black labels – a limited re-pressing carried a yellow label. An almost identical copy of the original pressing was made, except the inside photo is a horizontal photo of Bruce, and not the original one of Bruce, Clarence, Danny, Gary and Max live on stage. Originals are very rare.

God Save The Boss – (BOSS RECORDS)
Side one: 'He's Guilty'/'Goin' Back To Georgia'/'For You'/'Something In The Night'.
Side two: 'Action In The Streets'/'Drive All Night'/'I Don't Want To Go Home'/'Johnny Bye Bye'.
Source: Side one, tracks one and two – Bill Graham's Fillmore Records Studios, San Francisco, California, February 1970; track three – R.A.I. Building, Amsterdam, 23 November 1975; track four – Philadelphia Spectrum, Pennsylvania, 25 October 1976. Side two, track one – Boston Music Hall, Massachusetts, 25 March 1977; track two – Montreal Forum, 23 January 1981; tracks three and four – Byrne Meadowlands Arena, East Rutherford, 2 July 1981.
Cover: Deluxe colour.
Sound: Good.
Remarks: First two tracks are Steel Mill demos.

Good Rockin' That Night – (M 41)
Side one: 'Santa Claus Is Comin' To Town'/'Prove it All Night'.
Side two: 'Rave On'/'Fire'/'Candy's Room'/'Because The Night'.
Source: Paramount Theatre, Portland, Oregon, 19 December 1978.
Cover: Deluxe black and white.
Sound: Good/very good.
Remarks: Pressed on black vinyl with a limited edition on multi-coloured vinyl.

Greatest Rock Recordings Of The 80's – (BANDIDO RECORDS)
Side one: 'Wild Billy's Circus Story'/'Walking The Dog'.

Side two: 'New York City Serenade'.
Source: Liberty Hall, Houston, Texas, 10 March 1974.
Sound: Fair.
Remarks: A 10 album box set with one LP each by Bruce, Tom Petty, Kevin Rowland, Elliot Murphy, J. J. Cale, Dirk Hamilton, Van Morrison, Elvis Costello, Steve Ray Vaughan and Little Steven and the Disciples Of Soul (Rockpalast TV, West Germany, 15 May 1983).

The Great White Boss – (Hangman logo picture)
Side one: 'Tenth Avenue Freeze Out'/'Spirit In The Night'/'Then She Kissed Me'/'Growin' Up'/'It's Hard To Be A Saint In The City'.
Side two: 'E Street Shuffle'.
Side three: 'Every Time You Walk In The Room'/'She's The One'/'Born To Run'/'Thunder Road'.
Side four: 'Rosalita'/'4th Of July, Asbury Park (Sandy)'/'Quarter To Three'.
Side five: 'You Mean So Much To Me'.
Side six: 'Don't Look Back'/'Action In The Streets'.
Source: Bottom Line, New York City, 15 August 1975 (except sides five and six – see remarks). WNEW radio broadcast.
Cover: Box with insert.
Sound: Very good.
Remarks: Sides five and six are a 12" 45r.p.m. EP on white vinyl. Has often been copied in the same format, but with the black and white insert slightly out of focus. Side five recorded at My Father's Place, New York City, 31 July 1973. Side six recorded at Boston Music Hall, Massachusetts, 25 March 1977. Coloured vinyl. First pressing came with a Hanging Man label. Very rare in this form.

The Great White Boss – (GWHBS)
Side one: 'Tenth Avenue Freeze Out'/'Spirit In The Night'/'Then She Kissed Me'/'Growin' Up'/'It's Hard To Be A Saint In The City'.
Side two: 'E Street Shuffle'/'Circus Song'.
Side three: 'Every Time You Walk In The Room'/'She's The One'/'Born To Run'/'Thunder Road'.
Side four: 'Rosalita'/'4th Of July, Asbury Park (Sandy)'/'Quarter To Three'.
Source: Bottom Line, New York City, 15 August 1975 (except 'Circus Song' – see remarks).
Cover: Deluxe black and white photo from 1979.
Sound: Very good.
Remarks: 'Circus Song' is the version released on the promotional *Playback* EP (AS 52), recorded at the CBS three-day convention at the Ahmanson Theatre, Los Angeles, California, 1 May 1973.

The Great White Boss –(BLOCKHEAD RECORDS)
Remarks: One of the copies of the three – LP boxed set.

The Great White Boss – PICTURE DISC
Remarks: Same 1979 picture of Bruce and Clarence as on the two-LP set. Surprisingly, the record is *Live At The Roxy Theatre*.

Greetings From The Edge Of Darkness – (CNT)
Remarks: Re-pressing of sides 3–6 of the *1981 Box File* with a black and white insert.

Growin' Up Tour Legend – (SWINGIN' PIG)
Side one: 'Something In The Night'/'It's My Life'/'Point Blank'.
Side two: 'I Wanna Marry You'/'Mona' . . . 'She's The One'.
Source: Side one, track three – Portland, Oregon,

The
Great
White
Boss

BOTTOM LINE
8/15/75

Side One
1) Tenth Avenue Freeze Out
2) Spirit in the Night
3) And Then She Kissed Me
4) Growing Up
5) Saint in the City

Side Two
E Street Shuffle

Side Three
1) Everytime You Walk in the Room
2) Shes the One
3) Born To Run
4) Thunder Road

Side Four
1) Rosalita
2) Sandy
3) Quarter to Three

Side Five
You Mean So Much To Me
(Rare recording 1973 place unknown)

Side Six
1) Don't Look Back
2) Action in the Streets
(Rare recording 1973 place unknown)

25 October 1980. Side two, track one – Oakland, California, 27 October 1980. All other songs – The Masonic Auditorium, Detroit, Michigan, 15 February 1977.
Cover: Deluxe black and white.
Sound: Fair/good.
Remarks: Numbered edition on black vinyl.

He's Not An American Dreamer – (2–33–30)
Side one: 'For You'/'Walking In The Street'/'Song Of The Orphans'/'The Price You Pay'.
Side two: 'The E Street Shuffle'/'Stolen Car'/'Thunder Road'.
Source: Side one, track one – Atlanta, Georgia, 21 August 1975. Track two and side two, track three – Record Plant studios, New York City, recorded between October 1974 and August 1975. 'Song Of The Orphans' – recorded for a music publishing demo tape in 1972. Side one, track four – Stockholm, 8 May 1981. Side two, track two –

Stockholm, 7 May 1981. 'The E Street Shuffle' – London, 18 November 1975.
Cover: Deluxe colour.
Sound: Fair.
Remarks: All tracks copied from previous albums.

Happy New Year – (FP)
Side one: 'Night'/'Prove It All Night'/'Spirit In The Night'/'Darkness On The Edge Of Town'.
Side two: Independence Day'/'Who'll Stop The Rain?'/'This Land Is Your Land'/'The Promised Land'/'Out In The Street'.
Side three: 'Racing In The Street'/'The River'/'Badlands'.
Side four: 'Thunder Road'/'Cadillac Ranch'/'Sherry Darling'/'Hungry Heart'/'Merry Christmas Baby'.
Side five: 'Fire'/'Candy's Room'/'Because The Night'/'4th Of July, Asbury Park (Sandy)'.
Side six: 'Rendezvous'/'Fade Away'/'The Price You Pay'/'Wreck On The Highway'.
Side seven: 'Two Hearts'/'Ramrod'/'You Can Look'/'Held Up Without A Gun'/'In The Midnight Hour'/'Auld Lang Syne'.
Side eight: 'Rosalita'/'Santa Claus Is Comin' To Town'.

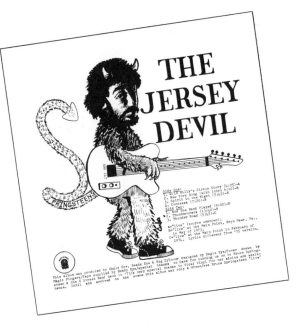

"THE LOST LIVE TAPES"

Side nine: 'Jungleland'/'Born To Run'.
Side ten: 'Devil With The Blue Dress' medley/'Twist And Shout'/'Raise Your Hand'.
Source: The Nassau Coliseum, Uniondale, New York, 31 December 1980.
Cover: Box set.
Sound: Excellent.
Remarks: Complete concert from Bruce and the E Street Band's epic New Year's Eve show. Also issued on red vinyl.

Harley In Heat – (TMQ)
Remarks: Copy of *Aint No One Here From Billboard Tonight*.

Hot Coals From The Fiery Furnace – (HAR 164)
Side one: 'It's Hard To Be A Saint In The City'/'The E Street Shuffle'.
Side two: 'New York City Serenade'/'Lost In The Flood'.
Side three: 'For You'/'Night'/'Tenth Avenue Freeze Out'/'Does This Bus Stop At 82nd Street?'/'You Never Can Tell'.
Side four: 'Wear My Ring Around Your Neck'/'It's My Life'/'Sha La La'/'Santa Claus Is Comin' To Town'/'It's Gonna Work Out Fine'/'Up On The Roof'.
Source: Side one, track one – The Main Point, 24 April 1973. Track two – Live, October or November 1975. Side two, track one and side three, track one – The Main Point, 5 February 1975. Side two, track two and side four, tracks two, three and four – C.W. Post College, Greenvale, New York, 12 December 1975. Side three, tracks two and three – Philadelphia, Pennsylvania, 31 December 1975. Track four – The Main Point, 24 April 1973. Track five – The Agora, Cleveland, Ohio, 3 June 1974. Side four, tracks five and six – The Bottom Line, New York City, 16 August 1975 (early show). Side four, track one – unknown live.
Cover: Orange and black insert.
Sound: Fair/very good.
Remarks: First pressing came on multi-coloured vinyl with picture label. Original copies are hard to find. Re-pressed on red and yellow vinyls.

Hot Coals From The Fiery Furnace – (TMQ 5468)
Remarks: Identical track listing to the original, but pressed on black vinyl.

Hungry Heart – (BS 526 602)
Side one: 'Out In The Street'/'The Ties That Bind'/'Darkness On The Edge Of Town'/'Follow That Dream'/'Two Hearts'.
Side two: 'Who'll Stop The Rain?'/'The Promised Land'/'This Land Is Your Land'/'The River'.
Side three: 'Badlands'/'Thunder Road'/'You Can Look'/'Cadillac Ranch'.
Side four: 'Sherry Darling'/'Hungry Heart'/'Fire'/'Because The Night'.
Side five: 'Prove It All Night'/'Factory'/'Independence Day'/'Johnny Bye Bye'/'Hungry Heart'/'Wreck On The Highway'.
Side six: 'Racing In The Street'/'Backstreets'/'Born To Run'/'Devil With The Blue Dress' medley.
Source: Sides one to four – Wembley Arena, London, 2 June 1981; sides five and six – Brighton, England, 26 May 1981.
Cover: Deluxe black and white photo, the same as the official sleeve for the single of the same name.
Sound: Good/very good.
Remarks: Cover claims it is a Japanese promo release. Black vinyl.

In Concert Hallenstadion Zurich – (UNKNOWN)
Remarks: Unconfirmed album; possibly a copy of *Live In Zurich*.

In Concert 1978 – (BS)
Remarks: Re-packaged copy of *Cry Me A River*, with black and white insert, pressed on both black and green vinyls.

I Was A Teenage Werewolf I & II
Remarks: Unsold copies of *The Agora Show*, parts I and II, in new sleeve. Worthless.

The Jersey Devil – (HAR 147)
Side one: 'Circus Song'/'New York Song'/'Spirit In The Night'/'Hey Santa Ana'.
Side two: 'Tokyo'/'Thundercrack'/'Thunder Road'.
Source: Side one, track one – The Ahmanson Theatre, Los Angeles, California, CBS convention, 1 May 1973. Side two, track three – partly from The Main Point, Bryn Mawr, Pennsylvania, 5 February 1975 (live) and part *Born To Run* LP version. All other songs – The Main Point, 24 April 1973.
Cover: Black and white insert.
Sound: Good/very good.
Remarks: 'Circus Story' from the CBS Playback series (AS 52). 'Thunder Road' starts off as the album version, then segues into a live performance. Original version on black vinyl with a silver label. Thought to be the very first unofficial release. HAR = Hoffman Avenue Records. (Also released as a black and white cartoon picture disc.)

The Jersey Devil – (BLOCKHEAD RECORDS)
Remarks: Pressed on both red and black vinyl. Copied from original, but with 'Thunder Road' and 'Circus Song' omitted. Similar insert.

The Jersey Devil – (PICTURE DISC – JRP 11773)
Side one: Interview – 'The Boss Nickname'/'E Street Shuffle' (part).
Side two: Interview – 'Billboard Sign'/'E Street Shuffle' (part).
Source: Interview with Dave Herman, KBFH radio, San Diego, 9 July 1978. 'E Street Shuffle' from The Bottom Line, New York City, 15 August 1975.
Disc: Great red and black photo of Bruce.
Sound: Poor.
Remarks: 'E Street Shuffle' is from the same source.

Just A Prisoner Of Rock 'N' Roll – (BOSS RECORDS)
Side one: 'Does This Bus Stop At 82nd Street?'/'Let The Four Winds Blow'/'Rosalita'.
Side two: '4th Of July, Asbury Park (Sandy)'/'Quarter To Three'/'Twist And Shout'.
Source: Side one, and side two, track three – Joe's Place, Boston, Massachusetts, 5 January 1974. Side two, tracks one and two – The Uptown Theatre, Milwaukee, Wisconsin, 2 October 1975.
Cover: Deluxe colour.
Sound: Good.
Remarks: Numbered edition. Also known as *Live In Milwaukee 1975*.

King Of The Alley – (TMQ 5466)
Remarks: Copy of *The Jersey Devil* on red vinyl.

King Of The Alley – (K & S 060)
Remarks: Pressed from the TMQ plates on black vinyl.

King Of The Alley – (BLOCKHEAD RECORDS)
Remarks: Copy of *The Jersey Devil*.

Live – (CORAL RECORDS NR 909–2)
Side one: 'Tenth Avenue Freeze Out'/'Spirit In The Night'/'Then She Kissed Me'/'Growin' Up'/'It's Hard To Be A Saint In The City'.
Side two: 'E Street Shuffle'/'Every Time You Walk In The Room'/'She's The One'.
Side three: 'Born To Run'/'Kitty's Back'.
Side four: 'Thunder Road'/'Rosalita'/'4th Of July, Asbury Park (Sandy)'/'Quarter To Three'.
Source: The Bottom Line, New York City, 15 August 1975 (WNEW radio broadcast). 'Born To Run' is, in part, the official LP version.
Cover: Superb colour gatefold.
Sound: Very good.

Remarks: Certainly the rarest of all Bruce bootlegs. Such was the high quality of its pressing and packaging (in 1976) that it prompted CBS, Bruce and The Bottom Line club to file suit against a record store caught selling it. On 10 September 1976 the case was 'amicably resolved' for an undisclosed sum. The album features the whole of Bruce's early show that night, although 'Thunder Road' is not in the correct sequence, 'Born To Run' is, as stated, partly the LP version, and between-song talk is omitted. Black vinyl, black labels with song titles on each side.

Live At The Bottom Line 8/15/75 – (NO LABEL)
Side one: 'Tenth Avenue Freeze Out'/'Spirit In The Night'/'Then She Kissed Me'/'Growin' Up'/'It's Hard To Be A Saint In The City'.
Side two: 'E Street Shuffle'.
Side three: 'Every Time You Walk In The Room'/'She's The One'/'Born To Run'/'Thunder Road'.
Side four: 'Rosalita'/'4th Of July, Asbury Park (Sandy)'/'Quarter To Three'.
Source: The Bottom Line, New York City, 15 August 1975. WNEW radio broadcast.
Cover: Deluxe black and white.
Sound: Very good.
Remarks: 'Kitty's Back' omitted from full concert. Black vinyl.

Live At The Bottom Line – (BLACK GOLD CONCERTS BG–909–2)
Cover: Deluxe black and white.

Live At The Hammersmith Odeon – (BS 1975)
Side one: 'Tenth Avenue Freeze Out'/'Spirit In The Night'/'Lost In The Flood'/'She's The One'.
Side two: 'Born To Run'/'E Street Shuffle'/'It's Hard To Be A Saint In The City'.
Source: Hammersmith Odeon, London, 18 November 1975.
Cover: Green and black insert.
Sound: Fair/good.
Remarks: Neat cover insert features a montage of some monkeys playing instruments with a photo of Bruce in the background. Black vinyl.

Live At The Roxy Theatre Hollywood 1978 – (RAVEN RECORDS BS 6895)
Side one: 'Badlands'/'Spirit In The Night'/'Darkness On The Edge Of Town'/'Candy's Room'/'For You'.

Side two: 'The Promised Land'/'Prove It All Night'/'Paradise By The Sea'/'Fire'/'Adam Raised A Cain'.
Side three: 'Adam Raised A Cain'/'Mona' . . . 'She's The One'/'Growin' Up'.
Side four: 'Heartbreak Hotel'/'Rosalita'/'Independence Day'/'Born To Run'.
Source: The Roxy, Los Angeles, California, 7 July 1978 (KMET radio broadcast).
Cover: Black and white insert.
Sound: Very good.
Remarks: Black vinyl. Cover lists songs as track listing for *Raises Cain* (OMEGA 917).

Live At The Roxy Theatre Hollywood 1978 – (LARTH 1978)
Remarks: Identical track listing to above. Deluxe black and white photo cover.

Live At The Roxy Theatre Hollywood 1978 – PICTURE DISC
Remarks: Sides two and three of LARTH 1978 with same black and white photo.

Live In Amsterdam – (DM 10002)
Side one: 'Night'/'Rendezvous'/'Spirit In The Night'/'Thunder Road'.
Side two: 'Tenth Avenue Freeze Out'/'Spirit In The Night'/'Lost In The Flood'/'She's The One'.
Source: Side one, tracks one–three – The Spectrum, Philadelphia, Pennsylvania, 25 October 1976. All other songs – R.A.I. Building, Amsterdam, 23 November 1975.
Cover: Plain white sleeve with title stamp.
Sound: Fair/good.
Remarks: Second pressing came in deluxe black and white cover. Title misleading, as only half of LP recorded in Amsterdam.

Live In Californiatown
Remarks: Worthless home-made re-packaging of *Live At The Roxy*.

Live In Philadelphia – (BS)
Cover: Original cover was a plain white sleeve with title stamp.
Sound: Good.
Remarks: Same record as *Cry Me A River*. Originally pressed on purple vinyl and re-released on black vinyl with a deluxe cover. Has been re-packaged and re-titled in various forms, but this is considered to be the original pressing and title.

Live In Philadephia Vol. II – (CESCO ELECTRONICS SS 13)
Side one: 'It's My Life'/'Something In The Night'.
Side two: 'Backstreets'/'Rosalita'.
Source: Possibly Monmouth Arts Centre, Red Bank, New Jersey, August 1976.
Cover: Deluxe colour.
Sound: Very good.
Remarks: Original copies on coloured vinyl. Excellent all-round package.

Live In Stockholm
Remarks: Three–LP box set, copied from *Teardrops On The City*, with same track listing. Black and white insert.

Live In The Promised Land – (SLIPPED DISC BS 2978)
Side one: 'Badlands'/'Streets Of Fire'/'Spirit In The Night'/'Darkness On The Edge Of Town'/'Factory'.
Side two: 'The Promised Land'/'Prove It All Night'/'Racing In The Steet'/'Thunder Road'.
Side three: 'Jungleland'/'Interview'/'The Ties That Bind'/'Santa Claus Is Coming To Town'.
Side four: 'The Fever'/'Fire'/'Candy's Room'/'Because The Night'/'Point Blank'.
Side five: 'Mona'/'The Preacher's Daughter'/'She's The One'/'Backstreets'/'Rosalita'.
Side six: 'Rosalita' (concluded)/'Born To Run'/'Devil With The Blue Dress' medley.
Source: Winterland, San Francisco, California, 15 December 1978. Interview recorded backstage at Tucson, Arizona, 13 December 1978 (KSAN radio broadcast).
Cover: Original copies came in box with insert. See remarks.
Sound: Excellent.
Remarks: First pressing in a limited box set. Second pressing in deluxe black and white gatefold sleeve. Has been copied in both types of cover several times, including a pressing on yellow vinyl.

Live In The Promised Land – (PISTE DISQUES)
Remarks: Deluxe black and white sleeve. Identical track listing to above.

Live In Zurich – (BOSS RECORDS FMF 001)
Side one: 'Factory'/'Out In The Street'/'Tenth Avenue Freeze Out'/'Darkness On The Edge Of Town'/'Independence Day'.

Maryland, 2 November 1978. Track four – Tempe, Arizona, 5 November 1980. Side two, tracks one to three – Richfield Coliseum, Cleveland, Ohio, 1 January 1979.

Cover: Deluxe colour.
Sound: Very good.

Luther – (SS 19)
Side one: 'Walking In The Streets'/'Rendezvous'/ 'Outside Looking In'/'Something In The Night'/'Because The Night'.
Side two: 'I Wanna Be With You'/'Darkness On The Edge Of Town'/'Racing In The Street'/'The Promise'.
Side three: 'Don't Look Back'/'Spanish Eyes'/'Let's Go Tonight'/'Streets Of Fire'/'Candy's Room'.
Side four: 'Sherry Darling'/'Candy's Boy'/ 'Badlands'/'Fire'.
Side five: 'Drive All Night'/'Something In The Night'/'Spanish Eyes'.
Side six: 'Roulette'/'Fade Away'/'Be True'/ 'Ramrod'/'I Wanna Marry You'/ 'I Wanna Marry You'.
Source: Sides one to five – studio out-takes from the Record Plant, N.Y.C., recorded between November 1977 and May 1978 (with the exception of side one, track one – October 1974 to July 1975). Side six – the Power Station Studios, N.Y.C., out-takes recorded between May 1979 and September 1980.
Cover: Box set with colour insert.
Sound: Poor/fair.
Remarks: Pressed on white, green and orange vinyl.

More Greetings From Asbury Park N.J. – (MOONBEAM RECORDS CBBS)
Side one: 'Blinded By The Light'/'Growin' Up'/'Mary, Queen Of Arkansas'/'Does This Bus Stop At 82nd Street?'/'Lost In The Flood'.
Side two: 'For You'/'Spirit In The Night'/'It's Hard To Be A Saint In The City'.
Source: Side one, track one – The Main Point, 31 October 1973; track two – unknown live; track three – WHFS studios, 2 June 1973; track four – My Father's Place, New York City, 31 July 1973; track five and side two, track one – Boston Music Hall, Massachusetts, 3 December 1975. Side two, tracks two and three – My Father's Place, New York City, 31 July 1973.
Cover: Black and white insert.
Sound: Poor.
Remarks: An attempt to re-create the official *Greetings . . .* in a live format (cover remarks on the absence of 'The Angel'). Poor sound quality makes it virtually unlistenable to.

Moving Up To Stockholm
Side one: 'Tenth Avenue Freeze Out'/'Darkness On The Edge Of Town'/'Independence Day'/'Who'll Stop The Rain?'
Side two: 'The Promised Land'/'This Land Is Your Land'/'The River'.
Side three: 'Thunder Road'/'Cadillac Ranch'/'Sherry Darling'/'Hungry Heart'/'Fire'/'You Can Look'.
Side four: 'Stolen Car'/'Racing In The Street'/'Backstreets'.
Side five: 'Rosalita'/'Born To Run'/'Devil With The Blue Dress' medley (includes 'High School Confidential').
Side six: Medley (concluded)/'Rockin' All Over The World'.

Side two: 'Who'll Stop The Rain?'/'You Can Look'/'The Promised Land'/'The River'/'Fire'.
Source: Hallenstadion, Zurich, 11 April 1981.
Cover: Deluxe colour.
Sound: Good/very good.
Remarks: First pressing was a numbered edition. Also known as *For My Friends*.

Live In Zurich – (OCEAN RECORDS SS3)
Side one: 'Tenth Avenue Freeze Out'/'Darkness On The Edge Of Town'/'Independence Day'/'Who'll Stop The Rain?'.
Side two: 'The Promised Land'/'This Land Is Your Land'/'The River'/'Thunder Road'.
Side three: 'Cadillac Ranch'/'Wreck On The Highway'/'Racing In The Street'/'Fire'.
Side four: 'Rosalita'/'Devil With The Blue Dress'

medley/'Rockin' All Over The World'.
Source: Hallenstadion, Zurich, 11 April 1981.
Cover: Deluxe black and white.
Sound: Very good.
Remarks: First pressing was a numbered edition on black vinyl. A second pressing came on orange and black vinyls.

The Lost Live Tapes – (CDS RECORDS AS 271 4–33–30)
Side one: 'Born To Run'/'It's Gonna Work Out Fine'/'The Ties That Bind'/'I Wanna Marry You'.
Side two: 'Santa Claus Is Comin' To Town'/'I Fought The Law'/'The Fever'/'Quarter To Three'.
Source: Side one, tracks one and two and side two, track four – Texas, September 1975. Side one, track three – Capital Centre, Largo,

Source: Isstadion, Stockholm, 7 May 1981.
Cover: Deluxe black and white.
Sound: Very good/excellent.
Remarks: Pressed on black vinyl. Incomplete concert from the same master tape that produced *Follow That Dream*. 'Fire' not listed on the cover.

Nassau – (S.F.E. RECORDS)
Side one: 'Merry Christmas Baby'/'Badlands'/'Two Hearts'/'Tenth Avenue Freeze Out'/'Darkness On The Edge Of Town'.
Side two: 'Independence Day'/'Who'll Stop The Rain?'/'The Promised Land'/'Out In The Street'.
Side three: 'Prove It All Night'/'Thunder Road'/'Cadillac Ranch'/'Sherry Darling'.
Side four: 'Fire'/'Because The Night'/'Stolen Car'/'Wreck On The Highway'.
Side five: 'Point Blank'/'The Ties That Bind'/'Ramrod'/'You Can Look'/'Rosalita' (part).
Side six: 'Santa Claus Is Comin' To Town'/'Jungleland'/'Born To Run'/'Devil With The Blue Dress' medley (part).
Source: Nassau Coliseum, Uniondale, New York, 29 December 1980.
Cover: Box with inserts (black and white photo, plus track list).
Sound: Fair.
Remarks: Incorrect track listing on insert. Black vinyl. Re-pressing came in single sleeve with colour insert.

Nassau – (PICTURE DISC)
Remarks: Sides five and six of the above. Red and black vinyl.

New York Palladium 1976 – (TOASTED RECORDS SS 12)
Side one: Murray the K opening/'Rendezvous'/'It's My Life'.
Side two: 'Something In The Night'/'Growin' Up'/'Rosalita'.
Single: 'We Gotta Get Outta This Place'/'Action In The Streets'.
Source: Sides one and two, and side one of the bonus 7" single – The Palladium, New York City, 4 November 1976. Side two of the single – Boston Music Hall, Massachusetts, 25 March 1977.
Cover: Deluxe black and white.
Sound: Good.

Remarks: Copy of *Paid The Cost To Be The Boss* in a limited edition on green vinyl. The 7" single is on orange vinyl.

The Night They Drove Old '80 Down – (WIL)
Side one: 'Night'/'Prove It All Night'/'Spirit In The Night'.
Side two: 'Darkness On The Edge Of Town'/'Independence Day'/'Who'll Stop The Rain?'/'This Land Is Your Land'.
Side three: 'Racing In The Street'/'The River'/'Badlands'.
Side four: 'Thunder Road'/'Cadillac Ranch'/'Sherry Darling'/'Hungry Heart'.
Side five: 'Merry Christmas Baby'/'Fire'/'Candy's Room'/'Because The Night'.
Side six: '4th Of July, Asbury Park (Sandy)'/'Rendezvous'/'Fade Away'.
Side seven: 'Wreck On The Highway'/'Two Hearts'/'Ramrod'/'You Can Look'/'Held Up Without A Gun'.
Side eight: 'In The Midnight Hour'/'Auld Lang Syne'/'Rosalita'.
Side nine: 'Jungleland'/'Born To Run'.
Side ten: 'Santa Claus Is Comin' To Town'/'The Promised Land'/'Twist And Shout'/'Raise Your Hand'.
Source: The Nassau Coliseum, Uniondale, New York, 31 December 1980.
Cover: Box set.
Sound: Excellent.
Remarks: Comes with leaflet containing photos and track listing.

1981 Box File – (CNT)
Side one: 'Prove It All Night'/'The Ties That Bind'/'Out In The Street'.
Side two: 'Darkness On The Edge Of Town'/'Independence Day'.
Side three: 'Johnny Bye Bye'/'Jackson Cage'/'Trapped'/'Two Hearts'.
Side four: 'The Promised Land'/'This Land Is Your Land'/'Badlands'.
Side five: 'Thunder Road'/'Cadillac Ranch'.
Side six: 'You Can Look'/'Sherry Darling'/'Hungry Heart'/'Fire'.
Source: Wembley Arena, London, 29–30 May 1981.
Cover: Box with black and white insert.
Sound: Fair/poor.
Remarks: Poor quality pressing on black vinyl. Also limited pressings on red, green and white vinyl.

1981 Box File
Remarks: Same as the box set, except that it came in a single white sleeve (stamped), with only two of the three records (mixed selection). A shoddy deal all round.

No Nukes – (NK)
Side one: 'Prove It All Night'/'Badlands'/'The Promised Land'/'The River'.
Side two: 'Sherry Darling'/'Rosalita'/'Born To Run'.
Side three: 'Stay'/'Devil With The Blue Dress' medley/'Rave On'/'Raise Your Hand'.
Side four: 'Raise Your Hand' (concluded)/'4th Of

July, Asbury Park (Sandy)'/'Does This Bus Stop At 82nd Street?'/'It's My Life'.
Source: Side one, side two and side three, tracks one, two and three – the M.U.S.E. concert at Madison Square Garden, New York City, 21 September 1979. 'Raise Your Hand' and 'Sandy' recorded at the Municipal Auditorium, Mobile, Alabama, 10 May 1976. Side four, tracks three and four – The Tower Theatre, Philadelphia, Pennsylvania, 30 December 1975.
Cover: Deluxe black and white.
Sound: Very good.
Remarks: 'Stay' is with Jackson Browne. 'Rosalita' is incomplete. Black vinyl.

October Stories – (CLASSIC FALL S–I)
Cover: High quality colour photostats of the three magazine covers that featured Bruce in October 1975 (notably *Time* and *Newsweek*).
Sound: Good/very good.
Remarks: A copy of *Prove It Every Night*. Black vinyl.

On The Prowl, New Jersey 1982
Remarks: Unconfirmed album. Track listing believed to be: 'Ready Teddy'/'From Small Things, Big Things One Day Come'/'(Come On) Let's Go'/'Come On Over To My Place'/'Around And Around'/'Lucille' . . . 'On The Prowl'/'Twist And Shout'. From a gig with Cats On A Smooth Surface at The Stone Pony, Asbury Park, N.J., 8 August 1982. Possibly other songs as well.

Paid The Cost To Be The Boss – (ESB 75 002 AB)
Side one: Murray The K opening/'Rendezvous'/'It's My Life'.
Side two: 'Something In The Night'/'Growin' Up'/'Rosalita'.
Source: The Palladium, New York City, 4 November 1976 (WCOZ radio broadcast).
Cover: Deluxe black and white photo.
Sound: Very good.
Remarks: Original pressing on purple/blue vinyl with Hanging Man labels – very rare in this form. Later re-pressed on both white and black vinyl. Great version of 'Something In The Night' with trumpet and a different lyric. The concert was recorded for radio broadcast at a later date in the Boston area. It's probable that a tape of this was used as the master for the album.

145

Palladium '76 – (BLOCKHEAD RECORDS)
Cover: Black and white insert.
Sound: Good.
Remarks: Copy of *Paid The Cost . . .* on black vinyl.

Philadelphia Special – (PHANTOM PRODUCTIONS IK)
Side one: 'Summertime Blues'/'Badlands'/'Spirit In The Night'/'Darkness On The Edge Of Town'/'Factory'.
Side two: 'The Promised Land'/'Prove It All Night'/'Racing In The Street'.
Side three: 'Thunder Road'/'Jungleland'/'Paradise By The Sea'.
Side four: 'The Fever'/'Sherry Darling'/'Not Fade Away' . . . 'Gloria' . . . 'She's The One'.
Side five: 'Growin' Up'/'Rosalita'/'Born To Run'.
Side six: 'Because The Night'/'Rave On'/'Quarter To Three'.
Source: The Spectrum, Philadelphia, Pennsylvania, 18 August 1978.
Cover: Box with insert.
Sound: Poor.
Remarks: Pressed on red, white and blue vinyl in a numbered edition. Gary Busey joins Bruce and the band for 'Rave On' and 'Quarter To Three'.

Piece De Resistance – (PISTE)
Side one: 'Badlands'/'Streets Of Fire'/'Spirit In The Night'/'Darkness On The Edge Of Town'/'Independence Day'.
Side two: 'The Promised Land'/'Prove It All Night'/'Racing In The Street'/'Thunder Road'.
Side three: 'Meeting Across The River'/'Jungleland'/'Kitty's Back'/'Fire' (part).
Side four: 'Candy's Room'/'Because The Night'/'Point Blank'.
Side five: 'Not Fade Away' . . . 'She's The One'/'Backstreets'/'Rosalita'.
Side six: '4th Of July, Asbury Park (Sandy)'/'Born To Run'/'Tenth Avenue Freeze Out'/'Devil With The Blue Dress' medley/'Raise Your Hand'.
Source: Capitol Theatre, Passaic, New Jersey, 19 September 1978 (WNEW radio broadcast).

Cover: Box with insert.
Sound: Excellent.
Remarks: First pressing in limited numbered edition. Several re-pressings have appeared with slight sound deterioration, and the number is written, not printed. A further re-press featured a different insert.

Porn In The U.S.A. – (INTERNATIONAL RECORDS RSR 208)
Side one: 'Badlands'/'Prove It All Night'/'Out In The Street'/'Atlantic City'.
Side two: 'Open All Night'/'Used Cars'/'Trapped'/'Glory Days'.
Side three: 'The Promised Land'/'Nebraska'/'The River'/'Born In The U.S.A.'.
Side four: 'Thunder Road'/'Cadillac Ranch'/'Hungry Heart'/'Dancing In The Dark'.
Source: National Exhibition Grandstand, Toronto, Canada, 24 July 1984.
Cover: Black and white insert.
Sound: Good.
Remarks: Unbelievable title.

Porn In The U.S.A. TOO – (FAN CLUB OF TAIWAN RSR 210)
Side one: 'Tenth Avenue Freeze-Out'/'No Surrender'/'Because The Night'/'I'm On Fire'.
Side two: 'Pink Cadillac'/'Bobby Jean'/'Racing In The Street'.
Side three: 'Rosalita'/'Jungleland'.
Side four: 'Born To Run'/'Street Fighting Man'/'Devil With The Blue Dress' medley.
Source: National Exhibition Grandstand, Toronto, Canada, 24 July 1984.
Cover: Black and white insert.
Sound: Good.

Prisoner Of Rock 'N' Roll – (PSYCHOBROTHERS RECORDS A/B)
Side one: 'It's Gonna Work Out Fine'/'When You Walk In The Room'/'Then She Kissed Me'/'Sha La La'/'Rave On'/'Summertime Blues'.
Side two: 'I Fought The Law'/'Who'll Stop The Rain?'/'You Never Can Tell'/'Mountain Of Love'/'Trapped'.
Source: Various live tapes, from 1974 to 1981.
Cover: Deluxe colour.
Sound: Very good overall.
Remarks: Has been copied on red vinyl with unlaminated cover.

The Promise
Side one: 'The Ties That Bind'/'Seaside Bar Song'/'Zero And Blind Terry'/'Because The Night'/'The Promise'/'Thunder Road'.

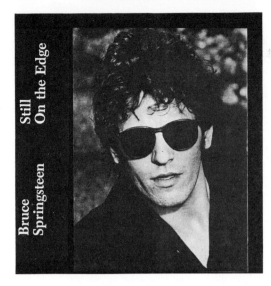

Side two: 'Independence Day'/'Point Blank'/'The Fever'/'Fire'/'Santa Claus Is Comin' To Town'.
Source: Side one, track one and side two (except 'Independence Day') – Winterland, San Francisco, California, 15 December 1978 (KSAN radio broadcast). Side one, tracks two and three – 914 Studios, Blaufelt, New York, 1973. Side one, tracks four and five – The Record Plant Studios, New York City, 1977–78; track six – The Record Plant Studios, New York City, 1974–75. Side two, track one – The Roxy, Los Angeles, California, 7 July 1978 (KMET radio broadcast).
Cover: Deluxe black and white.
Sound: Good.
Remarks: Very rare. A recent U.S.A. re-press features a yellow and black insert.

Prove It Every Night – (RETRO RBL–I)
Side one: 'Because The Night'/'Point Blank'.
Side two: 'Not Fade Away' . . . 'She's The One'/Interview/'Good Rockin' Tonight'/'The Fever'.
Source: Side one and side two, track one – The Capitol Theatre, Passaic, New Jersey, 19 September 1978. Side two, track three – Madison Square Garden, New York, 22 August 1978. 'The Fever' is the studio demo from 1973. Interview is KBFH radio, San Diego, California, 9 July 1978.
Cover: Black and orange insert.
Sound: Good.
Remarks: Black vinyl.

Race With The Devil – (S–21)
Remarks: Worthless home-made re-packaging of sides 3–4 of the *Stockholm Tapes* in a new deluxe black and white cover.

Ragamuffin Gunner – (TMQ 5468)
Side one: 'It's Hard To Be A Saint In The City'/'E Street Shuffle'.
Side two: 'New York City Serenade'/'Lost In The Flood'.
Side three: 'For You'/'Night'/'Tenth Avenue Freeze Out'/'Does This Bus Stop At 82nd Street?'/'You Never Can Tell'.
Side four: 'Wear My Ring Around Your Neck'/'It's My Life'/'Sha La La'/'Santa Claus Is Comin' To Town'/'It's Gonna Work Out Fine'/'Up On The Roof'.
Source: Inferior copy of *Hot Coals . . .*
Cover: Black and pink insert.
Sound: Fair.

Remarks: Black vinyl. Matrix number (HAR 164) in dead wax area.

Ragamuffin Gunner – PICTURE DISC
Remarks: Sides three and four of above.

Raises Cain – (OMEGA RECORDS 917)
Side one: 'Rave On'/'Badlands'/'Spirit In The Night'/'Darkness On The Edge Of Town'/'Candy's Room'.
Side two: 'For You'/'Point Blank'/'Prove It All Night'.
Side three: 'Racing In The Street'/'Thunder Road'/'Fire'/'Adam Raised A Cain'.
Side four: 'Growin' Up'/'It's Hard To Be A Saint In The City'/'Backstreets'.
Source: The Roxy, Los Angeles, California, 7 July 1978 (live radio broadcast on KMED).
Cover: Deluxe pink and white drawing.
Sound: Very good.
Remarks: Black vinyl. 'Backstreets' segues into an early verson of 'Drive All Night' ('Sad Eyes').

Rarities – (RECORD MAN 914)
Cover: Deluxe black and white, with photos from the Steel Mill era.
Sound: Fair.
Remarks: Copy of *Fire On The Fingertips*. Song titles again listed incorrectly on the cover.

Rescued – (BORNOBY RECORDS PL–14)
Cover: Deluxe colour sleeve.
Sound: Varies from fair to very good.
Remarks: Double LP. Copied from *Boss Of The Boardwalk* and *Roulette*.

Restless Nights – (PICTURE DISC VV II)
Side one: 'Be True'/'Rickie Wants A Man Of Her Own'/'Cindy'/'Roulette'/'Restless Nights'.

Side two: 'Loose Ends'/'Take Them As They Come'/'You Can Look (But You Better Not Touch)'/'Held Up Without A Gun'/'The Way'.
Source: Studio out-takes from *The River* sessions recorded at The Power Station Studios, New York City, between May 1979 and September 1980 (except 'The Way' which was recorded at the Record Plant between November 1977 and May 1978).
Sound: Very good/excellent.
Remarks: Great full colour picture.

Resurrected – (LONELY RECORDS LR 101)
Side one: 'Resurrection'/'Sister Theresa'/'Bright Lights, Big City'.
Side two: 'The Bishop Dance'/'You Mean So Much To Me'/'The Fever'/'Zero And Blind Terry'.
Source: Side one recorded at Steel Mill concerts *circa* 1970. Side two, track one – radio broadcast from Max's Kansas City, New York City, 30 August 1972; track two – WGOE studios, Richmond, Virginia, 31 May 1973; track three – 1973 demo; track four – The Main Point, 31 October 1973.
Cover: White sleeve with blue stamp, black and yellow insert.
Sound: Side one – Poor. Side two – Fair/good.
Remarks: Numbered edition on black vinyl.

Rock Crusade
Remarks: Unsold copies of *Ragamuffin Gunner* re-packaged with different black and white insert. Worthless.

Rockin' Days – (AMAZING PIG BS – 7AP009)
Remarks: Limited edition, copy of *Boss Hits The Sixties* on black vinyl.

Roulette – (ROUTE 9 RT–9–101)
Side one: 'Don't Look Back'/'Linda Let Me Be The One'/'Outside Looking In'/'Frankie'/'The Way'.
Side two: 'Thunder Road'/'I Wanna Be With You'/'Backstreets'/'Roulette'/'The Heist'.
Source: Side one, tracks one, three and five, and side two, track two – out-takes from The Record Plant, New York City, recorded between June 1977 and May 1978. 'Roulette' – The Power Station Studios, New York City, 1979. 'Frankie' – unknown live, 1976. All other songs – studio out-takes from The Record Plant, N.Y.C, 1974–75.
Cover: Red and white insert.
Sound: Good.
Remarks: Black vinyl, silver labels. 'The Heist' is the original title of 'Meeting Across The River'.

The Roxy In Stereo – (BS)
Side one: 'Rave On'/'Badlands'/'Spirit In The Night'/'Darkness On The Edge Of Town'/'Candy's Room'.
Side two: 'For You'/'Point Blank'/'Prove It All Night'.
Side three: 'Racing In The Street'/'Thunder Road'/'Fire'.
Side four: 'Growin' Up'/'It's Hard To Be A Saint In The City'/'Independence Day'.

Source: The Roxy, Los Angeles, California, 7 July 1978 (KMET radio broadcast).
Cover: Black and white insert.
Sound: Good/very good.
Remarks: Black vinyl, re-pressed on one red and one blue vinyls. Also known as *The Roxy 1978*. Also available in gatefold sleeve.

A Self Made Man – (VINYL SOUND RECORDS)
Side one: 'Roulette'/'Take Them As They Come'/'Cindy'/'Loose Ends'/'Rickie Wants A Man Of Her Own'.
Source: Studio out-takes, The Power Station Studios, New York City, recorded between May 1979 and September 1980.
Cover: Black and white insert.
Sound: Excellent.
Remarks: One-sided record. Numbered edition pressing.

Six Pack To Go
Remarks: Worthless home-made box set made up of unsold copies of the two *Agora* sets and the *Roxy (1978)* double. The re-packaging was admittedly well done, but it's still a shoddy deal.

Still On The Edge – (JERSEY RECORDS JER)
Side one: 'The Promise'/'Don't Look Back'/'Because The Night'/'Racing In The Street'.
Side two: 'Lets Go Tonight'/'Streets Of Fire'/'Candy's Room'/'Sherry Darling'.
Side three: Candy's Boy'/'Badlands'/'Fire'/'Drive All Night'.
Side four: 'Something In The Night'/'Spanish Eyes'/'Sherry Darling'/'Candy's Room'.
EP: 'Ramrod'/'Spanish Eyes'.
Source: Studio out-takes from The Record Plant, New York City, and The Power Station Studios, New York City, recorded between June 1977 and May 1978.
Cover: Deluxe colour gatefold.
Sound: Poor/fair.
Remarks: Poor sound quality spoils an otherwise well packaged set. 'Don't Look Back' is an instrumental version. Re-released without the EP and with insert cover.

The Stockholm Tapes
Cover: Box with insert.
Sound: Very good.
Remarks: Six album set. Sides one to six are a copy of *Follow That Dream*; sides seven to twelve are a copy of *Teardrops On The City*. Original pressing on coloured vinyl; further pressing on black vinyl.

TAKRL Anthology – (TAKRL BOZO 1)
Remarks: A double album 'best of' compilation featuring various artists such as the Beatles, Jimi Hendrix, David Bowie etc. The one Bruce song (side three, track one) is the 1973 demo version of 'The Fever'. Label states it as recorded in 1976. Also known as *T'anks For The Mammaries*.

Teardrops On The City
Side one: 'Run Through The Jungle'/'Prove It All Night'/'The Ties That Bind'/'Tenth Avenue Freeze Out'/'Darkness On The Edge Of Town'/'Independence Day'.
Side two: 'Factory'/'Who'll Stop The Rain'/'Two Hearts'/'Out In The Street'/'The Price You Pay'/'This Land Is Your Land'/'The River'.
Side three: 'The Promised Land'/'Badlands'/'Cadillac Ranch'/'Sherry Darling'/'Hungry Heart'.
Side four: 'Because The Night'/'You Can Look'/'Wreck On The Highway'/'Point Blank'.
Side five: 'Backstreets'/'Candy's Room'/'Ramrod'/'Rosalita'.
Side six: 'Born To Run'/'Devil With The Blue Dress' medley (includes 'High School Confidential')/'Can't Help Falling In Love'/'Rockin' All Over The World'/'Twist And Shout'.
Source: The Isstadion, Stockholm, 8 May 1981.
Cover: Superb colour gatefold.
Sound: Excellent.
Remarks: Excellent all round production makes this possibly the best bootleg ever made. The slight fade-out on some tracks and the omission of 'Rockin' All Over The World' from the cover listings are the only noticeable faults. Black vinyl with superb picture labels.

Thunder Rouge – (IMPOSSIBLE RECORDWORKS 1–23)
Side one: 'Point Blank'/'Spirit In The Night'/'Independence Day'/'Prove It All Night'.
Side two: 'Candy's Room'/'Fire'/'Born To Run'/'Tenth Avenue Freeze Out'/'Jungleland'.
Source: The Capitol Theatre, Passaic, New Jersey, 19 September 1978. WNEW radio broadcast.
Cover: Deluxe black and white.
Sound: Excellent.
Remarks: Cover states concert recorded at The Agora, Cleveland, 9 August 1978.

The Ties That Bind
Remarks: Worthless home-made re-packaging of *By The River*.

Tour Of Canada 1982 – (W 980)
Side one: 'Then She Kissed Me'/'Twist And Shout'/'Raise Your Hand'/'Ain't Too Proud To Beg'.
Side two: 'Devil With The Blue Dress' medley/'Quarter To Three'.
Side three: 'You Can't Sit Down'/'Rave On'/'Mountain Of Love'/'Back In The USA'.
Side four: 'Good Rockin' Tonight'/'Wear My Ring Around Your Neck'/'Little Queenie'/'Summertime Blues'/'Sweet Little Sixteen'.
Source: Side one, track one – The Bottom Line, New York City, 15 August 1975; track two – The Roxy, Los Angeles, California, 7 July 1978; track three – Capitol Theatre, Passaic, New Jersey, 19 September 1978; track four – The Palace, Detroit, Michigan, 4 October 1975. Side two, Largo, Maryland, 2 November 1978. Side three, track one – Capitol Theatre, Passaic, New Jersey, 31 December 1977; track two – The Roxy, Los Angeles, California, 7 July 1978; tracks three and four – The Main Point, Bryn Mawr, Pennsylvania, 5 February 1975. Side four, track one – Fox Theatre, Atlanta, Georgia, 30 September 1978; track two – Philadelphia, 30 December 1975; track three – Palace, Detroit, Michigan, 4 October 1975; track four – Agora, Cleveland, Ohio, 9 August 1978; track five – Louisville, 5 August 1978.
Cover: Deluxe black and white.
Sound: Fair to good.
Remarks: Title is misleading (to say the least). 'Little Queenie' is incorrectly listed as 'Party Store'. 'Wear My Ring . . ' not listed on the cover.

Truth O Trash – (S–22)
Remarks: Worthless home-made re-packaging of sides 5–6 of the *Stockholm Tapes* in a new deluxe black and white cover.

Visitation At Fort Horne – (ACME RECORDS SM 001)
Side one: 'He's Guilty'/'Goin' Back To Georgia'/'The Train Song'/'No Need'.
Side two: 'Marie'/'Visitation At Fort Horne'/'Night'/'Linda Let Me Be The One'/'Tokyo'.

THE BOSS

Source: Side one, tracks one to three – Steel Mill demos recorded at Bill Graham's Fillmore Records Studios, San Francisco, California, February 1970. Side one, track four and side two, tracks one, two and five – music publishing demos, *circa* 1972. Side two, tracks three and four – out-takes from the *Born To Run* sessions, recorded between October 1974 and August 1975.

Cover: Yellow and black insert.

Sound: Very good/excellent.

Remarks: Side two, track four is incorrectly listed as being from the *Darkness* . . . sessions. An otherwise excellent production.

Warriors Rest – (THUNDERBOLT RECORDS 303)

Side one: 'Paradise By The Sea'/'Fire'/'Sherry Darling'/'4th Of July, Asbury Park (Sandy)'.

Side two: 'Because The Night'/'Raise Your Hand'/'Twist And Shout'.

Source: The Agora, Cleveland, Ohio, 9 August 1978 (WMMS radio broadcast).

Cover: Deluxe black and white.

Sound: Very good.

Remarks: Cover states album is a promotion item. Black vinyl. Good all round production.

We Got A Long Night – (AR)

Side one: 'Jungleland'/'Two Hearts'/'Drift Away'.

Side two: 'Born To Run'/'Devil With The Blue Dress' medley/'Twist And Shout'/'Do You Love Me?'.

Source: Brendan Byrne Meadowlands Arena, East Rutherford, New Jersey, 20 August 1984.

Cover: Black and white insert.

Sound: Good.

Remarks: Little Steven guests on all the songs apart from 'Jungleland'. Limited numbered edition.

Who's Been Covered By The Boss? – PICTURE DISC – (JOUR DISCS)

Side one: 'Back In The U.S.A.' (5 February 1975)/'Sweet Little Sixteen' (5 August 1978)/'Night Train' (30 September 1978)/'A Love So Fine' (5 February 1975)/'Cupid' (29 October 1974).

Side two: 'Unknown'/'A Fine Fine Boy' (3 November 1976)/'Party Lights' (12 November 1975)/'Oh Boy' (29 July 1978)/'No Money Down' (13 July 1974)/'Chimes Of Freedom' (1 September 1978).

Side three: 'Needles And Pins'/'You Really Got Me'/'Cry To Me' (all 22 July 1975)/'Satin Doll' (31 May 1973)/'Haunted House' (31 October 1980).

Side four: 'Save The Last Dance For Me' (18 August 1978)/'On Top Of Old Smokey' (25 October 1980)/'Sock It To Me Baby' (13 July 1981)/'634–5789' (12 January 1974)/'Ballad Of Easy Rider' (20 August 1981)/'Kansas City' (5 February 1981)/'Be True To Your School' (3 November 1976).

Side five: 'Outer Limits' (31 October 1980)/'Waltz Across Texas' (9 November 1980)/'Call To Arms' (5 August 1978)/'Deportee' (28 August 1981)/'Proud Mary' (14 September 1981)/'Ring Of Fire' (12 January 1974).

Side six: 'Unknown'/'Ready Teddy' (6 August 1982)/'Lucille' (6 August 1982)/'Wooly Bully'/'Louie Louie'/'Rock Baby Rock It'/'Open All Night' (all 3 October 1982).

Source: Various live concerts, soundchecks, radio sessions, 1973 to 1982.

Cover: Deluxe leather bound.

Sound: Fair overall.

Remarks: Three picture discs featuring colour photos of Bruce, Clarence and Steve. Limited numbered edition.

Winterland 1978 – (8880)

Side one: 'Badlands'/'Streets Of Fire'/'Spirit In The Night'/'Darkness On The Edge Of Town'/'Factory'.

Side two: 'The Promised Land'/'Prove It All Night'/'Racing In The Street'/'Thunder Road'.

Side three: 'Jungleland'/'Interview'/'The Ties That Bind'/'Santa Claus Is Comin' To Town'.

Side four: 'The Fever'/'Fire'/'Candy's Room'/'Because The Night'/'Point Blank'.

Side five: 'Mona' . . . 'The Preacher's Daughter' . . 'She's The One'/'Backstreets'/'Rosalita'.

Side six: 'Rosalita' (concluded)/'Born To Run'/'Devil With The Blue Dress' medley.

Source: Winterland, San Francisco, California, 15 December 1978. KSAN radio broadcast.

Cover: Box with yellow and black insert.

Sound: Very good.

Remarks: Black vinyl. Limited number pressed on gold vinyl. Re-pressed in a very similar format.

Winterland – PICTURE DISC

Remarks: Sides five and six of the above.

With A Little Help From My Friends – (FC 001)

Side one: 'Thunder Road' (with Bob Seger, Ann Arbour, Michigan 3 October 1980)/'Jole Blon' (with Gary U.S. Bonds, East Rutherford, New Jersey (3 July 1981)/'Fire' (the Red Bank Rockers, Philadelphia, Pennsylvania 28 January 1982)/'You Mean So Much To Me' (with Ronnie Spector and the Jukes, Red Bank, New Jersey 13 May 1977)/'This Little Girl' (with Gary U.S. Bonds, East Rutherford, New Jersey 3 July 1981).

Side two: 'The Promised Land' (with Jackson Browne, Central Park, New York City 12 June 1982)/'In The Midnight Hour' (the Red Bank Rockers, Baltimore, Maryland 23 January 1982) /'Havin' A Party' (with Southside Johnny, Passiac, New Jersey 31 December 1977)/'Devil With A Blue Dress' medley (with Mitch Ryder, Detroit, Michigan 12 August 1981).

Source: See tracking listing.
Cover: Deluxe colour sleeve.
Sound: Good overall.
Remarks: Numbered edition on black vinyl.

You Can Trust Your Car To The Man Who Wears The Star – (SODD 001)

Side one: 'Incident On 57th Street'/'Mountain Of Love'/'Born To Run'.
Side two: 'E Street Shuffle'/'Thunder Road'/'I Want You'.
Side three: 'Spirit In The Night'/'She's The One'/'Growin' Up' (listed on label as being 'Blinded By The Light')/'It's Hard To Be A Saint In The City'.
Side four: 'Jungleland'/'Kitty's Back'.
Source: The Main Point, Bryn Mawr, Pennsylvania (5 February 1975). (WMMR radio broadcast).
Cover: Black and orange insert.
Sound: Very good.
Remarks: Features Suki Lahav on violin (to great effect). Black vinyl.

You Can Trust Your Car To The Man Who Wears The Star – (TAKRL 24903)

Remarks: 1978 re-issue of the above that came in a deluxe black and white cover (same drawing). Later re-pressings came in various shades of bright green. Original insert copies are hard to find.

You Can Trust Your Car To The Man Who Wears The Star – PICTURE DISC.

Remarks: Sides three and four of the green TAKRL 24903 release.

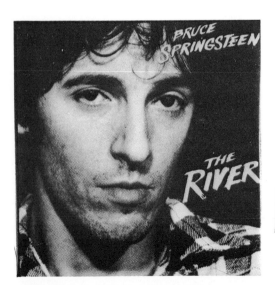

bruce springsteen

Sleeve design and artwork by Tim Tegge · Centerfold and rear sleeve photographs by Unicorn Productions

Imprimé en France

BRUCE
SPRINGSTEEN
DANCING IN THE DARK
WA 4436

Rockin' All Over The World

(*World Discography*)

U.S.A. DISCOGRAPHY

Regular Release

LP *Greetings From Asbury Park N.J.* COL. KC
31903 5 January 1973.
A 'Blinded By The Light'; 'Growin' Up'; 'Mary, Queen
Of Arkansas'; 'Does This Bus Stop At 82nd Street?';
'Lost In The Flood'; B 'The Angel'; 'For You'; 'Spirit In
The Night'; 'It's Hard To Be A Saint In The City'.
Promotion copies featured gold 'Not for Sale' stamp on

sleeve, timing strip and an info. sheet. (In other cases a
red 'demo only' stamp was used.) 'Visitation At Fort
Horn' believed to have been cut into early acetate
copies. No original chart placing though it did reach
Number 60 during the height of the 'Born To Run'
publicity campaign 18 October 1975.

45 **'Blinded By The Light'/'The Angel'** COL. 4–45805
23 February 1973.
Original issue in colour picture sleeve with lyrics on
rear. The white label promotion copies featured
Stereo/Mono versions of A side. No chart position.

45 **'Spirit In The Night'/'For You'** COL. 4–45864
11 May 1973.
No picture sleeve or chart placing. The white label
promotion copies were Stereo/Mono of A side.

LP *The Wild, The Innocent And The E Street Shuffle*
COL. KC 32432 11 September 1973.
A 'The E Street Shuffle'; '4th Of July, Asbury Park
(Sandy)'; 'Kitty's Back'; 'Wild Billy's Circus Story';
B 'Incident On 57th Street'; 'Rosalita (Come Out
Tonight)'; 'New York City Serenade'.
Promotion copies issued with either gold or red 'Not for

151

Bruce Springsteen
BLINDED BY THE LIGHT
From the Album: "Greetings From Asbury Park, N.J."

BRUCE SPRINGSTEEN: THE WILD, THE INNOCENT & THE E STREET SHUFFLE

featured white labels and timing strip. Reached number 6 in album chart 8 July 1978. Released as a compact disc in 1984.

45 **'Prove It All Night'/'Factory'** COL. 3–10763 9 June 1978.
No picture sleeve, promotion copies featured white label Stereo/Mono versions of A side. Reached number 33 in chart 15 July 1978.

45 **'Badlands'/'Streets Of Fire'** COL. 3–10801 14 August 1978.
No picture sleeve. No top 50 chart position. Promotion copies featured white label and Stereo/Mono version of A side.

LP **Born To Run** COL. HC 43795 and **Darkness On The Edge Of Town** COL. HC 45318 27 May 1980.
Issued on the Half Speed Mastered series. Superior sound quality alleged.

LP **The River** COL. PC2 36854 10 October 1980.
A 'The Ties That Bind'; 'Sherry Darling'; 'Jackson Cage'; 'Two Hearts'; 'Independence Day'; B 'Hungry Heart'; 'Out In The Street'; 'Crush On You'; 'You Can Look (But You Better Not Touch)'; 'I Wanna Marry You'; 'The River'; C 'Point Blank'; 'Cadillac Ranch'; 'I'm A Rocker'; 'Fade Away'; 'Stolen Car'; D 'Ramrod'; 'The

Sale' stamp on cover, and timing strip. Reached number 59 in chart 18 October 1975. Original copies featured the cover title in yellow ink (later changed to white).

LP **Born To Run** COL. PC 33795 25 August 1975.
A 'Thunder Road'; 'Tenth Avenue Freeze-Out'; 'Night'; 'Backstreets'; B 'Born To Run'; 'She's The One'; 'Meeting Across The River'; 'Jungleland'.
Originally sent out in a black envelope/folder with title graphics. The advanced white label promotion copies were printed in sepia and white gatefold sleeves with no lettering/credits apart from the front cover script title. A small insert with song titles (with 'The Heist' as the title for 'Meeting Across The River') was included, the inside photo covering almost all of one side of the fold. The more common promotion copy featured white label and timing strip. Several variants are to be found on the rear cover, with the misspelling of John Landau and the later corrected non credit of Suki Lahav. A further change saw a darker ink used. Reached number 3 in the chart 18 October 1975. Released as a compact disc in 1983.

45 **'Born To Run'/'Meeting Across The River'** COL. 3–10209 29 August 1975.
Reached number 23 in chart 1 November 1975. The lettering on the label varied slightly depending on which

plant it was pressed. White label promotion copies featured Stereo/Mono versions of A side. No picture sleeve.

45 **'Tenth Avenue Freeze-Out'/'She's The One'** COL. 3–10274 12 December 1975.
White label promotion copies featured Stereo/Mono versions of A side. Reached number 83 in chart 7 February 1976. No picture sleeve.

45 **'Born To Run'/Spirit In The Night'** COL. 13–33323 16 November 1976.
Released on the 'Hall of Fame' series with red label. Reissued in 1984 with grey label.

LP **Darkness On The Edge Of Town** COL. JC 35318 2 June 1978.
A 'Badlands'; 'Adam Raised A Cain'; 'Something In The Night'; 'Candy's Room'; 'Racing In The Street'; B 'The Promised Land'; 'Factory'; 'Streets Of Fire'; 'Prove It All Night'; 'Darkness On The Edge Of Town'. Acetate copies contained the song 'Don't Look Back'. Bruce rejected several colour variations and titles (inc. 'Badlands' and 'Racing In The Street'). The 'Badlands' sleeve was to have been the same as the sheet music of the single, both 'Racing In The Streets' and the final title had prototype sleeves made with the graphics running down the cover not across. Promotion copies

Bruce Springsteen
Born To Run

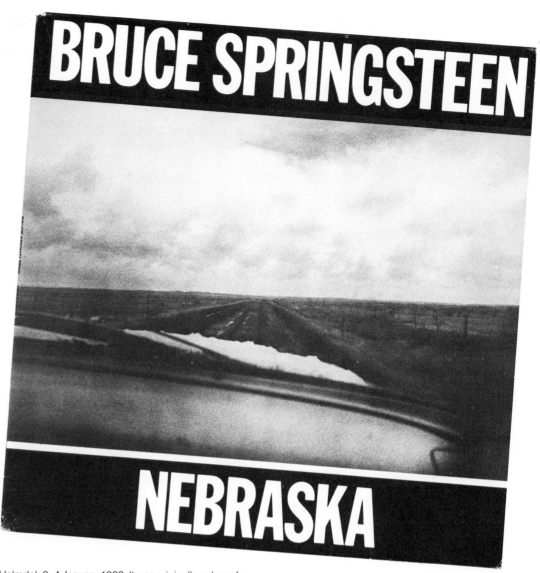

Price You Pay'; 'Drive All Night'; 'Wreck On The Highway'.
Original sleeves and press hand outs listed 'Held Up Without A Gun' as being on the record, it wasn't but almost sure to have been on acetate copies. Promotion copies on white labels. Reached number one in chart 15 November 1980.

45 **'Hungry Heart'/'Held Up Without A Gun'** COL. 11–11391 20 October 1980.
First top 10 single for Bruce when it reached number 5 on 17 January 1981. Issued in picture sleeve, the promotion copies were on white labels and featured Stereo/Stereo versions of A side.

45 **'Fade Away'/'Be True'** COL. 11–11431 3 February 1981.
Early pressings mistakenly titled B side as 'To Be True'. Promotion copies on white label with Stereo/Stereo versions of the A side. Issued in picture sleeve, it reached number 20 on 21 March 1981.

LP **Nebraska** COL. TC 38358 20 September 1982.
A 'Nebraska'; 'Atlantic City'; 'Mansion On The Hill'; 'Johnny 99'; 'Highway Patrolman'; 'State Trooper'; B 'Used Cars'; 'Open All Night'; 'My Father's House'; 'Reason To Believe'.
Totally solo album recorded at Bruce's N.J. home in

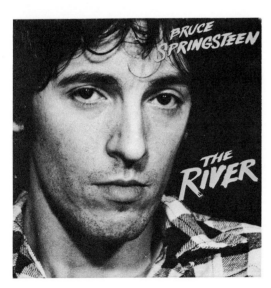

Holmdel, 3–4 January 1982. It was originally a demo for the band to work from, eventually the four track recording was mastered onto disc to Bruce's liking (with help from Chuck Plotkin and Mike Batlin). Promotion copies featured mainly gold stamp 'For demo only' with very few white labels pressed. Reached number 3 in chart 6 November 1982. No singles released in U.S. Released as a compact disc in 1984.

45 **'Hungry Heart'/'Fade Away'** COL. 13–03243 27 September 1983.
Issued on the 'Hall of Fame' series with red label. In 1984 reissued with grey label.

45 **Dancing In The Dark'/'Pink Cadillac'** COL. 38–04463 11 May 1984.
Reached number 2 in the U.S. chart 30 June 1984 (and stayed there for 4 weeks). Promotion copies featured Stereo/Stereo versions of the A side and were issued in the colour picture sleeve but with unique rear sleeve graphics.

LP **Born In The U.S.A.** COL. QC 38653 4 June 1984.
A 'Born In The U.S.A.'; 'Cover Me'; 'Darlington County'; 'Working On The Highway'; 'Downbound Train'; 'I'm On Fire'; B 'No Surrender'; 'Bobby Jean'; I'm Goin' Down'; 'Glory Days'; 'Dancing In The Dark'; 'My Hometown'.

Backed by a huge CBS marketing campaign that began on 1 May 1984 with Born In The U.S.A 6/'84. T-shirts were sent out, media 'listening parties' between 7–11 May, numerous TV and radio adverts and various promotional items including posters, baseball caps, badges and a 'Cover Me' 5'0" × 3'0" blanket (used to promote the 2nd single). But the music spoke for itself and peaked at number 1 in the U.S. chart 7 July 1984. No white label promotion copies pressed. Issued as a compact disc.

12" **'Dancing In The Dark'** (6.09 blaster mix)/**'Dancing In The Dark'** (4.50 radio) and **'Dancing In The Dark'** (5.30 dub) COL. 44–05028 June 1984.
Remixed by Arthur Baker. Superb 12" colour picture sleeve, back and front. Promotion copies featured a printed 'Demonstration-Not For Sale' on regular release labels. The best selling 12" of 1984.

45 **'Cover Me'/'Jersey Girl'** COL. 38–04561 31 July 1984.
Excellent colour picture sleeve featuring the present E Street Band line up (minus Patti Scialfa) posing by the car given to Bruce by Gary U.S. Bonds. Later pressings, minus the live 'Jersey Girl' introduction, reached number 10 in the U.S. chart 29 September 1984. Promotion copies featured Stereo/Stereo versions of A side and were issued in a colour picture sleeve with different rear side graphics.

12″ **'Cover Me'** (6.05 undercover mix) and **'Cover Me'** (4.02 dub 1)/'**Cover Me**' (3.46 radio) and **'Cover Me'** (4.15 dub 2) COL. 44–05087 August 1984.
All 4 versions remixed by Arthur Baker at the Hit Factory, New York City, using a total of 48 tracks and numerous effects such as echo, reverb, harmonizer and phasing. He also added new bass, keyboard, female vocals and various percussion tracks. Promotion copies featured a gold 'Not for Sale' stamp on cover only.

45 **'Born In The U.S.A.'/'Shut Out The Light'** COL. 38–04680 5 November 1984.
Colour picture sleeve. Reached number 9 in the U.S. chart 19 January 1985. Promotion copies featured a Stereo/Stereo of the A side and the picture sleeve had unique rear sleeve graphics.

12″ **'Born In The U.S.A.'** (7.20 freedom mix)/'same' (7.36 dub) and 'same' (6.10 radio) COL. 44–05147 December 1984.
12″ colour picture sleeve. 3 remixes by Arthur Baker. Promotion copies featured a gold 'Not for Sale' stamp on sleeve.

45 **'I'm On Fire'/'Johnny Bye Bye'** COL. 38–04772 4 February 1985.
Colour picture sleeve. Promotion copies featured Stereo/Stereo versions of the A side, and packaged as RR21 and RR23. Reached number 6 in the U.S. chart 13 April 1985.

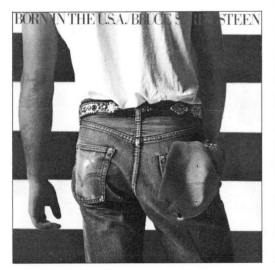

45 **'Glory Days'/'Stand On It'** COL 38–04924 22 May 1985.
Colour picture sleeve. Promotion copies featured Stereo/Stereo versions of A side.

Promotion Only

7″ **'Blinded By The Light'**/Andy Pratt song COL. Playback AS 45 12 January 1973.
Promotion release sent out to members of the Playback subscription club only. The 7″ record played at 33⅓rpm with light blue labels. 'Avenging Annie' by Andy Pratt was featured on other side.

7″ **'Circus Song'**/3 other songs COL. Playback AS 52 22 June 1973.
Bruce's first, live recordings of an original song. It was recorded at The Ahmanson Theatre, Los Angeles, California during the CBS 'Week of Music' convention on 1 May 1973. The Playback 7″ 33⅓rpm featured light blue labels and 3 other artists.

7″ **'Rosalita (Come Out Tonight)'/2 other songs** COL. Playback AS 66 29 January 1974.
Bruce's third and final inclusion on the promotion only Playback series, again with light blue labels and 33⅓rpm. The other side featured Johnny Winters and The Hollies.

7″ **'Spirit In The Night'** and **'Growin' Up'/'Rosalita (Come Out Tonight)'** COL. AE7 1088 2 June 1974.
White label promotion only released for DJs only in very limited form. 33⅓rpm.

LP **The Heavyweights** COL. A52 174 23 October 1975.
Double album white label compilation 'demonstration only' release that featured 17 songs including Bruce's 'Born To Run'.

12″ **'Rosalita (Come Out Tonight)'/'Rosalita (Come Out Tonight)'** COL. AS 330 unreleased.
Unreleased 12″ white label 45rpm. Originally scheduled for promotion only release 21 April 1977.

LP **Darkness On The Edge Of Town** Picture Disc COL. 35318 Summer 1978.
Colour picture disc that featured front and rear photos from the album cover. 1500 believed to have been pressed and sent out to various radio stations, DJs and press, although 5000 would seem a more plausible number of copies pressed. Some copies included lyric sleeve.

12″ **'Prove It All Night'/'Paradise By The Sea'** COL. AS 480 unreleased
Unreleased 12″ 45rpm promotion item, originally scheduled for release 14 July 1978 but never made it. Both sides were recorded live at the Berkeley Theatre, Berkeley, California, 1 July 1978.

12″ **'Devil With The Blue Dress Medley'**/Jackson Browne song ASYLUM AS 11442 December 1979.
12″ white label promotion only release. Recorded live at Madison Square Garden for the MUSE benefit on 21 September 1979. Jackson Browne's 'Before The Deluge' featured on the B side. The plain white sleeve featured a light brown sticker with title graphics.

LP **The Pitman Family Of Music – Our First 20 Years** COL. P 15663 December 1980.
Given to employees of CBS Records to mark the 20th anniversary of the Pitman plant. Numerous CBS/Columbia artists were featured in segmented versions of their songs, the Bruce track is about 20 seconds of 'Backstreets'. Colour sleeve and picture labels, it also carried a 16 page booklet.

LP **Hitline '80** COL. A2S 890 December 1980.
Double white label album featuring Columbia's top singles of 1980. Black and white gatefold sleeve, the one Bruce song was 'Hungry Heart' side 4, track 2.

LP **Mastersound Highlights** COL. Mastersound AS 902 March 1981.
White label with one Bruce song, 'Thunder Road', side 2, track 1. Issued by CBS to demonstrate the superior Half-Speed Mastered catalogue. Gatefold cover and 6 page booklet inside.

12″ **'Fade Away'/'Be True'** and **'Held Up Without A Gun'** COL. AS 928 April 1981.
12″ 45rpm that featured superb black and blue title labels. Issued in plain black sleeve with white sticker titles.

LP **As Requested Around The World** COL. AS 978 September 1981.
A 'Sherry Darling'; 'The River'; 'Cadillac Ranch'; 'Hungry Heart'; 'Out In The Street'; B 'Born To Run'; 'Badlands'; 'Prove It All Night'; 'Rosalita (Come Out Tonight)'.
Superb colour sleeve. The album featured 5 tracks from *The River* on side one and 4 songs from earlier albums on side two. Labels were unusual in as much as they were the regular Columbia red, and not the normal white used for promotion only items. Rear of sleeve featured black and white photo of Bruce and the E Street Band plus a world tour itinerary.

12″ **'Santa Claus Is Comin' To Town'/'Santa Claus Is Comin' To Town'** COL. AS 1329 December 1981.
12″ 33⅓rpm white label issue to promote the *In Harmony* album. Recorded live from the C. W. Post College, Greenvale, New York, on 12 December 1975. Released in plain black sleeve with red title sticker.

7″ **'Santa Claus Is Comin' To Town'/'Santa Claus Is Comin' To Town'** COL. AE7 1332 December 1981.
Same version as the 12″, but this time in a 7″ art sleeve, with record playing at 45rpm.

12″ **'Dancing In The Dark'/'Dancing In The Dark'** COL. AS 1862 June 1984.
Black and white picture sleeve. Both sides are the LP version (not the Arthur Baker remixes), pressed on regular coloured labels with a printed 'Demonstration–Not For Sale'. Plays at 33⅓rpm.

12″ **'Born In The U.S.A.'/'Shut Out The Light'; 'Pink Cadillac'; 'Jersey Girl'; 'Santa Claus Is Comin' To Town'** COL. AS 1957 November 1984.
12″ picture sleeve that features the *Born In The U.S.A.* LP sleeve but with totally different coloured overlay film and graphics. 'Jersey Girl' is an edited 5.56 version.

12″ **'Born In The U.S.A.'/'Born In The U.S.A.'** COL.

AS 1959 December 1984.
Both sides are LP versions and were pressed on white labels that came in a plain white sleeve.

12″ **'I'm On Fire'/'I'm On Fire'** COL. AS 2007 February 1985.
12″ black and white picture sleeve with unique rear side graphics. Pressed on regular coloured labels with a printed 'Demonstration–Not For Sale'. Plays at 33⅓rpm.

Various Artists Release

LP **No Nukes** ASYLUM ML 801 December 1979.
Triple album set recorded live from the Madison Square Garden MUSE concerts 19–23 September 1979. The two Bruce tracks were 'Stay' and 'Devil With The Blue Dress Medley'. 'Stay' featured a shared vocal with Jackson Browne with Rosemary Butler on back up vocals. The medley is a four and a half minute edited version. Promotion copies were on white labels. Bruce's contributions were from the 21 September 1979 show.

LP **In Harmony 2** COL. BFC 37643 December 1981.
Various artists album with part of the proceeds going to various children's charities. The one track by Bruce, 'Santa Claus Is Comin' To Town', was recorded live from C. W. Post College, Greenvale, New York 12 December 1975. Side 2, track 5. Promotion copies on white labels. The art sleeve originally featured a removable white sticker proclaiming 'Santa Claus Is Comin' To Town' only available on this album.

Radio Promotion Only Albums

Pressed by the radio station (or Armed Forces) for distribution to their various networks and overseas programmes, most albums/shows feature more than one artist, cue sheet, adverts, DJ talk and regular release LP or 45 fragmented 'cuts'.

The Rock Years – Portrait Of An Era WESTWOOD ONE RECORDS – Hour 33 features 'Born To Run', 'Thunder Road' and an interview with Jimmy Iovine. 'Darkness On The Edge Of Town' and 'The Promised Land' on Hour 41. 'Devil With The Blue Dress Medley' on Hour 44. 'The River' and 'Out In The Street' on Hour 47.

The Dick Clark Show Number 30 – Features a short interview with Bruce.

Christmas Album UNITED STATIONS – 3 cuts.

Top 30 Countdown DRAKE CHENAULT – 'Hungry Heart'.

Earth News Radio – Short interview with Bruce.

Third Annual Rock Radio Awards D.I.R. BROADCASTING – 4 LP show with 6 cuts by Bruce plus an acceptance speech by Jon Landau.

Rock On The Road D.I.R. BROADCASTING – 5 LP show that featured a live version of 'Prove It All Night' and 'Bishop Dance' plus an interview with Bruce.

Spectrum U.S. MARINE CORPS. – 'Two Hearts'.

Spectrum U.S. MARINE CORPS. – 'Hungry Heart'.

Christmas Album UNITED STATIONS – 3 cuts.

Off The Record WESTWOOD ONE RECORDS –

Bruce is featured on the September 1980 show, the September 1981 and the November 1981 shows. All are segments of interviews.

Top 30 Countdown DRAKE CHENAULT SHOW – 'Hungry Heart'.

Rock Quiz MAY 1983 – 1 cut.

Royalty Of Rock 2 LP set of cuts and interviews.

Rarities Radio Show includes the live 'Circus Song'.

American Top 40 CASEY KASEM SHOW – Box sets that logs all chart entries 'Born To Run' onwards.

Guest DJ ROCK STAR – Southside Johnny spins his favourite records, including one Bruce cut.

The Rolling Stone Continuous History Of Rock'N'Roll ROCK REVUE – A weekly radio report that has featured Bruce on numerous occasions, including – **East Coast Rock 1 & 2** (5 cuts and interviews with Roy Bittan and Southside Johnny), **Christmas Rocks** ('Santa Claus Is Comin' To Town' and Xmas message), **Rock Books** (Dave Marsh talks about *Born To Run*), **East Coast Rock-Labour Day Special 1 & 2** (5 cuts), **Critics Choice** (2 cuts and Dave Marsh interview), **Unusual Instruments** ('Born To Run'), **Rock Review** (*The River* LP reviewed), **Jimmy Iovine-Producer** (4 cuts), **Bruce Springsteen Bonus Hour** (1982 Labour Day Special).

Springsteen WESTWOOD ONE – 3 LP set featuring interviews and live music from the Sports Arena, Los Angeles, California, 1984.

U.K. DISCOGRAPHY

Regular release

LP ***Greetings From Asbury Park N.J.*** CBS 65480
9 March 1973.
Originally released with the old CBS plain orange labels, it had an Epic matrix number in the 'dead wax' area. Promotion copies featured the gold stamp 'Not for Sale' on the cover. No white label pressings are known.

LP ***The Wild, The Innocent And The E Street Shuffle***
CBS 65780 22 February 1974.
Original pressings featured a label misspelling '4th Of July, Ashbury Park (Sandy)' sic. Promotion copies with gold 'Not for Sale' stamp on cover. No white labels known.

45 **'Born To Run'/'Meeting Across The River'** CBS
3661 19 September 1975.
Reached number 58 in U.K. chart, 31 October 1975 after being subject to a massive hype campaign that failed dismally. No picture sleeve. White label promo copies believed to have been pressed.

LP ***Born To Run*** CBS 69170 10 October 1975.
Promotion copies again with gold 'Not for Sale' stamp on cover, although it is thought that a limited number of white labels were pressed. Credits on the rear of the sleeve were similar to the misspellings and omissions on the U.S. copies. Reached number 24 in the U.K. chart 1 November 1975. Also released on compact disc in 1983.

45 **'Tenth Avenue Freeze-Out'/'She's The One'** CBS
3940 6 February 1976.
No picture sleeve and no chart position.

LP ***Greetings From Asbury Park N.J.*** CBS 65480
5 December 1976 (reissued).
Reissued with same catalogue number but without the postcard jacket.

LP ***Darkness On The Edge Of Town*** CBS 86061
2 June 1978.
Reached number 18 in U.K. chart 8 July 1978. Promotion copies pressed with white label. Also released on compact disc in 1984.

45 **'Prove It All Night'/'Factory'** CBS 6424
9 June 1978.
Promotion copies pressed with white label. No chart position or picture sleeve.

45 **'Badlands'/'Something In The Night'** CBS 6532
21 July 1978.
Promotion copies pressed with white label. No chart position or picture sleeve.

45 **'The Promised Land'/'Streets Of Fire'** CBS 6720
27 October 1978.
Promotion copies pressed with white label. No chart position or picture sleeve.

45 **'Born To Run'/'Meeting Across The River'** CBS
7077 23 February 1979 (reissued).
Reissued on the 'Golden Decade' series. No white label promotion copies known.

LP ***Bruce Springsteen*** box set CBS 66353
November 1979.
The first three albums released with a deluxe colour box, wrapper wrongly states the title of *The Wild, The Innocent And The East Street Shuffle* (sic) and that the first LP is in its original sleeve. All albums carry their original catalogue numbers.

LP ***The River*** CBS 88510 17 October 1980.
Reached number 2 in the U.K. charts 1 November 1980. Actually carries two separate catalogue numbers, the official 88510 and 84622/3 on the labels and 'dead wax' area. Promotion copies pressed with white labels. Double album.

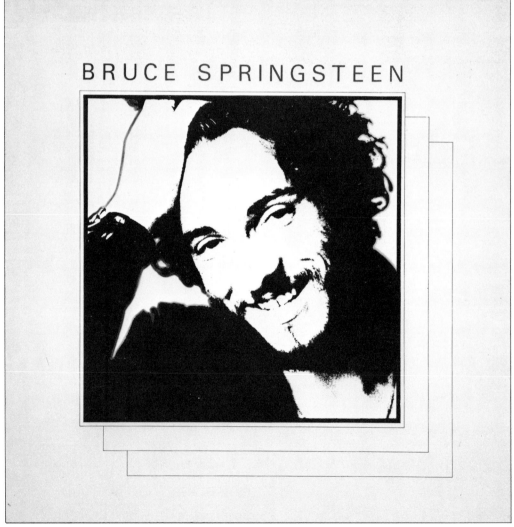

45 **'Hungry Heart'/'Held Up Without A Gun'** CBS 9309 31 October 1980.
Picture sleeve originally issued with blue lettering, but these were hastily withdrawn and replaced with black lettering on sleeves. Promotion copies pressed with white labels. Reached number 44 in the U.K. chart 22 November 1980.

45 **'Sherry Darling'/'Be True'** CBS 9568 20 February 1981.
Original promotion copies carried the wrong B side ('Independence Day') but were soon changed to the normal white label pressing. No chart position. Colour picture sleeve.

45 **'The River'/'Independence Day'** CBS A 1179 May 1981.
Promotion copies pressed with white labels. Picture sleeve. Reached number 35 in the U.K. charts 13 June 1981.

EP **'Rosalita (Come Out Tonight)'/'Born To Run'** and **The River'** CBS A13 1179 1 June 1981.
12″ 33⅓ rpm. Released to coincide with Bruce's U.K. tour. Original sleeve mistakenly named the band as the East Street Band (sic) twice! Promotion copies featured the gold 'Not for Sale' stamp.

45 **'Cadillac Ranch'/'Wreck On The Highway'** CBS A 1557 August 1981.

Colour picture sleeve. Promotion copies pressed with white labels. No chart position.

LP **Nebraska** CBS 25100 18 September 1982.
Very few white label promotion copies pressed, most came with the gold 'Not for Sale' stamp. Reached number 2 in U.K. chart 16 October 1982. Also released on compact disc in 1984.

45 **'Atlantic City'/'Mansion On The Hill'** CBS A 2794 24 September 1982.
Picture sleeve. Promotion copies pressed on white labels. No chart position.

45 **'Open All Night'/'The Big Payback'** CBS A 2969 20 November 1982.
B side released in Europe only. Picture sleeve. The normal U.K. promotion copy featuring both sides of the regular release but on white labels with a large A over the A side were dropped in favour of a plain white label stereo/mono version of 'Open All Night'. No chart position.

LP **Greetings From Asbury Park N.J.** CBS 32210 November 1982 (reissued).
Reissued in the Nice Price campaign with new catalogue number, with different rear sleeve design and no lyric sheet.

THE RIVER
BORN TO RUN
ROSALITA

LP **The Wild, The Innocent And The E Street Shuffle** CBS 32363 December 1983 (reissued).
Reissued in the Nice Price campaign with new catalogue number.

45 **'Dancing In The Dark'/'Pink Cadillac'** CBS A 4436 14 May 1984.
Colour picture sleeve. Promotion copies on white labels. Originally reached number 28 in the U.K. chart 2 June 1984 but with the aid of the video and a 1 hour Whistle Test TV special, 22 December 1984, it re-entered the chart and peaked at number 4 16 February 1985.

LP **Born In The U.S.A.** CBS 86304 4 June 1984.
Reached number 1 in the LP chart 16 February 1984, 9 months after its release! Promotion copies featured the gold stamp 'Not for Sale' on the sleeve. Oddly enough, initial copies of the LP were pressed in Holland.

PD **'Dancing In The Dark'/'Pink Cadillac'** – Picture Disc CBS WA 4436 11 June 1984.
12″ shaped colour picture disc of a pink cadillac, pressed in limited edition solely for the U.K. market. Repressed due to re-entry in U.K. chart of the 7″ single.

12″ **'Dancing In The Dark'** (6.09 extended mix) /**'Pink Cadillac'** CBS TA 4436 12 June 1984.

BRUCE SPRINGSTEEN

OPEN ALL NIGHT

BRUCE SPRINGSTEEN

Cadillac Ranch

Colour picture sleeve with lyrics to both songs on rear. Record plays at 45 rpm. Arthur Baker remix of the A side.

45 **'Cover Me'/'Jersey Girl'** CBS A 4662
24 September 1984.
Superb colour picture sleeve. B side recorded live at the Byrne Meadowlands Arena, 9 July 1981. No white label promotion copies pressed. Reached number 24 in U.K. chart 20 October 1984. Re-released in March 1985, re-entering charts at Number 10 on 30 March. The first 10,000 copies came in a poster bag, followed by a laminated sleeve. Both have slightly different rear graphics to the originals.

45 **'Cover Me'/'Jersey Girl' and 'Dancing in the Dark'/'Pink Cadillac'** CBS DA 4662 (twin pack)
24 September 1984.
Limited edition double pack in a sealed shrink-wrap bag. Both 7″ singles and sleeves identical to earlier releases, and catalogue number was printed on to a white overlay sticker. In March 1985, issued with the same catalogue number (CBS DA 4662), was 'Cover Me'/'Jersey Girl', 'Born To Run'/'Meeting Across The River'. A twin pack released to promote Bruce's earlier material.

12″ **'Cover Me' and 'Jersey Girl'/'Dancing In The Dark'** (5.30 dub) CBS TA 4662
24 September 1984.
Colour picture sleeve. The B side is the 5.30 dub version remixed by Arthur Baker. Plays at 45 rpm.

PD **'Cover Me'/'Jersey Girl'** – Picture Disc CBS WA 4662 Scheduled 1 October 1984 (unreleased).
Limited edition 12″ shaped picture disc due for a regular release but withdrawn at the last moment, thus making this a most sought after and collectable item. Plays at 33⅓ rpm. The B side is an edited 4.20 version. Came with a cardboard display that enabled the disc to stand up.

LP *Darkness On The Edge Of Town* CBS 32542
November 1984 (reissued).
Reissued in the Nice Price campaign with new catalogue number.

12″ **'Cover Me'** (undercover mix) and **'Cover Me'** (dub1) and **'Shut Out The Light'/'Dancing In The Dark'** (dub) and **'Jersey Girl'** CBS QTA 4662 March 1985.

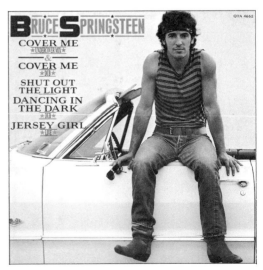

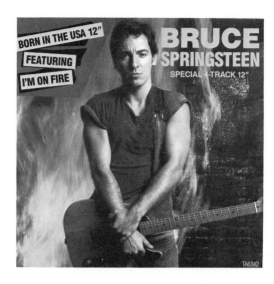

Totally different sleeve to the original 12″ and two additional tracks.

45 **'I'm On Fire'/'Born In The U.S.A.'** CBS A 6342
3 June 1985.
Laminated colour picture sleeve. Double A side. Original copies included a postcard competition to win concert tickets and had an overlay sticker announcing details.

12″ **'I'm On Fire'** and **'Rosalita'/'Born In The U.S.A.'** (freedom mix) and **'Johnny Bye Bye'** CBS TA 6342
3 June 1985.
Superb colour picture sleeve.

LP **Born In The U.S.A.** – Picture Disc CBS 11 86304
June 1985.
Limited edition that featured the LP picture on the face side (with different graphics) and a montage stars and stripes with track listing on the rear side. Possibly between 5–10,000 copies pressed.

PD **'I'm On Fire'/'Born In The U.S.A.'** – Picture disc CBS WA 6342 June 1985.
Limited edition 7″ picture disc released during Bruce's tour of the U.K. 1985.

(*Promotion Only*

LP **The Front Runners** CBS SPR 107 November 1975.
Various artists compilation LP available only through the post from the U.K. music paper Melody Maker. The one Bruce song is 'Born To Run', side 1 track 1. Rear sleeve featured a small photo of the *Born To Run* LP. Pressed with white labels.

45 **'Sherry Darling'/'Independence Day'** CBS 9568
20 February 1981.
The original white label promotion copy for the 'Sherry Darling' single release had the wrong B side and were hastily withdrawn. Believed to be only 100 pressed and even fewer were sent out with a colour picture sleeve that had 'Independence Day' printed on the front cover, making it the rarest U.K. item.

– **Showcase** – cassette only. CBS XPC 4003
August 1983.
Cassette only compilation that was issued to tie in with a Nice Price/U.K. store campaign promotion (buy one album and receive one free cassette). The one Bruce song is 'Blinded By The Light'.

LP **Nice Price Sampler** CBS/EPIC XPR 1262
October 1984.
White label various artists compilation LP that featured 'Rosalita (Come Out Tonight)' on side 1 track 1.

LP **CBS Preview** CBS XPR 1269 November 1984.
White label various artists compilation LP that featured 'Jersey Girl' on side 2 track 2.

Various Artists Release

LP **No Nukes** ASYLUM K 62027 December 1979.
Triple live album recorded at the M.U.S.E. concerts Madison Square Garden, New York, 19–22 September 1979. Bruce and the E Street Band's 2 contributions were 'Stay' and an edited 'Devil With The Blue Dress' medley. A film and video release of the same name featured 3 songs by Bruce, 'Thunder Road', 'The River' and 'Quarter To Three'. Promotion copies pressed on white labels.

LP **In Harmony 2** CBS 85451 10 December 1981.
Various artists compilation LP with part of the royalties going to a children's charity. The one Bruce song is 'Santa Claus Is Comin' To Town', recorded live at the C.W. Post College, Greenvale, New York, 12 December 1975 and produced by Bruce, Jimmy Iovine and Mike Appel.

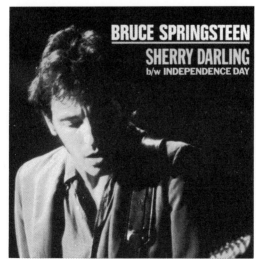

The following list includes every single, including promotion only releases and LPs released throughout the world that differ from the U.S.A./U.K. pressings.

Argentina
'Hungry Heart'/'Held Up Without A Gun' CBS 23.215 Titles in Spanish 1980. Promotion copies featured 'Not for Sale' printed on regular red labels.

Records of interest
Born To Run track listing in different order.
Oscuridad Al Borde De La Ciudad cover title of the **Darkness** LP.
'Dancing In The Dark'/'Born In The U.S.A.' CBS DEP 348. A promotion only 7″ that featured short versions of each song. 1984. Coloured sleeve.

Australia
'Born To Run'/'Meeting Across The River' CBS BA 222173 1975.
'Tenth Avenue Freeze-Out'/'She's The One' CBS BA 222193 1976.
'Prove It All Night'/'Factory' CBS BA 222430 1978.
'Badlands'/'Something In The Night' CBS BA 222445 1978.
'Hungry Heart'/'Held Up Without A Gun' CBS BA 222748 Black and white picture sleeve 1980.
'The River'/'I'm A Rocker' CBS BA 222789 1981.
'Fade Away'/'Be True' CBS BA 222801 1981.
'Atlantic City'/'Mansion On The Hill' CBS BA 222991 1982.
'Dancing In The Dark'/'Pink Cadillac' CBS BA 223189 Colour picture sleeve 1984.
'Dancing In The Dark' (blaster mix)/'same' (radio) and 'same' (dub) CBS BA 12093 12″ colour picture sleeve 1984.
'Cover Me'/'Jersey Girl' CBS BA 223223 Colour picture sleeve 1984.
'Cover Me' (undercover mix) and 'same' (dub 1)/'same' (radio) and 'same' (dub 2) CBS BA 12100 12″ colour picture sleeve 1984.
'Born In The U.S.A.'/'Shut Out The Light' CBS BA 223245 colour picture sleeve 1985.
'Born In The U.S.A.' (freedom mix)/'same' (dub) and 'same' (radio) CBS BA 121 12″ colour picture sleeve 1985.
'I'm On Fire'/'Johnny Bye Bye' CBS BA 223269 Colour picture sleeve 1985.
Promotion copies are pressed with white labels, except for 'Atlantic City' which features a printed 'Not for Sale' stamp on the regular release pressings.

Records of interest

Bruce Springsteen box set of first 3 LPs.
Rocktagon CBS Sampler 33 Octagonal shaped disc. Promotion only compilation LP with **'Hungry Heart'** 1980.
'Born In The U.S.A.'/**'Shut Out The Light'** and **'Pink Cadillac'**, **'Jersey Girl'** and **'Santa Claus Is Comin' To Town'**. CBS Sampler 9–3.
Promotional 12″ with colour picture sleeve with two songs on the A side.

Austria
All singles and LPs imported from Germany or Holland apart from –
'Sherry Darling'/**'The River'**/**'The Ties That Bind'** (live)/**'Hungry Heart'** CBS SHOL 3136 A 7″ one sided flexi disc issued with rock magazine Rennbahn Express, all songs are fragments. Plays at 33⅓rpm. 1981.

Belgium
All records imported from Holland.

Brazil
'Hungry Heart'/**'Stolen Car'** CBS 43043 Colour picture sleeve. Plays at 33⅓rpm 1980.
'Dancing In The Dark'/**'Pink Cadillac'** CBS 43.578 Black and white picture sleeve 1984.
Promotion copies feature printed 'Not for Sale' on regular release pressings.

Canada
'Born To Run'/**'Meeting Across The River'** COL. 3–10209 1975.
'Tenth Avenue Freeze-Out'/**'She's The One'** COL. 3–10274 1976.
'Prove It All Night'/**'Factory'** COL. 3–10763 1978.
'Badlands'/**'Streets Of Fire'** COL. 3–10801 1978.
'Born To Run'/**'Spirit In The Night'** COL. Hall Of Fame 13–33323 with both blue and red labels 1979.
'Hungry Heart'/**'Held Up Without A Gun'** COL. 11–11391 Black and white picture sleeve 1980.
'Fade Away'/**'Be True'** COL. 11–11431 Black and white picture sleeve, originally pressed with misprinted label of **'To Be True'** 1981.
'Atlantic City'/**'Mansion On The Hill'** COL. C4–8513 1982.
'Fade Away'/**'Be True'** COL. Hall Of Fame C4–1080 1983.
'Dancing In The Dark'/**'Pink Cadillac'** COL. 38–04463 Colour picture sleeve 1984.
'Dancing In The Dark' (blaster mix)/'same' (radio) and

'same' (dub) COL. 12CXP 5028 12″ colour picture sleeve 1984.
'Cover Me'/**'Jersey Girl'** COL. 38–04561 Colour picture sleeve 1984.
'Cover Me' (undercover mix) and 'same' (dub 1)/'same' (radio) and 'same' (dub 2) COL. 12CXP 05087 12″ colour picture sleeve 1984.
'Born In The U.S.A.'/**'Shut Out The Light'** COL. 38–04680 Colour picture sleeve 1985.
'Born In The U.S.A.' (freedom mix)/'same' (dub) and 'same' (radio) COL. 12 CXP 05147 12″. Colour picture sleeve 1985.
'I'm On Fire'/**'Johnny Bye Bye'** COL. 38–04772
'Glory Days'/**'Stand On It'** COL. 38–04924 Colour picture sleeve 1985.

Records of interest

Greetings From Asbury Park N.J. With full gatefold sleeve.
Bruce Springsteen Sampler COL. CDN 57 Promotion only LP A 'Born To Run'; 'The River'; 'Prove It All Night'; 'Blinded By The Light'; 'Cadillac Ranch'; B 'Rosalita (Come Out Tonight)'; 'Hungry Heart'; 'Spirit In The Night'; 'Candy's Room'; 'Thunder Road' 1983.
Give The Gift Of Music Compilation promotion only LP that featured 'Atlantic City' 1983.
'Born In The U.S.A.'/**'Shut Out The Light'**; **'Pink Cadillac'**, **'Jersey Girl'**, **'Santa Claus Is Comin' Town'** on COL. CDN 178. A promotion only 12″ with colour picture sleeve 1985.

China
No singles known to have been released. Albums from **Born To Run** onwards have been pressed and appear in thin glossy sleeves.

Denmark
All singles and LPs imported from Holland.

Finland
All singles and LPs imported from Holland.

France
'Hungry Heart'/**'Held Up Without A Gun'** CBS 9309 Black and white picture sleeve 1980.
'Cadillac Ranch'/**'Be True'** CBS A 1052 Colour picture sleeve 1981.
'The River'/**'Ramrod'** CBS A 1356 Colour picture sleeve 1981.

Records of interest
All LPs imported from Holland as are most singles.

Germany
'4th Of July, Asbury Park (Sandy)'/**'The E Street Shuffle'** CBS 3512 Colour picture sleeve 1974.
'Born To Run'/**'Meeting Across The River'** CBS 3661 Black and white picture sleeve 1975.
'Tenth Avenue Freeze-Out'/**'She's The One'** CBS 3940 Black and white picture sleeve 1976.
'Prove It All Night'/**'Factory'** CBS 6424 Colour picture sleeve 1978.
'Badlands'/**'Something In The Night'** CBS 6532 Colour picture sleeve 1978.
'Sherry Darling'/**'Be True'** CBS 9568 Black and white picture sleeve 1981.
'The River'/**'Independence Day'** CBS A 1179 Colour picture sleeve 1981.
Promotion copies issued up to CBS 3940 had unique picture sleeves with tracks and artist information on the front cover and a 'Blitzinformation' design on the back. CBS 6424 and CBS 6532 feature rear design only. All promotion copies pressed on white labels with a red thunderbolt on the A side.

Records of interest
Rock Archives a 10 LP box set that contained *Greetings From Asbury Park N.J.*

Greece
'Born To Run'/**'Meeting Across The River'** CBS 3661 Promotion only 1975.
'Cover Me' (undercover mix/**Cover Me'** (dub 1) and **'Jersey Girl'** CBS CASA 12 4662, 12″ plain black sleeve. 1984.

'The River'/'Independence Day' CBS A 1179 Colour picture sleeve 1981.
'The River'/'Ramrod' CBS A 1356 Colour picture sleeve 1981. Released for export only with a misprinted lyric on rear cover that mixed up 'The River' and 'You Can Look'.
'Santa Claus Is Comin' To Town'/Billy Joel song CBS PRO 151 Colour art sleeve 1981 promotion only.
'Atlantic City'/'Mansion On The Hill' CBS A 2794 Black and white picture sleeve 1982.
'Open All Night'/'The Big Payback' CBS A 2969 Black and white picture sleeve 1982.
'Dancing In The Dark'/'Pink Cadillac' CBS A 4436 Colour picture sleeve 1984.
'Dancing In The Dark' (blaster mix)/'same' (radio) and 'same' (dub) CBS A 12 4436 12″ colour picture sleeve 1984.
'Cover Me'/'Jersey Girl' CBS A 4662 Colour picture sleeve 1984.
'Cover Me' (undercover mix)/'Cover Me' (dub 1) and 'Jersey Girl' CBS A 12 4662 12″ colour picture sleeve 1984.

Records of interest
Born To Run issued in single jacket.
Darkness On The Edge Of Town featured black and white rear sleeve.

Holland
'Born To Run'/'Meeting Across The River' CBS 3661 Black and white picture sleeve 1975.
'Tenth Avenue Freeze-Out'/'She's The One' CBS 3940 Black and white picture sleeve 1976.
'Prove It All Night'/'Factory' CBS 6424 Colour picture sleeve 1978.
'Badlands'/'Something In The Night' CBS 6532 Colour picture sleeve 1978.
'Badlands'/'Candy's Room' CBS 6678 Colour picture sleeve 1978.
'Rosalita (Come Out Tonight)'/'Night' CBS 7753 Colour art sleeve 1979.
'Rosalita (Come Out Tonight)'/'Racing In The Street' and 'Night' CBS 12 7753 12″, colour picture sleeve, originally included a black and white poster 1979.
'Hungry Heart'/'Held Up Without A Gun' CBS 9309 Black and white picture sleeve 1980. Issued in 3 variations, the French export copy featured a textured sleeve with no LP photo on rear, the German export copy had a misspelt Jon Landan (sic) on rear credits.
'Sherry Darling'/'Be True' CBS 9568 Black and white picture sleeve 1981.

'Born In The U.S.A.'/'Shut Out The Light' CBS A 4920. Colour picture sleeve 1985.
'Born In The U.S.A.' (freedom mix)/'same' (dub) and 'same' (radio) CBS A 12 4920. 12″ colour picture sleeve 1985.
'I'm On Fire'/'Johnny Bye Bye' CBS A 6148 Colour picture sleeve 1985.
'I'm On Fire' and 'Johnny Bye Bye'/'Shut Out The Light' and 'Jersey Girl' CBS A 12.6148 12″ Colour picture sleeve 1985.

Records of interest
Rockwork CBS 88200 Double compilation LP that featured a 3.42 edited version of '4th Of July, Asbury Park (Sandy)' 1975.
The River 'Held Up Without A Gun' misprinted on inner sleeve.
Nebraska Superb gatefold sleeve.
'Born In The U.S.A.'/'Shut Out The Light', 'Pink Cadillac', 'Jersey Girl', 'Santa Claus Is Comin' To Town' CBS SAMP 89. Promotion only 12″ with colour picture sleeve 1985.

India
No details known apart from the single 'Born To Run', which is rumoured to exist.

Ireland
All singles and LPs pressed in England apart from:
Springsteen Pack issued in a plastic display wallet and

hastily withdrawn. Contents are –
'The Promised Land'/'Streets Of Fire' CBS 6720 Black and white picture sleeve.
'Born To Run'/'Meeting Across The River' CBS 7077 Black and white picture sleeve.
'Hungry Heart'/'Held Up Without A Gun' CBS 9309 Same as U.K. sleeve.
'The River'/'Independence Day' CBS A 1179 Same as U.K. sleeve.
All have plain orange labels and numerous mistakes on song titles and credits. 1983.

Israel
No singles believed to have been pressed.

Records Of Interest
Born To Run Issued in single jacket with lyric sheet.
The River Issued in a gatefold sleeve.
Dead End Street CBS DJ 428 One sided promotion only 12″ with picture sleeve from the film of the same name. Three songs, 'Jungleland'; 'Point Blank' and 'Hungry Heart'.

Italy
'Born To Run'/'Meeting Across The River' CBS 3661 Black and white picture sleeve 1975.
'Prove It All Night'/'Factory' CBS 6424 Black and white picture sleeve 1978.

161

'Badlands'/'Streets Of Fire' CBS 6532 Colour picture sleeve 1978.

'Hungry Heart'/'Held up Without A Gun' CBS 9309 Black and white picture sleeve 1980.

'Atlantic City'/'Mansion On The Hill' CBS A 2794 Black and white picture sleeve 1982.

'Dancing In The Dark'/'Pink Cadillac' CBS A 4436 Colour picture sleeve 1984.

'Cover Me'/'Jersey Girl' CBS A 4662 Colour picture sleeve 1984.

'Born In The U.S.A.'/'Shut Out The Light' CBS A 4920. Colour picture sleeve 1985.

'I'm On Fire'/'Johnny Bye Bye' CBS A 6148 Colour picture sleeve 1985.

Promotion copies featured promotion stamp on regular release labels.

Records of interest

Born To Run Promotion copies issued in a poster/sleeve with biography.

Il Ciocco CBS LP 195 promotion only compilation LP with 'Born To Run' 1975.

Bruce Springsteen Storia E Musica Cassette only release issued with companion magazine, A 'Blinded By The Light'; 'It's Hard To Be A Saint In The City'; 'Rosalita'; 'Tenth Avenue Freeze-Out'; B 'Thunder Road'; 'Jungleland'; 'Darkness On The Edge Of Town' Issued with colour sleeve 1982.

DJ Special Service CBS 12 PRM 019 'Hungry Heart' and 'I'm A Rocker'/'Born To Run' and 'Darkness On The Edge Of Town' 12" promotion only release.

'Born To Run'/Bob Dylan song CBS YD 452 Jukebox issue only

'Hungry Heart'/Love Unlimited Orchestra CBS JC 15045 Jukebox issue only.

Japan

'Born To Run'/'Backstreets' CBS/SONY SOPB 334 Black and white picture sleeve 1975.

'Tenth Avenue Freeze-Out'/'She's The One' CBS/SONY SOPB 350 Black and white picture sleeve 1976.

'Prove It All Night'/'Factory' CBS/SONY 06SP 232 Colour picture sleeve 1978.

'Badlands'/'Streets Of Fire' CBS/SONY 06SP 256 Colour picture sleeve 1978.

'Born To Run'/'Badlands' CBS/SONY 363 06SP Colour picture sleeve, issued on the Gold Star series 1979.

'Hungry Heart'/'Held Up Without A Gun' CBS/SONY 07SP 511 Originally issued in a colour picture sleeve, hastily withdrawn in favour of the U.K./U.S. style sleeve 1980.

'I Wanna Marry You'/'Be True' CBS/SONY 07SP 525 Black and white picture sleeve 1981.
'Atlantic City'/'Mansion On The Hill' CBS/SONY 07SP 657 Black and white picture sleeve 1982.
'Dancing In The Dark'/'Pink Cadillac' (mono) CBS/SONY 07SP 810 Colour picture sleeve 1984.
'Dancing In The Dark' (blaster mix)/'same' (radio) and 'same' (dub) CBS/SONY 12 AP 2889 12" colour picture sleeve 1984.
'Cover Me'/'Jersey Girl' CBS/SONY 07SP 831 Colour picture sleeve 1984.
'Cover Me' (undercover mix) and 'same' (dub 1)/'same' (radio) and 'same' (dub 2) CBS/SONY 12 AP 2930 Colour picture sleeve 1984.
'Born In The U.S.A.'/'Shut Out The Light' CBS/SONY 07SP 850 Colour picture sleeve 1985.
'Born In The U.S.A.' (freedom mix)/'same' (dub) and 'same' (radio) CBS/SONY 12 AP 12" Colour picture sleeve 1985.
'I'm On Fire'/'Johnny Bye Bye' CBS/SONY 07SP 875 Colour picture sleeve 1985.
Promotion copies are pressed with white labels.

Records and promotion only items of interest
The Wild, The Innocent And The E Street Shuffle Promotion copies came with a 5 page biography.
The Last American Hero CBS/SONY YAPC 95 Promotion only LP. A 'It's Hard To Be A Saint In The City'; 'Blinded By The Light'; 'Spirit In The Night'; 'New York City Serenade'; B 'Thunder Road'; 'Born To Run'; 'She's The One'; 'Tenth Avenue Freeze-Out';

'Jungleland'. Black and white picture sleeve 1978.
'Santa Claus Is Comin' To Town'/Barbra Streisand song CBS/SONY X DSP 93026 Promotion only release with superb colour picture sleeve 1981.
Killer Tracks From The River CBS/SONY X DAP 93030 12" promotion only release with black and white picture sleeve 1981 – A 'The River' and 'I Wanna Marry You' B 'Hungry Heart' and 'Point Blank'.
Nebraska First 1000 copies issued with a 24" × 36" colour poster.
'Dancing In The Dark'/(blaster mix) Bonnie Tyler song CBS/SONY XDAP 93110 12" promotion only release with colour picture sleeve 1984.
'Dancing In The Dark' (radio)/Laura Brannigan song CBS/SONY 12" promotion only release 1984.
All American Top 100 Monthly promotion only compilation LP. Bruce has appeared on the following – July 1978 'Prove It All Night', October 1978 'Badlands', February 1981 'Hungry Heart', March 1981 'Hungry Heart' and 'Fade Away', May 1981 'I Wanna Marry You', October 1982 'Atlantic City', June 1984 'Dancing In The Dark'.

Malaysia
No singles believed to have been pressed. Album titles available on cassette with catalogue numbers the same as U.S.A.

Mexico
'Hungry Heart'/'Stolen Car' CBS Colour picture sleeve 1980.
'Dancing In The Dark'/'Pink Cadillac' CBS 8604 1984 No picture sleeve.

New Zealand
'Born To Run'/'Meeting Across The River' CBS BA 461634 1975.
'Tenth Avenue Freeze-Out'/'She's The One' CBS BA 461649 1976.
'Prove It All Night'/'Factory' CBS BA 461858 1978.
'Badlands'/'Something In The Night' CBS BA 461872 1978.
'Hungry Heart'/'Held Up Without A Gun' CBS BA 222748 1980.
'Fade Away'/'The Ties That Bind' CBS BA 222801 Withdrawn 1981.
'Fade Away'/'Be True' CBS BA 222806 1981.
'The River'/'Point Blank' CBS BA 222843 1981.
'Atlantic City'/'Mansion On The Hill' CBS BA 222843 1982.
'Dancing In The Dark'/'Pink Cadillac' CBS BA 223189 Colour picture sleeve 1984.
'Dancing In The Dark' (blaster mix)/'same' (dub) and 'same' (radio) CBS BA 12100 12" colour picture sleeve 1984.
'Cover Me'/'Jersey Girl' CBS BA 223223. Colour picture sleeve 1984.
'Cover Me' (undercover mix) and 'same' (dub 1)/'same' (radio) and 'same' (dub 2) CBS BA 12100 12" colour picture sleeve 1984.
'Born In The U.S.A.'/'Shut Out The Light' CBS BA 223245. Colour picture sleeve 1985.
'Born In The U.S.A.' (freedom mix)/'same' (dub) and 'same' (radio) CBS BA 12" colour picture sleeve 1985.
'I'm On Fire'/'Johnny Bye Bye' CBS BA 223269 Colour Picture sleeve 1985.

Records of interest
Bruce Springsteen 3 LP box set.
Sampla Phonogram PHS LP2. Promotion only compilation LP that featured 'Born To Run'

Norway
All singles and LPs imported from Holland.

Records of interest
Bruce Springsteen 4 LP box set (all pressed in Holland) available only through a Norwegian book club promotion offer. Stunning colour sleeve 1983.

Philippines
'Hungry Heart'/'Held Up Without A Gun' believed to have been pressed 1980.
'Dancing In The Dark'/'Pink Cadillac' SCS 100037 1984.
'Dancing In The Dark' (blaster mix)/'same' (radio) and 'same' (dub) CE-EP 18006 1984.

Records of interest
Born To Run with different sleeve.
Greetings From Asbury Park N.J. with different rear sleeve.
The River issued with blue and white labels.
All records are on the Black Gold label.

Poland
Singles are pressed on picture postcards.
'She's The One'.
'Born To Run'.
'The Ties That Bind'.
'Meeting Across The River'.
'Tenth Avenue Freeze-Out'.
'Night'.
'Backstreets'.
'Jungleland'.
'Thunder Road'.
'Hungry Heart' (pressed as a 7" flexi disc).

Portugal
'Dancing In The Dark'/'Pink Cadillac' CBS 4436 Colour picture sleeve 1984.
'Dancing In The Dark' (blaster)/'same' (radio) and 'same' (dub) CBS A 12 4436 12" colour picture sleeve 1984.
'Cover Me'/'Jersey Girl' CBS A 4662. Colour picture sleeve 1984.
All LPs have been pressed here.

Singapore
No singles believed to have been pressed.

Last three albums available with catalogue numbers the same as U.S.A.

South Africa
'Born To Run'/'Meeting Across The River' CBS SSC 1420 1975.
'Prove It All Night'/'Factory' CBS SSC 1738 1978.
'Badlands'/'Streets Of Fire' CBS SSC 1759 1978.
'Hungry Heart'/'Wreck On The Highway' CBS SSC 5146 1980.
'Sherry Darling'/'Cadillac Ranch' CBS SSC 5178 1981.
'The Ties That Bind'/'I'm A Rocker' CBS SSC 5207 1981.
'Dancing In The Dark'/'Pink Cadillac' CBS SSC 5639 Colour picture sleeve 1984.
'Dancing In The Dark' (blaster mix)/'same' (dub) and 'same' (radio) CBS XSSC 5684 12" colour picture sleeve 1984.
'Cover Me'/'Jersey Girl' CBS SSC 5709 1984.
'Cover Me' (undercover mix) and 'same' (dub 1)/'same' (radio) and 'same' (dub 2) CBS XSSC 5739 12" colour picture sleeve 1984.
'Born In The U.S.A.'/'Shut Out The Light' CBS SSC 5756 Colour picture sleeve 1985.
'Born In The U.S.A.' (freedom mix)/'same' (dub) and 'same' (radio) CBS XSSC 12" colour picture sleeve 1985.
'I'm On Fire'/'Johnny Bye Bye' CBS SSC colour picture sleeve 1985.

Records of interest
The River issued with gatefold sleeve.

Spain
'Born To Run'/'Meeting Across The River' CBS 3661 Colour picture sleeve 1975.
'Tenth Avenue Freeze-Out'/'She's The One' CBS 3940 Colour picture sleeve 1976.
'Blinded By The Light'/'Spirit In The Night' CBS 5121 Black and white picture sleeve 1977.
'Prove It All Night'/'Factory' CBS 6424 Colour picture sleeve 1978.
'Badlands'/'Streets Of Fire' CBS 6838 Colour picture sleeve 1978.
'Hungry Heart'/'Held Up Without A Gun' CBS 9309 Black and white picture sleeve 1980.
'Sherry Darling'/'Be True' CBS 9568 Colour picture sleeve 1981.
'The River'/'Independence Day' CBS A 1179 Black and white picture sleeve 1981.
'Atlantic City'/'Mansion On The Hill' CBS A 2794 Black and white picture sleeve 1982.
'Open All Night'/'The Big Payback' CBS A 2969

Black and white picture sleeve 1982.
'Dancing In The Dark'/'Pink Cadillac' CBS A 4436 Colour picture sleeve 1984.
'Dancing In The Dark' (blaster mix)/'same' (radio) and 'same' (dub) CBS A 12 4436 12" colour picture sleeve 1984.
'Cover Me'/'Jersey Girl' CBS A 4662 Colour picture sleeve 1984.
'Cover Me' (undercover mix)/'same' (dub 4.02) and 'Jersey Girl' 12 4742 12" colour picture sleeve 1984.
'Born In The U.S.A.'/'Shut Out The Light' CBS A 4920 Colour Picture Sleeve 1985.
'Born In The U.S.A.' (freedom mix)/'same' (dub) and 'same' (radio) CBS A 12 4920 12" Colour picture sleeve 1985.
'I'm On Fire'/'Johnny Bye Bye' CBS A 6148 Colour picture sleeve 1985.

White label promotion copies pressed from 'Hungry Heart' onwards. In 1982 they became one sided pressings of the A side only.

Records of interest
Darkness On The Edge Of Town Different rear sleeve in black and white.
Especial FM Volume 1 CBS Especial Promotion only compilation LP with 'Prove It All Night' and 'Streets Of Fire' 1978.
Historia De La Musica Rock CBS LSP 15482 Reissue of the *Born To Run* songs with stunning sleeve 1983.
Oh Que Calor CBS PROMOCIONAL compilation LP, white label promotion copies pressed with 'Dancing In The Dark'.

Sweden
All singles and LPs imported from Holland.

U.S.S.R.
No records pressed.

Taiwan
No regular release singles known.
Super Hits SP 1054 4 track jukebox only issue featuring Eddie Money, K.C. and the Sunshine Band, Van Morrison and 'Badlands'.

Yugoslavia
'Prove It All Night'/'Factory' CBS/SUZY 6424 Picture sleeve 1978.

Records of interest
The last 4 LPs pressed here.

Jukebox Graduate

(*Other Artists' Songs Performed By Springsteen*)

Ever since the young Bruce Springsteen watched Elvis Presley's first appearance on the *Ed Sullivan Show* on 1 September 1956, he's been influenced by what he saw and heard on the television and radio (usually, station WCBS). His early guitar playing was influenced by the style of B. B. King and his Steel Mill years are sprinkled with cover versions of songs by Jimmy Reed, Otis Rush and Muddy Waters. The early and mid-seventies saw Bruce introduce into his live concerts the songs he'd bought from the local record store as a teenager in Freehold, New Jersey in the

1960s – Phil Spector's productions on the Philles label, the back catalogues from Stax and Atlantic, English bands like the Animals and Manfred Mann and the classic 'Quarter To Three' by Gary U.S. Bonds. In 1978 (and again in 1982) Bruce let his initial rock'n'roll influences flow free – Elvis Presley, Buddy Holly, Chuck Berry and Little Richard were a release to the overall starkness of *Darkness On The Edge Of Town* and *Nebraska*. On the latter part of the 1980–81 world tour, Bruce's choice of material reflected a more social and political awareness with Woody Guthrie's 'This

Land Is Your Land' being performed at almost every concert. Bruce Springsteen's choice of early material isn't the normal obligatory, end-of-concert oldies. It's much, much more than that, and what's more it shows a strong and living sense of musical history.

This section details as much as possible of Bruce's influences as reflected in his choice of non-original material for concerts and soundchecks. Included here are: song title; composer(s); original recording artist; label and catalogue number and year of release.

'A Fine Fine Boy (Girl)' (Spector, Greenwich, Barry) by Darlene Love (Philles 109) 1963.
Performed live about six times on the second tour of 1976.

'Ain't That A Shame' (Domino, Bartholomew) by Fats Domino (Imperial 5348) 1955.
Performed live with Beaver Brown in 1979 and 1982, both times in small New Jersey clubs.

'Ain't That Loving You Baby' (Reed) by Jimmy Reed (Vee Jay 168) 1955.
Performed at a couple of guest appearances with John Eddie and the Front Street Runners and Cats On A Smooth Surface in August 1983.

'Ain't That Peculiar' (Robinson) by Marvin Gaye (Tamla Motown 539) 1965.
Only known performance at the Student Prince, Asbury Park, New Jersey in 1971. Southside Johnny took lead vocals for a guest appearance with the Bruce Springsteen Band.

'Ain't Too Proud To Beg' (Whitfield, Holland) by The Temptations (Gordy 7054) 1966.
One performance, given to the lucky patrons of Michigan Palace, 4 October 1975, and another to an amazed audience at Patrix, a small club in New Brunswick, New Jersey, when Bruce guested with John Eddie and the Front Street Runners on 14 January 1984.

'All Aboard' (Berry) by Chuck Berry (Chess LP1480) 1961.
Bruce interpreted the lyric to suit his tour itinerary, always ending up with the name of the town where he was performing that night.

'Amen' (Traditional) by The Impressions (ABC-Paramount 10602) 1964.
Bridged into the beginning of 'Havin' A Party' at the Monmouth Arts Centre, 13 May 1977. Bruce and Miami Steve, backed by the Asbury Jukes, share lead vocals at one of the three Asbury All-Stars Revue gigs that took place during Southside Johnny's illness.

'Around And Around' (Berry) by Chuck Berry (Chess 1691) 1958.
First performed with the E Street Band at St. Petersburg, Florida, in July 1978. Bruce often included it in his guest appearances with various bands in and around the New Jersey bars in 1982 and 1983.

'A Teenager In Love' (Pomus, Shuman) by Dion and The Belmonts (Laurie 3027) 1959.
Bruce and Miami Steve sang one verse each when they joined Dion onstage as 'honorary Belmonts' at the Roxy, Los Angeles, California, September 1976.

'Auld Lang Syne' (Traditional)
Played, as one might expect, at New Year's Eve concerts only.

'Baby I Love You' (Spector, Greenwich, Barry) by The Ronettes (Philles 118) 1963.
Sung with Ronnie Spector when she guested at the Palladium, New York City on 4 November 1976 and again with Ronnie, plus Flo and Eddie, in Cleveland, Ohio, in February 1977.

'Back In The U.S.A.' (Berry) by Chuck Berry (Chess 1729) 1959.
Performed on a few rare occasions in 1975. The song was included as part of the first ever 'Devil With The Blue Dress' medley at the Hill Auditorium, University Of Michigan, Ann Arbor, 23 September 1975.

'Ballad Of Easy Rider' (McGuinn) by The Byrds (Columbia 44990) 1969.
One-and-only performance at the Vietnam Veteran's Benefit concert, the Sports Arena, Los Angeles, California, 20 August 1981.

'Bama Lama Bama Loo' (Penniman) by Little Richard (Speciality 697) 1964.
Bruce played guitar on this song at a gig by Dave Edmunds at Big Man's West, Red Bank, New Jersey, 18 September 1982.

'Be Bop A Lula' (Davis, Vincent) by Gene Vincent (Capitol 3450) 1956.
Performed at a gig with the Stray Cats at the Fast Lane, Asbury Park, New Jersey, 23 July 1982.

'Be My Baby' (Spector, Greenwich, Barry) by The Ronettes (Philles 116) 1963.
Performed with Ronnie Spector when she guested on a three-song 'Ronettes medley' at the Palladium, New York City, in 1976 and again with Ronnie plus Flo and Eddie in a four-song medley in Cleveland, Ohio, in February 1977.

'Be True To Your School' (Wilson) by The Beach Boys (Capitol 5069) 1963.
Used once, to intro 'Rosalita (Come Out Tonight)' at the Palladium, New York City, 3 November 1976.

'Blue Suede Shoes' (Perkins) by Carl Perkins (Sun 234) 1956.
One known performance, when Bruce joined John Eddie and The Front Street Runners onstage at the Brighton Bar, Long Branch, New Jersey, on 19 August 1983.

'Boom Boom' (Hooker) by John Lee Hooker (Vee Jay) 1960.
Performed with John Eddie and the Front Street Runners at Patrix, New Brunswick, New Jersey, on 14 January 1984 and with the Cats at the Stone Pony on 10 June 1984.

'Boys' (Dixon, Farrell) The Shirelles (Scepter 1211) 1960.
First song the Castiles learnt to play at rehearsals in 1965 and almost sure to have been included in their live concerts 1965–67.

'Bright Lights, Big City' (Reed) by Jimmy Reed (Vee Jay 398) 1961.
Performed live with the Bruce Springsteen Band, *circa* 1971–72. Made a surprise re-appearance when Bruce guested with John Eddie and the Front Street Runners at the Stone Pony on 1 June 1984.

'Brother John Is Gone' (Traditional)
Final encore at the 'Survival Sunday' concert, the Hollywood Bowl, Los Angeles, California, 14 June 1981.

'Can't Help Falling In Love' (Peretti, Creators, Weiss) by Elvis Presley (RCA Victor 47–7968) 1961.
One of Bruce's favourite Elvis songs, performed five times on the European tour of 1981, and again in 1985 during the first American leg of the world tour.

'Carol' (Berry) by Chuck Berry (Chess 1700) 1958.
Frequent 1975 concert encore. Bruce regularly used it on his guest appearances in the bar joints of New Jersey in 1982–83, most notably with Nils Lofgren at the Royal Manor North, 12 January 1982.

'C.C. Rider' (Rainey) by Gertrude ('Ma') Rainey (Paramount 12252) 1924.

Performed as part of the 'Devil With The Blue Dress' medley, first sung in September 1975. The medley has appeared on every tour since (sometimes only once, as in 1977), and in 1980–81 he closed *every* known show with it amongst the encores.

'Chimes Of Freedom' (Dylan) by Bob Dylan (Columbia 8993) 1964.
Only one live performance, at the Masonic Temple, Detroit, Michigan, on 1 September 1978.

'Come On Over To My Place' (Mann, Weil) by The Drifters (Atlantic 4023) 1965.
Performed about four times with Cats On A Smooth Surface at the Stone Pony, Asbury Park, New Jersey, August to October 1982.

'Cupid' (Cooke) by Sam Cooke (RCA Victor 47–7883) 1961.
From October 1974. Two renditions are known.

'Dancing In The Street' (Gaye, Stevenson, Hunter) by Martha and the Vandellas (Gordy 7033) 1964.
Regular opening song for Steel Mill, *circa* 1970. Last known performance at the Scene, New York City, 18 January 1971.

'Deportee (Plane Wreck At Los Gatos)' (Guthrie) by Woody Guthrie, *circa* 1940.
Bruce's choice of old material definitely showed signs of moral and political awareness during 1980–81. There was one performance only of 'Deportee' on 28 August 1981 at the Sports Arena, Los Angeles, California.

'Devil With The Blue Dress' (Long, Stevenson) by Shorty Long (Soul 35001) 1964.
The title song to the medley sometimes referred to (wrongly) as the 'Detroit Medley' has been a part of Bruce's stage material since 1975 and was released in an edited form on the *No Nukes* triple live album in 1979.

'Dirty Water' (E. Cobb) by The Standells (Tower 185) 1966.
Bruce joined Cats On A Smooth Surface onstage at the Stone Pony, Asbury Park, New Jersey, 8 April 1984 for a one and only performance of this 'punk classic'.

'Don't Be Cruel' (Blackwell, Presley) by Elvis Presley (RCA Victor 47–6604) 1956.
A version played at a soundcheck at the Capitol Theatre, Passaic, New Jersey, on 21 September 1978 was performed in a style similar to Billy Swan's country version.

'Down In The Valley' (Burke, Martin, Berns, Chivian) by Solomon Burke (Atlantic 2147) 1965.
Bruce played guitar and sang back-up vocals at a Southside Johnny show at the Stone Pony, Asbury Park, New Jersey, on 13 October 1977.

'Down The Road Apiece' (Raye) by Merril E. Moore (Capitol 3311) 1955.
One known performance with the Bruce Springsteen Band at the Back Door, Richmond, Virginia, in February 1972.

'Do You Love Me' (Gordy Jnr.) by The Contours (Gordy 7005) 1962.
First performed at the Forum, Montreal, 21 July 1984 where it was segued into a rousing version of 'Twist And Shout' and has since become a regular inclusion in the encores of the 1984–85 tour.

'Do You Wanna Dance?' (Freeman) by Bobby Freeman (Josie 835) 1958.

'Funky Broadway' (Christian) by Wilson Pickett (Atlantic 2430) 1967.
Originally part of Steel Mill's repertoire, it re-surfaced briefly when Bruce guested with New Jersey band, the Shots, at the Stone Pony, Asbury Park, New Jersey, on 4 September 1977.

'Further On Up The Road' (Veasey, Robey) by Bobby 'Blue' Bland (Duke 170) 1957.
Bruce appeared on back-up vocals and guitar when he guested with the Shots at the Stone Pony, Asbury Park, New Jersey, 4 September 1977.

'Give Me That Wine' (Hendricks) by Jon Hendricks (Arista) 1961.
First used when Bruce took time out to repair a guitar string at the Liberty Hall, Texas, 11 March 1974. One other known performance, at the Music Inn, Lenox, Massachusetts, in 1975.

'Gloria' (Morrison) by Them (Decca F 12018) 1965.
Introduced as part of the build up to 'She's The One' in July 1978, and last used with the E Street Band in November 1978 at the Utica Memorial Auditorium, New York. The last known version was with Cats On A Smooth Surface at the Stone Pony, Asbury Park, New Jersey, 10 June 1984.

'Goin' Back' (Goffin, King) by Dusty Springfield (Philips BF 1502) 1966.
Exclusively at the Roxy, Los Angeles, California, 16–19 October 1975. No other versions known.

'Good Golly Miss Molly' (Blackwell, Marascallo) by Little Richard (Speciality 624) 1958.
Performed as part of the 'Devil With The Blue Dress' medley.

'Good Rockin' Tonight' (Brown) by Roy Brown (De Luxe 1093) 1947.
Bruce opened several of his 1978 shows with this raucous rocker, including a classic interpretation at Madison Square Garden, 22 August, where due to a newspaper strike, the opening line 'Have you heard the news?' was built up by Bruce to a fever pitch before opening up with the full song. Occasionally used during 1981.

'Got My Mojo Working' (Morganfield) by Muddy Waters (Chess 1652) 1956.
Performed by both Steel Mill and the Bruce Springsteen Band, *circa* 1970–71.

'Hang On Sloopy' (Russell, Farell) by The McCoys (Bang 506) 1965.
A full version of the song was segued into 'Twist and Shout', the final encore of a guest appearance with John Eddie at Patrix, 14 January 1984. Also performed with the Del Fuegos at The Rhinoceros Club, Greensboro, North Carolina, in January 1985.

'A Hard Day's Night' (Lennon, McCartney) by The Beatles (Parlaphone R 5160) 1964.
Performed with Clarence Clemons and the Red Bank Rockers in April 1984, at the Expo Club, Mount Ivy, New York.

'Havin' A Party' (Cooke) by Sam Cooke (RCA Victor 47–8036) 1962.
Often performed with Southside Johnny in the smaller clubs at guest appearances. The first performance, backed by the E Street Band, was at the Civic Theatre, Akron, Ohio, on 8 August 1975. In 1982 Bruce included it in guest spots with Cats On A Smooth Surface in the New Jersey clubs.

Performed on a couple of occasions, to great effect, during Bruce's 'home tour' of the New Jersey bars, guesting with various local bands in 1982.

'Double Shot (Of My Baby's Love)' (Uncredited) by The Swingin' Medallions (Smash 2033) 1966.
For some great reason this song and 'Louie Louie' have always been performed at the Notre Dame University, South Bend, Indiana, from 1978 onwards.

'Drift Away' (Williams) by Dobie Gray (Decca 33057) 1973.
Two performances are known from when Little Steven guested with Bruce and the E Street Band. Debuted at the Brendan Byrne Meadowlands Arena, East Rutherford, New Jersey, on 20 August 1984 and again, at the Mid South Coliseum, Memphis, Tennessee, 13 December 1984.

'Follow That Dream' (Wise, Weisman) by Elvis Presley (RCA Victor EPA 4368) 1962.
Totally rearranged, with added lyrics by Bruce and augmented by a fair portion of Roy Orbison's 'In Dreams', this number was debuted in Paris on 19 April 1981, and was often used both in Europe and on the closing dates of the following U.S.A. tour.

'For What It's Worth' (Stills) by Buffalo Springfield (Atco 6459) 1967.
Steel Mill cover version, *circa* 1970.

'Forty Miles Of Bad Road' (Eddy, Casey) by Duane Eddy (Jaime 1126) 1959.
Brief snatches of this instrumental occasionally thrown into the live shows in 1978, segued into 'Paradise By The Sea'.

GARY US BONDS WITH **BRUCE SPRINGSTEEN**

JOLÉ BLON

'Haunted House' (Geddin) by Johnny Fuller (Speciality 655) 1958.
A special Halloween version was cooked up by Bruce for an appearance at the Los Angeles Sports Arena, 31 October 1980. Bruce opened the show by being carried on in a coffin, and then being chased by roadies in ghost attire.

'He's Sure The Boy I Love' (Mann, Weil) by The Crystals (Philles 109) 1962.
Only known performance at the Monmouth Arts Centre (previously called the Carlton Theatre), Red Bank, New Jersey, 1 August 1976.

'Heartbreak Hotel' (Axton, Durden, Presley) by Elvis Presley (RCA Victor 47–6420) 1956.
Performed with plenty of 'slapback' and echo, it was premiered with the E Street Band at the Roxy, Los Angeles, California, 7 July 1978, although a vocal shared with Robert Gordon at the Student Centre, New York City, on 2 December 1977 was Bruce's first known public performance.

'Heartful Of Soul' (Gouldman) by The Yardbirds (Columbia DB 7594) 1965.
Spontaneous version performed at a 1978 studio rehearsal.

'Higher And Higher' (Jackson, Smith) by Jackie Wilson (Brunswick 55336) 1967.
The brass-oriented version was first performed with the E Street Band and the Miami Horns at the Music Hall, Boston, Massachusetts, on 24 March 1977. An earlier working of the song took place at a soundcheck in Geneva, New York, in July 1975, the last performance being a shared duet with Chrissie Hynde at a Pretenders gig in Pasadena, California, in 1981.

'High Heel Sneakers' (Higenbottom) by Tommy Tucker (Pye 7N 25238) 1964.
Sung with Cats On A Smooth Surface at the Stone Pony, Asbury Park, New Jersey, in 1982.

'High School Confidential' (Hargrave, Lewis) by Jerry Lee Lewis (Sun 294) 1958.
Debuted in 1978 with great piano from Roy. In 1981 it made frequent appearances as part of the 'Devil With The Blue Dress' medley, also performed on the 1984–85 tour, notably on Halloween, as the show opener at the Sports Arena, Los Angeles.

'Honky Tonk Woman' (Jagger, Richard) by The Rolling Stones (Decca F 12952) 1969.

Only known version is from a Steel Mill show in 1971, where it was segued into a version of 'Dancing In The Street'.

'Hootchie Cootchie Man' (Dixon) by Muddy Waters (Chess 1560) 1953.
Only known performance with the Bruce Springsteen Band at the VCU Gym, Richmond, Virginia, *circa* 1970.

('I Can't Get No) Satisfaction' (Jagger, Richard) by The Rolling Stones (Decca F 12220) 1965.
Instrumental version known from a studio rehearsal in 1978.

'(I Don't Want To) Hang Up My Rock'n'Roll Shoes' (Willis) by Chuck Willis (Atlantic 1179) 1956.
Sadly only one version of this 'made to measure' song is known, a great bootlegged performance from Saginaw, Michigan, on 3 September 1978.

'I Don't Want To Go Home' (Van Zandt) by Southside Johnny & The Asbury Jukes (Epic LP 34180) 1976.
Often performed with Southside Johnny when Bruce guested with him onstage. In May 1977 Bruce and Miami Steve, backed by the Asbury Jukes, performed the song at the three 'Asbury All Stars' revues in Red Bank, New Jersey. More recently, with the E Street Band, Miami Steve took lead vocals at the Byrne Meadowlands Arena, East Rutherford, New Jersey, in July 1981.

'I Fought The Law' (Curtis) by The Crickets (Coral) 1960.
First performed in full at the Arena, Seattle, Washington, on 25 June 1978, this number has remained a constant part of Bruce's repertoire since, surfacing at irregular intervals throughout 1979, 1980, 1981, and 1984. A brief chorus was first heard on an acoustic radio session Bruce did back in April 1974.

'I Got You (I Feel Good)' (Brown) by James Brown (King 6015) 1965. Used in the 'Devil With The Blue Dress' medley on a couple of occasions in 1981.

'I'm Bad, I'm Nationwide' (Gibbons, Hill) by Z. Z. Top (Warner Brothers LP 3361) 1979.
Performed at the Stone Pony, Asbury Park, New Jersey on five occasions from 25 March 1984, on its debut with the Cats, up until the 22 August guest appearance with La Bamba's Hubcaps. It made a surprise E Street Band debut when it was played at the Spectrum, Philadelphia, Pennsylvania, in September 1984.

'I'm Into Something Good' (Goffin, King) by Earl Jean (Colpix 729) 1963.
One known performance with the Bruce Springsteen Band at the Back Door, Richmond, Virginia, in February 1972 when it was worked into a version of 'Take Out Some Insurance'.

'I'm Ready' (Lewis, Bradford, Domino) by Fats Domino (Imperial 5588) 1959.
Performed in concert in 1974 as the fade out to 'Let The Four Winds Blow', and again in 1980 as part of the 'Devil With The Blue Dress' medley.

'In The Mood' (Garland, Razaf) by Glenn Miller (RCA Bluebird 10416) 1939.
Played as the final number of the Castiles' first ever gig at the Wood Haven Swim Club, New Jersey, *circa* 1966. Bruce rearranged it to suit the band.

'I Sold My Heart To The Junkman' (Rene, Rene) by The Silhouettes (Ace 552) 1958.
Performed at the show that inspired Jon Landau's *Real*

Paper article (and that famous 'rock'n'roll future' quote) at the Harvard Square Theatre, Cambridge, Massachusetts, 9 May 1974.

'Is That All To The Ball Mr Hall' (Lewis) by Billy Lee Riley (Brunswick 55085) 1958.
Bruce began working out this great rockabilly number at a soundcheck for the opening show of the 1978 tour, Shea Theatre, Buffalo, New York. Unfortunately Bruce never chose to include it in concert!

'It's All Over Now' (Jagger, Richard) by The Rolling Stones (Decca F 11934) 1964.
Performed with Cats On A Smooth Surface at the Stone Pony, Asbury Park, New Jersey, 6 November 1983.

'It's All Over Now Baby Blue' (Dylan) by Bob Dylan (Columbia LP 9128 1965.
One known performance with Steel Mill, *circa* 1970. Believed to have been recorded at Carl 'Tinker' West's surfboard 'studio' (probably his garage) *circa* 1971–72, by the five-piece Bruce Springsteen Band (Bruce, Garry, David, Vini and Steve).

'It's Gonna Work Out Fine' (Seneca, Lee) by Ike and Tina Turner (Sue 749) 1961.
Best known from Bruce's performances in 1975. Bruce did the song once in 1978 and again in 1979 at Marc Brickman's wedding reception at the Whiskey, Los Angeles, California.

'It's My Life' (Atkins, D'errico) by The Animals (Columbia DB 7741) 1965.
Usually introduced with a tense narrative rap about Bruce's early teens and the problems he encountered with his father. Performed frequently from 1975 until its final rendition at the Capitol Theatre, Passaic, New Jersey, on 20 September 1978.

'I Want You' (Dylan) by Bob Dylan (Columbia 43683) 1966.
Performed by Bruce during Suki Lahav's time in the band, late 1974 to the summer of 1975. A completely slowed down arrangement and Suki's haunting violin make this one of the most memorable of all the cover versions Bruce has ever done.

'Jenny Take A Ride' (Johnson, Penniman, Crewe) by Mitch Ryder (New Voice 806) 1966.
Part of the 'Devil With The Blue Dress' medley, 1975 to 1985.

'Jersey Girl' (Waits) by Tom Waits (Asylum LP 6E 295) 1980.
A natural for Bruce, and for its debut at the Byrne Meadowlands Arena, East Rutherford, New Jersey, on 2 July 1981. Tom Waits joined Bruce and the E Street Band onstage for the song at the Sports Arena, Los Angeles, California, on 24 August 1981. A live version was released as the B side of the 'Cover Me' single in 1984.

'Johnny B. Goode' (Berry) by Chuck Berry (Chess 1691) 1957.
Performed with Dave Edmunds at Big Man's West in 1982, with Bruce on back-up vocal and guitar.

'Jole Blon' (Choates, York) by Harold Choates (Goldstar) 1946.
Originally recorded as a shared vocal duet on Gary U.S. Bond's album, *Dedication*. Bruce debuted a solo in-concert version at the Wembley Arena, London, 5 June 1981.

'Kansas City' (Leiber, Stoller) by Wilbert Harrison (Fury 1023) 1959.

First version known, from a 1981 show in Kansas, but it would seem likely that Bruce sang this on earlier trips there.

'Keep A Knockin'' (Penniman, Williams, Mays) by Little Richard (Speciality 611) 1957.
First performed with Cats On A Smooth Surface at the Stone Pony, Asbury Park, New Jersey, on 10 June 1983.

'Knock On Wood' (Cropper, Floyd) by Eddie Floyd (Atlantic 584 041) 1966.
Performed with Eddie Floyd in Memphis, Tennessee, on 28 April 1976.

'Land Of A Thousand Dances' (Kenner, Domino) by Chris Kenner (Atlantic) 1963.
Occasionally worked into the 'Devil With The Blue Dress' medley from 1980 onwards.

'The Last Time' (Jagger, Richard) by The Rolling Stones (Decca F 12104) 1965.
Performed at the Richfield Coliseum, Cleveland, Ohio, 1 January 1979 to mark the last night of a seven month tour that had lasted for most of 1978. There was a surprise performance with Cats On A Smooth Surface at the Stone Pony, Asbury Park, New Jersey, on 10 June 1984.

'(Come On) Let's Go' (Valens) by Ritchie Valens (Delfi 4106) 1958.
Performed with Beaver Brown and Cats On A Smooth Surface in the bars of New Jersey in 1982.

'Let's Talk About Us' (Blackwell) by Jerry Lee Lewis (Sun 324) 1959.
Performed with Dave Edmunds at Big Man's West, Red Bank, New Jersey, on 18 September 1982 (Bruce on back-up vocals and guitar).

'Let The Good Times Roll' (Theard, Moore) by Shirley and Lee (Aladdin 3325) 1956.
Known only from a guest appearance with Southside Johnny and the Asbury Jukes at the Stone Pony, Asbury Park, New Jersey, on 13 October 1977.

'Let The Four Winds Blow' (Domino, Bartholomew) by Roy Brown (Imperial 5439) 1957.
Excellent live versions known from 1974, probably included on the 1973 tour as well.

'Little Latin Lupe Lu' (Medley) by The Righteous Brothers (Moonglow 215) 1963.
Debuted on the 1977 tour at the Music Hall, Boston, Massachusetts, 23 March. It surfaced again for the guest appearances in New Jersey during 1982, 1983 and 1984.

'Little Queenie' (Berry) by Chuck Berry (Chess 1722) 1959.
Great song for Bruce, performed only in 1975 and last used as the final song of nine encores at the Hammersmith Odeon, London, 24 November. He played a fine, improvised version at the Uptown Theatre, Milwaukee – after a bomb scare he came back onstage at midnight and re-opened with this song.

'Lonesome Train' (Moore, Subotsky) by Johnny Burnette (Coral) 1956.
Sometimes mixed into the 'I Hear A Train' part of the 'Devil With The Blue Dress' medley from 1980 onwards.

'Long Tall Sally' (Johnson, Penniman, Blackwell) by Little Richard (Speciality 572) 1956.
Played on three guest appearances in New Jersey

during 1982 and 1983, once with the Stray Cats.

'Louie Louie' (Berry) by Richard Berry and The Pharoahs (Flip 321) 1957.
Debuted at Notre Dame University, 9 September 1978. Performed on rare occasions throughout 1981, and a couple of times with local bands in New Jersey during 1982 and 1983.

'Lucille' (Penniman, Collins) by Little Richard (Speciality 598) 1957.
Performed on rare occasions in 1975. It appeared regularly in and around the New Jersey Clubs when Bruce guested with numerous bands in 1982, 1983 and 1984.

'Memphis, Tennessee' (Berry) by Chuck Berry (Chess 1729) 1958.
Debuted at the Mid South Coliseum, Memphis, Tennessee, on 13 December 1984. It became the eleventh Chuck Berry song to be covered by Bruce.

'Merry Christmas Baby' (Baxter, Moore) by Johnny Moore and The Three Blazers (Exclusive) 1947.
Performed at each of the three shows Bruce and the E Street Band gave at the Nassau Coliseum, Uniondale, New York, on 28, 29 and 31 December 1980.

'Midnight Hour' (Pickett, Cropper) by Wilson Pickett (Atlantic 2289) 1965.
Soul classic, debuted at the Milwaukee Arena, 14 October 1980. Bruce unexpectedly called out for the E Street Band to play it.

'Mona' (McDaniels) by Bo Diddley (Checker 860) 1955.
Used consistently as the build-up to 'She's The One' from 1976 to 1979, it surfaced again in 1981 for its final performance at the Horizon, Rosemont, Illinois, on 10 October.

'Money' (Bradford, Gordy Jnr.) by Barrett Strong (Anna 1111) 1960.
Bruce took lead vocals at a guest appearance with Beaver Brown at Big Man's West, Red Bank, New Jersey, on 20 February 1982.

'Mony Mony' (James, Cordell, Gentry) by Tommy James and The Shondells (Roulette 7008) 1968.
Concluded the 'Devil With The Blue Dress' medley for the last four shows of 1981. A full version of the song was performed with the Iron City House Rockers at Big Man's West, Red Bank, New Jersey, on 24 July 1982.

'Mother-In-Law' (Toussaint) by Ernie K. Doe (Minit 623) 1961.
Played as a one-off at Mark Brickman's wedding reception, possibly with Rickie Lee Jones and Boz Scaggs (who also attended) at the Whiskey, Los Angeles, California, on 3 June 1979.

'Mountain Of Love' (Dorman) by Harold Dorman (Rita 1003) 1960.
A particular favourite of Bruce's that turned up at irregular intervals during the 1975 tour, and is often included in soundchecks.

'My Generation' (Townshend) by The Who (Brunswick 05944) 1965.
Known to have been performed by the Castiles, 1966–67.

'Mystery Train' (Parker) by Junior Parker (Sun 192) 1953.

The classic Presley version was added to the 'Devil With The Blue Dress' medley on one rare occasion at the Madison Square Garden, New York City, 28 November 1980.

'Mystic Eyes' (Morrison) by Them (Decca F 12281) 1965.
Another song known from Bruce's formative years with the Castiles.

'Night Train' (Forrest, Simkins, Washington) by Jimmy Forrest (Mambo 15340) 1955.
Instrumental played once at the Fox Theatre, Atlanta, Georgia, on 30 September 1978.

'No Money Down' (Berry) by Chuck Berry (Chess 1615) 1955.
Another Chuck Berry song, done in monologue fashion that really built. Performed live in 1974 and 1975 and in a few rare versions in 1980 as an introduction to 'Cadillac Ranch'.

'Nothing's Too Good For My Baby' (Stevenson, Cosby, Moy) by Stevie Wonder (Tamla 54130) 1966.
One known version, worked into the instrumental break of 'Kitty's Back' at the Music Hall, Houston, Texas, 13 September 1975.

'Not Fade Away' (Holly, Petty) by Buddy Holly and The Crickets (Brunswick 55035) 1957.
Used in 1978 only, sometimes on its own and sometimes with 'Mona' to introduce 'She's The One'.

'Oh Boy' (West, Tilghman, Petty) by Buddy Holly and The Crickets (Brunswick 55035) 1957.
Performed just once, when opening a show at the Bay Front Centre, St Petersburg, Florida, on 29 July 1978.

'On Top Of Old Smokey' (Traditional)
An unusual choice of material, even for the folks who live under its shadow in Portland, Oregon, but the one-time performance at the Memorial Coliseum, 25 October 1980 really worked.

'One By One' (Uncredited) by The Blues Magoos (Mercury 72692) 1966.
Castiles cover used as part of their audition set, and one of the songs that won them 29 prestigious gigs at New York's Cafe Wha in 1967.

'Only You Know And I Know' (Bramlett) by Delaney and Bonnie and Friends (Atco 6838) 1971.
Performed by the Bruce Springsteen band, *circa* 1971–72.

'Outer Limits' (Gordon) by The Marketts (Warner Brothers 5696) 1966.
Instrumental that opened the second half of the 31 October 1980 show at the Los Angeles Sports Arena, but never used again.

'Party Lights' (Clark) by Claudine Clark (Chancellor 1113) 1962.
Rarely performed song from the 1975 tour.

'Pretty Flamingo' (Barkan) by Manfred Mann (HMV Pop 1523) 1966.
Superb performances from the 1975 and 1976 tours with a great boy (doesn't) meet girl rap that led beautifully into the song. Last performance in Cleveland, Ohio, 31 January 1978 when it made a rare re-appearance into the live repertoire.

'Proud Mary' (Fogerty) by Creedence Clearwater Revival (Fantasy 619) 1969.
Performed twice on the latter part of the American 1981

Bruce Springsteen

Santa Claus Is Coming To Town

from the album
IN HARMONY 2
CBS 85451
containing tracks from the following artists:

BILLY JOEL
JAMES TAYLOR
LOU RAWLS AND DENIECE WILLIAMS
TEDDY PENDERGRASS
JANIS IAN
CRYSTAL GAYLE
DR. JOHN
KENNY LOGGINS
CARLY AND LUCY SIMON
BRUCE SPRINGSTEEN

for promotion only
not for sale

tour, and on three guest appearances with John Eddie in New Jersey in 1982 (one) and 1984 (two).

'Quarter To Three' (Barge, Guida, Anderson) by Gary U.S. Bonds (Legrand 1008) 1961.
Probably the most famous of all Bruce cover versions, this was a regular encore from 1974 to 1981. An edited version can be seen in the film *No Nukes* from one of the M.U.S.E. concerts at the Madison Square Garden, New York City, on 22 September 1979.

'Raise Your Hand' (Floyd, Cropper, Isbell) by Eddie Floyd (Stax 208) 1967.
Great encore from Bruce and the E Street Band in 1976 and 1977 (with the Miami Horns in attendance). Bruce occasionally brought the song back in 1978, and again on the U.S. part of the 1980–81 world tour.

'Raunchy' (Justis, Manker) by Bill Justis and his Orchestra (Phillips International 3519) 1957.
Instrumental that Tex Vinyard, the Castiles' manager, liked so much that he got them to include it into their stage performances, *circa* 1966.

'Rave On' (West, Tilghman, Petty) by Sonny West (Atlantic 1174) 1957.
First performed at the live KMET broadcast from the Roxy, Los Angeles, California, on 7 July 1978, it has surfaced at irregular intervals ever since.

'Ready Teddy' (Blackwell, Marascalco) by Little Richard (Speciality 579) 1956.
Debuted as the opening song of the 1978 show at the Maple Leaf Gardens, Toronto, on 16 November. It became a regular part of the New Jersey guest spots in 1982 and 1983.

'Ring Of Fire' (Carter, Kilgore) by Johnny Cash (Columbia 42788) 1963.
One known version from 1974, but Peter Knobler's article in the *Crawdaddy* of March 1973 mentions a live version from as early as 1972.

'Rip It Up' (Blackwell, Marascalco) by Little Richard (Speciality 579) 1956.
One known performance with Sonny Kenn on lead vocals in New Jersey, 1982.

'Rock Baby Rock It' (Carroll) by Johnny Carroll (Phillips International) 1957.
Obscure rockabilly song that Bruce sang once at the 14-song guest appearance with Cats On A Smooth Surface at the Stone Pony, 3 October 1982.

'Rockin' All Over The World' (Fogerty) by John Fogerty (Asylum 45274) 1975.
Appropriately, Bruce closed the majority of his European shows of the world tour in 1981 with this song. It was also performed in the latter part of the U.S. shows that year and again in 1982, 1983 and 1984 around the New Jersey shore.

'Route 66' (Troup) by Nat King Cole (Capitol) 1958.
Performed with Sonny Kenn at Big Man's West, Red Bank, New Jersey, on 12 June 1982.

'Run Through The Jungle' (Fogerty) by Creedence Clearwater Revival (Fantasy 641) 1970.
Heard only on the 1981 European tour, as the opening song to three of the shows in Rotterdam, Gothenburg and Stockholm.

'Running On Empty' (Browne) by Jackson Browne (Asylum 45460) 1978.
Bruce supplied back up vocals and guitar for Jackson Browne at the Nuclear Disarmament Rally in Central Park, New York City, on 12 June 1982. Bruce and Jackson have appeared together on various occasions, the last time being at Madison Square Garden, New York City, on 2 August 1983 when this song was again performed.

'Run Shaker Life' (arr. Havens) by Richie Havens (Verve LP 3034) 1968.
This Steel Mill cover from 1970–71 is often incorrectly referred to as 'I'll Be Your Saviour' and credited as an original Bruce Springsteen song.

'Santa Claus Is Comin' To Town' (Gillespie, Coots) by The Three Suns 1952.
This became the fourth live song to be released by Bruce when it appeared on the various-artists album *In Harmony 2* in 1981. It was also featured as a promotion only release in both 7″ and 12″ formats in the U.S. It has been regularly featured onstage around Christmas time (and as early as September!) since its first performance at the Boston Music Hall on 2 December 1975.

'Satin Doll' (Ellington) by Duke Ellington (RCA Victor) 1940.
Instrumental that opened four acoustic radio sessions that Bruce and members of the band played in 1973 and 1974. Prior to that, the tune was used in at least one Steel Mill concert, *circa* 1969.

'Save The Last Dance For Me' (Pomus, Shuman) by The Drifters (Atlantic 2071) 1960.
Performed live in 1974 and at a soundcheck at the Spectrum, Philadelphia, Pennsylvania, on 18 August 1978.

'Say Goodbye To Hollywood' (Joel) by Billy Joel (Columbia 02518) 1976.
Ronnie Spector and Flo and Eddie joined Bruce onstage in Cleveland, Ohio, in 1977 for this song. Backed by the E Street Band and produced by Miami Steve, Ronnie released the song as a single in 1977.

'Sea Cruise' (Smith, Vincent) by Frankie Ford (Ace 554) 1958.
Opened the second half of an outdoor gig in Red Rocks, Denver, Colorado, 16 August 1981.

'Sha La La' (Taylor, Moseley) by The Shirelles (Scepter 1267) 1964.

Performed fairly regularly in concert, 1975.

'Shake' (Cooke) by Sam Cooke (RCA Victor 47–8486) 1965.
Made its debut as part of the 'Devil With The Blue Dress' medley in London 1981, and has been used in the medley on several subsequent occasions.

'Shout' (Isley, Isley) by The Isley Brothers (RCA Victor 47–7588) 1959.
Bruce would occasionally mix this number into the fade-out part of his own composition, 'A Love So Fine' in 1975.

'Sitting On Top Of The World' (Carter Jacobs) by Howlin' Wolf (Chess 1679) 1957.
Performed by the Bruce Springsteen Band in February 1972.

'634–5789' (Floyd, Cropper) by Wilson Pickett (Atlantic 2289) 1965.
One known performance, at Parsippanny, New Jersey, on 12 January 1974.

'Sock It To Me Baby' (Crewe, Brown) by Mitch Ryder (New Voice 820) 1967.
Introduced into the tail end of the 'Devil With The Blue Dress' medley in the latter stages of the 1981 U.S. tour.

'Something You Got' (Kenner) by Chris Kenner (Instant 3237) 1961.
Performed on the 1973 and 1974 tours.

'Soothe Me' (Cooke) by Sam and Dave (Stax 218) 1966.
Known only from a couple of soundchecks in 1975, but it would seem likely Bruce did a live version or two between 1973 and 1975.

'Spanish Harlem' (Leiber, Spector) by Ben E. King (Atco 6185) 1960.
Terrific version premiered at the Capitol Theatre, Passaic, New Jersey, on 18 October 1974. One other version is known, both prominently featuring Suki Lahav on violin.

'Stand By Me' (King, Glick) by Ben E. King (Atco 6194) 1960.
Performed when Bruce guested with the Del Fuegos at The Rhinoceros Club, Greensboro, North Carolina, in January 1985.

'Stay' (Williams) by Maurice Williams and The Zodiacs (Herald 552) 1960.
Vocal duet with Jackson Browne, debuted at the Madison Square Garden, New York City, for the two M.U.S.E. concerts Bruce did in 1979, and released on the *No Nukes* triple live album.

'Strawberry Fields Forever' (Lennon, McCartney) by The Beatles (Parlophone R 5570) 1967.
During the U.K. part of the 1981 world tour, Bruce played the song during soundchecks to at least three of the shows, but it has never materialised in a concert performance.

'Street Fighting Man' (Jagger, Richard) by The Rolling Stones (Decca LP LK 4955) 1968.
Debuted on the first night of the 1984–85 tour at the Civic Centre, St. Paul, Minnesota, on 29 June 1984 and has since become a regular addition to the encores.

'Summertime Blues' (Cochran, Capehart) by Eddie Cochran (Liberty 55144) 1958.
Debuted at Miami, Florida, 28 July 1978, it became a regular opening number that summer. Also sung in and around the New Jersey joints in 1982.

'Sweet Little Rock'n'Roller' (Berry) by Chuck Berry (Chess 1709) 1958.
One performance with Sonny Kenn and the Wild Ideas at Big Man's West, Red Bank, New Jersey, on 31 July 1982.

'Sweet Little Sixteen' (Berry) by Chuck Berry (Chess 1683) 1958.
Another great Chuck Berry song and a regular part of Bruce's live act in the summer of 1978. Duetted on a couple of shows in 1980 with Jackson Browne, and sung at least three times during the New Jersey 'bar blitz' of 1982 and twice in 1983, once as a duet with Jackson at Madison Square Garden, New York City, on 2 August.

'Sweet Soul Music' (Redding, Conley) by Arthur Conley (Atco 6463) 1967.
First played in whole in Paris, 19 April 1981, and then included as part of the 'Devil With The Blue Dress' medley on four of the following U.K. shows and most of the U.S. gigs. Also occasionally performed on the 1984–85 tour.

'Take Me Out To The Ballgame' (Norworth, Von Tilzer) by Frank Sinatra and Gene Kelly 1949.
Apart from the Bruce Springstone parody, the real Bruce Springsteen actually did perform an acapella version of this song with the E Street Band in Binghampton, New York, on 12 June 1973.

'Take Out Some Insurance' (Singleton, Hall) by Jimmy Reed (Vee Jay 314) 1959.
One known performance with the Bruce Springsteen Band at the Back Door, Richmond, Virginia, in February 1972 when it was mixed into another cover version, 'I'm Into Something Good'.

'Tallahassee Lassie' (Cannon) by Freddy Cannon (Swan 4031) 1959.
Performed at the Sportatorium, Tallahassee, Florida, 7 December 1984.

'Then He Kissed Me' (Spector, Greenwich, Barry) by The Crystals (Philles 115) 1963.
First known performance at the Bottom Line, New York City, in July 1974. It became a regular choice for the summer months of Bruce's 1975 tour.

'This Land Is Your Land' (Guthrie) by Woody Guthrie circa 1940.
Debuted at the Nassau Coliseum, Uniondale, New York, in 1980, originally in a slightly faster version than the one played at all (except Hamburg) European shows and the remaining U.S. dates of the 1980–81 world tour.

'Trapped' (Cliff) by Jimmy Cliff (Island 6132) 1972.
This superb re-arrangement by Bruce was debuted in London, 29 May 1981, and went on to become a frequent part of the remaining shows of 1981. It was again performed during the 1984–85 tour. A live version was released on the We Are The World LP in April 1985.

'Travelin' Band' (Fogerty) by Creedence Clearwater Revival (Fantasy 637) 1970.
Since its debut at the Joe Louis Arena, Detroit, Michigan in July 1984 it has become a regular addition to the 'Devil With The Blue Dress' medley and often includes the band namechecks during the song.

'Tutti Frutti' (Penniman, La Bostrie) by Little Richard (Speciality 561) 1955.
One known performance with local band Midnite Thunder at the Headliner, Neptune, New Jersey, on 16 July 1983.

'Twist And Shout' (Medley, Russell) by The Isley Brothers (Wand 124) 1962.
Bruce's superb rendition of this song never fails to please the audience almost as much as he enjoys singing it. It has been performed on numerous occasions and included in every tour except 1977's. On the 1984–85 tour Bruce segued 'Do You Love Me' into the middle break to great effect.

'Turn On Your Love Light' (Scott, Marlene) by Bobby 'Blue' Bland (Duke 344) 1962.
Performed with Steel Mill, circa 1970–71.

'Up On The Roof' (Goffin, King) by The Drifters (Atlantic 2162) 1962.
Featured a slowed-down arrangement by Bruce and performed on the 1975 tour.

'Uptight (Everything's Alright)' (Cosby, Moy, Wonder) by Stevie Wonder (Tamla 54124) 1965.
Worked into the 'Devil With The Blue Dress' medley at the Spectrum, Philadelphia, Pennsylvania, on 6 December 1980.

'Walking In The Rain' (Spector, Mann, Weil) by The Ronettes (Philles 123) 1964.
Another song originally recorded on Bruce's seemingly favourite record company – Phil Spector and Lester Sill's Philles label. Performed with Ronnie Spector in 1976, and again with Ronnie and Flo and Eddie in Cleveland, Ohio, in 1977.

'Walking The Dog' (Thomas) by Rufus Thomas (Stax 140) 1963.
First known live performance with the Bruce Springsteen Band in 1971, and performed with the E Street Bands of 1973 and 1974.

'Waltz Across Texas' (Tubb) by Ernest Tubb (Decca) circa 1940.
One performance at the Special Events Centre, Austin, Texas (where else!), on 9 November 1980.

'Wabash Cannonball' (A.P. Carter) by The Carter Family, circa 1935.
Performed as part of the 'Devil With The Blue Dress' medley at the Sports Arena, Los Angeles, California, on 1 November 1980.

'Wear My Ring Around Your Neck' (Carrol, Moody) by Elvis Presley (RCA Victor 47–7240) 1958.
Used as one of the encores from late 1974 and occasionally in 1975. Last performed at the Tower, Philadelphia, Pennsylvania, on 30 December 1975.

'Wedding Bells' (Boone) by Hank Williams (MGM) 1949.
Known from a soundcheck at the Capitol Theatre, Passaic, New Jersey, in September 1978.

'We Gotta Get Out Of This Place' (Mann, Weil) by The Animals (Columbia DB 7639) 1965.
Just one known version with the E Street Band from the last night of the 1976 tour, at the Palladium, New York City, 4 November. But is was performed with Cats On A Smooth Surface at the Stone Pony, 10 June 1984, when Bruce and Nils guested.

'When You Walk In The Room' (De Shannon) by Jackie De Shannon (Liberty 55645) 1964.
Debuted at the Bottom Line, New York City, in August 1975, this became a fairly regular part of the live act up until its final performance at the Hammersmith Odeon, London, on 24 November 1975.

'Who'll Stop The Rain?' (Fogerty) by Creedence Clearwater Revival (Fantasy 637) 1970.
First performed at Madison Square Garden, New York City, on 19 December 1980, and played at all the following shows on the 1980–81 world tour except three (two in London, and the 5 August 1981 show in Largo, Maryland). Occasionally performed on the 1984–85 tour.

'A Woman's Got The Power' (Notte, Bush) by The A's (Arista SP 107) 1981.
A one-off performance when Red Bank Rocker mainstay J. T. Bowen guested with the E Street Band at the Brendan Byrne Arena, East Rutherford, New Jersey, on 9 August 1984.

'Wooly Bully' (Domingo) by Sam The Sham and The Pharoahs (MGM 13322) 1965.
Played on guest appearances with Cats On A Smooth Surface twice in 1982 and once in 1983. Debuted by the E Street Band during the 1984–85 world tour.

'The Yellow Rose Of Texas' (Wise, Starr) by Mitch Miller (Columbia 40540) 1955.
Instrumental version debuted at the Reunion Arena, Dallas, Texas, 8 November 1980 and used once again the following night in Austin, Texas.

'You Can't Sit Down' (Clark, Upchurch, Muldrow) by Phil Upchurch Combo (Boyd 3398) 1961.
Consistent part of the encores, from 1976 to 1978. In 1981 it was added to the 'Devil With The Blue Dress' medley during the latter part of the U.S. dates.

'You Know My Love' (Rush) by Otis Rush (Chess 1759) 1960.
Bruce Springsteen Band cover version circa 1971.

'You Never Can Tell' (Berry) by Chuck Berry (Chess 1906) 1964.
Performed on the 1974 tour and possibly on the 1973 tour as well.

'Yum Yum I Want Some' (Floyd, Rice, Cropper) by Eddie Floyd (Stax 909) 1968.
A one-off performance of this obscure song was at the Ellis Auditorium, Memphis, Tennessee, 29 April 1976 when Eddie Floyd joined Bruce onstage and segued it into 'Knock On Wood'.

The E Street Shuffle

(*The E Street Band Discography*)

Roy Bittan – Piano
(E Street Band September 1974 to present)
Bruce Springsteen:
Album releases: *Born To Run* 1975. *Darkness On The Edge Of Town* 1978. *The River* 1980. *Born In The U.S.A.* 1984.
Single releases: 'Held Up Without A Gun' 1980. 'Be True' 1981. 'Pink Cadillac' 1984. 'Jersey Girl' 1984. 'Shut Out The Light' 1984. 'Johnny Bye Bye' 1985. 'Stand On It' 1985.

Tracks: *Even A Broken Clock Is Right Twice A Day* Capitol 1118 U.S. Roy's first band 1972.
Niki Aukema: *Niki Aukema* 1974.
David Bowie: *Station To Station* 1975.
Jackson Browne: *The Pretender* 1977.
Russel Morris: *Russel Morris 2* 1977.

Ronnie Spector and the E Street Band: 'Say Goodbye To Hollywood'/'Baby Please Don't Go' 1977.
Meatloaf: *Bat Out Of Hell* 1977.
Peter Gabriel: *Two* 1978.
Ian Hunter: *You're Never Alone With A Schizophrenic* 1979.
Various artists: *No Nukes* 1979.
Dire Straits: *Making Movies* 1980.
David Bowie: *Scary Monsters And Super Creeps* 1980.
Garland Jeffreys: *Escape Artist* 1980.
Stevie Nicks: *Belladonna* 1981.
Meatloaf: *Dead Ringer* 1981.
Jim Steinman: *Bad For Good* 1981.
Gary U.S. Bonds: *Dedication* 1981.
Various artists: *In Harmony 2* 1981.
Jimmy Mack and the Jumpers: *Jimmy Mack and the Jumpers* 1981.

Ellen Foley: *Spirit Of St. Louis* 1981.
Gary U.S. Bonds: *On The Line* 1982.
Donna Summer: *Donna Summer* 1982.
Bob Seger: *The Distance* 1983.
Bonnie Tyler: *Faster Than The Speed Of Light* 1983.
Stevie Nicks: *Wild Hearts* 1983.
Chris Mancini: *Chris Mancini* 1983.
U.S.A. For Africa: *We Are The World* 1985.

Ernest 'Boom' Carter – Drums
(E Street Band February 1974 to August 1974)
Bruce Springsteen:
Album releases: *Born To Run* (title song only) 1975.

David Sancious: *Forest Of Feelings* 1975.

David Sancious: *Transformation* 1976.
David Sancious: *Dance Of The Age Of Enlightenment* 1976.
Southside Johnny and the Asbury Jukes: *This Time It's For Real* 1977.
David Sancious: *David Sancious* 1977.
David Sancious: *True Stories* 1978.
David Sancious: *Just As I Thought* 1979.
Billy Squire: *A Tale Of The Tape* 1980.
Various artists: *The Sounds Of Asbury Park N.J.* 1980.
David Sancious: *The Bridge* 1981.
Southside Johnny and the Asbury Jukes: *Trash It Up* 1983.
Little Bob Story: *Too Young To Love Me* 1984.

**Clarence Clemons – Saxaphone
(Five piece band August 1972 to present E Street Band)**
Bruce Springsteen
Album releases: *Greetings From Asbury Park N.J.* 1973. *The Wild, The Innocent And The E Street Shuffle* 1973. *Born To Run* 1975. *Darkness On The Edge Of Town* 1978, *The River* 1980. *Born In The U.S.A.* 1984.
Single releases: 'Circus Song' 1973; 'Held Up Without A Gun' 1980; 'Be True' 1981; 'Pink Cadillac' 1984; 'Jersey Girl' 1984; 'Shut Out The Light' 1984 'Johnny Bye Bye' 1985. 'Stand On It' 1985.

Vibratones: Unknown single, recorded at the Philadelphia Studios, Broad Street, *circa* 1964.
Norman Seldin and the Joyful Noise: *Norman Seldin and the Joyful Noise* 1969.
Dan Hartman: *Images* 1976.
Pez Band: *Pez Band* 1977.
Ronnie Spector and the E Street Band: 'Say Goodbye To Hollywood'/'Baby Please Don't Go' 1977.
Scarlet Rivera: *Scarlet Rivera* 1977.
Intergalactic Touring Band: *Intergalactic Touring Band* 1977.
Carlene Carter: *Two Sides To Every Woman* 1979.
Janis Ian: *Night Rains* 1979.
Truth: Unreleased demos produced by Clarence for this local New Jersey band. 1979.
Various Artists: *No Nukes* 1979.
Michael Stanley Band: *Heartland* 1980.
Joan Armatrading: *Me, Myself, I* 1980.
Various Artists: *In Harmony 2* 1981.
Greg Lake: *Greg Lake* 1981.
Gary U.S. Bonds: *Dedication* 1981.
Schwartz: *Schwartz* 1981.
Blue Steel: *Nothing But Time* 1981.
Gary U.S. Bonds: *On The Line* 1982.
Little Steven and the Disciples Of Soul: *Men Without Women* 1982.
Ian Hunter: *All The Good One's Are Taken* 1983.
Joe Cerisano: *Trouble At Home* 1983.
Michael Stanley: *Poor Side Of Town* 1984.
U.S.A. For Africa: *We Are The World* 1985.

Clarence Clemons:
'There's Still Christmas', unreleased single recorded at the Kajem Studios, Pennsylvannia 1982. Royalties were to have gone to a New Jersey charity.

Clarence Clemons and the Red Bank Rockers:
Rescue (CBS 25699 – U.K., COL. BFC 38933 – U.S.) 1983.
A 'Jump Start My Heart'; 'Rock'N'Roll DJ'; 'Money To The Rescue'; 'A Woman's Got The Power' B 'A Man In Love'; 'Heartache 99'; 'Savin' Up'; 'Resurrection Shuffle'.
'Resurrection shuffle'/'Money To The Rescue' CBS A 3803 U.K. 1983.
'A Woman's Got The Power'/'Summer On Signal Hill'

COL. 38–04359 U.S. 1983.
'Savin' Up'/'Summer On Signal Hill' CBS A 3928 U.K. 1983.

**Danny Federici – Organ
(Child 1969 to Steel Mill January 1971 and the E Street Band 1972 to present)**
Bruce Springsteen:
Album releases: *The Wild, The Innocent And The E Street Shuffle* 1973. *Born To Run* (title song only) 1975. *Darkness On The Edge Of Town* 1978. *The River* 1980. *Born In The U.S.A.* 1984.
Single releases: 'Circus Song' 1973. 'Held Up Without A Gun' 1980. 'Be True' 1981. 'Pink Cadillac' 1984. 'Jersey Girl' 1984. 'Shut Out The Light' 1984. 'Johnny Bye Bye' 1985. 'Stand On It' 1985.

Ronnie Spector and the E Street Band: 'Say Goodbye to Hollywood'/'Baby Please Don't Go' 1977.
Various artists: *No Nukes* 1979.
Joan Armatrading: *Me, Myself, I* 1980.
Graham Parker: *The Up Escalator* 1980.
Garland Jeffreys: *Escape Artist* 1980.
Various artists: *In Harmony 2* 1981.
Gary U.S. Bonds: *Dedication* 1981.
Gary U.S. Bonds: *On The Line* 1982.
Little Steven and the Disciples Of Soul: *Men Without Women* 1983.
U.S.A. For Africa: *We Are The World* 1985.

**Suki Lahav – Violin
(E Street Band September 1974 to March 1975)**
Bruce Springsteen:
Album releases: *The Wild, The Innocent And The E Street Shuffle* (backing vocals on '4th Of July, Asbury Park (Sandy)' and 'Incident on 57th Street') 1973. *Born To Run* (violin on 'Jungleland') 1975.

**Nils Lofgren – Guitar
(June 1984 to present)**
Paul Dowell and the Dolphin: 'Get Together'/? Sire 1969.
Paul Dowell and the Dolphin: 'It's Better To Know You'/'The Last Time I Saw You' Sire 1969.
Neil Young: *After The Goldrush* 1970.
Grin: *Grin* Spindizzy 30321 (U.S.) Epic 64272 (U.K.) 1971.
Crazy Horse: *Crazy Horse* Reprise RS 6438 (U.S.) K 44114 (U.K.) 1971.
Stephen Stills: *Stills Two* 1971.
Grin: *One Plus One* Spindizzy 31038 (U.S.) Epic 64652 (U.K.) 1972.
Grin: *All Out* Spindizzy 31701 (U.S.) Epic 65155 (U.K.) 1972.
Grin: *Gone Crazy* A&M SP 4415 (U.S.) 64415 (U.K.) 1973.
Kathy McDonald: *Insane Asylum* 1974.
Neil Young: *Tonights The Night* 1975.
Nils Lofgren: *Nils Lofgren* A&M SP 4509 (U.S.) 64509 (U.K.) 1975.
Nils Lofgren: *Back It Up* A&M SP 8362 (U.S.) Authorized bootleg 1975.
Charlie and the Pep Boys: *Daddy's Girl* 1976.
Nils Lofgren: *Cry Tough* A&M SP 4573 (U.S.) 64573 (U.K.) 1976.
Nils Lofgren: *I Came To Dance* A&M SP 4628 (U.S.) 64628 (U.K.) 1977.
Nils Lofgren: *Night After Night* A&M SP 3707 (U.S.) 69439 (U.K.) 1977.
Nils Lofgren: *Nils* A&M SP 4756 (U.S.) 64756 (U.K.) 1979.

Nils Lofgren: *Night Fades Away* MCA MCF 3121 (U.K.) 1981.
Neil Young: *Trans* 1982.
Nils Lofgren: *Wonderland* MCA/*Backstreet* MCF 3182 (U.K.) 1983.
U.S.A. For Africa: *We Are The World* 1985 (vinyl debut with the E Street Band on 'Trapped'.
Nils Lofgren: 'Secrets In The Street'/'From The Heart' and 'Message' (live)/'Little Bit O Time' (live) twin pack single. Towerbell TOWG 68 1985.
Nils Lofgren: *Flip* Towerbell TOW LP11 (U.K.) 1985.

Bootleg Albums
For Your Live (RUTHLESS RHYMES). . . . Single LP recorded in Philadelphia Pa. 1976.
Old Grey Whistle Test (DEATH 534). . . . Single LP recorded from TV show, England 1976.
In London (K&C RECORDS 025). . . . Limited edition made from the DEATH 534 plates.
Live, An Authorized Bootleg (SP 8362). . . . Pirate version of the promotion release, issued on at least two other labels (TAKRL) 1999, FLAT 8239).

**Vini Lopez – Drums
(Child 1969 to the E Street Band February 1974)**
Bruce Springsteen:
Album releases: *Greetings From Asbury Park N.J.* 1973. *The Wild, The Innocent And The E Street Shuffle* 1973.
Single releases: 'Circus Song' 1973.

Bill Chinook: *Badlands* 1978.
Various artists: *The Sounds Of Asbury Park N.J.* 1980.

**Vini Roslyn – Bass
(Child 1969 to Steel Mill March 1970)**
Motiffs: 'Molly' single released on a local New Jersey label 1966.

**David Sancious – Piano
(E Street Band July 1973 to August 1974)**
Bruce Springsteen:
Album releases: *Greetings From Asbury Park N.J.* 1973. *The Wild, The Innocent And The E Street Shuffle* 1973. *Born To Run* 1975 (title song only).

Lenny White: *Venusian Summer* 1975.
Stanley Clarke: *Journey To Love* 1975.
Stanley Clarke: *Schooldays* 1976.
Les Dudek: *Say No More* 1977.
Narada Michael Walden: *Garden Of Love Light* 1977.
Jack Bruce and Friends: *I've Always Wanted To Do This* 1980.
Billy Squire: *A Tale Of The Tape* 1980.
Ray Gomez: *Volume* 1980.
Various artists: *The Sounds Of Asbury Park* 1980.
Cozy Powell: *Tilt* 1981.
Santana: *Appearances* 1984.
David Sancious:
Forest Of Feelings Epic 33441 U.S. 1975.
Transformation Epic 33939 U.S. 1976.
Dance Of The Age Of Enlightenment Epic 34130 U.S. (scheduled 1977, unreleased).
David Sancious Chelsea 548 U.S. (early demos-unauthorised release) 1977.
True stories Arista 4201 U.S. (Arista SPART 1082 U.K.) 1978.
Just As I Always Thought Arista 4247 U.S. 1979.
The Bridge Electra K 52403 U.K. 1981.

Patti Scialfa – Backing vocals
(E Street Band June 1984 to present)
Bruce Springsteen: No releases as yet, although Patti did sing on an unreleased version of 'Dancing In The Dark' 1984.

Narada Michael Walden: *Garden Of Love Light* 1977.
Narada Michael Walden: *Awakening* 1979.
David Sancious: *Just As I Thought* 1980.
Southside Johnny and the Asbury Jukes: *Love Is A Sacrifice* 1980.
David Sancious: *The Bridge* 1981.
U.S.A. For Africa: *We Are The World* 1985.

Garry W. Tallent – Bass
(Dr Zoom and the Sonic Boom February 1971 to present)
Bruce Springsteen:
Album releases: *Greetings From Asbury Park N.J.* 1973. *The Wild, The Innocent And The E Street Shuffle* 1973. *Born To Run* 1975. *Darkness On The Edge Of Town* 1978. *The River* 1980. *Born In The U.S.A.* 1984.
Single releases: 'Circus Song' 1973; 'Held Up Without A Gun' 1980; 'Be True' 1981; 'Pink Cadillac' 1984; 'Jersey Girl' 1984; 'Shut Out The Light' 1984. 'Johnny Bye Bye' 1985. 'Stand On It' 1985.

David Sancious: *David Sancious* 1977.
Ronnie Spector and the E Street Band: 'Say Goodbye To Hollywood'/'Baby Please Don't Go' 1977.
Ian Hunter: *You're Never Alone With A Schizophrenic* 1979.
Various artists: *No Nukes* 1979.
Various artists: *The Sounds Of Asbury Park N.J.* 1980.
Gary U.S. Bonds: *Dedication* 1981.
Various artists: *In Harmony 2* 1981.
Southside Johnny and the Asbury Jukes: *Reach Up And Touch The Sky* 1981.
Gary U.S. Bonds: *On The Line* 1982.
Little Steven and the Disciples Of Soul: *Men Without Women* 1982.
U.S.A. For Africa: *We Are The World* 1985.

Robbin Thompson – Vocals
(Steel Mill December 1970 to January 1971)
Robbin Thompson:
Robbin Thompson Nemperor 440 U.S. 1976.
Two B's Please Ovation OV 1759 U.S. 1980.

Steve Van Zandt – Guitar
(Steel Mill March 1970 to the Bruce Springsteen Band February 1972 and the E Street Band May 1975 to May 1984)
Bruce Springsteen:
Album releases: *Greetings From Asbury Park N.J.* (feedback on 'Lost In The Flood') 1973. *Born To Run* (backing vocals on 'Thunder Road' and horn arrangement for 'Tenth Avenue Freeze-Out') 1975. *Darkness On The Edge Of Town* 1978. *The River* 1980. *Born In The U.S.A.* 1984.
Single releases: 'Held Up Without A Gun' 1980. 'Be True' 1981. 'Pink Cadillac' 1984. 'Jersey Girl' 1984. 'Shut Out The Light' 1984.

Southside Johnny and the Asbury Jukes: *I Don't Want To Go Home* 1976.
Southside Johnny and the Asbury Jukes: *Jukes Live At The Bottom Line* 1976.
Southside Johnny and the Asbury Jukes: *This Time It's For Real* 1977.

Ronnie Spector and the E Street Band: 'Say Goodbye To Hollywood'/'Baby Please Don't Go' 1977.
Flame: *Queen Of The Neighbourhood* 1977.
Southside Johnny and the Asbury Jukes: *Hearts Of Stone* 1978.
Southside Johnny and the Asbury Jukes: *Havin' A Party* 1979.
Various artists: *No Nukes* 1979.
Gary U.S. Bonds: *Dedication* 1981.
Various artists: *In Harmony 2* 1981.
Gary U.S. Bonds: *On The Line* 1982.
Gary U.S. Bonds: *Standing In The Line Of Fire* 1984.
Lone Justice: *Lone Justice* 1985.

Little Steven and the Disciples Of Soul:
Men Without Women EMI America ST 17086 U.S. and EMI AML 3027 U.K. 1982. A 'Lyin' In A Bed Of Fire'; 'Inside Of Me'; 'Until The Good Is Gone'; 'Men Without Women'; 'Under The Gun' B 'Save Me'; 'Princess Of Little Italy'; 'Angel Eyes'; 'Forever'; 'I've Been Waiting'.
'Forever'/'Caravan' EMI America B–8144 U.S. colour picture sleeve 1982.
'Forever'/'Men Without Women' EMI EA 148 U.K. colour picture sleeve 1982.
'Lyin' In A Bed Of Fire'/'Angel Eyes' EMI EA 155 U.K. 1982.
'Solidarity'/'Under The Gun' EMI EA 161 and EMI EA 12 161 (12") black and white picture sleeve – Europe only 1983.
Voice Of America EMI America ST 17120 U.S. and EMI EJ240 1511 U.K. 1984.
A 'Voice Of America'; 'Justice'; 'Checkpoint Charlie'; 'Solidarity'; 'Out Of The Darkness'. B 'Los Desaparecidos'; 'Fear'; 'I Am A Patriot'; 'Among The Believers'; 'Undefeated'.
'Out Of The Darkness'/'Fear' EMI America B–8207 U.S. and EMI EA 174 U.K. colour picture sleeve 1984.
'Out Of The Darkness'/'Out Of The Darkness' and 'Fear' EMI IA KO52 2001606 (12") colour picture sleeve – Europe only 1984.
'Vote That Mutha Out'/'I Am A Patriot' EMI IA 006 2004227 colour picture sleeve – Europe only 1984.

Promotion only releases
'Lyin' In A Bed Of Fire'/'Lyin' In A Bed Of Fire' EMI America SPRO 9846 12" black and white picture sleeve 1982.
'Under The Gun'/'Under The Gun' EMI America SPRO 9918 12" plain sleeve with title sticker 1982.
'Out Of The Darkness'/'Out Of The Darkness' EMI America SPRO 9111–2 black sleeve with title sticker 1984.
'Undefeated'/'Undefeated' EMI America SPRO black sleeve with title sticker 1984.

Steve Van Zandt Song Discography

'Among The Believers': Released on the *Voice of America* LP in 1984.
'Angel Eyes': Released on debut LP and as a B side to U.K. single 1982.
'Baby Please Don't Go': Recorded by Ronnie Spector 1977.
'Checkpoint Charlie': Released on the *Voice of America* LP in 1984.
'Daddy's Come Home': Recorded by Gary U.S. Bonds on the *Dedication* LP 1981.
'Fear': Released on the *Voice of America* LP in 1984.
'First Night': Recorded by Southside Johnny for his second album 1977.
'Forever': Released on debut album and as a single in the U.K. and U.S. 1982.
'Got To Be A Better Way Home': Recorded by Southside Johnny for the *Hearts Of Stone* LP 1978.
'How Come You Treat Me So Bad': Recorded by Southside Johnny on his debut LP 1976.

'I Ain't Got The Fever No More': Recorded by Southside Johnny for the second LP 1977.
'I Am A Patriot': Released on the *Voice of America* LP in 1984. Incredibly the U.K. labels listed the song as 'I Am Not A Patriot'.
'I Don't Want To Go Home': Title song of Southside Johnny's debut LP 1976. Also performed live by Bruce and the E Street Band in 1981.
'Inside Of Me': Released on debut LP 1982.
'I Played The Fool': Recorded by Southside Johnny for the *Hearts Of Stone* LP 1978.
'I've Been Waiting': Released on the debut LP 1982.
'Justice': Performed live in 1983 and released on the *Voice of America* LP in 1984.
'Last Time': Recorded by Gary U.S. Bonds for the *On The Line* LP 1982.
'Light Don't Shine': Recorded by Southside Johnny for the *Hearts Of Stone* LP 1978.
'Little Girl So Fine': Co-written with Bruce Springsteen for Southside Johnny's second album 1977.
'Little Sister': Written in 1983 and as yet, unreleased.
'Los Desaparecidos': Released on the 1984 LP *Voice of America*.
'Love On The Wrong Side Of Town': Co-written with Bruce for the second Southside Johnny LP 1977.
'Lyin' In A Bed Of Fire': Released on the debut LP 1982. Also issued as a single in the U.K. and as a 12" promotion only U.S. release (SPRO 9846).
'Men Without Women': Title track of the debut LP 1982. Also released as B side of a U.K. single.
'Next To You': Recorded by Southside Johnny for the *Hearts Of Stone* LP 1978.
'Out Of The Darkness': Released on the *Voice of America* LP in 1984 and as a single in most parts of the world.
'Princess Of Little Italy': Released on the debut LP 1982.
'Rock'N'Roll Rebel': Performed as the opening number of the 1982 and 1983 tours. Recorded at the ICP Studios, Brussels, Belgium, 13 April 1983. Unreleased as yet.
'Save Me': Released on the debut LP 1982.
'She Got Me Where She Wants Me': Recorded by Southside Johnny for his second LP 1977.
'Solidarity': Released in Europe in 7" and an extended 12" version in 1983. Released on the *Voice of America* LP in 1984.
'Somethings Just Don't Change': Recorded by Southside Johnny for his second LP 1977.
'Standing In The Line Of Fire': Title song of Gary U.S. Bonds' 1984 LP.
'Sweet Sweet Baby': Recorded by Lone Justice on their debut LP 1985.
'Sweeter Than Honey': Recorded by Southside Johnny on his debut LP and also released on the *Jukes Live At The Bottom Line* promotion only album. 1976.
'Take It Inside': Recorded by Southside Johnny for the *Hearts Of Stone* LP 1978.
'That's How I Feel': Performed live with the Asbury Jukes in 1974.
'That Woman's Gonna Break Your Heart': Written and performed live during Steve's time as a member of the Asbury Jukes, 1974.
'This Time Baby's Gone For Good': Recorded by Southside Johnny for the *Hearts Of Stone* LP 1978.
'This Time It's For Real': Title track of Southside Johnny's second LP 1977.
'Trapped Again': Co-written with Bruce and John Lyon for the Southside Johnny album, *Hearts Of Stone* 1978.
'Undefeated': Released on the *Voice of America* LP in 1984.
'Under The Gun': Released on the debut LP in 1982. Also issued on the promotion only 12" U.S. release (SPRO 9918). Live version released in Europe 1983.
'Until The Good Is Gone': Released on the debut LP 1982.

'Voice Of America': Title track of Steve's second LP released in 1984.

'Vote That Mutha Out': Released as a single in Europe only, 1984, and hastily withdrawn.

'When You Dance': Originally written by Bruce Springsteen and performed with the Bruce Springsteen Band in 1972. It was recorded by Southside Johnny on his second LP in an updated (co-written by Bruce and Steve) version 1977.

Max Weinberg – Drums
(E Street Band September 1974 to present)

Bruce Springsteen:
Album releases: *Born To Run* 1975. *Darkness On The Edge Of Town* 1978. *The River* 1980. *Born In The U.S.A.* 1984.

Single releases: 'Held Up Without A Gun' 1980; 'Be True' 1981; 'Pink Cadillac' 1984; 'Jersey Girl' 1984; 'Shut Out The Light' 1984. 'Johnny Bye Bye' 1985. 'Stand On It' 1985.

Secrets: 'Everyday' (Red Bird label) Max's college band 1967.
Ides Of Love: 'Hey Mr. Wiseman' (Talmu Records) Single release with one of Max's formative bands *circa* 1968.
Blackstone: *Blackstone* (Epic 30470 – U.S.) Max's first professional band 1971.
Danny Toan: *First Serve* 1977.
Meatloaf: *Bat Out Of Hell* 1977.
Ronnie Spector and the E Street Band: 'Say Goodbye To Hollywood'/'Baby Please Don't Go' 1977.
Southside Johnny and the Asbury Jukes: *Hearts Of Stone* 1978.
Ian Hunter: *You're Never Alone With A Schizophrenic* 1979.
Various Artists: *No Nukes* 1979.
Jim Steinman: *Bad For Good* 1981.
Meatloaf: *Dead Ringer* 1981.
Gary U.S. Bonds: *Dedication* 1981.
Various artists: *In Harmony 2* 1981.
Southside Johnny and the Asbury Jukes: *Reach Up And Touch The Sky* 1981.
Gary U.S. Bonds: *On The Line* 1982.
Little Steven and the Disciples Of Soul: *Men Without Women* 1982.
Bonnie Tyler: *Faster Than The Speed Of Light* 1983.
Meatloaf: *Midnight At The Lost And Found* 1983.
Various artists: *Streets Of Fire* 1984.
U.S.A. For Africa: *We Are The World* 1985.

Southside Johnny Discography

Southside Johnny and the Asbury Jukes are included here due to the close working relationship they have with Springsteen and the E Street Band. They are an essential branch of the family tree.

I Don't Want To Go Home Epic PE 34180 (U.S.) EPC 81515 (U.K.) 1976.
A 'I Don't Want To Go Home'; 'Got To Get You Off My Mind'; 'How Come You Treat Me So Bad' (with Lee Dorsey); 'The Fever'; 'Broke Down Piece Of Man' B 'Sweeter Than Honey'; 'Fanny Mae'; 'It Ain't The Meat (It's The Motion)'; 'I Choose To Sing The Blues'; 'You Mean So Much To Me' (with Ronnie Spector).
Recorded at the Record Plant, New York City. Produced by Steve Van Zandt.

Live At The Bottom Line Epic AS 275 (U.S.) promotion only 1976.
A 'Got To Get You Off My Mind'; 'Without Love'; 'Searchin''; 'Sweeter Than Honey'; 'Snatching It Back' B 'Little By Little'; 'It Ain't The Meat (It's The Motion)'; 'The Fever'; 'Havin' A Party'; 'You Mean So Much To Me' (with Ronnie Spector).
Recorded at the Bottom Line. New York City on 16–17 October 1976. Produced by Steve Van Zandt.

This Time It's For Real Epic PE 34668 (U.S.) EPC 81909 (U.K.) 1977.
A 'This Time It's For Real'; 'Without Love'; 'Check Mr Popeye' (with the Coasters); 'First Night' (with the Satins); 'She Got Me Where She Wants Me' B 'Some Things Just Don't Change'; 'Little Girl So Fine' (with the Drifters); 'I Ain't Got The Fever No More'; 'Love On The Wrong Side Of Town'; 'When You Dance'.
Recorded at Studio 49, CBS, New York City. Produced by Steve Van Zandt.

Hearts Of Stone Epic JE 35488 (U.S.) EPC 82994 (U.K.) 1978.
A 'Got To Be A Better Way Home'; 'This Time Baby's Gone For Good'; 'I Played The Fool'; 'Hearts Of Stone'; 'Take It Inside' B 'Talk To Me'; 'Next To You'; 'Trapped Again'; 'Light Don't Shine'.
Recorded at the Secret Sound Studios, New York City. Produced by Steve Van Zandt.

The Jukes Mercury 3793 (U.S.) 9100 067 (U.K.) 1979.
A 'All I Want Is Everything'; 'I'm So Anxious'; 'Paris'; 'Security'; 'Living In The Real World' B 'Your Reply'; 'The Time'; 'I Remember Last Night'; 'Wait In Vain'; 'Vertigo'.
Recorded at Muscle Shoals Studio, Alabama. Produced by Barry Beckett.

Love Is A Sacrifice Mercury 3836 (U.S.) 9111 081 (U.K.) 1980.
A 'Why'; 'Love When It's Strong'; 'Goodbye Love'; 'Murder'; 'Keep Our Love Simple' B 'Restless Heart'; 'Why Is Love Such A Sacrifice'; 'On The Beach'; 'Long Distance'; 'It Hurts'.
Recorded at the House Of Music, West Orange, New Jersey. Produced by John Lyon and Billy Rush.

Reach Up And Touch The Sky Mercury 8602 (U.S.) 6619 052 (Europe) 1981.
A 'I'm So Anxious'; 'Talk To Me'; 'All I Want Is Everything'; 'Hearts Of Stone' B 'Trapped Again'; 'Why Is Love Such A Sacrifice'; 'Restless Heart'; 'Vertigo' C 'I Don't Want To Go Home'; 'The Fever'; 'Stagger Lee' D Sam Cooke medley – 'Only Sixteen'/'Wonderful World'/'You Send Me'/'A Change Is Gonna Come'; 'Bring In On Home To Me'; 'Havin' A Party'; 'Back In

The U.S.A.'; 'Havin' A Party' (reprise).
Recorded on the 1980 U.S. tour. Produced by John Lyon and Stefan Galfas.

Trash It Up Mirage 90113–1 (U.S. release only) 1983.
A 'Trash It Up'; 'Can't Stop Thinking About You'; 'Get Your Body On The Job'; 'My Baby's Touch' B 'The Beast Within'; 'Ain't Gonna Eat Out My Heart Anymore'; 'Slow Burn'; 'Ms Park Avenue'; 'Bedtime'.
Recorded at the Atlantic Studios, New York City. Produced by Nile Rogers.

In The Heat Mirage 90186–1 (U.S.) Polydor 823747–1 (U.K.) 1984.
A 'Love Goes To War'; 'New Romeo'; 'Love Is The Drug'; 'Captured'; 'I Can't Live Without Your Love' B 'Over My Head'; 'Don't Look Back'; 'Tell Me Lies'; 'Action Speaks Louder Than Words'; 'New Coat Of Paint'.
Recorded at the House Of Music, West Orange, New Jersey. Produced by John Lyon and Billy Rush.

Selected records of interest:
Havin' A Party Embassy 31772 (U.K.) Compilation LP of the first 3 LPs and a live version of the title song 1979.
Superstar Radio Network Presents A Conversation With Southside Johnny and Ronnie Spector Epic AS 362 (U.S.) Recorded at the Alpha Studios, Philadelphia, Pennsylvania 18 April 1977.
Grand Slam – DJ Only EP Epic AE7 1106 'I Don't Want To Go Home' and 3 other songs 1976.
'Little By Little'/'Havin' A Party' Epic AE7 – 1122 promotion only 1977.

Acknowledgements

It is often an impossible task to thank all the people who have helped to create a book. This is especially the case in a book such as *Bruce Springsteen: Blinded By The Light*.

Many people have lent their voices here, but we must first make a friendly salute to the man himself, Bruce Springsteen.

For their continued help editorially we would like to thank Steve Adamson and Heather Shackleton for their insight and suggestions; Nicky Adamson for things too numerous to mention; and Lisa Hardy and Ken Kitchen who put in endless labour, thought and consideration. All of these people helped pull the book into shape.

For their help and assistance visually, we would like to thank Steve Rapport for his photograph of Bruce used on the front cover, Richard Manning for the hand-tinting of it, and Alan Dempsey for lettering.

We would also like to thank the following newspapers and magazines:

Time, Newsweek, Rolling Stone, Rock and Folk, People Magazine, New Musical Express, New York Times, Crawdaddy, Rockscene, Creem, Imagine, Grooves, and the *New York Sunday Times*.

The following individuals, collectors and picture agencies all contributed to the gathering of photographs for this book and we would like to extend our special gratitude to them:

Steve Rapport, London Features International, Frank Spooner Agency, Brian Magid for lending us his rare posters, Chuck Pulin, Photofeatures, Pictorial Press, The Photo Source, Lawrence Kirsch/Sparrow Photos, Adrian Boot, Geoff Nagle, Retna, Robert Zimmerman, Joe Stevens, Mike O'Mahony, Robert Ellis, Tom McElroy, Hans-Erik Eriksson, Neil Gibson, Mike Zabaroff, Max Soden, Paul Tabbenner, Mary Speed, Dan French, Dave Percival, 'Miami' Ron Cowell, Joe Kivak, Tom Beach, Billy Ramone, Jack Weinstein, Mats Ericsson and Sharon Wheeler at CBS.

It has not been possible in all cases to trace the copyright sources, and we would be glad to hear from any such unacknowledged copyright holder.

For all their efforts, assistance, phone calls, letters and above all friendship, I would like to give enormous thanks to the following people, without whom this book, for my part, would not have been possible:

This is 'For You' . . . Rene Slegers, Mary Speed, Holly Cara, Albert v/d Sanden, Cliff Breining, Bryan Carter, Chantal Constant, Matt Allan, Alma Cooper, Paul Williams, Candy Gandolfi, Tony Young, Martin Eagles, Frans Van de Pol, Kris Aleshnikova, Steve Fowler, Peter Papageorgantis, Mark Swift, Ruby Ong, Vera Dehnke, John Mokrzycki, Cary Judd, Graham Richards, Peter Jackson, Geoff Nagle and Antonio Giannetto. Grateful appreciation goes to Easy Listening, Acocks Green, Birmingham (John and Richard Corbett), Dave at the Music Market, Cheltenham, Vinyl Dreams, Birmingham (Barry), Craig at the Record Peddler, Manchester, Discovery Records, Solihull and Radio Radio Records, Arlington Va.

For spreading the name Asbury Park to all parts of the universe (and possibly beyond!) a big thanks to all the fanzine editors . . . Dan French (*Point Blank*), Gary Desmond (*Candy's Room*), Charles Cross (*Backstreets*), Jeff Mathews (*Rendezvous*), Paul Limbrick (*Jackson Cage*), Jon Munson (*Out In The Street*), Salvador Trepat Andres (*Thundercrack*) and especially Dave Percival (*The Fever*), whose enthusiasm and hard work has been of enormous help throughout (Cheers mate).

Special mention also to David, Jocelyn, Veronica and Mike at the W.M.A.M.S., Linda Tabbenner, Frank and Jill O'Hagan, Julian 'Max' Soden and Sally, Joy and Elizabeth Cowell, John ('Let Him Roll') Sansome and Pat, Rose and Alan Shelley, Kath and Arthur Carran, the Mason clan, Richard Martin, Tony Moody and Ian (180) Holden.

A very special 'thank you' to Hans-Erik Eriksson, Neil and Larna Gibson, 'Miami' Ron Cowell, Joe Kivak, Michael Zabaroff, Rick Howell, Dave Percival, Mats Ericsson, Paul Tabbenner and to Brian Magid whose help, contribution and enormous effort has added so much to this book. Thanks to Lawrence Kirsch for getting things into motion and for the introduction to Patrick Humphries (we finally got there!).

Dedicated to Sheila, Tony, Peter and above all Angela, Winnie and Rebecca Louise.

Finally, thank you Plexus for letting the dream come true.

Chris Hunt, May 1985

To Neil Gibson, Mike Zabaroff, Dan French, John Marriott, Gary Desmond, Dave Percival, Martin Eagles, Roger Scott, Mark Barnes and Paolo Hewitt, for being fans, and steering me in the right direction.

Chris Hunt, for his indefatigable good humour, wisdom and level head; and for the immortal line: 'There's this Czechoslovakian picture disc of "Born To Run" I'd like to get in somewhere!' Lawrence Kirsch, for forging the link. Kit Buckler and Sharon Wheeler, for being the acceptable face of CBS London, and still remaining fans. Bill and Kathy, for their valued friendship; Richard and Claire Wootton, for sound advice on music and builders; Andrew and Nicki Whitfield, for the good times. Lisa Hardy, Sandra Wake and Annie Hayman, for knocking it (me!) into shape. Uncle Bernard and Suki Paradise, for style counsel. Eric Humphries, for all those years of support. Vicky and Bruce George, for being such good neighbours. Finally, Peter K. Hogan my agent for coercing, and for keeping my rock'n'roll heart beating. Final finally, for Sue Parr, with love above and beyond the call of duvet, and for two of the happiest years of my life.

To the memory of my late uncle, Dr J. W. Lusk, OBE, MD, ChB, and to Mary and Roger with love.

Patrick Humphries, May 1985